Hate Spin

Information Policy Series

Edited by Sandra Braman

The Information Policy Series publishes research on and analysis of significant problems in the field of information policy, including decisions and practices that enable or constrain information, communication, and culture irrespective of the legal siloes in which they have traditionally been located as well as state-law-society interactions. Defining information policy as all laws, regulations, and decision-making principles that affect any form of information creation, processing, flows, and use, the series includes attention to the formal decisions, decision-making processes, and entities of government; the formal and informal decisions, decision-making processes, and entities of private and public sector agents capable of constitutive effects on the nature of society; and the cultural habits and predispositions of governmentality that support and sustain government and governance. The parametric functions of information policy at the boundaries of social, informational, and technological systems are of global importance because they provide the context for all communications, interactions, and social processes.

Hate Spin

The Manufacture of Religious Offense and Its Threat to Democracy

Cherian George

The MIT Press
Cambridge, Massachusetts
London, England

This book was set in Stone Sans and Stone Serif by Toppan Best-set Premedia Limited. Printed and bound in the United States of America.

Library of Congress Cataloging-in-Publication Data

Names: George, Cherian, author.
Title: Hate spin : the manufacture of religious offense and its threat to democracy / Cherian George.
Description: Cambridge, MA : MIT Press, 2016. | Series: Information policy | Includes bibliographical references and index.
Identifiers: LCCN 2016014335 | ISBN 9780262035309 (hardcover : alk. paper)
Subjects: LCSH: Offenses against religion—Law and legislation. | Offenses against religion—Political aspects. | Freedom of speech. | Political persecution. | Hate speech—Law and legislation
Classification: LCC K5305 .G46 2016 | DDC 345/.0288—dc23 LC record available at https://lccn.loc.gov/2016014335

10 9 8 7 6 5 4 3 2 1

To the memory of Ibrahim Haji Kader Mustan (1925–1976)

Contents

Series Editor's Introduction

Sandra Braman

Elisabeth Noelle-Neumann, in her influential and still important work *The Spiral of Silence*, asked just how it is that extreme positions of hate against entire populations—hate speech—can come to dominate politically. Her question was inspired by the Nazis, but her insights into the psychology of public speech, from what may begin as very small and highly deviant groups expressing extreme views, have helped us understand humanitarian disasters such as the genocidal war between the Hutus and the Tutsis, so clearly driven by a deliberate radio campaign. Jacob Shamir and Michal Shamir, in *The Anatomy of Public Opinion*, explores ways in which differences in knowledge base prior to exposure to extreme speech can affect how individuals engage with or are affected by these processes, and others who study public opinion have added to our understanding of individual-level dynamics that lead to mass mobilization via extreme speech. Mark Granovetter's sociological work on "Threshold Models of Collective Behavior" valuably extends the argument to decisions made by individuals in groups that turn from speech to extreme behavior, as when violence erupts during a political demonstration.

In these public opinion and sociology literatures, researchers and theorists are concerned with the *effects* of extreme speech on individual expression and action. The focus is on what has happened in historical hate speech campaigns and their consequences—the figure in the figure/field configuration that always characterizes our research subjects. By contrast, in *Hate Spin*, Cherian George starts by looking at the field, noting that there must be additional dynamics in play because there have been myriad instances in which expressions of hate speech have generated no social consequences at all. His in-depth research in three of the world's largest democracies clearly explains that what makes the difference—what triggers hate speech campaigns and their genocidal effects—are choices made by political entrepreneurs to deliberately use opportunities to take offense to achieve other political goals. His focus is not on the effects of hate speech, but its *use as a political tool*. The analyses provided here identify specific individuals, historic moments, and decisions of these kinds in qualititively different social, economic, political, and legal environments—as well as examples of opportunities to use this political tool that were not taken, either because there was no immediate political advantage to be gained or because there was no appropriately positioned political entrepreneur in place to take advantage of the moment.

George's theory of hate spin provides an original, persuasive, and valuable framework for thinking about these phenomena and the processes they unleash. He peels back the big and often overly simple narratives characterizing much of what is said publicly about matters such as responses to Danish publication of cartoons about the Prophet Mohammed. What he makes visible are the very specific political motives and decisions of individual actors in particular contexts that led to social explosions when and where they took place. Developments in each of the three countries studied are contextualized within the long histories of the pertinent societies, with acute observations into historical events and contemporary forces that create the contexts within which hate spin has come to be seen as such a useful political tool.

This author's insights into the dynamics in play provide a foundation for a critique of existing laws and regulations intended to deal with the deliberate giving of offense (hate speech) and the deliberate taking of offense, which together comprise "hate spin." George argues that the law is not only, in many places, inadequate for contemporary social dynamics, but it also can provide affordances for conflict. The book builds upon its theory, analysis of the social processes underway, and significant case studies to offer an exploration of what the media, civil society, and the law are—and could be—doing. All three are important to each of us as individuals and to society as a whole.

From the perspective of the Information Policy series, the analyses of the history, development, and current status of laws and regulations that can facilitate or impede the ability to engage in hate spin are of particular value. For those in the information policy / law and society domains, this book identifies a research agenda of great significance and urgent immediate need. The subject of information policy and the refugees and displaced persons who are on the move precisely because of successful uses of hate spin is also of interest to the series.

This is important work. We are riven, today, with violence unexpected and projected, immediate and far away, singly and in multiples, small children and large populations, all too often justified by claims that it is the legitimate and only response to hate speech. In *Hate Spin*, Cherian George removes the veil from one of the most powerful political dynamics of our times, tells us how it works in its specifics in the world's major democracies, and makes concrete and operationalizable recommendations about what we might do as next steps in an effort to reverse the trends.

Preface

Several years ago in Malaysia, a large crowd assembled by hard-line Muslim activists disrupted a forum on religious freedom. The police arrived to restore order—by instructing the organizers of the dialogue to abandon their meeting so as not to provoke the protesters further.[1] When I heard about this incident occurring in a country with a deserved reputation for tolerance of diversity, I was taken aback. I would have been less surprised if the religious conservatives had been incensed by a rock concert or some other perceived assault on family values. Instead, they were outraged at the idea of an interfaith initiative. Somehow, these members of the country's majority faith—the state religion—had convinced themselves that their status was under threat. And somehow, the authorities decided that the proper way to resolve the dispute was to side with those loudly professing righteous indignation, and to silence perfectly respectable speech.

Until then, my personal antenna had been tuned to more conventional types of government censorship. Working as a journalist and an academic in the illiberal environment of my native Singapore had made me all too familiar with officials' desire to restrict political discourse and the expression of popular grievances. But here was something else. The protesters were exhibiting the dark side of people power—a public opinion convinced of its virtue, intolerant of difference, and using democratic space to smother the freedom of others. I began to notice it happening everywhere. At a time when few challenges are more urgent and universal than learning to live with diversity, opportunists are using hate propaganda to create delusions of pure communities in need of protection from adulteration by others. Some of this takes the form of hate speech, which instigates harms against a vilified group. In other cases, hate propaganda manifests as outbursts of mass indignation against perceived offense. Protesters demand government intervention or engage in vigilante reprisals to salve wounded religious feelings.

Observers usually describe these conflicts as primordial, rooted in tribal psychology and reinforced by the messages of prophets and preachers. In this interpretation, the instincts of man, plus the word of God, are sufficient to explain these seemingly spontaneous and inevitable events. My inquiry started from a different intuition: perhaps, many large-scale episodes of group vilification and indignation are not organic responses to human diversity, but rather sophisticated campaigns manufactured by political entrepreneurs working to further their own strategic interests. It soon became clear to me that their orchestrations of offense-giving and offense-taking make up a double-sided technique of political contention. Unable to find a term to describe this phenomenon, I decided to call it hate spin.

This book is a study of how hate spin operates and how democracies should deal with it. In its eight chapters I analyze major transnational episodes, typified by the 2005–06 controversies surrounding the publication of cartoons of the Prophet Muhammad. I also investigate several domestic conflicts within the world's three largest democracies. The Hindu Right in India, the Muslim Right in Indonesia, and the Christian Right in the United States all include accomplished users of hate spin, adapting their methods to suit their respective legal and social environments. I show how practitioners of hate spin use the freedom and tolerance provided by democracy to push an agenda that undermines democratic values. Hate spin agents assert themselves in the public sphere, claiming victimhood and demanding respect—even as they deny others the right to participate as equals in the life of society, or even to be treated with the basic dignity owed to fellow human beings.

Democracies must develop legal, political, media, and civic responses to hate spin. Notwithstanding the need to protect free speech, they have to prohibit incitement. This book will show how vulnerable communities are terrorized when authorities fail to live up to this obligation. But dealing with offendedness is a different matter. We'll see that laws against blasphemy or the wounding of religious feelings are highly counterproductive. They allow exponents of hate spin to hijack the coercive powers of the state by staging performances of righteous indignation. Thus, misguided policies toward hate spin can doubly disadvantage vulnerable groups. On the one hand, inadequate policing of incitement leaves them exposed to hate campaigns that result in discrimination and violence. On the other, their own religious or cultural practices may be declared offensive to the dominant group, and then suppressed through the selective use of insult laws.

Commentators, analysts, and policymakers have been paying close attention to the unsteady dance between religion and free speech. The cost of mismanaging that relationship is plain to see—in bitter divisions over art and literature, in polarized elections that leave no room for compromise, and in dehumanizing rhetoric that culminates in mass murder. To improve our prospects for peaceful coexistence in societies that are not getting any less crowded or diverse, good intentions are not enough. We also need to grasp the underlying dynamics that shape religious intolerance. Understanding hate spin and how it works is a small step in that direction.

Acknowledgments

This book would not have come about but for the support of many organizations and individuals. A residency at the Rockefeller Foundation's Bellagio Center in 2011 gifted me the time to crystallize the concept of hate spin. Programs organized by the Asia-Europe Foundation and the Open Society Foundations introduced me to leading thinkers and activists working in the areas of freedom of expression and the politics of religion. When my research and writing reached its most demanding phase, each level of my current institution—the Department of Journalism in the School of Communication, Hong Kong Baptist University—was generous with financial support and professional encouragement.

My exploratory research benefited greatly from early consultations with Eric Barendt, the late Kevin Boyle, Agnes Callamard, Jeffrey Haynes, Arif Jamal, Frank La Rue, Tarlach McGonagle, Sejal Parmar, Robert Post, and Arch Puddington. I also gained insights from Sayeed Ahmad, Shahzad Ahmad, Susan Benesch, Nighat Dad, Goh Lih Shiun, John Keane, Toby Mendel, Kamran Reza, Naomi Sakr, and Lokman Tsui.

My research on India was guided by Bhairav Acharya, Chinmayi Arun, Saurav Datta, Roxy Gagdekar, Varghese George, Mohd Aamir Khan, Milind Kokje, Harsh Mander, Siddharth Narrain, Cedric Prakash, Geeta Seshu, Teesta Setalvad, Imran Siddiqui, R. B. Sreekumar, Shyam Tekwani, Romila Thapar, and Deepal Trivedi. The Indonesia chapter owes much to Ihsan Ali-Fauzi, Endy Bayuni, Donald Emmerson, Abdul Malik Gismar, Bambang Harymurti, Sidney Jones, Edwin Lubis, Zulfiani Lubis, Megi Margiyono, Husni Mubarak, Mohamad Guntur Romli, and Bonar Sigalingging. In the United States, I was fortunate to learn from Ossama Bahloul, Miranda Blue, Randy Brinson, Nicholas Gaxiola, Eric Johnston, Nathan Lean, Tara Morrow, Peter Montgomery, Mark Potok, Corey Saylor, Saleh Sbenaty, Faheem Shaikh, Yasmine Taeb, Ashfaq Taufique, and Sara Wicht.

Thanks are also due to my research assistants, Parul Sharma in India, Yasmin Purba in Indonesia, and Pearl Liu Fangfei, Nathaniel Suen, and Bridgette Hall in Hong Kong. Audra Wolfe improved the manuscript substantially with her editing skills. Mary Bagg was meticulous in giving it a final polish. Over drinks, many academics will exchange notes about the frustrations of book publishing. If I emerge from this experience with no dismal stories to share, it is mainly due to Sandra Braman, who "got" my project, solicited this monograph, and shepherded it into the capable hands of Gita Devi Manaktala and her team at the MIT Press.

The bulk of the writing was done during my first year in the entirely new environment of Hong Kong. It might have been too unsettled a period for intense concentration, were it not for the constancy of my wife, Zuraidah. Her companionship and confidence in me has been my compass through every new experience. I dedicate this book to a person who adored her long before I did, her late father. I never met Ibrahim Haji Kader Mustan but by all accounts he was someone who honored the written word and carried within him the ultimate antidote to intolerance—a desire to just get along.

1 Hate Spin as Politics by Other Means

An offensive video is released; violent protests follow. Elsewhere, a mob heeds a preacher's call to attack members of a minority sect. Meanwhile, a politician leads a rally against migrants and refugees, describing their religious values as alien and dangerous.

Such eruptions of intolerance have become all too common around the world. In response, commentators have produced mountains of analysis, trying to make sense of the trend. According to one fairly common perspective, we are in the throes of a clash of civilizations. Surely, these events are driven by the visceral emotions and primordial instincts unleashed when deep-seated religious beliefs come into conflict with one another and with secular modernity. It is time to trim back freedom of expression to show more respect for religion, some commentators propose. Others urge a muscular liberalism that tells religious groups to live with hate speech as a price of democratic citizenship.

To anyone who has followed the debates surrounding events like the 2015 *Charlie Hebdo* killings, such statements sound all too familiar.

In this book I argue that these claims—though commonplace—are wrong. They misdiagnose the causes of religious disputes, misinterpret the role played by freedom of expression, and mistakenly prescribe speech-related cures that could make matters worse. I show instead that major episodes of religious offense and offendedness are not the natural, spontaneous product of human diversity, but rather performances orchestrated by political entrepreneurs in their quest for power. These opportunists selectively tease out citizens' genuine religious emotions and encourage expressions of the popular will, the better to mobilize them toward anti-democratic goals. This is people power, used against itself. I argue that the law should not permit the abuse of free speech to inflict the harms of discrimination or violence upon vulnerable groups. But neither should the law pander to opportunistic outbursts of righteous indignation by suppressing whatever has been deemed offensive. Democracies need to protect the public space for vigorous debate of opposing viewpoints—including about religious values—while also guaranteeing people of all faiths the right to participate fearlessly as equals in the life of a society. The democratic values of freedom and equality are undermined not only when the state abrogates its basic responsibility of providing security to its most vulnerable communities, but also when it intervenes too hastily to protect the feelings of groups that loudly profess outrage at perceived insult.

Expressions of religious intolerance are distressingly common. Consider Hungary and other parts of Europe, where a variety of groups are expressing flamboyant anti-Semitism.[1] Nativists and extreme nationalists have found unlikely allies in some radical Muslim immigrants. The latter promote hostility against another religious minority while protesting against the bigotry they themselves face. In Russia, meanwhile, the authorities have been enthusiastically policing religious offense. At the behest of a Russian Orthodox cleric, authorities cracked down on an avant-garde opera that included an image depicting Jesus Christ's crucifixion between a naked woman's legs. Criminal charges were brought against the director and theater manager. Both were acquitted, but the theater manager was fired by the culture minister.[2]

Similar tensions afflict every continent on the globe. In one Egyptian village, five Christian students performed a skit that made fun of IS, the Islamic State. After their teacher's phone was stolen, his video recording of the skit was discovered, and the Copts' homes were attacked. He, and four students who were all under eighteen, were charged with contempt of religion.[3] In Nigeria, the 2015 presidential election was plagued by hate speech. Bishop David Oyedepo, one of Africa's wealthiest pastors, came out in support of the incumbent Goodluck Jonathan, a Christian from the south, who was being challenged by the Muslim northerner Muhammadu Buhari, the eventual winner. In one sermon before the election, the bishop told a congregation that he had been anointed to fight the jihadists. "If you catch anyone that looks like them, kill him! Kill him and pull out his neck."[4]

In Brazil, an aggressive evangelical movement has produced a spike in intolerance against homosexuals and religious minorities, such as followers of the traditional Afro-Brazilian Candomblé religion. The victims included an eleven-year-old girl who was struck by a stone flung by Bible-waving men shouting that her kind should burn in hell.[5] In the United States, the anti-Islam campaigner Pamela Geller taunted Muslims by organizing a Muhammad Art Exhibit and Cartoon Contest, professedly to take a stand for free speech in the aftermath of the *Charlie Hebdo* killings. Two gunmen who took the bait and attempted an attack at the exhibit were shot dead outside the venue.[6] Geller went on to try to buy advertising space for a cartoon of the Prophet in the Metro system of Washington, DC, prompting the transit authorities to ban all issue-oriented ads because of safety concerns.[7]

In Myanmar, an anti-Muslim campaign fronted by such radical Buddhist monks as Ashin Wirathu has begun to reach the definition of genocide.[8] When United Nations Secretary-General Ban Ki-Moon called for more protection of the Rohingya minority, parliamentarians accused him of referring to a nonexistent ethnic group, and thus insulting Myanmar's sovereignty.[9] In Singapore—in a case alarming more for its pettiness than its extremity—authorities sprang into action when a blogger made disparaging references to Jesus Christ within a profanity-laced YouTube rant against the country's recently deceased leader Lee Kuan Yew. The blogger was convicted and sentenced to jail after Christians lodged complaints with the police. The focus of their ire: a sixteen-year-old student.[10]

This small sampling of incidents occurred within six months on either side of the *Charlie Hebdo* incident, suggesting that the murders in Paris epitomize a global phenomenon. The cases have certain elements in common, including deep intolerance of difference; identity-related offense; appeals to an in-group; and censorship or oppression of a target group. All these are classic ingredients of "hate speech," a category of extreme speech that has been studied for decades. Hate speech can be defined as *the vilification of a group's identity in order to oppress its members and deny them equal rights.* The extreme right's anti-Semitic rhetoric in Europe fits this description, as does Bishop Oyedepo's call to kill anyone who "looks like" a jihadist and the Venerable Wirathu's calm claim that monks should react to Muslims as they would to human excrement.[11]

In other cases, however, the same elements are present but are configured differently. Recall that in classic hate speech, the eventual harm—exclusion or violence—is inflicted on the same group that was targeted by the vilifying expression. In contrast, when bloggers and journalists are attacked or films and operas are censored because they are deemed offensive, the tables are turned. The professed victims of insult retaliate with a force far greater than any measurable harm instigated by the original expression. The words go one way, but the sticks and stones fly in the opposite direction. If conventional hate speech is strategic offense-*giving* by those who are intolerant of diversity, this other type of aggression comprises indignant offense-*taking.* The former overtly victimizes a target community; the latter is about playing the provoked victim, with malicious intent.

So far, we've lacked a vocabulary to deal with this double-sided use of offense by the forces of intolerance. I call it hate spin, a term that encompasses both hate speech and its 180-degree-flipped cousin. I define hate spin as *manufactured vilification or indignation, used as a political strategy that exploits group identities to mobilize supporters and coerce opponents.*

Many agents of hate deftly deploy both offense-giving and offense-taking, often in parallel. The word "spin" is meant to conjure up this freewheeling quality of their campaigns. The contemporary, colloquial meaning of spin also applies: hate spin is a form of calculated, deceptive propaganda. This is a truth that is lost in many popular interpretations of religious intolerance—including the kinds of statements I presented in the opening paragraphs of this chapter. Cameras focus on the hotheaded men raging against books, films, temples, and peoples that they cannot abide. Their photogenic fury may not be completely inauthentic or insincere. But, as we shall see, in practically all large and sustained disturbances, the agitation is neither spontaneous nor inevitable. Scratch the surface, and we find spin doctors at work. These are the political entrepreneurs who play with communities' visceral emotions but are themselves coldly calculating in their use of the techniques of persuasion, from the ancient tricks of rhetoric to the latest tools of social media. Hate spin agents are usually elites—leaders of political or religious organizations, sometimes even government officials—who find it expedient to cloak their power-seeking motives in the guise of popular outpourings of religious sentiment. When these opportunists succeed, they can unleash forces that are much more intimidating and irresistible than ordinary public relations campaigns.

In this book I examine the global phenomenon of hate spin and its implications for the regulation of expression in democracies. The policy challenge in confronting hate spin is part of a broader balancing act: How can freedom of expression be protected and promoted in a way that appreciates its vital importance, while also recognizing the responsibility that comes with it? Within this larger debate, there is probably no question more contentious than how to deal with speech that is disrespectful of religion. There is no consensus on this issue, even within the Western, liberal democratic family, either philosophically or in law and policy.

It is tempting to treat both kinds of hate spin—conventional hate speech as well as manufactured offendedness—as problems demanding similar remedies. After all, when the practical outcome of religious offense is violence, it may seem immaterial whether the mobs are rallying around the expression or raging against it. This is, however, a crucially important detail. Free speech shouldn't be absolute or unconditional, and hate speech that incites listeners to rob others of their rights is a reasonable place to set a legal limit. But misapplying this incitement threshold to cases of indignation amounts to flawed logic and bad policy. It is expressed in blasphemy laws and other legislation that prohibits the wounding of religious feelings. Such laws are harmful not only because they choke the work of artists, journalists, and others on whom open societies depend, but also because they allow a dominant group to suppress marginalized minorities by deeming their voices as "offensive" to mainstream values.

It is all too easy to confuse incitement and indignation. Consider a 2012 editorial in *Social Identities*, a scholarly journal devoted to the study of race, nation, and culture. Discussing troubling developments in "the politics of free speech," the editors concluded: "Surely, public interest demands that, when so many innocent people are killed across the world, governments act with rapidity to remove materials that incite hatred and violence."[12] This statement is roughly in line with international norms of human rights that require the prohibition of incitement.[13] The problem, though, is that the editorial was a response to the mayhem that followed the release of a film titled *Innocence of Muslims* on YouTube earlier that year. This crass video certainly vilified Islam, but the lawbreaking that ensued was in reaction to the video, not incited by it. The Pulitzer-winning cartoonist Gary Trudeau made the same error in an otherwise excellent essay in the *Atlantic* in response to the *Charlie Hebdo* affair. Noting that hate speech "directly incites violence," he said: "Well, voila—the 7 million copies that were published following the killings did exactly that, triggering violent protests across the Muslim world, including one in Niger, in which ten people died." This, again, is conflating the giving of offense with the taking of it.[14]

An Overview

In this book I examine hate spin dynamics at the international level and within the religiously diverse megademocracies of India, Indonesia, and the United States. My key claims are as follows:

• Hate spin is a technique of contentious politics that involves the strategic use of offense-giving and offense-taking. Hate spin exploits democratic freedoms by harnessing group identities as a resource for anti-democratic collective action.

• Hate spin needs to be resisted to preserve democracy's twin pillars: liberty, including the freedom to share provocative ideas; and equality, including the capacity to take part in public life unhindered by unfair discrimination or intimidation.

• Under-regulation of hate speech allows its exponents to incite harms against vulnerable groups with impunity. International human rights norms require the state to protect people from incitement to discrimination and violence.

• Over-regulation of insult encourages the manufacture of offendedness as a political weapon. The deliberate giving of religious offense can be immoral, but it is too subjective to be declared illegal.

• The best way to enshrine respect for religion is to protect the right to freedom of religion and belief, guaranteed to every individual. Equality-enhancing, antidiscrimination measures—and the prohibition of actual hate crimes—do more for religion than laws prohibiting offense.

• Religious vilification cannot be eradicated, but it can be nudged out of the mainstream by an assertive pluralism that combines legal measures, political leadership, civic activism, and media cooperation.

A Synopsis of the Book

In this book I combine conceptual discussions with in-depth case studies. I focus in chapter 2 on laws and constitutions. I explain the modern human rights norm, which calls for protections against offensive expression, plus prohibition of incitement to serious harms. This is the general approach adopted by the United Nations Human Rights Committee, the European Court of Human Rights, and the domestic courts of most Western democracies. I contrast it with the tradition of punishing blasphemy and the wounding of religious feelings. This approach persists in many countries, some of which have attempted to incorporate it into international law through the principle of "defamation of religions." At one level, this is part of a debate over the role that religious norms should play within modern constitutional orders. I end chapter 2 with a review of what scholars have said about this larger question.

In the following four chapters I present detailed case studies of hate spin, In chapter 3, I analyze several major cross-border episodes, including the conflicts surrounding Salman Rushdie's *Satanic Verses* and the Danish newspaper cartoons of Prophet Mohammed. The Internet provides a global platform for hate spin; in this chapter I also consider the role of such intermediaries as Google in allowing hate spin to flourish.

In chapters 4, 5, and 6, I look respectively at India, Indonesia, and the United States—the world's three largest democracies. My goal is not to produce comprehensive national reports on religious intolerance in these three countries, but rather to study how hate spin unfolds in different contexts. Hate spin probably has the nastiest effects in nondemocracies, which lack independent institutions for conflict resolution and for protecting human rights. In such societies, however, the problem is not analytically challenging. Where there is no respect for legitimate speech to start with, offense is just another reason to clamp down further on freedom of expression; the debate over how to manage it is "hollow or even mere play-acting, its outcome preordained," as the Hungarian writer and human rights advocate Miklos Haraszti notes.[15] In contrast, hate spin poses a genuine conundrum in more open societies that are committed to maintaining a vibrant environment for free speech. To varying degrees, this describes India, Indonesia, and the United States, all three of which are highly allergic to government control of media and communication. Each of these countries has a different majority faith, showing that hate spin is not confined to any one religion.

With the final two chapters I zoom out from the case studies and attempt to identify patterns. In chapter 7, I examine the role of media and civil society in facilitating or resisting hate spin. These—like the law—can be either part of the solution or part of the problem. In chapter 8, I synthesize the book's findings. To resist hate spin, democracies must appreciate the sophistication with which political entrepreneurs apply this strategy. I show how their strategic, versatile, and networked approach makes it extremely difficult to regulate forms of hate spin that should be prohibited. Legal solutions are sometimes necessary, but are almost always insufficient. Therefore, resisting hate spin also requires political and civic responses. These need to be built on a clear, normative commitment to a cosmopolitan, inclusive vision of nationhood.

A Democratic Dilemma

Mention religious conflict and most people will think of terrorism. This study, however, deals with other dangers. They are not as spectacular as the harms caused by terrorists; they may not generate as much disruption and fear. They are nevertheless not trivial. Each year, many more thousands suffer as a result of religious violence and discrimination than are killed or injured by terrorists—who, by definition, amplify the symbolic and psychological impact of their actions by using attention-grabbing methods that compensate for their limited capacity to overcome their opponents. Besides, our sensibilities should allow various forms of injustice and suffering to register, even if they are not the most bloody. Hate spin has negative impacts that are electoral (fearmongering as a winning campaigning strategy), social (the marginalization of religious minorities) and ideological (censorship of books and art that challenge dominant narratives). Such harms deserve public concern, even when they don't culminate in the horror of genocide or the terror of a suicide bomb.

Also at stake is democracy's ability to deal with religious diversity. Many of the conflicts I describe in this book are over opposing ways of imagining the nation. On one side are the equal rights contained in modern, secular constitutions, designed for the complex challenge of living with difference; on the other, religious nationalisms promising a simple, pure, and stable sense of belonging in unsettling times. We find this contest in the Christian-majority United States, Hindu-majority India, and Muslim-majority Indonesia. This is a clash, yes; but a clash of civilizational values, not civilizations.

The numbers game of democracy compounds the hate spin challenge. Unscrupulous politicians vying to mobilize a majority find the strategy irresistible. Even highly principled leaders struggle to fight it. On two occasions in Myanmar, I sat in the audience before Aung San Suu Kyi, moved by her inspiring, unequivocal call for freedom and democracy. But when reporters asked her about the plight of Rohingya Muslims in Rakhine State, she transformed into a study of bureaucratic evasiveness. She would only speak in general terms about the importance of rule of law, gingerly avoiding any assignment of blame. She and her party clearly felt that they could not afford to alienate a majority influenced by Buddhist nationalism as well as deep prejudices against Muslims, who make up around 5 percent of the population. A year later, her National League for Democracy fielded no Muslims among its 1,151 candidates for the historic 2015 elections.[16]

In the United States, a landmark hate spin campaign occurred in 2010, after Muslims in New York announced a project to build a community center and prayer hall a few blocks from the old World Trade Center site. Despite strong local support for the project, hate propagandists engineered a protest against what they dubbed the "Mosque at Ground Zero." President Barack Obama responded with what the *New York Times* interpreted as a "strong defense" of the proposal.[17] "Ground Zero is, indeed, hallowed ground," he acknowledged in his White House speech celebrating the start of the Muslim holy month of Ramadan. "But let me be clear: as a citizen, and as President, I believe that Muslims have the same right to practice their religion as anyone else in this country. That includes the right to build a place of worship and a community center on private property in lower Manhattan, in accordance with local laws and ordinances. This is America, and our commitment to religious freedom must be unshakeable."[18] But barraged by criticism from the right, Obama moderated his views the very next day. "I was not commenting and I will not comment on the wisdom of making the decision to put a mosque there," he told reporters. "I was commenting very specifically on the right people have that dates back to our founding."[19]

The philosopher Martha Nussbaum took a dim view of the flip-flop, calling it "a failure of leadership."[20] Obama made erudite speeches in attempts to build bridges between the West and Islam. He contested stereotypes associating Muslims with terrorism. But there were limits to how much he was prepared to do to stand up for a small minority, what with perceptions that he himself was really a Muslim. Only in the final year of his presidency did he decide it was politically safe to avail himself of a photo opportunity in an American mosque.[21] He and Aung San Suu Kyi, incidentally, were among the small handful of active politicians to have received the Nobel Prize for Peace. When we see even Peace Prize laureates flinch in the face of hate spin, we begin to realize the odds that democracies are up against.

An Interdisciplinary Approach to Hate Spin

Research for this book has taken some years, several thousand miles of travel, and restless forays into an eclectic range of scholarly literatures. Here, I identify the distinct intellectual wellsprings from which I have drawn. Nonacademic readers may prefer to skip this section and rejoin the chapter at "Offense-Giving: Hate Speech and Its Harms."

Insights from Social Sciences and Legal Studies

My starting point was communication studies, which has long had an interest in freedom of expression and public discourse. Many societies' media and communication policies treat religion as a special case of expression; religious offense is not given the same latitude as other types of provocative criticism. This is certainly the dominant view in my own country, Singapore, which happens to be the most religiously diverse country in the world.[22] There, a laudable desire to preserve religious harmony has translated into broad public support for censorship of provocative expression. This consensus troubled me, and I began looking more closely at the supposed harms caused by offensive speech.

Within communication studies, discourse analysis has helped us deconstruct hate speech and understand how it works.[23] Media studies research can help explain news professionals' ambiguous role in relation to such democratic values as giving voice to minorities.[24] Research in this field has also helped us understand journalists' ritualistic professional practices, including how they decide what constitutes "news" and, thus, whose voices and which events get publicized.

I have drawn extensively on legal scholarship. The law tells political actors what they can or cannot get away with if they choose to use hate speech; and what support they can expect from the state if they decide to take offense at a painting, a film, or a church. Legal studies have probably devoted more attention to extreme speech than any other discipline.[25] This is in part because of the growth of the field of international human rights law, in which genocide and its promotion through hate speech are recognized as a particularly important problem. Disputes over less serious forms of hate speech, as well as over offensive material, regularly reach national and regional courts. The jurisprudence on human rights is still evolving, generating intense scholarly discussions. Internet law is another growth area within academic and policy circles, and hate speech is never far from the top of the agenda.

This study is not, however, primarily an exercise in legal analysis, since the law constitutes only one set of influences on political behavior. As a rule, we cannot assume that discussions among jurists, lawmakers, and judges reflect the world that is really out there. Eric Posner has been searing in his rebuke of this naiveté in human rights law. "In the legal literature, a hundred papers parsing human rights doctrine to ever finer degrees are written for every paper that takes an empirical approach," the University of Chicago law professor alleges. "Lawyers mainly read and discuss judicial opinions—which hardly affect anyone at all—while ignoring the actual behavior of governments, NGOs, and individuals."[26]

For a picture of how laws and constitutions play out on the ground, we need to cross from legal studies into other fields in the social sciences. Political science has had a strong interest in the role of free speech in democracies, the relationship between religion and politics, and the tension between majority rule and minority rights, all of which are among my key concerns in this book. Much of that research is Eurocentric, but since the end of the Cold War, a cluster of political scientists has been trying to make sense of the diversity of democratic systems sprouting across the world. The subfield of comparative politics has rejected the assumption that states would or should ultimately converge to resemble the American liberal model. The comparativists have instead tried to understand the various combinations of constitutional forms, institutional arrangements, and cultural norms that can support viable democratic societies.[27] Taking into account the disintegration of many transitional societies, some studies have concluded that majority rule needs to be balanced with constitutions

that accommodate minority interests. On their own, elections simply identify the majority and the minority, without ensuring either tolerance or
civility.[28]

Other comparativists have looked anew at the relationship between
church and state, highlighting not only the potentially destabilizing contest between religious and secular authority, but also rejecting the notion
that religion has no place in a democratic public sphere.[29] In common with
much of this work in comparative political science, I have tried to take the
countries I'm studying on their own terms, shelving any preconceptions
about ideal or template laws and institutions.

Through the Lens of Contentious Politics

The field of political sociology has proven most hospitable to my project.
Scholars in this subdiscipline have tried to understand unruly forms of
collective political struggle such as protests, social movements, and revo-
lutions. They use the term "contentious collective action" to capture the
confrontation between resource-challenged insurgents and elites, authorities, and other better-equipped opponents.[30]

Midway through my exploration of potentially useful intellectual traditions, I realized that hate spin could be regarded as a technique of contentious politics. Social movement studies have tended to spotlight progressive
causes, such as civil rights and environmental activism. Conceptually, however, there is no reason why the same concepts and analytical tools cannot
be applied to anti-democratic causes, since movements are identified not
by their goals but rather by their methods—their engagement in contentious politics as an adaptation to their relative weakness or exclusion from
elite forums.[31]

Looking through this lens, it became clear that hate spin agents, like
leaders of social movements, try to get people thinking about a situation in
ways that produce solidarity and support for their cause.[32] To achieve this,
they engage in cultural framing work and cognitive interventions.[33] As the
sociologist William Gamson has argued, "injustice frames" can be particularly effective for mobilizing supporters. Injustice frames create narratives
that persuade an in-group that powerful outsiders are violating its interests
and values.[34] Anchoring injustice frames on powerful symbols increases
their ability to resonate with the group. Injustice symbols may be enduring, as is the case with the Holocaust for Jews, but many have a shorter
shelf life, requiring activists to be constantly on the lookout for fresh ones.
This can explain the enthusiasm with which hate spin agents declare a
book or video to be intolerably offensive to their community. The political

scientist Thomas Olesen has arrived at similar conclusions in his study of such events as the publication of the Prophet Muhammad cartoons and the Guantanamo Bay prisoner abuse scandal, both of which, he argues, were turned into transnational injustice symbols.[35]

Studies of contentious politics have also given us the concept of "repertoires" of contention, which comprise a range of protest methods that are already part of the culture. Activists tend to draw from these repertoires while also innovating at the margins. Thus, in 2014, when my students in Hong Kong joined in the mass civil disobedience campaign for political reform, they used sit-in tactics developed by earlier generations of protesters a world away; chose as their anthem the Cantonese version of "Do You Hear the People Sing?" from the musical *Les Misérables* that recalled the Paris Uprising of 1832; and turned umbrellas, which they had wielded to fend off tear gas canisters, into an original icon. We should expect hate spin agents to be no less creative—even if much less uplifting—in borrowing methods of contention that are already circulating, while also improvising to suit local conditions.

The sociological approach to contentious politics has favored thick, comparative descriptions of episodes of contention, with a view to identifying causal mechanisms and processes.[36] I've adopted a similar methodological approach. In this book I engage mainly in the middle, or "meso," level of analysis, examining why different organizations and institutions act the way they do. This is not to dismiss the value of microlevel, social-psychological research. For example, the "spiral of silence" theory in political communication helps explain why moderates fearing social isolation may fail to speak out against a vocal, intolerant minority.[37] The burgeoning field of behavioral science has revealed psychological biases that predispose people to feel correct even when the facts say otherwise.[38] Such insights shed light on how it is possible for individuals to behave immorally when other communities are targets of hate. On the other end of the spectrum, macrolevel analyses that treat hate spin episodes as outcomes of broad historical and geopolitical trends also contribute a useful perspective.

Offense-Giving: Hate Speech and Its Harms

Hate speech and the taking of offense are two sides of the same coin. Of the two, the former has attracted more attention, by far. Hate speech earned its infamy with its role in laying the ground for the Holocaust and other genocides. More routinely, it helps spread bigoted attitudes and converts such attitudes into actual discrimination, intimidation, and oppression. Hate speech is hardly new, but its harms are felt more acutely at a time when equality has been gaining recognition as a universal value: all modern theories of justice, notes Amartya Sen, prize equality in some form or other.[39]

Defining Hate Speech

Despite agreement that the term refers to something real and important, a consensus definition of hate speech remains elusive. Most of the debate centers on its legal meaning. As I show in chapter 2, it has proven impossible to settle on a globally accepted definition of hate speech that can distinguish between what must be legally restricted from what is permissible, even if extremely unpleasant.

Scholars nevertheless agree on how hate speech works and the harms it can cause. Hate speech communicates extremely negative ideas about a group, or a representative of that group, as defined by identity markers such as race, religion, and sexual orientation.[40] The Council of Europe—which concerns itself not only with hate speech law but also with social and political responses to it—has defined hate speech as covering "all forms of expression which spread, incite, promote, or justify racial hatred, xenophobia, anti-Semitism, or other forms of hatred based on intolerance, including: intolerance expressed by aggressive nationalism and ethnocentrism, discrimination and hostility against minorities, migrants, and people of immigrant origins."[41] The legal scholar Alexander Tsesis calls it "misinformation that is disseminated with the express purpose of persecuting targeted minorities."[42]

Based on these definitions, vilification would only qualify as hate speech when it is directed at vulnerable groups. Usually, these vulnerable groups are numerical minorities. But extreme hate groups sometimes have fewer members than their targets. It is also possible for grossly outnumbered elites to exercise hegemonic power, as in the case of Brahmin Hindus in India. In analyses of hate speech, therefore, the term "minority" should be treated as shorthand for target groups that are historically disadvantaged or oppressed. Members of such groups find themselves handicapped by history when they try to counter misinformation about their communities in the open marketplace of ideas. For this reason, they may require society to intervene when they are subject to demeaning attack. Which groups should be considered deserving of special accommodation—a sort of affirmative action in public discourse—is a contentious question. Most societies acknowledge the danger in racist speech more than homophobic or xenophobic speech, for example. I will say more in chapter 2 about how thinking on this matter has evolved.

Regardless of whether we are operating in the realm of theory or policy, certain forms of expression should be excluded from even the most expansive definitions of hate speech. For example, expressions of anger, which are more spontaneous and which can coexist with positive feelings—even love—need to be distinguished from hate speech, which taps on more total and enduring emotions and prompts more deliberate action.[43] Neither does the term apply to political dissent targeted at governments. This should go without saying. Yet, one unfortunate reason why hate speech has risen in the global agenda is because the term resonates with governing elites who are on the receiving end of hateful online attacks that they cannot abide. Improving the quality of debate and maintaining civility in public discourse are worthy objectives—but these are separate issues from regulating hate speech. Government leaders are not historically disadvantaged groups by a long shot, and no criticism of those in power, no matter how defamatory or vicious, should be confused with hate speech.

Even when vulnerable groups are the targets, we should not be too quick to count as hate speech any expression that wounds their feelings. People should certainly try to avoid such expression and empathize with those at the receiving end of offensive speech. That being said, offense and hurt feelings are inevitable consequences of living in open societies. They are not in themselves indications of a systemic problem within free speech, any more than financial losses and bankruptcies indicate a failure of market-based economics. The concept of hate speech should be understood as an attempt to create a space within the discourse about democracy where we acknowledge a serious type of market failure in the marketplace of ideas—a failure that involves the abuse of free speech in ways that rob people of their status as equal citizens, thus eroding one of the foundational pillars of democratic life. Therefore, even in a nonlegalistic sense, hate speech should be narrowly defined as that which not only offends and hurts, but also at the same time leads to more objective harms such as discrimination, intimidation, oppression, violence, and systematic exclusion of a vulnerable group from the full enjoyment of its democratic rights.

As we will see in chapter 2, First Amendment doctrine in the United States defines illegal hate speech even more narrowly, to cover direct incitement of immediate violence; it protects public discourse that incites the lesser evils of discrimination and hostility. Scholars working within this framework consider the term "hate speech" to be unhelpfully broad. Susan Benesch, for example, carves out for special attention a subset of language she calls "dangerous speech"—"inflammatory speech that precedes violence, especially outbreaks of mass violence like genocide."[44] Such a formulation makes sense for policy discussions concerned with these most extreme of harms. In this book, however, I consider the full range of hate propaganda that threatens equality. Just as too broad a definition opens the door to regulating wounded feelings at the expense of democratic freedoms, an ungenerously narrow one belittles the problem of discrimination and exclusion. Contemporary anti-Semitism in Europe probably won't escalate into another genocide.[45] But that would hardly justify indifference to any increase in the hostility that Jews are facing again.

Comparing various definitions of hate speech, we can see some blurriness at the margins. For example, can something be considered hate speech if it comprises purely factual statements? This is the kind of subtlety that would be important in a legal definition. (To take the analogy of defamation law, truth is a defense in democratic societies, but not in all nondemocracies.) Sociologically speaking, though, the definitional differences are not as stark. What we know about the processes of stereotyping and framing tells us that towering untruths can be cultivated from cherry-picked facts. For example, repeatedly emphasizing that a certain minority group controls most of the business in a country and harping on cases where one or two of those businesses have engaged in exploitative labor practices—while neglecting to mention that most members of that community are not well-off and that its businesses are no less ethical than those owned by the majority community—can make it a target for attack, as documented in Amy Chua's work on "market-dominant minorities."[46]

Hate Speech Motives and Effects

Cultivating group-wide hatred serves a variety of goals. Most obviously, hate speech intimidates an out-group and lays the ground for persecution. Hate speech has a long history in association with large-scale massacres or subjugation of defenseless communities, from the ethnic cleansing of Native Americans and Aboriginal Australians by white colonists, to the enslaving of Africans, the extermination of Jews in Nazi Germany, and the Rwandan genocide of 1994. Often, though, the main purpose of hate speech is to build in-group support. Any harm inflicted on the out-group is just collateral damage, not the strategic objective. By accentuating the difference between Us and Them, and constructing the out-group as the enemy, hate groups appeal to new recruits, build solidarity, and mobilize members around their political agenda. Hate speech is thus an instrument of identity politics.

Scholars have described a systematic process by which propaganda makes reasonable people willing to inflict horrendous harms on others. Cees

Hamelink deconstructs a "spiral of conflict escalation."[47] It starts with a collective sense of anxiety that renders people vulnerable to manipulation. This could be rooted in an objective cause for concern, such as economic decline, or cultural unease over the erosion of reassuring social mores. Leaders then agitate to construct a collective identity at the expense of an out-group that is portrayed as the object of the community's anxiety. A process of alienation follows, in which the out-group is dehumanized to the point that it is no longer seen as deserving of empathy or moral obligation. Finally comes "accusation in a mirror"—a term used in the tribunal investigating the Rwandan genocide—which involves convincing the in-group that the out-group is the real aggressor, and that eliminating the other would be an act of self-defense and even a matter of survival. Such escalation, it should be stressed, is not unplanned or uncoordinated. Although media outlets commonly describe ethnic violence as if it were a spontaneous eruption of subterranean forces, it invariably results from deliberate actions by actors who stand to gain from such ruptures. Thus, Rita Whillock has described hate speech as a "stratagem" or trick that creates a "symbolic code for violence": "its goals are to inflame the emotions of followers, denigrate the designated out-class, inflict permanent and irreparable harm to the opposition, and ultimately conquer."[48]

A major challenge for regulators is that hate speech is never self-contained. It does not arrive in a discrete package with a clear return address. Prosecutors have a hard time establishing legal accountability because the process is both long-term and distributed. Tsesis notes, "The most dangerous form of bigotry takes years to develop, until it becomes culturally acceptable first to libel, then to discriminate, and finally to persecute out-groups."[49] In Rwanda, the radio station RTLM fanned the flames of hatred from the time it started operating in July 1993, several months before the April 1994 eruption of mass violence that killed approximately 800,000 people. In that case, the propaganda was so explicit, and the cause-and-effect connections so clear, that the international tribunal was able to convict media chiefs for their roles in organizing the genocide. At the height of the genocide, the station was even broadcasting hit lists. In most cases, though, prosecutors may not be able to join the dots between speech and harm.

The dispersed nature of hate speech has also been well documented. More often than not, hate groups divide their labor, with more moderate-sounding groups tilling the ground for racist ideas. One study has shown how the white supremacist website Stormfront systematically portrayed Jews and African Americans as inferior, manipulative, tyrannical, genocidal, and false martyrs. The site nevertheless avoided blatantly racist statements and employed less virulent rhetoric than the extreme groups to which it is linked. It tried to appear scientific and rational, often quoting (or misquoting) reports from such credible media as the *New York Times* and the *Wall Street Journal*. Stormfront thus provided stepping-stones to hate through "'reasonable racism,' a tempered discourse that emphasizes pseudorational discussions of race, and subsequently may cast a wider net in attracting audiences."[50] The regulatory challenge of dealing with distributed and long-term hate speech will surface in the case studies; I also discuss it in detail in the final chapter.

Offense-Taking: Manufactured Indignation

Scholars and policymakers understand much less about the manufacture of offendedness than they do about hate speech. While the aggressive motivation behind hate speech is unmistakable, deliberate offense masks itself in victimhood. The indignant mob may seem hypersensitive and downright intolerant, but its sincerity is rarely doubted. Observers assume that they are witnessing genuine, uncontrollable anger at perceived provocations. But things are not always as they seem. Instead, arresting displays of indignation are quite likely to be instances of hate spin. I'm not referring to cases where individuals or small groups lash out at provocations in face-to-face encounters—what American jurisprudence calls "fighting words." And I don't doubt the sincerity of many people who sign a petition or take to the streets to protest how their community has been disrespected by some movie or building plan. But when such campaigns are sustained and take sensational forms, we should be on the lookout for political entrepreneurs with an agenda quite separate from the grievances being expressed. They call for censorship, but their real goal may be to mobilize followers or corner opponents. The resulting agitation is neither spontaneous nor inevitable.

The Myth of Spontaneous Rage

The manufactured quality of hate spin is usually lost on the media, whose news reports often describe the event as a kind of chemical reaction or mechanical response. Reporting on the *Innocence of Muslims* YouTube video in 2013, for example, the *Guardian* said that the film "triggered mayhem in the Muslim world";[51] the *New York Times* said it "ignited bloody protests in the Muslim world."[52] There are multiple problems with this sort of shorthand. Among other things, it paints the world's Muslims as homogeneously susceptible to violent outrage, when in fact only an extremely small minority expresses anger in extreme ways or supports those who do. Indeed, these same newspapers, in their more considered editorials and opinion columns, object strenuously to such stereotyping. The *Guardian's* Sunday publication, the *Observer*, criticized as "almost racist" the notion of "Muslim rage" that, the paper said, had dominated the debate over the video. It pointed out that the lack of a nuanced understanding of Muslims' responses to religious insult perpetuates the impression of a community beyond reason, thus inviting the West to continue relating to Muslims "through the language of hostility alone."[53]

Even when we qualify our accounts by attributing violent acts to only small extreme groups rather than the whole "Muslim world," it is still misleading to liken extremists' reactions to an explosion that is sparked, triggered, or ignited by an inflammatory provocation. Such accounts exclude agency—the deliberate choices made by political middlemen to use the opportunity to instigate an over-the-top reaction. By failing to recognize the decisive roles played by these actors, societies paint themselves into a regulatory corner: if indeed religious conservatives were programmed by their beliefs to wreak havoc when confronted with provocative content, the only options available for peace-loving societies would be to go to war with those groups or censor materials that offend them. If, instead, hate spin is an act of political entrepreneurship, as I hope to demonstrate, different policy options become available. We no longer face a futile battle against transcendent forces, but a rather less epic contest with politicians and activists who can be countered with enough determination and sagacity.

The myth of spontaneous and automatic offense-taking has been cultivated not only by hate spin agents but also their hard-line opponents. Both benefit from brushing aside the many voices of reason and portraying extreme and intolerant offendedness as authentic and natural expressions of that religious community's opinions. Hate spin agents profit when others treat them as genuine spokesmen of their communities, even though their views are usually quite unrepresentative. Their mirror-image opponents gain as well, because exaggerating the clout of extremists helps to justify their own hard-line intolerance.

Puncturing such codependent mythmaking takes some doing. The clearest counterevidence is the sheer inconsistency of offense-taking, especially its patchy distribution over time and space. Offense rarely infects all believers, and there is invariably a time lag between the appearance of the offending work and the first outbreak of outrage against it. One of India's most respected artists, the late Maqbool Fida Husain, sketched a nude Saraswati, the Goddess of Learning, in the mid-1970s. But it was only in 1996 that Hindu chauvinists accused the drawing of offending Hinduism, leading to attacks on galleries, serial police investigations of Husain, and his eventual exile. The timing had more to do with the ascendant Hindu nationalists' need for symbols to show the supposed dangers of secularism than with anything represented in the actual drawing, as the writer and freedom of expression advocate Salil Tripathi points out. Before the relatively recent rise of Hindu nationalism, blasphemy had been a concept alien to the religion. Backed by Hinduism's highly individualized understanding of how devotees should relate to deities, Hindus have erected temples adorned with scenes of not just naked goddesses but even sexual intercourse, including bestiality. By comparison, Husain's paintings were tame. "Neither lascivious nor derisive, Husain's sketch of Saraswati had stirred admiration. But times had changed," Tripathi says.[54]

The Role of Middlemen

If provocative symbols do not always and everywhere produce strong reactions, it must follow that some other intervening factor affects how people in a given time and place respond. This intervention comes in the form of middlemen who decide whether it is in their interests to transform a potential provocation into a full-blown protest. Political scientist Paul Brass showed this in his ethnographic study of collective violence in rural India.[55] At first glance, the routine spectacle of Hindu–Muslim violence in India appears to support the theory of inherently incompatible and mutually offensive religious beliefs. However, Brass found that village disputes in rural Uttar Pradesh escalated into full-blown communal riots only in some cases. Converting a minor squabble to a major incident requires what he calls an "institutionalized riot system" at the local level. The process is directed by a network of specialists with both the capacity and the motivation to interpret events in ways conducive to mass violence. They mobilize the masses, who serve as a "large cast of extras" who believe they are acting in their own interests but are usually the ultimate losers—poor villagers often end up harassed, beaten, or killed by police. Through such processes, an everyday fight among thieves over a statue, for example, can be transformed into a defense of Hindu faith of millennial import. "Riots, therefore, are partly organized, partly spontaneous forms of collective action designed to appear or made to appear afterwards as spontaneous expressions of popular feeling."[56]

These scholarly observations are corroborated by individuals with experience in managing such crises on the ground. One such person is the former police officer R. B. Sreekumar, in India's Gujarat state. He was head of intelligence of the Gujarat police in 2002 when one of the ugliest pogroms of the twenty-first century claimed between one and two thousand lives, mainly of Muslims.[57] The state government, led by Narendra Modi, denied any responsibility. It claimed that the violence was an understandable reaction to a fatal train fire, blamed on Muslim arsonists, in which dozens of Hindu pilgrims died. But Sreekumar turned whistleblower, handing over reams of evidence pointing to high-level political direction and police complicity in the riots. Among other facts, Sreekumar revealed the uneven geographic distribution of fatalities. In places where honest law enforcers followed standard procedures for dealing with communal disturbances, few to zero deaths occurred, even in areas with a history of communal violence.[58] Another senior official, Harsh Mander, also broke ranks to speak out. "This was not a spontaneous upsurge of mass anger. It was a carefully planned pogrom," he wrote in a blog that was subsequently published in mainstream media.[59] The idea that the Indian state lacks the capacity to suppress mass violence has no credibility, he says. "No riot can go on for more than a few hours without a complicit state. This was a state-sponsored massacre."[60]

In this book I focus not on communal violence alone, but on the broader category of religious offense. Nevertheless, what scholars and activists have discovered about riots is eminently transferable to the kinds of incidents explored here. Offendedness, like the instigation of collective violence, is a political strategy—no matter how convincingly wrapped in what Brass calls "the discourse of faith and sentiment."[61] It shows the same kind of selectivity and sophistication on the part of political actors whose choices are shaped by more prosaic interests than the defense of their God. Indeed, the "institutionalized riot system" may be a misnomer, for it suggests a mechanism designed to produce only episodic collective violence. Violent conflict between ethnic communities is only one possible output in the system's repertoire. The button that agents choose to push could instead unleash mob demands for censorship, attacks on publishing houses, and so on.

The law cannot treat offense-taking as it does hate speech. The state should act against incitement, but laws against religious insult in effect enshrine a right to take offense, compelling the state to come to the aid of those who loudly profess their righteous indignation. Such a system might pass muster if nobody ever cries wolf—if people complain only when they believe the offense is an early symptom of much more serious harms. The system would also require an ethic of reciprocity: people have to respect others' feelings as much as they want their own feelings respected by others. Unfortunately, there is scant evidence that groups use a right to be offended in either a restrained or a reciprocal fashion. In this book I show how, on the contrary, hate spin agents politicize righteous indignation in unbridled bids to increase their own groups' power over others. This can produce a culture of offendedness that undermines the values of tolerance and mutuality that democracy requires.

A Growth Industry?

In November 2013, I spoke on a panel in Bangkok with the Pakistani social activist Sabeen Mahmud. Mahmud had had a busy year. She talked about her "Hugs for YouTube" social media campaign, protesting the ban that Pakistani authorities had imposed on the video-sharing platform after the *Innocence of Muslims* video was released.[62] She had also launched a campaign mocking the government's ban on celebrating Valentine's Day and developed a crowd-sourced website to name and shame those who posted hate speech online. Joyful and generous, she was herself a walking, smiling icon of the cosmopolitan values found in liberal sections of Pakistani civil society, as well as a living antidote to hate spin.

In April 2015, Sabeen Mahmud, aged thirty-nine, was shot dead in her car. Authorities produced a suspect who said her murder was in retaliation for her Valentine's Day campaign, appearing to confirm police statements that Mahmud had been targeted by religious extremists.[63] The journalist Veengas Yasmeen is one of many inside Pakistan who do not buy that story. "Why now? The Valentine's Day protest was two years earlier," she said.[64] Skeptics like her are convinced Mahmud was killed because she had, just a few hours earlier, hosted a human rights forum discussing abuses in Balochistan, where the Pakistani military is engaged in brutal counterinsurgency operations.[65]

Sabeen Mahmud's murder is a particularly nasty—but otherwise not unique—case of the nexus between religious intolerance and political opportunism. Around the same time as Mahmud's murder, "atheist" bloggers were being hacked to death in separate attacks in Bangladesh.[66] To most observers, this looked like another open-and-shut case of religious zealots tipped over the edge by offensive expression. But according to journalists and human rights defenders, the bloggers had become targets not for their religious views as such, but because of their influential role in public protests demanding the death penalty for an Islamist leader convicted in Bangladesh's divisive war crimes trials.[67] This was the context of the smear campaign vilifying them as anti-Islamic—a campaign in which a government-formed committee played an instrumental role in compiling a list of eighty-four offending bloggers.[68] They were pawns, crushed in the jostling between the governing Awami League and Islamist groups that it is trying to appease and neutralize. The bloggers' killings remain somewhat shrouded in mystery, but the "secularists vs. extremists" narrative favored by most news reports obscures more than it reveals.[69]

We will be oblivious to these underlying dynamics as long as we are satisfied with accounts that simplistically ascribe violence to mass intolerance and outrage. Indeed, our tendency to uncritically accept the more superficial narrative is probably one reason that hate spin exponents cultivate it so assiduously. The irrational religious mob makes a compelling cover story for political actors who want to conceal their selfish interests. They can hide behind the clash of civilizations idea, which makes any manifestation of religious intolerance—censorship, riots, murders—appear to be just another illustration of colliding values. Such a framing also allows them to invoke the people's name, not just God's. They can take advantage of rising populism, which rewards political actors who are seen to represent large and raucous crowds.[70]

A second reason we should expect religious hate spin to grow in prevalence in the coming years is religion's utility in the framing work that all collective action requires. "Because it is so reliable a source of emotion, religion is a recurring source of social movement framing," says the political sociologist Sidney Tarrow. "Religion provides ready-made symbols, rituals, and solidarities that can be accessed and appropriated by movement leaders."[71] Such connections can be a powerful force for good. Consider, for example, the use of Christian frames by the Reverend Martin Luther King Jr. and Archbishop Desmond Tutu in advancing the cause of human equality in the United States and South Africa respectively. In the hands of movement leaders, any religion is a malleable resource—for good or ill. Hate spin agents can manipulate it to promote intolerance.

Third, hate spin may be growing in reaction to globalization. Globalization doesn't only expand opportunities for people; it also disrupts on grand and intimate levels.[72] It forces people to confront strangers and their values, both in person and through the media. People who fear the changes wrought by globalization often crave simple ideas that offer a reassuring sense of stability. Hate spin responds to that need with its vision of a tight community united against a common enemy. It converts rational, defensive anxieties into a paranoid attack mode, which could involve hate speech against a minority group, manufactured indignation over some injustice symbol, or both. "Fear is implicated in most bad behavior in the area of religion," Martha Nussbaum points out.[73]

Finally, in an age of slower world economic growth, leaders who are struggling to deliver material promises may turn to the politics of identity as a recession-proof alternative, thereby creating the conditions for hate spin. The subjective quality of offense makes hate spin a versatile tool. Although many political scientists regard the economy as the main factor shaping people's political behavior, it can be difficult for politicians to muster winning economic arguments. Many simply lack the capacity to do so. And, there is a limit to how much a politician can bend economic reality. His claims that a community is suffering intolerable material hardship, for example, will not make an impact if it does not tally with the community's own lived experience, or if it is countered by tangible government programs. Economic promises designed to appeal to one segment of voters are likely to come at some cost to another—especially in conditions of low or no economic growth.

Religious offendedness, in contrast, is an extremely elastic resource that can be used with very little political cost. It can be manufactured virtually out of thin air. If the intended audience does not immediately see the threat that the politician purports to see, this can be to his political advantage. He can then present himself as the savior perceptive enough to have spotted the disguised enemy, says Nussbaum: "The corollary of the idea of hidden evil is the idea of superior insight."[74] Once conjured up, offendedness is difficult for others to neutralize. If they try to challenge a community's justification for its outrage, this will probably deepen its sense of being under siege.

This book went to press amidst alarm and incredulity at the Donald Trump phenomenon in the 2016 American presidential election. Trump's racial and religious fearmongering was a logical, if grotesque, outcome of electoral dynamics that reward enterprising political actors who are prepared to use hate spin to give them a competitive edge. Democracies need to resist this destructive form of politics. In part, this depends on adopting the right constitutional provisions and laws, the subject of the next chapter.

2 By What Rules? Human Rights and Religious Authority

Constitutional and legal frameworks shape the practice of hate spin. Laws protecting freedom of expression expand the space for hate speech, while those that prohibit incitement restrict it. When the state bans blasphemy or the wounding of religious feelings, this creates opportunities for hate spin agents to manufacture righteous indignation as a political weapon.

Hate speech regulation is a complex and contentious area of public law. The challenge lies in simultaneously protecting liberty and equality, the two basic pillars of democracy. Bad laws can threaten either or both by restricting the freedom to engage in socially valuable public discourse and by compromising the rights of minorities to live as equal members of society. It is important to get these laws right.

Unlike, say, toxic chemicals or radioactive waste, words and symbols are not inherently hazardous. Whether they cause harm depends on a number of contextual factors that are open to cultural interpretation. Even the public expression of flagrantly bigoted opinions can have positive effects, by alerting society to the existence of hate groups, prompting counter-speech, and allowing such ideas to be defeated through open debate. Like fire, provocative expression has both creative and destructive potential, and laws must somehow find a way to facilitate the former while limiting the latter.

Human rights principles provide the most promising guideposts. International human rights treaties require states to prohibit incitement to discrimination or violence—but do not support the idea of banning religious offense. The latter half of the prescription is more controversial than the first. To some persons of faith, a government's refusal to protect religions from disrespect seems like a grave injustice. It should be stressed, though, that we are referring here only to *legal* responses. Treating religious offense as legally permissible does not mean it has to be socially or politically tolerated. A United Nations human rights report emphasizes this point: Government officials and political party leaders "should have the courage to systematically condemn hate speech publicly," even when that speech is protected by the law.[1]

In this chapter I first explore the human rights standard in detail, after which I discuss the American First Amendment tradition. These two frameworks, while distinct, belong in the broad category of modern liberal approaches to hate speech regulation. In contrast, a more traditional set of policies is much less protective of free speech, allowing governments wide latitude to police offense and insult. The most serious and sustained challenge to the international human rights perspective, which I discuss toward the end of this chapter, has been Islamic nations' attempt to incorporate the notion of "defamation of religion" into international law. This debate raises the larger question of how constitutions should accommodate religious rationales for law. Drawing insights from the sociology of religion and comparative political science, I argue that a plural and tolerant democracy does not require religion to be forced out of the public sphere. But the balance between religious and secular authority must give primacy to the rule of law.

The Human Rights Perspective

International human rights law provides a framework for balancing freedom of expression and the rights potentially violated by hate speech. This framework is sensitive to the harms that can be inflicted when group identities are vilified, but resists the idea that the law should protect anyone's religion from offense. This approach is prescribed by the International Covenant on Civil and Political Rights (ICCPR), which has been ratified by almost nine out of ten UN member states.[2] Nevertheless, the ICCPR must still compete with more traditional ideas about regulating speech. After all, human rights norms are neither the only nor the most established systems of morality available to societies. Long before these norms were developed, most people intuitively recognized the moral responsibility to help others, and certainly to avoid harming them. This commitment, however, tended to be limited to people within their own groups, whether families, tribes, or nations. The radical idea behind human rights is that we owe obligations to strangers and enemies as well, on the basis of our shared humanity.[3] The international system would therefore have to recognize not only the sovereignty of nation-states, but also the sanctity of each and every person, regardless of the status that any state gives or denies to individuals within its borders.

This principle was enshrined in the preamble of the United Nations Charter, which affirms faith "in the dignity and worth of the human person, in the equal rights of men and women and of nations large and small."[4] In 1948, the UN General Assembly adopted the Universal Declaration of Human Rights (UDHR), an unenforceable assertion of fundamental principles.[5] "All human beings are born free and equal in dignity and rights," states Article 1. The UDHR was reinforced by the ICCPR, which was adopted by the General Assembly in 1966.[6] By the end of 2015, 168 states had ratified the treaty, effectively agreeing to be bound by it. The UDHR and ICCPR, together with the International Covenant on Economic, Social and Cultural Rights, collectively make up what is referred to as the International Bill of Human Rights. Regional groupings of European and American nation-states have their own human rights instruments. The forty-seven-member Council of Europe applies the European Convention on Human Rights, while the Organization of American States, comprising thirty-five states in North and South America, uses the American Convention on Human Rights. Their approaches to free speech are closely aligned with the UN treaties.

A network of supporting institutions has emerged around these international and regional instruments. The Human Rights Council, an intergovernmental body of forty-seven member states, derives its authority from the UN Charter. It provides a formal avenue to discuss human rights issues, to conduct periodic reviews of the human rights situations in all member states, to hear complaints from individuals and groups, and to make recommendations. The Human Rights Council has appointed a network of Special Rapporteurs—independent experts who are given free rein to report annually to the General Assembly on situations of concern. The Guatemalan activist Frank La Rue played a key role in articulating a human rights perspective on hate speech during his term as the Special Rapporteur on the Promotion and Protection of the Right to Freedom of Opinion and Expression from 2008 to 2014.[7] The UN also has a separate Human Rights Committee to which anyone can bring complaints of alleged violations in states that are party to a relevant treaty. The Council of Europe's Convention and its supporting institutions have been described as "the most comprehensive and developed system for supranational human rights protection."[8] The European Court of Human Rights has produced several groundbreaking decisions relating to offense and incitement, some of which I refer to in this chapter. The standard-setting body for the European Convention, the Council of Ministers, has issued detailed opinions on this issue.[9] Civil society organizations and academic experts have collaborated with officials to develop norms for dealing with hate speech and religious intolerance that are consistent with international human rights treaties. These discussions have produced the so-called Camden Principles, prepared in 2009 by the London-based NGO that calls itself Article 19, and the Rabat Plan of Action, drawn up under the auspices of the UN Secretariat's Office of the High Commissioner for Human Rights in 2012.[10]

International and regional human rights treaties and their supporting institutions and policy documents address societies with extremely diverse historical experiences, cultural traditions, and political systems. Not surprisingly, levels of treaty implementation vary greatly across the world. Even liberal democratic jurisdictions differ from one another in their interpretations of human rights law. The human rights approach, nonetheless, contains certain broad normative principles that are relevant to all open societies seeking to manage religious hatred. Four aspects merit detailed discussion. First, the approach includes a strong commitment to freedom of expression. Second, it enshrines people's right to be free of discrimination and hatred, allowing—or even requiring—states to act in defense of that right, including by restricting expression. Third, it provides a framework for balancing these rights, emphasizing that any restrictions on free speech must satisfy strict conditions. And fourth, it associates freedom of expression with freedom of religion, viewing them as complementary rights. Both are undermined when speech is censored in the name of respect for religion.

Freedom of Expression

The ICCPR's Article 19(2) upholds freedom of expression. Echoing Article 19 of the UDHR, it states, "Everyone shall have the right to freedom of expression; this right shall include freedom to seek, receive, and impart information and ideas of all kinds, regardless of frontiers, either orally, in writing or in print, in the form of art, or through any other media of his choice."[11] The American Convention, adopted three years after the ICCPR, contains virtually identical wording in its Article 13.[12] The European Convention, drafted in 1950, provides a similar right in its Article 10.[13]

These treaties establish freedom of expression as intrinsically valuable to every human being. Freedom of expression is required as "a means to claim and enjoy all other rights" and as "a critical foundation of democracy, which depends on the free flow of diverse sources of information and ideas."[14] It is not, however, an absolute right. While it is a fundamental right of every individual, each person exists in a social context without which one's full development is not possible. The ICCPR and European Convention therefore speak of freedom of expression carrying with it "duties and responsibilities." Accordingly, states can set certain limitations and restrictions on freedom of expression. Article 19(3) of the ICCPR says that restrictions are permitted: "(a) For respect of the rights or reputations of others; (b) For the protection of national security or of public order (ordre public), or of public health or morals." Article 13(2) of the American Convention and the European Convention's Article 10(2) contain similar wording.

These lists of exceptions are meant to be exhaustive and not open-ended. Note that they do not mention the feelings of a community or the stature of their religious beliefs as legitimate concerns for speech restrictions. Rather, the right to freedom of expression protects "forms of expression that are offensive, disturbing, and shocking."[15] If it didn't, the right would be superfluous, since expression that does not trouble anyone would not face any resistance. Speech needs legal protection precisely because it is sometimes upsetting, especially to powerful interests and dominant values. Such speech can have worth, since only if the new and unfamiliar are given leeway to challenge the old and settled is it possible to have human progress and creativity.

Protection Against Incitement to Hatred

Hate speech regulation is premised on the idea that individuals can be unfairly handicapped by their group identities. Certain groups in society may have been subject to neglect or oppression to such a degree that, even if their members now enjoy formal equality, they continue to be systemically disadvantaged by prejudice. For these persons, achieving the goal of substantive equality requires some kind of affirmative action. Hate speech regulation, then, can be thought of as a type of positive discrimination for society's traditional scapegoats.

None of the major international or regional treaties on human rights include the term "hate speech." The term is too broad and unwieldy for legal purposes. Instead, international human rights law refers to "incitement" to hatred. The ICCPR says in Article 20(2): "Any advocacy of national, racial or religious hatred that constitutes incitement to discrimination, hostility or violence shall be prohibited by law." Note that this article goes beyond merely permitting states to impose restrictions on harmful speech; it obliges them to do so. The American Convention echoes the ICCPR's wording, except that it mentions only incitement "to lawless violence or to any other similar action," and not discrimination. The European Convention does not contain an explicit prohibition of incitement, but the European Court has derived a similar standard from its reading of the treaty. The free speech provision itself, in Article 10(2), allows restrictions to protect the rights of others. Article 14, which rules out discrimination, has also been cited to uphold restrictions on hate speech. The European Court has also turned to Article 17, which says that there is no right to engage in activities aimed at the "destruction of any of the rights and freedoms" contained in the treaty. This provision is meant to counter the risk that democratic freedoms are abused to undermine democratic values. Based on this article, hate speech can be disqualified from free speech protection.

Definitions of key terms—"incitement," "discrimination," and "hostility"—vary. The nongovernmental Camden Principles define "incitement" as calls to action that "create an imminent risk."[16] Some European jurisdictions use the terms "provocation" or "threatening speech" instead of "incitement."[17] The terms "hatred" and "hostility" refer to "intense and irrational emotions of opprobrium, enmity and detestation towards the target group," say the Camden Principles.[18] Frank La Rue, the former UN Special Rapporteur for Freedom of Expression, defines "discrimination" as any identity-based "distinction, exclusion or restriction ... that has the effect or purpose of impairing or nullifying the recognition, enjoyment or exercise, on an equal footing, of all human rights and fundamental freedoms in the political, economic, social, cultural, civil or any other field of public life."[19]

While hate speech laws vary, there is a broad consensus among liberal democracies that what needs to be prohibited is speech that results in objective harms done to actual, living people—and not to religions or belief systems as such, or their prophets, holy books, or icons, no matter how precious and central they are to believers' identity. Expression that is merely insulting or offensive cannot be treated as dangerous. "Since not all types of inflammatory, hateful or offensive speech amount to incitement, the two should not be conflated," La Rue says.[20]

Balancing of Rights

At first glance, the ICCPR's provisions dealing with free speech and incitement may appear to contradict each another. In a 2011 General Comment, the UN Human Rights Committee sought to correct this impression with a definitive statement: "Articles 19 and 20 are compatible with and complement each other."[21] It points out that Article 19(3) already recognizes that protecting the rights of others is one of the legitimate rationales for state restrictions on free speech. Hate speech could be restricted under this provision, or for reasons of public order or national security.[22] Article 20 addresses an important set of situations in which restrictions are especially warranted. In only one respect does Article 20 go beyond Article 19: In the special case of incitement to hatred, states are required, not just permitted, to impose legal prohibitions. Article 20 must still comply with Article 19, which circumscribes the kind of restrictions that states can impose. Article 19(3) says that the right to freedom of expression may be "subject to certain restrictions, but these shall only be such as are provided by law and are necessary" for specified purposes, as noted above.

Based on a close reading of Article 19, experts say that any proposed government interference must be subject to a so-called three-part test of legality, legitimacy, and proportionality.[23] First, any restriction must be explicitly "provided by law." The law must be precisely and clearly worded so that people can regulate their own conduct accordingly. The law must not give unlimited discretion to regulators; it must set out unambiguously what expression they can and cannot restrict.

Second, government restrictions on freedom of expression must serve at least one of the societal interests that international law explicitly recognizes as legitimate: namely, to protect the rights or reputations of others, national security or public order, or public health or morals. Although governments routinely abuse such justifications to further their own political interests, well-drafted laws and independent courts can contain such risks.[24]

Third, the government must be able to show that its chosen intervention is the least restrictive way to achieve its stated aim. The American Convention elaborates on this principle of proportionality, stating that restrictions on expression may entail "subsequent imposition of liability" but not "prior censorship," except for the sole purpose of regulating access to public entertainments to protect children and adolescents.

As a general principle, states attempting to strike a balance between competing rights and interests are supposed to be faithful to the overarching principles enshrined in constitutions and covenants. In line with this requirement, Article 29(2) of the UDHR and Articles 9(2) and 10(2) of the European Convention state that limitations of rights and freedoms are allowable if they are necessary "in a democratic society." Like Article 17 of the European Convention, these insertions can be thought of as safety mechanisms that deter bad-faith treaty interpretations that undermine the document's core democratic values.

Human rights defenders argue that even in the extreme cases of incitement to violence, the value of free speech is not negated. In the run-up to the Rwandan genocide, for example, it was a lack of media freedom that permitted hate-filled government radio to monopolize the media space in many parts of the country.[25] Societies need to be able to respond to hate speech with counter-speech. It is more likely that hate speech will escalate unchallenged when there are barriers to setting up media outlets, constraints on policy debates, and a stifling of social condemnation of incivility.[26]

Freedom of Religion

Hate spin targeting or perpetrated by religious communities has implications for another human right—freedom of religion. Article 18 of the ICCPR upholds a person's right to freedom of thought, conscience, and religion. This includes a person's right "to manifest his religion or belief in teaching, practice, worship and observance." The European and American Conventions provide similar guarantees in Article 9 and Article 12, respectively.

Since the loudest objections to blasphemous expression usually come from devout believers, freedom of religion may appear to be in conflict with freedom of expression. From a human rights perspective, however, this is a false opposition. "Freedom of religion or belief and freedom of opinion and expression are interdependent, as is the whole body of human rights norms," UN experts have noted.[27] Without free speech, religious communities cannot exercise their faiths freely, since all have some beliefs and practices that others find offensive. Practically all of today's world religions evolved by challenging and breaking away from preexisting belief systems. Early adherents suffered for it, and some continue to do so. Defenders of the human right to religious freedom are therefore united with free speech advocates in opposing the idea of "suffocating criticism of a religion by making it punishable by law" or "preventing ideas about religions from being expressed."[28]

States that see no contradiction between speech suppression and religious freedom are invariably those that discriminate in how they apply both. They give favored religious communities the freedom to express their own beliefs, including in ways that shock or offend others, while denying that latitude to individuals of other persuasions. The strongest proponents of using the law to punish disrespect to religion tend not to respect the religious freedoms of other sects, denominations, and faiths.

Such discrimination violates the principle of human equality at the heart of international human rights law. Article 2 of both the UDHR and the ICCPR state that everyone is entitled to the rights and freedoms contained in these documents, "without distinction of any kind," including those of race and religion. Article 14 of the European Convention and Article 1 of the American Convention provide similar guarantees of nondiscrimination in respecting people's rights and freedoms. Once we insist that freedom from discrimination be wedded to freedom of religion and belief, it becomes readily apparent why the latter cannot exist without freedom of expression.

Only when the law protects the robust discussion of religious doctrines and practices as well as the questioning of one another's values—including in ways that some find upsetting—can religious freedom be enjoyed by all. This is also why religious freedom provisions include the words "or belief." Those who believe in no god cannot be denied freedoms held by people of faith—a principle that is violated when atheists are persecuted.

Dimensions of Difference

The human rights approach is relatively new, having crystallized only within the past few decades. Many signatories to the ICCPR deviate significantly from its principles. Even democracies vary in how they interpret the above norms, based on their particular historical contexts and how they prioritize different rights. Vestiges of more traditional approaches—such as blasphemy laws—survive to this day, even in some Western democracies. Most legislators and jurists recognize that complete standardization is unrealistic for matters relating to culture and values. The European system acknowledges this in its key principle of "margin of appreciation," which refers to the latitude that the European Court is prepared to accord to member states when deciding how best to protect individual rights. This latitude applies particularly to freedom of expression, given that states have no identical conception of morals. National courts are presumed to be better able than a supranational judge to weigh questions of morality as well as the necessity of restrictions.[29]

National approaches to regulating free speech vary on several dimensions: which risks the law seeks to contain, including whether to prohibit religious offense; which groups and interests it seeks to protect; at what point the state should forcibly intervene; and who should be held liable for the harms caused by speech. On each of these dimensions, some countries adopt a modern, liberal approach compatible with human rights norms, while others lean toward more traditional answers. The range of approaches is explored in this section, and the key differences are summarized in table 2.1.

Which Risks to Contain

Laws dealing with offensive or vilifying speech vary in the kinds of risks that they try to address. Offense is the oldest justification for censorship; it's where many countries continue to draw the line. Many nations still have blasphemy laws on the books. Typically, such laws are themselves discriminatory, protecting only the state-sanctioned or dominant religious

Table 2.1

Comparing the traditional and modern human rights perspectives on religious offense.

	Traditional approach	Modern approach
Which risks to contain	Law insulates people's feelings from expression that offends them.	Law is reserved for protecting people from incitement to hatred, especially violence.
Whether to protect religion	Law protects the dominant religion's orthodoxy and punishes heresy and blasphemy.	Law cannot shield beliefs. Respect for religion should be encouraged, not forced.
Which groups to protect	Law sides with the majority and preserves mainstream culture and values.	Law helps the vulnerable; dominant groups can help themselves.
When to intervene	States have wide latitude to restrict speech as soon as any risk of harm is apparent.	States can restrict speech only if the threat is direct and imminent.
Whom to hold accountable	Anyone who disseminates the offending expression is liable for punishment.	Intent matters: news media must be free to perform their informational function.

doctrine, for instance the Orthodox Church in Greece and Sunni Islam in Malaysia. The victims are frequently adherents of sects, denominations, and other minority faiths whose practices are deemed to be an affront to the orthodoxy. A 2011 study found that several countries—Bahrain, Iran, Kuwait, Pakistan, and Saudi Arabia—filtered websites belonging to religions or sects that are not state sanctioned. Several others, including Bangladesh, Indonesia, Oman, Qatar, Sudan, Tunisia, the United Arab Emirates, and Yemen, filtered content perceived as blasphemous, offensive, or contrary to Islam.[30]

As discussed above, international human rights law rejects offense as a legitimate justification for restricting speech. Liberal jurisdictions consider criticism of particular ideas and institutions to be protected speech, even if expressed in extreme and hurtful language. Liberal norms now recognize only flesh-and-blood victims of hatred, not abstract concepts or deities. In England, the offenses of blasphemy and blasphemous libel were abolished in 2008. Liberal democracies that still criminalize blasphemy—such as Canada—have not enforced these laws for decades. Countries applying the ICCPR standard draw the line instead at incitement. There is a consensus that incitement to violence—and certainly genocide—calls for state intervention. Policies toward incitement to discrimination, however, vary markedly. Most forms of racist propaganda are protected by the US Constitution, as discussed further below.[31] In contrast, Canada's commitment to multiculturalism means that the government can take legal action against hate speech that compromises the target group's acceptance in the larger society and that cultivates intolerance among others.[32]

The European Court's position is complicated by the margin of appreciation principle, by which it is prepared to cede discretion to national courts. In 2005, it did not object to Turkey's imposition of a fine on a publisher found guilty of publishing a book insulting to God, Islam, the Prophet, and the Quran. The European Court said that although believers should tolerate criticisms of their religion, the book contained not just provocative but also abusive attacks on the Prophet, and that "believers could legitimately feel that certain passages of the book in question constituted an unwarranted and offensive attack on them."[33]

One tricky distinction that laws may or may not make is between violence that is incited by hate speech and violence that is provoked by offensive speech. Both jeopardize public order, and the maintenance of public order—as opposed to the rights of vulnerable groups—is one of the main rationales for hate speech regulation in many societies. In the United Kingdom, for example, hate speech prohibitions evolved from the Public Order Act 1986 and continue to be framed in breach-of-peace terms. Germany's Criminal Code, similarly, prohibits speech that incites hatred in a way "capable of disturbing public peace."[34]

The problem with regulating speech through the lens of public order is that it can unfairly penalize speakers for outcomes they did not intend, and over which they have no control. The strategy of manufactured indignation makes this is a very real possibility. It is not difficult for hate spin agents to instigate violent outrage at a political opponent's speech, thus triggering restrictions against the speaker. Before applying the rationale of public order, the state should instead satisfy the remaining parts of the "three-part test." In most cases, censorship does not meet the test of necessity, since the state could instead use its coercive powers against those who threaten to break the law with their violent outrage.

Which Groups to Protect

Traditionally, nations regulated offensive speech to preserve the standing of individuals in power and the culture and values of the majority community. Within the Western world, the first insult law was probably that of seditious libel, which banned any writing that could foster hatred or contempt for rulers.[35] Over time, this bias for the status quo has been overturned by the rise of democratic principles that require the weak to be able to challenge the strong peacefully. From a modern human rights perspective, a community whose beliefs are already dominant does not need the law to defend its members against insult or ideological attack.

Over time, therefore, liberal jurisdictions have turned the traditional approach on its head. Instead of insulating already-powerful elites or mollycoddling majority feelings, the law creates space for dissent and protects marginalized groups against majoritarian attacks. The United Kingdom illustrates this trend. Back in the 1960s, the first person prosecuted for hate speech under the Race Relations Act of 1965 was a black man who cursed a white policeman. In 1968, a leader of the Black Liberation Movement was sentenced to a year in prison for a speech calling whites "vicious and nasty people."[36] In more recent decades, however, courts in the UK and other Western democracies would be more likely to brush off such offensive speech by minorities as understandable responses to racism in a white-dominated society. In Australia in 2003, for example, the court dismissed a Race Discrimination Act application by a white prison officer. It said that the act's purpose was to protect vulnerable minorities, whereas whites are dominant in Australia. Similarly, the European Court has tended to uphold prohibitions on hate speech attacking minorities, but challenged governments that punish minorities for using extreme speech in ongoing conflicts, for instance Turkey's crackdown on Kurdish dissidents.[37]

Liberal democratic jurisdictions still acknowledge that mainstream norms cannot be totally disregarded in censorship matters. In the United States, for example, states are allowed to legislate different standards for the public display of pornographic magazines. The US courts' "Miller test" for obscenity includes consideration of the viewpoint of the "the average person, applying contemporary community standards."[38] The Miller test, however, only applies to works that lack serious literary, artistic, political, or scientific value—in other words, when giving in to community standards would amount to no great loss for those who disagree.

At the other extreme are illiberal societies that maintain a traditional bias for dominant interests, regardless of the cost to minority rights. In Pakistan, for example, blasphemy laws have been applied disproportionately to non-Muslims and to the Shia Muslim minority.[39] Punishments are more severe when Muslims take offense than when other religious communities' sensibilities are hurt. Under Pakistan's Penal Code's Section 295A—inherited from India—someone who intentionally outrages the religious feelings of any community could be jailed for ten years. But under Section 295B the penalty rises to life imprisonment for derogatory use of the Quran. Section 295C allows the death penalty to anyone who "by any imputation, innuendo, or insinuation, directly or indirectly, defiles the sacred name of the Holy Prophet Muhammad."

Liberal societies recognize that, in principle, any identifiable group with entrenched disadvantages might need protection from hate speech. In practice, the question of which types of groups should be recognized is a matter of evolution and debate. The ICCPR's Article 20 explicitly mentions only "national, racial or religious hatred," while Canada's more expansive hate speech law refers to any "identifiable group," which means "any section of the public distinguished by colour, race, religion, national or ethnic origin, age, sex, sexual orientation, or mental or physical disability."[40] India's Penal Code and its Protection of Civil Rights Act cover the unique problem of caste-based hate speech. Liberal societies have gradually broadened their antidiscrimination and hate speech protections to include more and more groups, usually starting with ethnic minorities. Migrant workers and sexual minorities have tended to lag in their struggle for recognition as groups deserving protection. This is especially the case at the international level. Table 2.2 shows the sequence of core UN human rights instruments dealing with the rights of specific groups. It reveals racism as probably the earliest form of discrimination to be universally abhorred. The hate speech provision in the International Convention on the Elimination of All Forms of Racial Discrimination (ICERD) is stronger than the ICCPR's Article 20. It requires states to "criminalize" (as opposed to broadly "prohibit") "the dissemination of ideas based on racial superiority or hatred" and "incitement to racial discrimination."

The international community is more divided on the issue of religious discrimination. In 1981, the UN General Assembly adopted without a vote a Declaration on the Elimination of All Forms of Intolerance and of Discrimination Based on Religion or Belief. It was nonbinding, but Iraq nonetheless lodged a reservation on behalf of the Organization of the Islamic Conference over perceived contradictions between the declaration and Islamic law.[41] A stronger UN convention addressing religious discrimination is unlikely, since the dominant religion is core to the national identity of several member states.

Thresholds for Legal Intervention

The harm caused by hate speech depends not only on its content but also its context, making it impossible to predict with complete certainty the effects

Table 2.2
Core international human rights treaties protecting vulnerable groups.

To protect	Treaty name	Year adopted by General Assembly	Years taken to enter into force*	Number of state parties**
Racial groups	ICERD: International Convention on the Elimination of All Forms of Racial Discrimination	1965	4	177
All human beings	ICCPR: International Covenant on Civil and Political Rights	1966	10	168
	International Covenant on Economic, Social and Cultural Rights	1966	10	164
Women	CEDAW: Convention on the Elimination of All Forms of Discrimination against Women	1979	2	189
Children	CRC: Convention on the Rights of the Child	1989	1	196
Migrant workers	ICMW: International Convention on the Protection of the Rights of All Migrant Workers and Members of Their Families	1990	13	48
Persons with disabilities	CRPD: Convention on the Rights of Persons with Disabilities	2006	2	160

*A UN treaty enters into force when it receives its 20th ratification.
**As at December 7, 2015. State parties are those that agree to be bound by the treaty.

of any particular utterance. States vary in the timing of their legal interventions. The "incitement" threshold favors downstream interventions, when harms are imminent. Alternatively, prudence may pressure regulators to act upstream, closer to the source of the speech and long before its worst-case effects are certain. For example, although experts agree that Rwanda's genocidal RTLM radio station was not entitled to free speech protection, they disagree over when the station should have been banned or jammed—only once the killing started, or months earlier when it commenced its hate campaign.[42]

The history of identity-based conflict in any given country has a dramatic effect on how its domestic laws are formulated. India, for example, is prepared to punish the promotion of "disharmony" between different religions, long before any resulting harms are imminent.[43] This is not because disharmony as such is anathema to Indian society, but because a history of communal conflict has made the state averse to the risk that discord will escalate into violence. Similarly, history has persuaded some Western democracies to ban denial of the Holocaust. In 1993, the UN's Human Rights Committee ruled that France did not violate Article 19 of the ICCPR by convicting a university professor, Robert Faurisson, for promoting the idea that the Holocaust was a fabrication.[44] The Human Rights Committee was persuaded that Holocaust denial in the context of contemporary France could constitute a form of incitement to anti-Semitism, violating the Jewish community's right to live in society with full human dignity.

Since attacks on historically oppressed groups are often accompanied by revisionist accounts of the past, the Camden Principles explicitly recognize that the condoning or denying of genocide, crimes against humanity, and war crimes can constitute hate speech and, as such, should be prohibited.[45] Such denial, also called negationism, can be considered a special category of racist speech. The human rights standard usually demands that the would-be censor or prosecutor establish a direct causal link between the expression he wants to suppress and the imminent harm he means to avoid. But, as the case of Holocaust denial shows, states may be prepared be more elastic in applying the principle of causal proximity. American free speech doctrine, in contrast, demands a "clear and present danger" test: only if violence would otherwise be virtually inevitable would government regulation of hate speech be justified.

Courts have evolved some general indicators to help ascertain the likelihood of harm from hate speech. These include not only the content of the expression but also the status and social role of the speaker, the size of the audience, the mode of dissemination, and the context of the speech. Politicians, parties, public officials and preachers addressing large, polarized audiences can be assumed to have a greater impact than lesser-known citizens reaching out to smaller groups in a stable environment. Applying such criteria, the European Court of Human Rights has ruled that even patently violent language deserves protection if it does not amount to a credible call to arms.

Take, for example, the European Court's 1999 judgment on the Turkish government's jailing of a Kurdish poet, under its antiterrorism law. The court recognized that his poems contained aggressive pleas, for instance "to join the martyrs of Kurdistan." The judges acknowledged, "Taken literally, the poems might be construed as inciting readers to hatred, revolt, and the use of violence." They nonetheless argued that the poet was a private individual whose works addressed a very small audience. Such factors substantially limited the poems' potential impact on national security and public order, making them "less a call to an uprising than an expression of deep distress in the face of a difficult political situation."[46] The court therefore found the conviction inconsistent with the European Convention's free speech provisions.

Accountability for Harmful Speech

Hate speech is often mediated by journalists and, increasingly, online platforms. States that are serious about protecting freedom of expression would target the original source of hate propaganda and not punish those who merely transmit messages either with good intentions or without knowledge. Other states, however, use the circulation of inflammatory views as an opportunity to clamp down on media that carry diverse viewpoints as part of their informational role. Consider an incident in Malaysia in 2008, when a ruling party politician declared at a public event that the country's large Chinese minority were squatters who did not deserve equal rights. The government used the Internal Security Act to make an arrest—not of the politician, but of a journalist from a national Chinese-language daily who accurately reported the speech.[47] Faced with an instant outcry, the government released the reporter and claimed that she had been detained for her own protection. But its illiberal instincts were plain to see.

In the landmark case of *Jersild v. Denmark*, the European Court recognized that journalists reporting on incidents of hate speech should not be treated the same as the speakers themselves. Danish courts had convicted a reporter whose television documentary about the far right quoted extremists' racist opinions.[48] The European Court judged that the reporter should not have been found guilty of aiding the dissemination of hate speech, since the press has a duty to raise public awareness and generate debate about hate groups. This, though, does not imply any blanket immunity for the media. The European Court did not rule Turkish authorities out-of-bounds when they fined the owner of a weekly publication that had published two inflammatory letters in a climate of conflict and tension.[49]

For Internet intermediaries, the issue is more complicated; I explore it in detail in chapter 3.

The intent of the speaker is a key factor in deciding culpability. Artists, like journalists, have a social role that may require them to produce provocative content. "Artistic expression should be considered with reference to its artistic value and context, given that individuals may use art to provoke strong feelings but without the intention of inciting violence, discrimination or hostility," notes Frank La Rue.[50] Horrendous human rights violations occur in states with sweeping offense laws that pay no heed to the speaker's intent. In Pakistan, for example, the blasphemous libel laws originally only criminalized deliberate and malicious acts.[51] Under President Zia ul-Haq in the 1970s and 1980s, however, harsher and more sweeping provisions were added that made no distinction between intended and unintended offense. In 2002, a man was sentenced to death for declaring that Muhammad was a false prophet, despite indications that he was mentally ill (he also claimed he was a reincarnation of Jesus Christ).[52]

The US First Amendment: A More Liberal Standard

The American deviation from the international human rights position on freedom of expression is best characterized as a family dispute within the liberal clan. However, its tilt in favor of free speech is pronounced enough to have generated a library of comparative legal analysis, raging quarrels between civil rights defenders, and complex court cases. One practical outcome of regulatory disparities is that many European hate groups park their websites on US servers to enjoy freedoms that they might not in their home countries. Ironically, therefore, the United States, with its deserved reputation as the world's leading salesman of democratic values, is also among the biggest exporters and conduits of antidemocratic intolerance. Other liberal democracies have had to make peace with the US position. "There is no prospect politically of the First Amendment to the Constitution being rolled back," notes Mark Potok of the Southern Poverty Law Center, an American anti-hate watchdog group. "Support for it is absolutely broad; it goes from the far left to the far right, right across the board."[53]

Freedom of expression is not an absolute right in the United States, but the protected space is far more expansive than in any other country. The First Amendment of the US Constitution declares, "Congress shall make no law … abridging the freedom of speech, or of the press." Since its adoption in 1791, and especially as interpreted in landmark US Supreme Court rulings in the latter half of the twentieth century, the First Amendment's Free

Speech Clause has evolved into the world's most powerful bulwark against censorship of public discourse. Private actors can impose their own rules and restrictions, and corporations are free to fire employees who speak out of turn; news media can and do drop commentators who offend ethnic sensibilities. But government suppression of viewpoints in public discourse is almost always unconstitutional. In comparison, the ICCPR's loophole-ridden free speech protection looks "practically useless," says the American legal scholar Robert Post.[54] Prevailing First Amendment doctrine leaves only a few types of political speech unprotected, on the grounds that they infringe on others' rights: "when it amounts to a true threat of violence, when it incites its audience to imminent lawbreaking, when it recklessly defames a public figure, or when it negligently defames a private person."[55]

The United States does not even prohibit racist speech as such. Taking a position that many American legal scholars have questioned and most non-Americans find perverse, the US Supreme Court does not allow government to suppress racist speech to give nonracist speech an advantage in public discourse, as this in its view would amount to unconstitutional discrimination against a given viewpoint. In one extraordinary 1992 case, the court struck down a city ordinance against hate symbols, which had been used to convict a white youth who burnt a cross on a black family's lawn. It acknowledged that the government had a legitimate interest in protecting members of groups that had suffered discrimination, including ensuring that they could live in peace wherever they wished. The justices' problem with the ordinance was that it discriminated against hateful viewpoints. The authorities should instead use content-neutral means to protect the rights of minorities, the court opined.[56]

When the United States ratified ICERD in 1994, it lodged a reservation against Article 4, which, as quoted above, requires states to criminalize the dissemination of racist ideas or race hatred. It said it would not accept any obligation under the convention to restrict free speech rights that were protected by the US Constitution and its laws. The United States posted similar reservations regarding the ICCPR's anti-incitement Article 20 when it finally ratified the treaty in 1992—nineteen years after Germany and sixteen years after Canada.

First Amendment doctrine does agree with the international human rights norm that those who incite violence should not be granted free speech protection. However, the two part ways on the incitement to discrimination and hatred, which the ICCPR requires governments to prohibit and the US Constitution prohibits government from restricting when such speech occurs in the course of public debate. Even incitement to violence is interpreted exceptionally strictly by the United States. The term is reserved for public statements that produce an imminent risk of violence. It is distinguished from "advocacy," which refers to the intentional promotion of violence. Advocacy of violence would be protected speech if it does not also incite. This was the line drawn by the Supreme Court in its 1969 *Brandenburg v. Ohio* decision.[57] This case involved Ku Klux Klan members who staged a rally in which speakers told blacks to return to Africa and Jews to Israel, and said that if the government did not act, the Klan would. The Supreme Court unanimously overturned a criminal conviction against the organizers, arguing that this statement did not amount to incitement. It relied on a distinction it drew in a 1957 case involving communist advocacy of overthrowing the government by force.[58] To cross the line of incitement, the statement must be likely to prompt its hearers to take unlawful action. According to the court, advocacy or the teaching of abstract doctrines is too removed from concrete action to be lawfully suppressed, even though the speaker may hope that his statements ultimately lead to violent revolution.

The extraordinary constraints that US law places on governmental responses to hate speech derive from the special status that American democracy gives to speech—or, more precisely, to public discourse. "The reason why we impose such odd rules on public discourse is that it is the precise location in which the 'self' in 'self-government' is created," Robert Post explains. "It is the location in which we collectively decide what is and what is not fundamental. And if that question is already decided and imposed upon public discourse, then we lose the capacity collectively to think through the problem."[59] Good speech must be given the opportunity to conquer bad speech, and this is always preferable to state intervention, the thinking goes. Only when there is no opening for counter-speech to make a difference, and when the government would not be able to prevent the resulting harms—as in the exceptional case of incitement to imminent violence—might restrictions on discourse be justified.

This doctrine is also designed to meet the procedural requirements of democracy. Only if public discourse is wide open and no viewpoint forcibly suppressed can outcomes be regarded as democratic. When the state stands up for the rights of minorities against the wishes of hate groups, the argument goes, its legitimacy is derived partly from having allowed the bigots their say. The late philosopher and constitutional scholar Ronald Dworkin explained this principle elegantly. "We may and must protect women and homosexuals and members of minority groups from specific and damaging consequences of sexism, intolerance, and racism," he said. "But we must not try to intervene further upstream, by forbidding any expression of the attitudes or prejudices that we think nourish such unfairness or inequality, because if we intervene too soon in the process through which collective opinion is formed, we spoil the only democratic justification we have for insisting that everyone obey these laws, even those who hate and resent them."[60]

In addition to its idiosyncratic position on hate speech, the United States has developed an unusual perspective on defamation. Civil defamation law is consistent with Article 19 of the ICCPR, since it serves the legitimate purpose of protecting people's reputations. But the United States raises the bar for public figures who want to sue for defamation. They must show not only that the statements are false, but also that they were published with knowledge that they were false, or with reckless disregard for their truth or falsity—conditions that are very difficult to meet. According to this view, individuals who hold powerful positions or who have thrust themselves into a controversy of public significance should not be entitled to the same level of protection provided to ordinary citizens under defamation law, explains the First Amendment scholar Kyu Ho Youm. "Instead, he should be strong enough to fight back in the open marketplace of ideas because of his pervasive influence or his active agenda-setting role," Youm says.[61] The landmark judgment that created this standard, *New York Times v. Sullivan*, struck a blow in favor of civil rights by preventing racist public officials from using defamation suits to stifle allegations against them.[62] The law, however, can cut both ways. It leaves spokesmen of small minority communities vulnerable to vicious misinformation campaigns by hate groups.

Although American society treats the First Amendment as almost sacred, the prevailing US doctrine on hate speech continues to be debated. For example, the American legal scholar Alexander Tsesis has argued for new hate speech legislation that would go beyond incitement to violence and, mirroring the ICCPR, target "anyone inciting others to discriminate, persecute, oppress, or commit any similar acts against members of an identifiable group."[63] Convicted perpetrators could be sent to prison for three months to three years, and assigned up to four hundred hours of community service, he suggests.

Critiques of current First Amendment doctrine come from several angles. Perhaps the most relevant for this study is the argument from within democratic theory itself, that hate speech must be regulated to allow its targets fair and equal means to participate in public life. Public discourse is already loaded with systemic and historical inequalities, which hate speech exacerbates. Critical race and feminist theories have long argued that the country's dominant free speech doctrine is a product of white male hegemony, which has failed to protect vulnerable minorities. Law professor Frederick Schauer, for example, challenges the conventional wisdom that the legal toleration of speech-related harm is a price society must pay for free speech protection. That "price" is not distributed evenly, he says. Instead, it is disproportionately borne by victims of hate speech—usually members of historically marginalized groups—who do not necessarily gain the most from existing free speech protections.[64] In the same vein, scholars of religion have observed that the US secular constitutional order is colored by its Protestant roots.[65]

The legal philosopher Jeremy Waldron questions Dworkin's proposition that democracy would lose its legitimacy as a fair system of dispute resolution if laws discriminated against racist speech. This might be a good reason for allowing extreme views to be expressed about "contestable elements" such as affirmative action or welfare policies.[66] Waldron suggests, however, that the premises underlying those policies—that racism and racial inequality are wrong—can be treated as settled convictions. Fundamentals of justice and rights—such as racial and gender equality, human dignity, and freedom from intimidation—are foundational matters, in the sense that social life collapses without them: "I think we are now past the stage where we are in need of such a robust debate about matters like race that we ought to bear the costs of what amount to attacks on the dignity of minority groups—or, more importantly, *require individuals and families within those groups* to bear the costs of such humiliating attacks on their dignity and social standing—in the interests of public discourse and political legitimacy."[67]

These debates are substantive, but American exceptionalism should not be exaggerated. The US and international human rights approaches to free speech are more similar than different. The First Amendment's extreme resistance to government regulation applies to the narrow domain of public discourse and not the entire public sphere. In television broadcasting, for example, American standards are not necessarily more permissive than European.[68] Once we take into account how private actors enforce norms of civility in American public life, it is difficult to make the case that the United States is, on the whole, more hospitable to hate speech than Western Europe or Australia, for example.

The US Constitution and the ICCPR have much in common. Both are informed by Enlightenment values that deny belief systems—including religions, political ideologies, and scientific orthodoxies—legal immunity from criticism and insult. Both insist that there is no right not to be offended in a democracy. Both fix freedom of expression as a default setting that governments can override only to protect people from objective harms, and even then only with independent courts providing checks and balances against arbitrary intervention. Finally, both pressure states to enlarge the embrace of equality, to protect more and more communities from discrimination.

Defamation of Religion: The Traditionalist Challenge

A much more fundamental challenge to the international human rights standard than US First Amendment doctrine comes from the opposite end of the ideological spectrum. Traditionalists believe the ICCPR places too much emphasis on individuals' right to free speech at the expense of harmonious community ties, resulting in impunity for outrageous assaults on people's feelings. At the United Nations, this view has been championed most persistently by the Organisation of Islamic Cooperation (OIC; formerly called the Organization of the Islamic Conference). This lobby of fifty-seven Muslim countries was initiated by Saudi Arabia—incidentally, one of eight UN members that abstained when the Universal Declaration of Human Rights was put to a vote in 1948, and which has never signed the ICCPR.

In 1990, the organization adopted the Cairo Declaration of Human Rights in Islam, supposedly based on Islamic codes instead of international law.[69] The Cairo Declaration includes commitments to equality and nondiscrimination (irrespective of religious belief). Article 22(a) upholds freedom of expression only insofar as it does not contradict Islamic law (sharia): "Everyone shall have the right to express his opinion freely in such manner as would not be contrary to the principles of the Shari'ah." Article 22(c) bans religious offense, stating that information "may not be exploited or misused in such a way as may violate sanctities and the dignity of Prophets, undermine moral and ethical values or disintegrate, corrupt or harm society or weaken its faith." The Cairo Declaration is thus diametrically opposed to the modern human rights view that the law must not shield religions from insult or criticism. Articles 24 and 25 subject all rights and freedoms in the declaration to sharia, which is to be the only reference point for clarifying any of its articles.

Not content with merely declaring OIC members' rejection of international human rights principles, the organization then embarked on a mission to change those global norms. Its leaders were goaded by the sense that Islam and its adherents had become easy targets of denigration and discrimination. Starting in 1999, the OIC persuaded the UN Commission on Human Rights (the predecessor to the Human Rights Council) to adopt annual resolutions condemning "defamation of religions." When *Jyllands-Posten* published the Prophet Muhammad cartoons in 2005, the OIC became convinced of the need to revise international law, and not just issue toothless declarations. Many in the West agreed that the Danish newspaper's act was unnecessarily offensive. Yet, Western laws offered no recourse against Islamophobia. "As a result of this rising trend, Muslims, in the West in particular, are being stereotyped, profiled, and subjected to different forms of discriminatory treatment," the OIC said. "The most sacred symbols of Islam are being defiled and denigrated in an insulting, offensive, and contemptuous manner to incite hatred and unrest in society."[70]

The OIC escalated its campaign to the General Assembly. Blasphemy should be regarded by the international community as a social ill requiring legal intervention, it began to argue. Religions needed "protection from contempt."[71] This change in tenor was greeted with immediate pushback, led by the United States. In 2009, an international coalition of more than two hundred civil society organizations, including Muslim ones, urged the Human Rights Council to reject the resolutions. Its arguments are instructive. "Although we are sympathetic to the stated goals of the resolutions of combating intolerance, racism, and religious hatred, we believe that such resolutions do not serve to achieve these goals but rather limit the ability of individuals to raise questions, concerns, and even criticisms at a time when people of all faiths need to engage in more, not less, dialogue," the petition said.[72]

The OIC resolutions were basically attempts to equate religious insult to racism in the eyes of international law. The civil society petition noted, however, that criticism of religion could not be likened to racist hate speech. "Unlike immutable race, religion involves the freedom to follow one's conscience, and implies dialogue and debate with others about the truth claims involved," it said.

The petition pointed out that each religion makes truth claims, some of which contradict other religions. The conventional understanding of "defamation," which refers to the spreading of untruths, cannot really be applied to religion, since it is impossible to prove which of these claims are true or untrue. A law against defamation of religion could be used to ensnare any idea that contradicted or offended others' religious beliefs. The toll on freedom of expression is obvious. But there would also be a cost to freedom of religion, which must include not only the right to hold beliefs privately but also the right to express them openly, even if those beliefs offend others. Governments charged with combating defamation of religion would end up picking and choosing from among faiths, protecting some while suppressing others. Already, countries with such domestic laws tended to favor the majority religion over minority religions. "The application of similar legal mechanisms at the international level would not only legitimate such existing problematic domestic legislation, but would result in a greater proliferation of such legislation to other countries," the civil society groups warned.

The OIC resolution would also place unnecessary limits on people's ability to address their differences through peaceful debate, scuttling initiatives at interreligious dialogue. "Such restrictions will have the opposite effect of increasing religious intolerance and hatred than what the resolutions on 'combating defamation of religions' are purportedly designed to combat," the petition said. It also quoted a joint report from the UN's Special Rapporteurs on Freedom of Religion and on Racism, reiterating international human rights norms: "Freedom of religion primarily confers a right to act in accordance with one's religion but does not bestow a right for believers to have their religion itself protected from all adverse comment."[73]

Altogether, the UN's human rights bodies and the General Assembly adopted seventeen resolutions on religious defamation.[74] OIC states—supported by China, the Philippines, Russia, and South Africa—consistently voted in favor of new internationally binding instruments. But Western states and human rights groups were gradually able to win over countries that had previously abstained. The Vatican initially supported the resolutions but did an about-face in 2009. Several Latin American countries followed suit. As the tide turned, the OIC was persuaded to shelve the controversial concept of defamation of religion—as well as the vaguer notion of vilification that it had hoped might be more acceptable.[75] In return, the OIC secured commitments from member countries to combat religious intolerance.[76] These resolutions reaffirmed the protection of persons rather than their beliefs as the rightful focus of international law, marking an important defense of human rights norms.

At one level, the defamation of religions proposal was part of a larger implicit claim that religion could serve as the basis for legal order, says the legal scholar Lorenz Langer.[77] This had been "the default option" through much of human history, he notes.[78] Societies that have gone this route have incorporated such categories of religious offense as sacrilege, profanity, blasphemy, heresy, and apostasy into their laws. The OIC's defamation of religion campaign can be seen as an attempt by those societies to extrapolate their religion-based domestic laws to the international level in response to the fact that religious offense has become a transborder phenomenon. It may have also been a way to fight back against the international community's assertion of secular human rights norms. "Prohibiting defamation of religions is an attempt to reassert the legitimacy of religious norms in the face of constant criticism of such norms by human rights bodies," Langer observes.[79]

The OIC's 2011 retreat at the UN General Assembly did not mean it had been won over. Defamation of religions was expected to resurface in international fora. Besides, the successful defense of international norms barely made a dent on domestic legislation in states determined to punish religious insult. At the risk of oversimplification, the clash is between the "rule of law" and the "rule of identity," says David Kaye, a law professor who was appointed the UN Special Rapporteur on Freedom of Expression in 2014. The modern construct of rule of law holds that objective rules, adopted through the democratic process, cover all spheres and extend to the rights of minorities. The rule of identity, on the other hand, is the traditional principle of organizing politics and law around the powerful pull of group affiliations such as religion. "In practice, it is destined to be discriminatory," Kaye notes. "We live in a transitional moment, a time when we see modern and traditional views both colliding and changing."[80]

Religion and Democracy

The "rule of law" and the "rule of identity"—or, more pointedly, the "rule of God"—remain in tension as competing bases for societal order.[81] Democratic theory and modern human rights principles argue unequivocally for the primacy of the rule of law. But this then raises the question of how democracy should relate to religion, which shows no sign of disappearing from the scene. This brings us to the final topic I explore in this chapter.

There is no shortage of opinion on this subject, much of it polemical. Secular humanists sometimes claim that intolerance is the inevitable outcome of organized religion. An even more widespread suspicion is that the problem lies with certain monotheistic religions—and Islam in particular. Hate, they believe, is not manufactured selectively by political actors but programmed into fundamentally evil religious ideologies. That conclusion finds easy support in citations from holy books that recommend intolerance toward nonbelievers. Texts, however, never determine behavior. Therefore, no amount of theological exegesis can reveal a religion's potential impact in the world. This section, then, draws from the fields of comparative politics and the sociology of religion, which have churned out at least two decades' worth of studies examining the relationship that actually exists between religion and democracy.

The role religion should play in contemporary public life is one of the most contentious issues in democratic theory and practice. The debate has not been helped by social scientists' century-old assumption that modern societies would outgrow the need for God. "We live in a world that is not supposed to exist," the international relations scholar Scott Thomas notes wryly. "Religion was supposed to decline with modernization and economic development."[82] Instead, rapid modernization and economic globalization have filled many people with an "existential insecurity" that pushes them to seek comfort in organized religion, argue the political scientists Pippa Norris and Ronald Inglehart.[83] For believers who do not wish to reject modernity entirely, there are many forms of religious revivalism that fit into modern consumer culture, complete with the use of communication technologies to popularize and broaden access to spiritual services.[84] The global resurgence of religion is also partly a response to the growth of state power.[85] As we'll see in later chapters, the religious Right in the United States believes it is simply rising to the defense of the nation, in response to the courts' aggressive imposition of an immoral secular agenda. In Indonesia and many other countries, the higher public profile of religion is very much due to politicians' use of religion to legitimize their status.

The Twin Tolerations Framework

If religion is here to stay, the question is how it should relate to the political sphere. It is unhelpfully simplistic to think of religion as being in a head-to-head conflict with secularism. For one, this binary formulation underestimates the degree to which dominant religious values have already been inscribed into supposedly secular systems. José Casanova, one of the world's leading scholars of the sociology of religion, has challenged what he calls the "European secular foundation myth," which ignores how religious identities shaped state formation.[86] Even countries with low church attendances, like Denmark, possess "an implicit confessional identity, a residual manifestation of a long historical pattern of fusion of church, state, and nation"—a pattern that reveals itself in discrimination when confronted by alien religions.[87] In the same vein, Eric Michael Mazur notes that so-called church-state disputes involving minority faiths in the United States tend to overlook the fact that the state—through such conventions as recognizing Sunday as a day of rest—is already tilted in favor of the historically dominant Protestant Christian majority.[88]

Contrary to the myth that democracy requires a total separation between church and state, Western political systems have developed various ways to resolve the tension between secular and religious authority.[89] If the European Enlightenment hungered for freedom *from* religious belief, its American counterpart was about freedom *to* believe.[90] The United States developed a uniquely strict separation of religion and state, allowing neither government support for, nor government restrictions on, religious practices. The French model of *laïcité*, in contrast, delegitimizes even the appearance of religion in public life. Several of France's European neighbors, though, have an established or official church. Democracies also answer policy questions relating to media and culture differently when determining, for instance, whose religious content (if any) can be broadcast on public television, and whether religious messages, symbols, and dress are permitted in public schools. These decisions by themselves do not have a discernable effect on the relative quality of democracy.

Analyzing the overall pattern, Alfred Stepan concludes that secularism and the separation of church and state are not central to democracy. Instead, democracy depends on a more subtle and flexible form of accommodation with religion that he calls the "twin tolerations." The twin tolerations require a negotiated settlement between religious and political authorities:

> Democratic institutions must be free, within the bounds of the constitution and human rights, to generate policies. Religious institutions should not have constitutionally privileged prerogatives that allow them to mandate public policy to democratically elected governments. At the same time, individuals and religious communities ... must have complete freedom to worship privately. In addition, as individuals and groups, they must be able to advance their values publicly in civil society and to sponsor organizations and movements in political society, as long as their actions do not impinge negatively on the liberties of other citizens or violate democracy and the law.[91]

The twin tolerations principle is consistent with the rule of law—the supremacy of constitutions that protect equality. It is not compatible with what other scholars have called the "rule of God" or "political theology"— "a doctrine that legitimates public authority, and the institutions that exercise it, on the basis of a divine revelation."[92]

In most countries, including all three republics studied in this book, religion competes with modern human rights principles to supply underlying "norm-rationales" for legal systems.[93] This is not to say that religious norm-rationales are totally incommensurate with human rights. Modern human rights owe a debt to religious principles concerning the inviolable, God-given dignity of man. Religion has also inspired efforts at building peace and resolving conflict.[94] But religious norm-rationales become a severe problem when articulated in absolute and exclusive terms. This is the kind of distorted thinking that the theologian William Schweiker calls "hypertheism"—a supreme conviction in one's own human interpretations of divine will. "It is the attempt to simplify and unify beliefs about God into one form that is then used to structure the rest of social, political, and personal life," Schweiker says.[95] This is an antithesis of Stepan's "twin tolerations."

These ideas can serve as normative benchmarks as we assess the agendas of the hate spin agents featured in this book. We should not be alarmed by their religiosity as such, or even by their desire to align national policies with their religious values. It is their democratic right to try to do so. Rather, the threat they pose to democracy stems from their unwillingness to share such rights with those who differ from them. Out of their exclusivist and absolutist convictions grow a politics that denies equal dignity to their opponents, and rejects the accommodation and compromise that are central to democratic life.

The Myth of In-Built Intolerance

Some religions tend to give more authority than others to textual sources. These religions might seem more inclined toward hypertheism, and therefore away from the twin tolerations. Many commentators portray Islam as particularly problematic in this regard. This perspective has been stated most memorably by the political scientist Samuel Huntington, whose "clash of civilizations" thesis provided an intellectual hook for fears that friction between Islam and the West would be a key driver of future conflict.[96] The rise of the Islamic State has worsened the religion's reputation, to put it mildly. The death cult's extensive use of Quranic messages has made it harder for observers to absolve the religion of blame. As a 2015 cover story in the *Atlantic* observed, "The reality is that the Islamic State is Islamic. *Very* Islamic."[97]

But while Islamic State zealots may believe that they are following the Quran's dictates to the letter, the notion that theirs is either the most authentic or the most representative reading of Allah's will is contradicted by the vast majority of devout Muslims. Large-scale empirical studies, particularly by Jonathan Fox at Israel's Bar-Ilan University, provide scant support for the view that Islam is inherently or uniquely antidemocratic or prone to violence.[98] Political attitudes do not differ greatly between citizens of the Muslim world and the West.[99] Studies show that correlations between Islam and violence are better explained by nonreligious factors, including asymmetric conflict that makes peaceful dispute resolution appear impossible.[100]

As for the tendency to take violent offense, it is certainly striking that practically every major transborder hate spin episode of recent decades, starting with *The Satanic Verses*, has featured intolerant Muslims in an ignominious starring role. Palestine has been a potent injustice symbol for decades, and, rightly or wrongly, many Muslims associate Western hegemony with the perpetuation of political and economic wrongs in their own societies. Also relevant is the fact that Muslims are twice as likely as Christians to be living in countries where they are a minority community, making them far more likely to confront dominant value systems that contradict their own beliefs.[101]

When we move from the international to the domestic stage, it becomes much clearer that intolerance is not the preserve of any one religion. The three national case studies in this book feature different religious majorities. The Hindu Right in India, the Muslim Right in Indonesia and the Christian Right in the United States are all quite capable of antidemocratic, exclusivist attitudes and actions. The American religious Right is certainly less violent than its Asian cousins—domestically, that is; internationally, the wars it has championed in the twenty-first century have killed more noncombatants than any terrorist organization. But the spilling of fellow citizens' blood in religious conflicts is probably a function of the general level of militarization and political violence within the given society, and, again, not an outcome of theology. When societies have a habit of resorting to violence to settle differences, religious disputes are more likely to take a bloody turn. Examining democratic Indonesia's dismal record of ethnic and religious violence, the political scientist Abdul Malik Gismar notes, "Put in the pot of violence generally, it is a tiny drop. Indonesian society is violent, period—mostly against officials."[102]

Several religions go beyond moral principles to establish specific laws. While few commentators object to religious laws that govern, say, diet, many secularists warn against those that prescribe public behavior. Islam's sharia has especially been a target of criticism, but experts clarify that sharia is not a specific legal code as much as a body of scholarship from which laws can be articulated. The degree to which it is open to interpretation and innovation has always been a matter of contestation within and between different Muslim communities, as well as within the individual believer.[103] The Pakistani legal scholar Shaheen Sardar Ali acknowledges that Islamic legal tradition may be "systemically closed" in that it "operates within the boundaries of a divinely prescribed framework and endeavors to jealously guard those systemic origins." Importantly, though, "the application of these systemically closed channels of legal rules is cognitively open to the imperatives of evolving norms, the 'living law,' and changing needs of people and time."[104]

The Indian case is particularly instructive on the question of the supposedly inherent tendencies dictating how religions relate to democracy. Even Hinduism—a belief system that any comparative religion text would describe as essentially open and eclectic—can be fashioned into intolerant hypertheism. The same has been true of Buddhism in Myanmar and Sri Lanka. The oxymoron of Buddhist extremism prompted the comedian Trevor Noah of *The Daily Show* to ponder a question on many observers' minds, and answer it with only slight exaggeration: "What do extremist Buddhists do? What, do they clap with one hand loudly? No, silly, they want all Muslims to die."[105]

Huntington's "clash of civilizations" thesis is based on the unsupportable assumption that each religion offers only one path from which true believers do not deviate. But all religions are "multivocal," says Stepan, with elements that can be used for either the construction or the sabotage of the twin tolerations.[106] William Schweiker concurs, pointing out that even those who treat divine revelation seriously as a guide to organizing public life are not restricted to a single, antidemocratic path. No religion commands a "single idea of God somehow dictated by 'revelation' because the 'revelation' is a welter of ideas, images, and metaphors that have to be interpreted."[107] Indeed, Schweiker notes, the requirement for human interpretation is inescapable within all monotheistic religions—they all claim that God transcends reality and cannot be fully known. Therefore, due to human limitations, thinking about God cannot be equated with God.

The multivocal thesis is borne out by history. Even if religious worldviews differ in their attitudes toward secular authority, these have not led to fundamentally different outcomes. A large part of Christian history reveals the church claiming authority over temporal power, or supposedly secular authorities adopting religious norm-rationales, notes Langer. "In what used to be part of Christendom, severe sanctions for religious offence have long been an important part of the law," he adds.[108] Conversely, the homeland of Judaism, Israel, has not ceded complete legal authority to religious Zionists or Orthodox Jews, whose preferences have had to be balanced with those of secularists. Similarly, most majority-Muslim states are not governed by sharia.

It is nevertheless undeniable that today's Muslim communities have had a hard time reining in absolutists and extremists. John Anderson, a scholar of religion and politics, offers a nuanced interpretation of this phenomenon. Reflecting the scholarly consensus, he rejects the idea that any major religion is divinely preordained to repel democratic values. He acknowledges, however, that the dominant streams of a religion as they actually exist at a particular moment may contradict democratic principles. He argues that though religions are multivocal, "at any one point in time the dominant voices and practical political circumstances may work more or less in support of democratisation efforts."[109] While its role has often been overblown, religion is not irrelevant to politics. "In the short term what tradition is dominant in a country may—subconsciously or as deliberately fostered by religious and/or secular leaders—help to shape the outcome of democratic processes," Anderson says.[110]

Thus, scholars working on the history, sociology, and politics of religion concur that religion matters in politics. However, its impact is determined not by the contents of sacred texts, but by how believers interpret its precepts. Religious conflict is not the result of irreconcilable worldviews. A large body of research has convincingly shown that "identities, attachments, loyalties, values, and even emotions are socially, culturally and discursively created, changing in time and space."[111] No amount of doctrinal analysis of divine revelation can explain why some groups in some situations choose "hypertheistic" political positions that deny the rights of others. Even when a belief is sincerely held to be the only true reading of God's intent, it is only one among many parallel interpretations of a faith.

For all these reasons, I do not engage in close reading of sacred texts, or in trying to divine the true intentions of the founders of faiths, or the deepest beliefs of the faithful. These are dead ends in trying to explain hate spin. The notion that any religion is "inherently" anything fails to grasp the inescapable role of human interpretation in religious beliefs. Instead, applying insights from the study of collective action, I treat religion as a malleable resource in the hands of political entrepreneurs. From a policy perspective, it is neither necessary nor desirable to regulate the religious beliefs of individuals. What matters is how believers act. The democratic test is a practical one: whether or not people pursue their values and interests in ways that respect the basic rights of others. As the following chapters show, hate spin agents fail this test.

3   God, Google, and the Globalization of Offendedness

On July 1, 2012, a fourteen-minute movie, *Innocence of Muslims*, debuted on the world's most popular video sharing platform. It was a drop in the ocean that is YouTube, representing perhaps 0.00025 percent of the content that would have been uploaded to the network just that single day.[1] With no discernable appeal, *Innocence of Muslims* was never going to be a viral phenomenon like the Korean performer Psy's "Gangnam Style," which was released the same month. The global reaction to *Innocence*—mostly by people who never saw it—nevertheless ensured its place in any analysis of twenty-first-century religious offense.

The film was undoubtedly an intentional assault on Islam. But its effectiveness as a piece of hate propaganda was debatable. Such a crude and over-the-top production was unlikely to influence viewers' attitudes toward the religion and its adherents. All the same, individuals within some Muslim societies seized upon the film as offensive and encouraged their communities to express their indignation, loudly and violently. So familiar was the pattern that US officials initially blamed the video for provoking the deadly assault on their diplomatic compound in Benghazi, Libya, on September 11, 2012. The Benghazi incident turned out to be an unrelated militant attack. In various other locales, though, some seventy-five people were killed in riots organized in reaction to the film. *Innocence of Muslims* was thus an archetypal cross-border case of hate spin. The video was also an important landmark in Internet governance: the controversy resulted in an unprecedented flurry of take-down orders. Some countries blocked access to YouTube altogether.

The cross-border trade in hate ideology is now firmly on the radar of international security experts and is generating a great deal of interest among scholars of communication. Most of the discussion centers on classic hate speech—propaganda that incites violence. Internet-assisted "self-radicalization" of jihadist terrorists dominates the agenda.[2] The Internet did not start this global flow, and still does not monopolize it. As a US Senate report notes, "Printed materials, videos of terrorist activities, including operations and training, and recordings of sermons and speeches espousing the virtues of the violent Islamist ideology have been distributed and sold around the world for decades."[3]

Cross-border hate propaganda has also infected other ethnic communities. One chilling example is found in the manifesto of the Norwegian mass murderer Anders Behring Breivik, who killed seventy-seven people on a single summer day in 2011 in protest against his country's tolerance of Muslims and other immigrants. The document that he cobbled together, *2083: A European Declaration of Independence*, quotes liberally from the leading American manufacturers of anti-Muslim misinformation. Their citation counts would have done the US Islamophobia network proud, were it a university department. Robert Spencer and his Jihad Watch blog are cited 162 times; Daniel Pipes and the Middle East Forum, 18 times; Frank Gaffney and his Center for Security Policy, 7 times.[4] The ideological attraction seemed mutual: Pamela Geller, cited 12 times in Breivik's document, later said that the youth camp targeted by the shooter was an anti-Israel "indoctrination training center."[5]

In this chapter I focus on an aspect of cross-border hate spin that is less-studied than incitement: manufactured offendedness. Obvious complexities arise in regulating speech that offends populations across national boundaries. One question is whose laws and social norms should prevail. Because of cultural differences, different national populations attach different meanings to messages and symbols. Take, for example, the chic Buddha Bar lounges that have spread from Paris to several cities in Europe and the Middle East. Giant statues of the Buddha anchor these "exotic" bars. Although supposedly inspired by a love for the cultures of the Asia-Pacific region, predominantly Christian Manila is the only city in that part of the world to feature a Buddha Bar. Franchises have not taken off in countries with large Buddhist populations, where residents may find it difficult to reconcile their understanding of the Buddha's message of moderation with the steady flow of alcohol or all-you-can-eat Sunday brunches. In Indonesia—where Buddhism accounts for less than 1 percent of the population but is nonetheless accorded constitutional recognition—Jakarta's franchise swiftly attracted opposition that led to its closure. In Buddhist-majority Myanmar in 2015, three enterprising individuals—evidently trying to cash in on the Buddha Bar concept's appeal to Western tourists—were jailed for their Facebook posts showing a Buddha wearing headphones and advertising their pub's shisha and "Bottomless Frozen Mararita [sic]."[6]

Such conflicts between different notions of propriety are inevitable. "In this late modern world of ours the stranger's otherness is constantly in our face: in the lived reality of urban spaces, in the imagined and communicated realities of mediated places," observed the late media scholar Roger Silverstone. "There is a huge debate emerging as to how this new world can be, and should be, lived in."[7] Hate spin agents have exploited these frictions as opportunities to produce transborder offendedness. As a way to understand the phenomenon, I examine in this chapter three stand-out cases of politicized transnational indignation: Salman Rushdie's award-winning novel, *The Satanic Verses*, the Prophet Muhammad cartoons published by the Danish newspaper *Jyllands-Posten*, and the *Innocence of Muslims* YouTube video. Because online offense has become a key part of this story, I will also look at the role of Google and other global Internet intermediaries that regularly confront the problem of uneven laws and social norms.

Salman Rushdie's *The Satanic Verses*

Cross-border religious offendedness existed before the Internet was there to foster it. Published in Greek in 1953 and in English in 1960, *The Last Temptation of Christ* was greeted by a transnational storm of protest. The novel by Nikos Kazantzakis depicted Jesus Christ as divine, but tortured by human doubts and longings, which he ultimately overcomes. Kazantzakis's literary license with the biblical story incensed religious conservatives. He was excommunicated by the Eastern Orthodox Church, and the book was placed on the Catholic Church's *Index of Forbidden Books*.[8] An even more intense controversy followed when the prominent Hollywood director Martin Scorsese made a movie version in 1988. But this was nothing compared with the outrage that followed the publication of another literary masterpiece the same year.

This was Salman Rushdie's *The Satanic Verses*. Set in contemporary India and Britain, its main theme is the tension in the postcolonial experience between migrant and national identities.[9] Written in Rushdie's magical realism style, the book contains dream sequences, one of which features the life of Mahound "the Messenger," clearly based on the Prophet Muhammad. The Messenger pronounces polytheistic ideas, but later retracts them as having been inserted by the devil. One of his companions confesses to having altered portions of the sacred text dictated to him. Critics disagree as to whether such content was actually blasphemous. Rushdie's lawyer Geoffrey Robertson has pointed out that a private prosecution failed to make the case, even when blasphemy law existed in England. The six alleged blasphemies were each "based either on a misreading or on theological error." For example, although Rushdie was attacked for calling the Prophet "a conjuror," "a magician," and a "false prophet," these epithets were placed in the mouth of "a drunken apostate, a character with whom neither author nor reader has sympathy."[10] A separate dream sequence features a fanatical religious leader reminiscent of Iran's Ayatollah Khomeini in his Parisian exile. While Rushdie has never denied that the novel was intended to be provocative, he has insisted that his target was not religion per se, but rather the hypocrisy of some believers.

Viking Penguin published *The Satanic Verses* in September 1988. Rushdie was already one of the world's most celebrated novelists, so the book quickly gained worldwide attention. In his native India, the government banned the book's sale and distribution within a fortnight of its release. The book won the prestigious Whitbread Prize in early November, intensifying the sense of impotence some Muslims felt and heightening their desire to lash out against the perceived insult. In January 1989, Muslim residents in Bradford, England, burned copies of the book. A month later, six people were killed in violent demonstrations in Pakistan. It was Ayatollah Khomeini, however, who escalated the conflict into a global clash of values. On February 14, 1989, he issued a stunning edict ordering the death of Rushdie and his editors. "I call on all zealous Moslems to execute them quickly, wherever they find them, so that no one will dare to insult the Islamic sanctions. Whoever is killed on this part will be regarded as a martyr, God willing," the fatwa declared.[11]

Mehdi Mozzafari, a political philosophy professor, suggests that the fatwa was the product of Khomeini's uncompromising division of the world into good and evil, his conviction that the Quran contains all necessary truths, and his sense that he faced unique responsibilities as the Muslim world's only religious leader who was simultaneously a head of state. Regardless of the sincerity of Khomeini's outrage, however, the political context was significant. Iran at the time was emerging from its eight-year war with Iraq, one of the most debilitating conflicts of the twentieth century. Two months before the publication of Rushdie's book, Iran had accepted a ceasefire. The war had not ended gloriously. Iran lost not only millions of its citizens but also some of the prestige that its 1979 revolution had earned it among Muslim countries. The war devastated the decade-old Islamic Republic; even among the clerics, dissent was growing.[12] In this light, Iran's response to *Satanic Verses* was less a Quranic imperative than a page from the classic political playbook: faced with a loss for answers, produce a common enemy, internal or external. It was "the type of response one might get when a civilization is in its final decline or when it is unable to reenvision itself," as the political scientist Sohail Inayatullah puts it.[13]

Khomeini's attempt to publicly crowdsource the assassination of the citizen of another country stunned the international community and forced Rushdie into hiding. In recent years, the author has spoken out against the "culture of offendedness" of which he was a victim, and which is a key concern of this book.[14]

The *Jyllands-Posten* Prophet Muhammad Cartoons

The case of the Danish cartoons exemplifies the friction between fundamentally different sets of laws and social norms governing religious offense. Denmark's original blasphemy law, dating from 1683, resembled those currently operating in Saudi Arabia and elsewhere. Danish law tied together the status of religion, the king, and the state, such that preserving the legitimacy of earthly rulers required protecting God's name. By the 1920s, blasphemous expression was still regarded as uncivilized, but parliamentarians believed that Danish society had, for the most part, matured to the point that such speech could be regulated without resorting to the force of law.[15] By the late 1920s, Danish parliamentarians and legal scholars agreed that the law should step in only to protect peace between different communities, not to preserve harmony between man and God. Reformers held up the Protestant reformer Martin Luther and the Danish philosopher Soren Kierkegaard as positive examples of blasphemers who had contributed to societal progress through their mocking of convention. The last time a Danish court convicted anyone for blasphemy was in 1938, when the law was used to protect a minority group: the case involved anti-Semitic propaganda by Danish Nazis.

In the 1970s, the artist Jens Jorgen Thorsen tested this liberal culture. In 1973 he released a film script, *The Many Faces of Jesus Christ*, which depicted Jesus as a drunk with a wild sex life. Danish embassies in Madrid and Rome were targets of threatened and actual violence. Under pressure, the government forced the Danish Film Institute to withdraw funding for the film project, but the authorities never actually charged Thorsen with any crime. Nor was he prosecuted for a 1985 mural in which he depicted Jesus with an erection.[16]

In its evolving attitudes toward religious offense, Denmark represents the liberal universe in microcosm. As I discussed in chapter 2, the legitimate focus of law and policy in modern jurisprudence pivoted away from the protection of elite and majority feelings toward accommodation for minority communities and contrarian viewpoints. In the Danish case, however, the country's troubled experience with immigration has complicated this trend. Unhappy with the intolerant attitudes of some immigrants, Danish liberals came to pit the argument for freedom of expression against the principle of minority protection, such that blasphemy debates became about the "artistic right *to offend religious minorities*," as Signe Larsen, a cultural scholar at Aarhus University, puts it.[17] In this mindset, blasphemers are no longer seen as the "other," manifesting a "counter-identity" that may or may not play a positive social function but should in any case be tolerated by a mature society; instead, blasphemous expression fulfills "an attribute of contemporary Danishness."[18]

The right-wing Danish People's Party pushed this line aggressively, arguing that the country's secular principles and Lutheran tradition—born out of heresy against the Catholic Church—were threatened by creeping Islamization. And indeed, some Muslims challenged the value that Danish society attached to freedom of expression. In 2004, for example, some tried to take legal action when Danish television stations broadcast Theo van Gogh's short film *Submission*, which criticized the treatment of women in Muslim societies. The Dutch filmmaker's brutal murder in Amsterdam later that year forced liberal Europeans to confront the reality that some immigrants and their children were rejecting the values of their host nations. "This sorry tale raises a big issue not just in the Netherlands, but across Europe: how far should liberal societies tolerate the intolerant?" the *Economist* noted at the time.[19]

The Escalation of a Controversy

This was the context in which journalists at the newspaper *Jyllands-Posten* conceived of the Prophet Muhammad cartoons. The journalists were disturbed to hear that the publisher of an innocuous children's book about Muhammad could not find an artist willing to illustrate it. They felt that such fear and self-censorship should have no place in Denmark. The paper's cultural editor, Flemming Rose, invited members of the Danish Newspaper Illustrators' Union to submit drawings of Muhammad, as they saw him. On September 30, 2005, the paper devoted a full page to twelve cartoons under the headline, "The Face of Muhammad." Some of the cartoons, like one depicting a schoolboy named Muhammad, traversed the minefield gingerly. The most provocative, by Kurt Westergaard, showed the Prophet wearing a turban shaped like a bomb.

As would later be the case with writers at *Charlie Hebdo*, doubts have since been expressed about the sincerity of the journalists' motivations: critics suspect an underlying anti-immigrant bias.[20] But in its front-page article, the paper took the high ground of protecting Danish freedom of expression. "Some Muslims reject modern, secular society," it complained. "They demand a special position, insisting on special consideration of their own religious feelings. This is incompatible with secular democracy and freedom of expression, where one has to be ready to put up with scorn, mockery and ridicule."[21] Flemming Rose's article below the cartoons repeated the concern that some Muslims wanted special treatment of a kind that threatened the free exchange of ideas. By publishing the cartoons, *Jyllands-Posten* took a deliberately provocative stand in the debate on whether Islam should be treated any differently from other religions.

And provoke it did. Danish Muslims mounted a peaceful protest. One of the protesters was a young activist named Ahmed Akkari. Akkari's group was hardly the most influential or representative organization of Muslims in Denmark; a more prominent Danish Muslim was the parliamentarian Naser Khader, a proponent of integration and vocal critic of radicalism. Akkari's chosen course of action was probably influenced by his need to compete for influence against more established figures in the Danish Muslim community.

Within a week of the cartoons' publication, Akkari's group reached out to the embassies of Muslim countries in Copenhagen. Eleven ambassadors representing Muslim-majority nations wrote to the Danish prime minister on October 19, asking for an urgent meeting. The prime minister replied— stating that those who felt wronged were welcome to lodge a blasphemy complaint—but did not accede to their request for a meeting. The Egyptian government was the most receptive to Akkari's pleas. Hosni Mubarak's government in Egypt began lobbying the United Nations, the European Union, and the Organization for Security and Coordination in Europe to condemn the cartoons and discrimination against Muslims in general. Egypt also urged the Arab League and the Organisation of the Islamic Conference to keep up diplomatic pressure on Denmark.[22]

The cartoons had appeared in a landmark year for Egypt's military-backed regime. Mubarak, in power since 1981, had been pressured to allow multicandidate presidential elections for the first time. His victory was a foregone conclusion—he was declared the victor with almost 89 percent of the vote in early September 2005—but the upcoming parliamentary elections in November–December were less predictable. The biggest threat came from candidates linked to the banned Muslim Brotherhood.[23] To counter them, the state needed opportunities to portray itself "almost as Islamic as the Islamist opposition," noted one analyst.[24] The legislative elections were just weeks away when the Egyptian government received word of the Akkari's appeal to its embassy in Copenhagen. The temptation to ride on the cartoons as an injustice symbol must have been irresistible. "My impression is Mubarak sought to use the Danish cartoons to promote Egypt's Islamic credentials, and neutralize Muslim Brotherhood's ascendancy in general elections for parliament," recalls an Asian diplomat based in Cairo at the time.[25]

Meanwhile, Akkari continued campaigning. He led delegations to Cairo, Damascus, and Beirut in December 2005 to publicize the case. They brought with them a forty-three-page dossier, which contained not only the twelve published cartoons but also three other images of dubious provenance. "I was ready to get the whole world moving," Akkari mused later. "I was surprised that it moved so quickly."[26]

In the first three months after the cartoons' publication, though, the protests were peaceful, legitimately using democratic and diplomatic spaces to register Muslims' unhappiness at what they felt was an unjust provocation. The controversy entered an uglier phase in late January 2006, after the influential satellite television channels Al-Jazeera and Al-Arabiya covered the story. It was then picked up in Friday sermons in Egypt, Saudi Arabia, and Iraq. Reports about the affair were circulated frenziedly, embellished with false rumors and doctored images suggestive of the persecution of Muslims by the West. In late January and February 2006, serious violence occurred on three continents, either in belated response to the original publication of the cartoons by *Jyllands-Posten*, or their republication by various other papers in Europe—among them, *Charlie Hebdo*, which added several more cartoons to the set as part of a sixteen-page cover feature in February 2006. Embassies were attacked in Indonesia, Iran, Lebanon, and Syria, and protesters died in Afghanistan, Libya, and Pakistan. Around a hundred Nigerians were killed in sectarian Muslim–Christian violence linked to the publication of the cartoons. Extremists threatened and attacked individuals and organizations implicated in the publication of the cartoons.

Choosing to Explode

At the height of protests, behind the semblance of spontaneous combustion, there is evidence of options being weighed and choices being made. In Egypt, two popular television preachers publicly debated what stand to take on the cartoon controversy. Amr Khaled favored dialogue with the Danes; he even organized a conference in Copenhagen. But Youssef al-Qaradawi, an older, conservative cleric, chided Khaled, arguing that the time was not right to make peace. Significantly, al-Qaradawi expressed his position not in the form of a moral imperative, but in terms of political strategy: the outrage provoked by the cartoons was an opportunity to unify the Muslim world and deal with others from a position of strength.[27] Here was an activist mindful of the cartoons' potential as a "transnational injustice symbol."

Most commentators at the time pointed to Islamic prohibitions on depictions of the Prophet as an explanation for Muslim outrage. The scriptural basis for this position is itself interesting, but is not particularly illuminating for our purposes here. If indeed the prohibition were absolute, with no room for interpretation and no accounting for context, we would not expect to find any republication of the cartoons in Muslim media. This was not the case. As early as October 17, 2005, a Cairo newspaper, *El-Fagr*, republished six of the cartoons to accompany an article condemning the Danes for their blasphemy, and was not punished for doing so (though the paper later removed the images from its website).[28] A Saudi tabloid printed three of the cartoons in the midst of the furor in February 2006, to accompany an interview with a cleric who was calling for a boycott of Denmark. Although the Saudi authorities suspended the paper's publication soon after, the editor's original decision belies the theory of an absolute prohibition, internalized by all believers.

In Indonesia, the online news site of *Rakyat Merdeka*, part of the large Jawa Pos group, published the cartoons twice that October alongside stories about the controversy. "Nobody seemed to care about it," recalls its editor, Teguh Santosa.[29] When he did the same in February 2006, though, about three hundred members of the hard-line Islamic Defenders Front (FPI, Front Pembela Islam) besieged his office. After public complaints, the authorities charged Santosa with blasphemy, though nothing came of this. Santosa—himself a leading member of one of Indonesia's largest Muslim organizations, Muhammadiyah—had felt he needed to publish the cartoons to help inform his readers about what he realized was a brewing storm. He successfully convinced hard-liners of the purity of his intentions. Thanks to his persuasive skills, the FPI activists who appeared at his office with chants of "Kafir! Kafir!" departed with the cheer, "Viva *Rakyat Merdeka*!" Because he believes in keeping communication channels with radicals open, Santosa even spoke about his editorial decisions with Abu Bakar Bashir, the spiritual leader of the militant group, Jemaah Islamiyah, which had been responsible for Southeast Asia's worst terrorist incidents. "At that time, he was just out of prison. We met in a mosque, I told him what I had done. He said this was not a blasphemy toward the Prophet or the religion, what you have to show in the court is that you are a good Muslim, that's all," Santosa told me.

Such cases suggest that the philosophical approach to extreme speech in Muslim societies is not as different from the secular West as it is sometimes made out to be. As in the West, Muslim societies treat the intention of the publisher and the context of the communication as seriously as the content of the expression. That, in turn, opens the door to interpretation and the negotiation of meaning. There is no necessary, mechanistic cause-and-effect relationship between provocative speech, offense, and violent retribution. In between are middlemen such as Abu Bakar Bashir in Indonesia and Youssef al-Qaradawi in Egypt, who decide whether or not to push the moral panic button. Adept navigators of these complex terrains, like Teguh Santosa, know that their fate rests not only with God and the law, but also the brokers of hate spin, who determine which incidents are appropriate for escalation.

As for Ahmed Akkari, the hate spin agent who had worked assiduously to turn a dubious editorial decision into a global scandal, he made a stunning about-face in 2013. He declared that he now valued Denmark's freedom and apologized to the editor Flemming Rose, the artist Kurt Westergaard, the politician Naser Khader, and the nation at large.[30]

The *Innocence of Muslims* Video

As one of the first instances of violent offendedness against online content, *Innocence of Muslims* was a controversy whose time had come. More than a decade had passed since the global Internet superimposed a dense network of fluid, open exchange on a world map still divided by different ways of living and thinking. The contradiction between borderless communication and bounded cultures offered plenty of hate spin potential. The earlier cases described above showed how globalization allowed transnational hate spin even with older media technologies. The Internet would create new opportunities for offendedness.

In most other respects, though, the *Innocence* case followed the same pattern as *Satanic Verses* and the *Jyllands-Posten* cartoons. The initial release of the video was followed by a time lag, after which the temperature of the controversy spiked, with violent protests that strained democracies' commitment to freedom of expression.

Innocence was a 2012 trailer for a full-length feature film that was still in the works. The film was produced by Nakoula Basseley Nakoula, an American from Egypt's Coptic Christian community. In an interview with the *New York Times* later, he said that the persecution of Copts in Egypt drove him to make the film.[31] An earlier version of his script went by the title

The First Terrorist. The video portrays Islam as a violent religion and depicts Prophet Muhammad as an ambitious and foolish man who condones sexual abuse of children. The character is shown having sex with his wife and other women. The film suggests that his wife Khadija had an instrumental role in creating the Quran.

The project was supported by Media for Christ, a nonprofit organization. The director they hired had a body of work comprising primarily soft-core pornographic flicks. The filming took place in Los Angeles over fifteen days. Nakoula misled actors into participating in the film: the script they worked with had nothing to do with Islam; it was purportedly about an ancient tribal leader named George. The producers dubbed the final dialogue over the original soundtrack.

Nakoula's son posted the video on Facebook and YouTube on July 2, 2012; other American activists with a history of denigrating Islam, including Terry Jones, the Florida preacher behind the 2010 "International Burn a Koran Day" campaign, joined him in promoting the video.[32] The Arab media picked it up two months later, in September 2012, just in time for the anniversary of the 9/11 terror attacks. The riots kicked off soon after, starting in Cairo, where around 350 Egyptians attacked the US Embassy on September 11. At that point, the video's origins were still unclear. On September 12, the Associated Press reported claims that Jewish investors had bankrolled the film. The agency issued a correction two days later, but by then the myth of a Jewish conspiracy had already spread.[33]

There were also violent protests in Dhaka (Bangladesh), Karachi (Pakistan), and Kabul (Afghanistan). Initial reports suggested that the film provoked the rocket attack that killed a US ambassador and others in Benghazi on September 11. It later emerged that the militant attack had been planned earlier; protesters interviewed at the scene were unaware of the film.[34] Nevertheless, the Benghazi attack added to the overwhelming impression that the film had crossed a line and that the situation was spinning out of control.

Governments and Google Respond

The predictable liberal response to the video and its aftermath was to reaffirm the value of legally protected free speech while also emphasizing the need to respect religion. The US government was less dismissive of Muslim outrage than Denmark had initially been. Perhaps American officials had learned from Denmark's mistakes. But perhaps more to the point, the United States relies heavily on the cooperation of Muslim countries for its military and counterterrorism operations and therefore cannot afford to alienate them. In 2010, for instance, faced with the threat of Terry Jones' Quran-burning campaign, President Barak Obama appeared on the ABC television network's *Good Morning America* program to say that the pastor's "stunt" was "completely contrary to our values" and a "destructive act" that could "greatly endanger our young men and women in uniform."[35]

The *Innocence* controversy forced Obama into damage-control mode once again. His administration took the unprecedented step of creating a television commercial—starring the president and Secretary of State Hillary Clinton—to "reject" a privately produced video.[36] The administration's counter-video was aired on Pakistani television. The US government, as well as those of Australia and Egypt, also asked Google to check whether the video violated its company's content guidelines. Given that the international controversy would almost certainly have prompted the company to review the video even without any governmental prompting, the US officials' request was probably symbolic, to disassociate the state from the acts of some of its citizens.

Google decided that *Innocence* did not violate the YouTube Community Guidelines regarding offensive speech, which were broadly in line with the liberal position on freedom of expression, prohibiting attacks on living people but not on belief systems: "We encourage free speech and defend everyone's right to express unpopular points of view. But we don't permit hate speech (speech which attacks or demeans a group based on race or ethnic origin, religion, disability, gender, age, veteran status, and sexual orientation/gender identity)."[37] Nevertheless, the company took the extraordinary step of unilaterally restricting the video from view in Egypt and Libya, "due to difficult circumstances."[38] This move has since been treated as an anomaly, and not reflective of YouTube policy. Top management appears to have made the decision in a fit of panic, against the advice of colleagues who cautioned against setting such a precedent.

Google actions in eight other countries were more in keeping with its protocol. In response to government requests—as opposed to taking unilateral action—YouTube blocked the video from view in Indonesia, India, Jordan, Malaysia, Russia, Saudi Arabia, Singapore, and Turkey. In three other countries—Afghanistan, Bangladesh, and Pakistan—governments opted for the kill switch, blocking the entire YouTube platform.

In all these countries, Muslims formed majorities or politically significant minorities. Their governments' responses fit the narrative of religious offense whose inflammatory effects could only be contained through censorship. But a closer look suggests that this may not have been authorities' primary motivation in every case. In Bangladesh, the government had been itching to crack down on YouTube, which was being used to circulate reports on the explosive political issue of war crimes, notes Faheem Hussain, a Bangladeshi scholar who researches technology and society.[39] A similar situation unfolded in Pakistan: YouTube videos had been exposing the scandalous behavior of politicians and human rights violations by the army, says Nighat Dad, director of the Digital Rights Foundation. Citizen videos of extrajudicial killings and torture in Balochistan, for example, had contributed to the US government's decision to withhold funding from tainted Pakistani units.

Singapore's response showed the impact of international relations on censorship decisions. With a Muslim population of around 15 percent, its government initially responded to the controversy by expressing faith that level heads would prevail. "I am confident that Singaporeans will react to this film in the same rational and calm manner as they have done previously," said Teo Chee Hean, the deputy prime minister and security czar, on September 14.[40] The following day the prime minister, Lee Hsien Loong, continued to maintain a policy of detachment. "It doesn't matter what happens elsewhere in the world," he said. "These are not our quarrels and we should continue living peacefully, harmoniously together, among ourselves and nurture and preserve our harmony."[41] On September 19, however, the government announced that it was requesting Google to block online access to the video: "The continued circulation of this film is likely to cause disharmony or feelings of ill-will between different groups in Singapore."[42]

This curious U-turn, although ostensibly responding to an internal security threat, was probably performed to keep Singapore in step with its two closest neighbors, Indonesia and Malaysia. This would not have been the first time that Singapore expressed such neighborly solidarity. In 2002, it banned the Hollywood comedy *Zoolander* citing "controversial elements"—almost certainly because the film involved a conspiracy to kill a fictional Malaysian prime minister, which had already earned it a ban across the border.[43] Or, it may have felt that the time had come to take a symbolic stand against the West's export of its liberal doctrine. Whatever the reason for Singapore's decision, it is unlikely to have been based on an assessment of the immediate risk of public disorder. A full week had passed since the controversy broke, with no disturbances in Singapore.

The Instigators of Indignation

The public order argument for state action received support among commentators in the West. The Chicago Law School professor Eric Posner, critiquing the way the First Amendment was being applied, suggested that there might, in fact, be circumstances when the US government should intervene "in the spirit of prudence" when contemplating foreign relations crises like the *Innocence* video.[44] It is simplistic, however, to conclude that greater cultural sensitivity and stricter hate speech laws alone can address the kind of challenge posed by the *Innocence* video. Such policy prescriptions are based on an incomplete reading of the case, one that focuses on the givers of offense without interrogating the strategy of offense-taking. As in the earlier cases discussed above, the manufacture of indignation required disseminators and brokers who actively turned an obscure video into an international cause célèbre.

Initial reports pointed the finger at Sheikh Khaled Abdullah, a presenter on an influential religious satellite TV channel, al-Nas. The Egyptian state-owned satellite network, NileSat, carried the Saudi-owned station. Sheikh Khaled had a track record of portraying the United States as an aggressor against Islam, and of attacking Egypt's Coptic Christian community.[45] On September 8, his program aired clips from the video dubbed into Arabic. The segment soon spread online. Sheikh Khaled's program was not, however, the first media organization to publicize the existence of the *Innocence* video. According to an investigative report in the *Columbia Journalism Review* by Emad Mekay, the video was first reported in Egypt on September 6, by secular media controlled by supporters of the old Mubarak regime.[46] The reports appeared in the newspapers *Youm7* and *El-Fagr*, the latter of which had held the dubious honor of being probably the first newspaper to republish *Jyllands-Posten*'s infamous cartoons. Editors at both papers appear to have been driven by an interest in discrediting the Islamists in the new government. *Youm7* was so intent on stirring the pot that it provided expanded coverage on September 8.

Other pro-Mubarak outlets soon followed up. Even a website owned by a wealthy Egyptian from the very community whose American brethren had been behind *Innocence*, the Christian Copts, published articles needling the Islamists for not responding to the insult. A liberal newspaper that ordinarily speaks up for Egypt's Christians, *Wafd*, goaded Islamists with the headline, "Muslim Brotherhood Lets the Prophet Down." While a mix of anti-US sentiment and religious fervor helped ensure the video's value as an international injustice symbol, detailed forensics reveal that those who did the most to push that narrative out were motivated primarily by domestic political interests.

Regulating Internet Intermediaries

The *Innocence* case evokes a sense of déjà vu, in that its dynamics resemble any number of earlier international controversies involving religious offense. It also foreshadowed the *Charlie Hebdo* affair of 2015. In one respect, though, *Innocence* was groundbreaking. The ensuing policy debate centered on a whole new kind of player—the global Internet intermediary. Intermediaries are the entities that "offer the facilities and services that help people access, transmit, host, store, cache, index, and locate information on the Internet."[47] In addition to Internet service providers, they include search engines, video sharing sites, blogging platforms, and social media sites. Internet intermediaries do not create the content that draws hundreds of millions of users to their screens every day—the messages, news stories, home videos, selfies, songs, games, comments, or items for sale. Without intermediaries, however, the Internet would be the minority pastime of geeks and the habitat of organizations with the time and money to swim through the ocean of data; the scientist Clifford Stoll would have been right when he scoffed at technohype in a 1995 *Newsweek* column titled, "The Internet? Bah!"[48]

In the early years of the World Wide Web, the technology was highly decentralized, creating the perception that it would be almost impossible to regulate. As it grew, however, the provision of Internet services became more capital intensive and subject to economies of scale, resulting in a highly concentrated sector more easily targeted by regulators.[49] And the biggest target of all was Google. "The secret is out: if you can regulate Google, you can regulate the Internet," notes Uta Kohl of Aberystwyth University.[50]

Google started out as a search engine that was very much in the background of the Internet user's experience. It grew into a household name, with the boundless ambition to "organize the world's information and make it universally accessible and useful."[51] As early as 2003, Thomas Friedman of the *New York Times* was asking, "Is Google God?"[52] Google bought YouTube in 2006. By 2010, Google was being dubbed the most powerful company in the world and receiving the attention of dedicated watchdog groups.[53]

Even after heavily discounting for hype, it is clear that transnational hate spin gets more interesting—and complex—when it is Internet assisted. The main issue is whose standards global Internet intermediaries like Google should be expected to follow. The question also has a practical dimension: whether it is technically possible for governments, or even the intermediary itself, to filter the fire hose of online content.

Yahoo! and Nazi Memorabilia

As the crucial role of intermediaries became apparent, their responsibilities became the subject of policy debate. In 2000, a landmark court case in France involved Yahoo!, Google's predecessor as the world's most popular Internet company. Buyers and sellers were using Yahoo!'s online auction site to trade Nazi memorabilia, ranging from flags and uniforms to mouse pads and cushions. Although authorities might have been able charge Yahoo! under the French criminal code, which prohibits the display of Nazi items, they chose not to. Instead, two civil society organizations pursued the matter as a civil action.

The company tried several arguments in its defense, none of which persuaded the French court.[54] First, Yahoo! claimed that the French judge had no jurisdiction over the American company. The judge dismissed this, noting that the firm had a 70-percent stake in a French subsidiary, that it was publishing French-language advertising targeting a French audience, and that items advertised on its auction site could be bought within France. Second, Yahoo! argued that it was merely a passive conduit and could not be held accountable for content hosted on its sites. But Yahoo! was found to have monitored and edited portions of its auction site, belying its claim to be nothing more than a common carrier, like a phone company. Third, Yahoo! tried pointing to the First Amendment. The company claimed that the US Constitution prevented it from censoring what its users could see, and that Nazism and racism were best countered in the free marketplace of ideas. Since the First Amendment refers only to restrictions by public authorities and not private individuals or media owners, however, and since Yahoo! already had in place various bans on its auction site— including restrictions on trading live animals, drugs, weapons, and even used underwear—these arguments were not particularly persuasive. Finally, after the French court ordered Yahoo! to take steps to prevent users in France from accessing Nazi merchandise on its auction site, the company argued that such a move would be prohibitively expensive. The judge held firm, ordering Yahoo! to comply to a "reasonable degree" within three months.

The French ruling helped establish the principle that, "while the Internet enables actors to reach a geographically dispersed audience, the Internet should not change the accountability of those actors for their conduct within national borders," as the legal scholar Joel Reidenberg put it.[55] It was also a step toward forcing "technical elites to respect democratically chosen values and the rule of law."[56] The court ruling could be seen a repudiation, from within the moral universe of Western democracies, of John Perry Barlow's 1996 "Declaration of Independence of Cyberspace."[57] The decision reaffirmed traditional notions of jurisdiction for the Internet age. Technical developments in the following years showed that Internet intermediaries could indeed apply reasonably effective geographic filtering of online content.[58]

In one respect, though, Yahoo! was proven right: such restrictions are incompatible with American courts' reading of the First Amendment. To establish this point, the company sued the French plaintiffs in California. Yahoo! got what it wanted: a court declaration that the French decision could not be recognized in the United States. Interestingly, though, months before this action, in January 2001, Yahoo! unilaterally banned the sale of Nazi memorabilia from its US auction sites, stressing that this decision was not in response to any court order. The company hoped to demonstrate that it would challenge unreasonable legal restrictions as vigorously as it could, but that it was also willing to exercise social responsibility on a purely voluntary basis. It had been under pressure at home from anti-hate organizations such as the Simon Wiesenthal Centre and the Anti-Defamation League.[59]

Regulatory Principles

In some ways, the issues raised by Internet intermediaries are conceptually similar to those affecting other transnational corporations navigating a world with varied environmental standards and rules on corruption. Parallels can also be drawn to the regulation of international aviation, which has a similar interest in facilitating safe cross-border carriage. But policies concerning Internet intermediaries cannot be neatly modeled on any of these more established sectors.

First, there is no way to create a global rule-making body for Internet content like the International Civil Aviation Organization (ICAO) since, for a start, there is no agreement as to what "safety" means in Internet communication. Based on scientific tests, ICAO since 2015 has prohibited the carriage of lithium metal batteries packed on their own as cargo on passenger planes.[60] In contrast, there is no agreed way to determine what counts as explosive or inflammatory online content, and what to do about it. Second, the business of Internet intermediaries differs from most other international activities in that it implicates users' rights to freedom of expression. In his 2011 report to the UN General Assembly, the Special Rapporteur for freedom of expression Frank La Rue noted that although Internet access was "not yet a human right as such"—implying, remarkably, that it could one day be—it should be treated as one necessary means for exercising free speech rights. Given that it was already "an indispensable tool for full participation in political, cultural, social and economic life," states had an obligation to make the Internet widely available and accessible.[61]

Like other human rights, freedom of expression, in principle, transcends the laws of the land of which one is a citizen. The Universal Declaration of Human Rights (UDHR), proclaimed in 1948, marked a conceptual break in international law and global ethical discourse: it challenged the traditional idea that the international system could only deal with sovereign states. The UDHR instead stressed the primacy of individuals. States' wishes are not supposed to trump citizens' "freedom to hold opinions without interference and to seek, receive, and impart information and ideas through any media and regardless of frontiers," as the UDHR puts it. In practice, the international system has had very limited power to interfere in domestic affairs to uphold human rights, even when millions of lives are at stake, as in today's Syria or previous genocides in Bosnia, Rwanda, or Cambodia. The penetrating reach of the Internet, however, offers a unique opportunity to realize human rights principles. By design, Internet architecture challenges centralized authority and empowers end users to an unprecedented degree. States can meddle with that architecture within their territories, but for a change they are at a major technical disadvantage.

Far more than with print or broadcast media—where states write policy with little regard for international norms or industry interests—the regulation of Internet intermediaries has been intensely debated in international forums. One basic question is whether an intermediary can be held responsible for the speech of others. If so, it would have to protect itself from punishment by vetting any content that anyone wants to distribute through its services. This, of course, is no different from the gatekeeping routinely practiced by newspapers and television stations. Those who think of YouTube as a media distribution company would not be alarmed by the idea of imposing this form of liability on an Internet intermediary.

If, however, one understands YouTube as something closer to a telecom company, the implications are rather different. Most people would probably find abhorrent the idea of a phone company listening in to calls, and deciding to cut the line when it feels the conversation might be breaking a law. Thus, attitudes to liability vary depending on how one conceives of an intermediary—as a publisher with gatekeeping responsibilities, or as a common carrier obliged to stay completely neutral with regard to content. Not surprisingly, Google prefers the telephone analogy: "We don't hold the telephone company liable when two callers use the phone lines to plan a crime. For the same reasons, it's a fundamental principle of the Internet that you don't blame the neutral intermediaries for the actions of their customers."[62]

The comparison is somewhat disingenuous, because phone calls are mostly private instances of one-to-one communication, while online expression can have a public reach larger than that of traditional mass media. Nor can Google persuasively claim to be content neutral. Google's processes may be automated, but they still bear traces of human decision making. The algorithms behind its search functions are manmade organizing principles, "and like other organizing principles they reflect biases towards some content over other content," notes the legal scholar Uta Kohl.[63] If its algorithms do not discriminate against illegal sites, Kohl argues, this is the result of a "systematic corporate intentionality" to "accord a value of zero to the factor of legality within the automation process."[64]

That said, Google has two features that make it more like a phone company than a publisher. First, the sheer volume of content it traffics is many orders of magnitude greater than, say, a satellite television network like MTV or a news agency like Reuters. Prescreening content for problematic expression would require massive and prohibitively costly resources, compelling intermediaries to turn away most user-generated content if they want to stay in business.[65] As we see in chapter 7, some news organizations have voluntarily taken this route. For companies like YouTube and Twitter, however, which exist solely to provide an intermediary role, prescreening is not realistic. The second reason that search engines and major social media platforms are more like telephone companies than publishers is that they have become part of the infrastructure on which Internet users depend. For many users, Google is so central to their online experience that it "is" the Internet—it is the indispensable utility that makes it possible to navigate what is out there, like "the light that allows us to see cyberspace."[66]

Google's Internal Policies

Google's policies in the run-up to the *Innocence* crisis attempted to strike a compromise between opposing visions for the Internet. On the one hand, the company maintained the libertarian instincts associated with the early architects of the World Wide Web. On the other, it exhibited a grudging acceptance of national jurisdiction, and acknowledged that total denial of responsibility for content posted through its sites is untenable. Google's policy on controversial content declares a "bias in favor of free expression," but also recognizes limits. All its products, for example, ban child pornography. "But in other areas, like extremism, it gets complicated because our products are available in numerous countries with widely varying laws and cultures," it says.[67] Its search tool adheres to separate policies from its publishing platforms such as YouTube.

> For Search—where we are simply indexing content—we take down as little as possible because helping people find information goes to the heart of our mission. We remove webpages from our search index when required by law, and we post a notice to Chilling Effects when we do so. For example, if we're notified about specific pages that glorify Nazism, which is prohibited by German law, then we remove those specific pages from Google.de (our German domain).

On YouTube and Google+, for example, the company doesn't merely link to content but actually hosts. These platforms therefore have guidelines encouraging users to behave responsibly:

> For example, no hate speech, no copyright-infringing content, no death threats, no incitement to violence. And when we're notified about content that either violates those guidelines or breaks the law—for example, we receive a court order—we will remove it, or restrict it in the country where it's illegal.

Generally, Google entertains requests to restrict controversial content in countries where the company's lawyers assess that the relevant service has a presence, such as a localized version or a physical office. It interprets demands as narrowly as possible, and challenges those that seem unreasonable. In addition, Google only restricts views in jurisdictions where the request is made. This ensures that no single government gets to decide what users in other countries get to access. In the reporting period prior to the *Innocence* video, Google had complied with around half of the requests it received.[68] *Innocence* prompted an unprecedented number of challenges, from seventeen countries on four continents. Google complied with eight and rejected the rest.

Google's approach continues to be attacked from both ends of the ideological spectrum. To those who attach a low priority to freedom of expression on the Internet, its guidelines are too insensitive to the harms done by offensive expression. Some states explicitly want to apply their national standards beyond their own borders. Turkey is a prominent example: a prosecutor tried to force Google to extend worldwide the country's ban on insulting the republic's founder, Mustafa Kemal Ataturk, to protect the feelings of the Turkish diaspora.[69] Similarly, authorities in Thailand wanted intermediaries to get its *lèse majesté* standard applied globally. Google has thus far resisted such pressure.

To digital freedom advocates, though, most intermediaries are not putting up enough of a fight against censorship. The local laws that Google obeys are often not consistent with international human rights standards.

The fear is that, as a commercial actor, Google lacks accountability and is likely to make decisions that are more pragmatic than principled. Google—more than Facebook and other intermediaries—has acknowledged that the situation is far from ideal. In response, the company has steadily increased transparency around the requests it receives from governments and other actors.

In 2008, Google, Yahoo!, and Microsoft, together with several research institutions and NGOs devoted to freedom of expression, formed the Global Network Initiative (GNI) to address the challenge of complying with national laws while also protecting human rights.[70] Its industry members now additionally include Facebook and LinkedIn. GNI members have publicly committed themselves to freedom of expression principles modeled on international human rights standards—although, like those international treaties, the GNI principles may be more aspirational than a direct reflection of realities on the ground.

Spoilers, Trolls, and Symbolic Targets

With more people of more diverse cultures living closer together in physical and informational space, we can expect debates about offense to continue, and possibly intensify. US Internet giants may need to de-Americanize their internal rules. Take YouTube's Community Guidelines, quoted above. Its definition of hate speech includes speech that demeans a group based on "veteran status." There may be reasons for this in a US context, but YouTube's global policy to protect the sensibilities of former combatants (and presumably only those who fought on the American side), even as it claimed that it sees no violation in the Muslim-bashing *Innocence*, smacks of a bias toward mainstream American cultural values.

At the same time, we need to be realistic about what greater sensitivity toward others' feelings can and can't achieve. Trying harder to avoid offense may satisfy most members of communities that are weary of sustained racism and xenophobia purveyed against them through the media and in public life. Being generally respectful of others' beliefs and identities shouldn't need any special justification, other than that it's the right thing to do. It would be naïve, however, to expect government censorship, self-censorship, or self-restraint to end the phenomenon of religious outrage. Such an expectation ignores the existence of hate spin agents who have no interest in avoiding indignation, as long as it can serve as a useful political resource.

Such actors may not be acting in good faith. They can be likened to what the international relations field calls "spoilers"—saboteurs intent on subverting peace processes.[71] Alternatively, drawing from Internet culture, we could think of them as "trolls." Trolls are users who enter forums to provoke emotional reactions that will cause the discussion to degenerate into verbal conflict. The term is usually applied to those who harass other users or insert inflammatory comments. But just as offensiveness can be substituted with offendedness in the versatile strategy of hate spin, the objectives of trolls can be achieved not just through garden-variety hate speech, but alternatively through fiery displays of indignation. The Internet analysts Rebecca MacKinnon and Ethan Zuckerman point out that the satisfaction of trolls is often "directly proportional to the unnecessary conflict they are able to create."[72] Therefore, experienced online moderators warn newcomers not to "feed the trolls" by giving them the attention they crave. "Censoring trolls rarely succeeds—they tend to return, even more disruptive than before, using new monikers. Instead, the best way to silence trolls is to ignore them."[73]

Government and Google as Targets

The troll analogy tells us that, whether online or off, responses toward campaigns of righteous indignation need to be measured, taking into account the motives and methods of the actors involved. The cases we've analyzed in this chapter suggest that we need to rethink some conventional views about media and power. For more than twenty years, scholars and journalists investigating digital media have focused on the question of whether and how these new technologies bypass traditional regulatory and editorial controls. Especially in undemocratic regimes, scholars have mainly studied the Internet as a means of evading authority. This is certainly an important function of digital space, but it should not blind us to other creative applications of the Internet.

In the strategy of hate spin, political opportunists use the Internet to magnify claims on the state—not to avoid it. The Internet excels at the rapid crowdsourcing of hate spin. Through it, hatemongers can distribute the search for potential injustice symbols globally. The Internet is the mother lode of offense, both intended and unwitting. And, when the right cause has been identified, the Internet facilitates moral panics. In these circumstances, the state would often prefer to evade attention. In most conservative societies, governments know that they lack the capacity to enforce morals. They opt for a kind of Victorian hypocrisy whereby all manner of questionable conduct is allowed to take place in the shadows; governing elites feign ignorance.

But by dragging offensive expression into the open, hate spin practitioners force the authorities to act. Then, hear-no-evil, see-no-evil is no longer tenable as a coping strategy for balancing the live-and-let-live tolerance of a cosmopolitan society with the conservative values of large segments of the population. In some cases, governments itching to crack down on media can exploit such situations, as Pakistan and Bangladesh did when *Innocence* presented them with an opportunity to block YouTube. But in Southeast Asia, authorities in Indonesia, Malaysia, and Singapore were probably compelled to take symbolic action, even if they preferred to look the other way.

The Internet has also presented hate spin agents with a completely new target for claim making: Google itself. With more wealth and greater name recognition than many nation-states, Google's profile is hardly that of a characterless public utility provider or infrastructure builder. People on all sides of the free speech debate view Google as a powerful institution in its own right. This unique position thrusts Google directly into hate spin campaigns, sometimes cast in the role of a formidable co-conspirator in the liberal plot against a besieged community. Protest banners and placards condemning Viking Penguin or *Jyllands-Posten* would hardly have the same global impact as those with slogans like "Google is a worldwide web TERRORIST" or "GOOGLE, YOUTUBE ARE PART OF THE HATRED CAMPAIGN AGAINST ALL MUSLIMS" (pictures of which you can find online— via Google Images, of course).

Symbolic Purification

In a simpler world, offendedness is a learned response that helps humans avoid harm, a culturally evolved analog to the revulsion reflex. But this impulse to purify has never been as mechanistic as it might seem. In her 1966 study, the anthropologist Mary Douglas showed that traditional religious communities' concepts of pollution and taboo are culturally sophisticated, and not just motivated by some physiological need for hygiene.[74] Rules of purity are expressive, symbolic statements for maintaining social systems. They are not rigid or uncompromising. For example, communities have simple cleansing rituals to ensure that violations do not bring life to a standstill. Dirt and pollution are not taken too literally.

Understanding the offense-taking side of hate spin may require a similar mental shift from a hygiene frame to a symbolic frame. Protests against offensive messages, no matter how furious, may not be aiming for total eradication or complete quarantine, as if they are dealing with a deadly toxin. They are making a political point—after which the protesters can stand down. This is why we see agitators publicizing the existence of offending material in the same breath that they call for its censorship—behavior that would make no sense if the real motive were to shield their community from exposure to that content. State responses are also more complex than mere protection. States and their leaders perform their reactions for domestic and international audiences. Whether they actually succeed in shutting out the content or in fact draw more attention to it is not as important as being seen to react.

Sometimes, the interests of hate spin agents and government officials are aligned in acting against offensive content. But this stand is not permanent, if for no other reason than each has other priorities and interests to attend to. So, at other times, the same parties may show total indifference to the same provocation that had previously incensed them. In many cases, content that religious groups violently opposed remains freely available through some parallel medium—without any protest.

Take the case of Pakistan, where hard-liners can always be depended on for loud indignation at religious insult. Not surprisingly, *The Satanic Verses* is banned in Pakistan. But when I asked my friends at a digital freedom NGO, Bytes for All, to check whether the book is available online, they found copies readily available via Amazon. The Wikipedia entry on the *Jyllands-Posten* controversy, which includes a scan of the full page containing the twelve cartoons—was also freely accessible. They reached this content through PTCL, an Internet service provider majority-owned by the government.

In Indonesia, I tested the country's moral fences personally. I found that the full version of the *Innocence of Muslims* video was available on YouTube, just a few years after the trailer had been condemned as blasphemous. This can't be because Indonesians are IT novices. The country's citizens are some of the world's biggest users of social media, and hard-line Muslim groups are as adept as liberal secularists at using these technologies. No, these are examples of conservatives and governments choosing to look the other way, as deliberately as when they decide to fixate on something and take offense.

The violence in the words and actions of offense-takers suggests an uncompromising, instrumental intent. Offense-takers give the impression that they are motivated by an all-consuming desire to keep their homelands free of the insults and corruption that globalization brings. A closer look at their conduct, though, reveals that while their methods may be physical in the extreme, their goals are largely symbolic. Just as the performance of offendedness can emerge out of the blue, it usually fades into oblivion. Neither the onset nor the termination of protest bears a direct relation to the arrival or removal of the offending material. Their conduct conforms with Joseph Gusfield's description of Prohibition in the United States: the ban on alcohol was pushed as part of a "symbolic crusade" that did not particularly care whether or not alcohol actually remained available.[75] It is no different in the Internet age. Campaigns of offendedness have no doubt included many supporters with a strong personal desire to cleanse their countries of sinful practices. But hate spin dynamics are unintelligible without skeptical scrutiny of hate spin agents' interests and a critical analysis of political context.

4 India: Narendra Modi and the Harnessing of Hate

On May 26, 2014, Narendra Modi was sworn in as India's fifteenth prime minister. Government turnovers are nothing new in this constantly contested democracy. But the manner and meaning of Modi's victory was revolutionary. Modi's Hindu nationalist Bharatiya Janata Party (BJP) won an outright majority of parliamentary seats—282 out of 543—without any help from the twenty-plus minor parties in the center-right National Democratic Alliance. In a country whose fractious diversity suggested the inevitability of coalition politics, this marked the first time in thirty years that a party's right to govern did not depend on support from allies. With just forty-four seats, the Indian National Congress—the party of the founding fathers of the republic—had never found itself in a hole so deep or at such a loss for answers. Inspired by its Great Soul or "Mahatma," Mohandas K. Gandhi, the Congress doctrine had always emphasized minority rights, especially for historically disadvantaged classes and castes, but also for religious minorities. India is the birthplace of more major religions—Hinduism, Buddhism, Jainism, and Sikhism—than any other civilization. Its Muslim population is larger than any other country's save Indonesia and, perhaps, Pakistan.[1]

Opposing the accommodationism of the Congress Party, the BJP aims to shift the political center of gravity decisively toward the four-in-five Indians who identify with the Hindu faith. Modi's was not the first BJP-led government. But, in its previous stints, from 1996 to 2004, the BJP was restrained by the need to appease its coalition partners, resulting in a central government that was still recognizably Indian in its diversity. Modi's term represented a radical break from the past, in that he came to the office with a strong majoritarian mandate. The 282 BJP Members of Parliament elected in 2014 included not a single Muslim. As a result of the BJP wave, the 543-member House included just 20 Muslims (less than 4 percent), in a country where Muslims account for around 14 percent of the population.

Modi did not land in office solely because of religion. By a factor of three to one, Indians believed that the BJP would do a better job than the incumbent Congress government in creating jobs, fighting corruption, and reining in inflation.[2] Modi's image as the man most likely to get India working again was the main factor behind his ultimate victory at the polls nationally. Even so, the BJP played the religious card assiduously in key states.[3] Nor could Modi have emerged as the BJP's unquestioned leader without brandishing his reputation as a Hindu chauvinist. He shot to prominence in 2002 as chief minister in the state of Gujarat, where under his watch perhaps a thousand Muslims were massacred, ostensibly in revenge for the burning of a train carrying Hindu pilgrims and activists.[4]

Politicians had used religion for electoral gain prior to Modi's election. Despite its lofty ideals, the Congress Party was an early practitioner of what Indians call "communal" politics—dangerous, ethnic-based sectarianism. In 1984, Congress politicians instigated attacks on Sikhs to avenge the assassination of Prime Minister Indira Gandhi by her Sikh bodyguards. More than 2,700 Sikhs were killed.[5] But, while others played occasionally with the fire of communalism, the BJP immersed itself in it and defined itself by it.[6] Together with its allied movements, the BJP embraced hate spin as a key strategy. Indeed, in probably no other democracy today can one witness hate spin at work to the extent that it is practiced in Modi's India.

Hate propaganda was an essential part of Narendra Modi's rise to the leadership of the world's largest democracy. His movement's vilification of the Muslim minority through classic hate speech mobilized the far right and helped unite the caste-riven Hindu majority behind the upper-caste BJP. The Hindu Right also conducted a systematic campaign to manufacture extreme offendedness against historical writing perceived as defaming their religion. What is remarkable about the Indian case is not just the regularity of incitement and manufactured indignation. It is also the systemic, high-level use of this strategy that sets India apart.

The Rise of Hindu Nationalism

In Mahatma Gandhi's fabled riverside ashram in Ahmedabad, Gujarat, is a poster recalling his stand against majoritarianism: "I do not believe in the doctrine of the greatest good of the greatest number. It means in its nakedness that in order to achieve the supposed good of fifty-one percent, the interest of forty-nine percent, may be, or rather should be sacrificed. It is a heartless doctrine and has done harm to humanity."

The quote reflects Gandhi's conviction—shared with the architect of the Indian Constitution, the formidable Bhimrao Ramji Ambedkar—that political life "was inconceivable without an unconditional equality in moral and social relations," as the historian Aishwary Kumar puts it.[7] India's commitment to religious equality took on geopolitical significance after independence. Pakistan is the "other" of Indian nationalism, so it was important to demonstrate that Muslims who stayed behind in secular India instead of heading to Islamic Pakistan upon partition had made the right decision. However, the secular anticolonial nationalism of Congress was always challenged.[8] The Muslim separatism that created Pakistan would continue to thrive in Kashmir. And there was Hindu nationalism. The same Gujarat that claims India's greatest son would also produce Narendra Modi.

In the 1920s, Gandhi's Ahmedabad was the spiritual center for the political principles of nonviolence and nondiscrimination. Eighty years later, Ahmedabad would be ground zero for one of India's bloodiest communal massacres since partition. After that, in the new normal presided over by Chief Minister Modi, the city was divided by physical, institutional, and cultural walls completely antithetical to India's founding vision. Muslims are ghettoized in the suburb of Juhapura, which is denied municipal services. "It is almost impossible for Ahmedabad's Muslims to obtain a housing loan for a home in a Hindu area, and the city government of Ahmedabad has designated most of Juhapura as an agricultural zone. Muslims are therefore not only pushed on the margins of the city but also towards illegality," says Zahir Janmohamad, an American human rights worker who witnessed the 2002 pogrom and has written a book about contemporary Ahmedabad.[9]

Modi's Bharatiya Janata Party (BJP) was formed in 1980. Like India's other nationalisms, however, its roots go back to the late nineteenth century. The BJP is the political wing of a formidable network of groups referred to collectively as the Sangh Parivar ("family of organizations" in Hindi). The movement's main driver is the Rashtriya Swayamsevak Sangh (RSS), an all-male Hindu chauvinist organization founded in 1925. At its most benign, the RSS is a disciplined force of volunteers dedicated to social service, usually among the first to offer help in natural disasters. But RSS militants are also at the forefront of extreme intolerance, leading the charge in violence against minorities, organizing forced conversions, and attacking writers and artists.

Pradip Jain, a smartly dressed lawyer, is the RSS spokesman in Gujarat. Sitting cross-legged on a divan in an office in Ahmedabad, he tells me that the role of the RSS is simply to spread good values and build good human beings, who would in turn build the nation. "Just like every family has a head, every society has a head, and religion is its head." He explains that, while the country is ordered by its constitution, the nation is ruled by dharma, loosely translated as life-sustaining cosmic order. This is, he says, what sets India apart from other nations. "In India, dharma is supreme."[10]

This self-understanding, of being both separate from and superior to the trivialities of electoral politics, makes the RSS an uncompromisingly ideological organization. It has no political agenda as such, Jain insists: it inculcates values and does not interfere with the state. This, however, is not some isolationist sect. The RSS may not want to govern—that is the BJP's job—but it obviously relishes power, and does not mind being feared. It has mastered its unique place in Indian life, everywhere and nowhere, fluid and iron. The RSS doesn't even have a formal membership system, Jain says, but that does not stop him from giving a small, satisfied smile when I point out that it is reputedly the largest voluntary organization in the world. And even as he insists that the RSS does not tell its followers what to do, Jain notes that each is required to give back something to the society in his own sphere. "The person who has built his persona through Sangh will not leave any stone unturned," Jain says with the same smile. You get the sense that the chill invoked by this choice of words was probably not accidental.

The RSS and its family of organizations are seized by the perceived threat to the status of India's majority religion. And like other fascist groups throughout history, the Hindu Right believes that the best defense is a good offense. It projects a muscular Hinduism that would wrest India into a new era of glory if given power, and brooks no dissent from those—including Hindus of a more liberal persuasion—who stand in their way. Violence is meted out or instigated by members of the Vishva Hindu Parishad (VHP) and other extreme groups within the family of right-wing organizations.

The Sangh Parivar's ideology is dubbed Hindutva ("Hinduness"), to distinguish it from Hinduism. The movement does not demand a theocratic state or any explicit embrace of Hinduism as the state religion. Hindutva is a national-cultural rather than a religious category, seen as synonymous with the idea of India. Indians of other faiths, including Muslims, should therefore have no trouble accepting Hindutva, according to the Sangh Parivar. If they choose not to, they must be traitors to the nation. The Sangh Parivar's main grievance is that India's Congress-architected secularism has been too accommodating to Muslims and other minorities. One major symbolic sticking point is the state's recognition of Muslim personal law for marriage and inheritance, while other Indians are subject to a uniform civil code. The Sangh Parivar claims to seek formal equality, and wants to remove policies intended to protect minority rights.[11] But the movement has a record of religious discrimination, even in distribution of disaster relief, as well as extreme intolerance backed by physical violence.[12]

BJP-led coalitions had brief moments in power in 1996 and 1998, followed by a full five-year term from 1999. The demolition of a sixteenth-century mosque in Ayodhya in 1992 contributed to the BJP victory by energizing RSS members on the ground. The Babri Mosque had allegedly been erected on the site of an ancient Hindu temple believed to have marked the birthplace of Rama, an avatar of the Hindu god Vishnu and the hero of the epic *Ramayana*. In 1990, BJP president L. K. Advani embarked on a 10,000-kilometer journey across northern India to Ayodhya, where he said he would build a new temple. He and his entourage were arrested before they could do any damage. In December 1992, however, the authorities felt they had no choice but to step aside when up to 200,000 activists descended on the sacred site. Although the attackers were initially characterized as a frenzied mob, journalists later revealed that Sangh Parivar leaders coordinated the group and the attack. "Volunteers were trained, logistics painstakingly put in place and the assault on the disputed shrine launched using large surging crowds with volunteers skilled in demolishing structures embedded in it," reported the *Times of India*.[13]

The appeal of BJP to Indian voters has never been guaranteed because Hindus in India do not generally behave as a vote-bank—they have not traditionally voted as a unified bloc. Varghese K. George, the political editor of the *Hindu*—a national newspaper that, despite its name, is one of Indian journalism's stoutest champions of secular democratic values—identifies three structural weaknesses in the Sangh Parivar that, historically at least, limited its electoral prospects.[14] First was the tension between Hindu traditionalists focused on the transcendental and a middle class impatient for higher standards of living. Second, caste divisions within Hindu society limited the appeal of BJP elites among less privileged groups. Third, there was an uneasy balance of power between the dogmatic RSS and the electoral pragmatism of the BJP.

Narendra Modi provided an answer to all three dilemmas, George says. For a start, he bridged the traditional and the modern. With the Gujarat pogrom of 2002, the state's chief minister had already established his credentials as an unflinching defender of the faithful. He would spend the next decade cultivating the second part of what one commentator called his "two-in-one package of rabid Hindutva and pro-reform smartness."[15] Modi aggressively pursued economic growth while championing largely symbolic religious causes, for instance, opposing the slaughter of cows. Hindutva 2.0, as George calls it, breaks from the past mainly in its embrace of neoliberalism. Under Modi, Gujarat resisted redistribution policies and embraced economic growth. "Going by Mr. Modi's public pronouncements over several years, Hindutva 2.0 is a particular variant of neoliberalism that dovetails religious nationalism with economic progress," he says.[16]

The second problem, caste, had been the major obstacle to the BJP's achieving power in India's poorer states. Backward castes—such as the Dalits, traditionally treated as outcastes or untouchables—felt better represented by the national Bahujan Samaj Party and state-level organizations such as the left-leaning Samajwadi Party in Uttar Pradesh. To woo them, Modi flaunted his own backward caste origins, significantly broadening his appeal. But to foster Hindu unity, it was also necessary for Modi to conjure up a common enemy.[17] Muslims—already associated with Pakistan and global terrorism—readily served that purpose. Modi's predecessors recognized this when they tore down the Ayodhya mosque. The Supreme Court banned building anything in its place, so the site remained a potent injustice symbol for cultivating fear and loathing of Muslims.

Modi was also able to transcend the RSS–BJP tension. As a member of RSS since the age of eight, his pedigree was unquestioned. The first BJP prime minister, Atal Behari Vajpayee, had tried to keep the extremist tendencies RSS at bay. Unable to stomach the 2002 pogrom in Gujarat, he had even tried to oust Modi as the state's chief minister.[18] But by then, Modi was already untouchable in Gujarat. In 2013–14, he contemptuously brushed aside his rivals within the BJP. He had emerged as the Sangh Parivar's best hope for returning to power. "In the persona of the Gujarat chief minister—who projects a masculine Hindu pride while seeming to embrace a pragmatic economic philosophy and sporting a Movado watch, Bulgari spectacles, and Montblanc pens—the RSS may have found a way to resolve, or at least dissipate, the tensions between its ethos and the exigencies of contemporary political life," noted the journalist Dinesh Narayan.[19]

If the BJP's road to Delhi in 1998 was paved with the shattered stones of the Babri Mosque, its stunning return in 2014 detoured through the blood-soaked streets of Ahmedabad as well as the supportive boardrooms of major corporations. Within 150 days of Modi becoming chief minister of Gujarat, Hindu hard-liners there were massacring Muslims. An investigation into the riots by the Campaign Against Genocide—a network of civil society organizations that includes Hindu and other faith-based groups—found the state government "complicit and culpable at the highest level."[20] Modi has never been able to live down his association with the 2002 pogrom. Not that he has tried to. For a significant section of his core constituency, the Gujarat pogrom was about finally teaching Muslims a lesson, a long-overdue turning of the tables against a dangerous minority. Moderates in the Hindu population were horrified, but—as politicians around the world understand—moderates don't make the most effective army for an election campaign. The troops whose enthusiasm Modi needed most were members of the RSS, which had founded the BJP in 1980. Only with their blessings could Modi achieve preeminence within the BJP. Even after he emerged as the clear front-runner, when prudence might have suggested that he position himself as a more moderate and inclusive PM-in-waiting, Modi's campaign burnished his image as a Hindu strongman. The giving and taking of religious offense continued unabated.

Sectarianism and the Regulation of Offense

Before we examine how Modi and the BJP rolled out hate spin for the 2014 election, we should map India's unique legal landscape. As I noted in earlier chapters, hate spin can be both constrained and facilitated by the law. India's laws are a hybrid of its democratic commitment to freedom of expression and its instinct to protect the religious feelings of its citizens, a response conditioned by its history of sectarian conflict. The Indian Constitution and Supreme Court have always taken freedom of expression seriously, and its political culture prizes the right to dissent vociferously against governmental authority. It outperforms most of the Global South in political rights and civil liberties, and it is only one of five territories in Asia rated "free" by Freedom House.[21] India is closer to the United States than to, say, Pakistan or Russia in the formal protection it offers to freedom of expression.[22] At the same time, India deviates from liberal democratic norms in its desire to police offense. While the United States reacted to its legacy of sectarian conflict by developing an extreme allergy to state intervention in theological quarrels, Indian lawmakers adopted the opposite response, diving in to push apart contesting communities, refereeing their religious disputes, and creating no-go areas in what otherwise remained a colorfully contested public sphere.

Although contemporary commentators frequently speak of the Hindu–Muslim conflict as an almost timeless, ontological constant, historians of India generally consider it an outcome of British rule. Precolonial history was not free of violence, of course, but the colonial government's administrative classifications and its policy of divide-and-rule had the effect of freezing previously fluid identities and making them more salient.[23] Self-consciously sectarian conflict is therefore more recent, with Hindu–Muslim riots dating back only to the last quarter of the nineteenth century, when there was growing competition between then-dominant Muslim elites within the colonial administration and the rising educated class of Hindus in northern India. Once the state recognized communally defined publics and accorded their representative organizations and leaders the status of legitimate interlocutors, they would develop a life of their own. Thereafter, when the nationalist leaders Jawaharlal Nehru and Mahatma Gandhi tried to shape an all-encompassing Indian identity, they had to accept the political reality that the leaders of various religious and linguistic groups would insist on holding on to their own constituencies.[24]

Sectarian competition was tragically written into the narrative of independence. The crude, cruel partition into Muslim-majority Pakistan and Hindu-majority India led to the largest migration in history. The upheaval escalated into violent clashes, killing an estimated one million civilians. The trauma of partition, together with the assassination of Mahatma Gandhi by a Hindu extremist, gave urgency to the secularist project, but failed to inoculate India against future outbreaks of communal violence. Inter-religious riots have remained part of the soundtrack of the Indian story, mostly in the background as low-intensity conflicts, but occasionally erupting into mass violence. "India may be an officially secular state, but Indian society is defined by religious identities and riven by communal mistrust and hatreds," notes Robert Hardgrave, a scholar of South Asian politics.[25]

The Indian Constitution gives all citizens the right to freedom of speech and expression in Article 19(1)(a). However, Clause (2) allows restrictions "in the interests of the sovereignty and integrity of India, the security of the State, friendly relations with foreign States, public order, decency, or morality or in relation to contempt of court, defamation, or incitement to an offence." By democratic standards, notes the constitutional lawyer Bhairav Acharya, this is an exceptionally long list of permissible limitations. "We do not have a consistent or coherent free speech doctrine," he says.[26] The new republic retained colonial-era restrictions designed to keep order between communities. The Indian Penal Code has numerous sections curtailing freedom of expression that threatens the peaceful coexistence of religious groups. Under Section 153A, individuals can be fined or jailed up to three years for any attempt to promote "enmity between different groups on grounds of religion, race, place of birth, residence, language, etc., and doing acts prejudicial to maintenance of harmony."

Section 295A is the closest thing India has to a law against blasphemous libel. The colonial government devised it in 1927, in response to Muslim groups' outrage over a controversial pamphlet on the life of Prophet Muhammad. The authorities had failed to secure the publisher's conviction under the older Section 153A, which the judge said was "intended to prevent persons from making attacks on a particular community as it exists at the present time and was not meant to stop polemics against deceased religious leaders."[27] Within months, as Muslims' anger continued unabated, Section 295A was introduced to plug the perceived gap in the Penal Code, covering "deliberate and malicious acts, intended to outrage religious feelings of any class by insulting its religion or religious beliefs." With that, says Acharya, the right to offend was taken away. "The idea that government must bow to street protest was born here," he says.[28] "This is not the right to give offense. This is expanding the right to take offense." The outcome was the product, explains Acharya, of the colonial government's hallmark impulse to maintain public order by keeping communities separate—a governance approach that carries on to this day. While the modern concept of defamation is meant to protect the reputation of individuals, India has grafted onto it "an inchoate and as yet undefined notion of community honor," he adds.[29]

Penal Code prohibitions against offense are also contained in Section 505(1)(c), which amounts to a group libel law dealing with statements, rumors, and reports that incite one class or community to commit any offense against any other class or community. Section 505(2) penalizes anyone who "makes, publishes, or circulates any statement or report containing rumour or alarming news" likely to create or promote "feelings of enmity, hatred or ill-will" between different castes or communities. Most of these Penal Code offenses are punishable with jail terms of up to three years, with stiffer penalties if committed in a place of worship.

But despite the multilayered defenses against religious offense, India's political system and culture cannot be characterized as thin-skinned. Indian political tradition embraces a long history of contestation between conservative and liberal impulses, and a multitude of positions in between and at either extreme. Even in 1927, when Indian legislators passed Section 295A, they were practicing what the historian Neeti Nair calls "legislative pragmatism." Nair points out that while the colonial authorities felt compelled to prohibit religious insult, Indian lawmakers representing diverse interests and perspectives were under few illusions that this would solve the problem of communal conflict. Significantly, legislators entertained many proposed amendments to the bill to ensure that the new legislation would not punish sincere criticism of religion, calls for social reform, or historical research.[30]

Since independence, India's higher courts have on many occasions thwarted the abuse of insult laws. Judges, recognizing the value of historical and artistic explorations of communal themes, have struck down attempts to censor expression deemed offensive. When one of the conspirators in the 1948 assassination of Mahatma Gandhi wrote a book explaining his actions, the Bombay High Court invalidated the government's decision to confiscate all the copies. In its 1971 ruling, the court noted that the author was dealing with past history and not contemporary issues, and that the book should be assessed in its entirety and not solely on passages taken out of context.[31] In 1988, the Supreme Court ruled that the instructional benefits of a television serial portraying religious extremism leading up to the partition of India outweighed its alleged inflammatory potential.[32] Similarly, when authorities censored a documentary film on the 1984 massacre of Sikhs on the ground that it would stir communal tension, the Bombay High Court objected. In its 1997 ruling, the court said that the film's message of peace deserved the protection of the Constitution's free speech provision.[33] In 2005, the Calcutta High Court rejected the state government's arguments for confiscating a book decrying the plight of women in Muslim Bangladesh. The government had claimed that the book violated Section 295A of the Penal Code, as it would outrage religious feelings and insult the beliefs of Muslims in India. The court ruled, however, that the book should be read in the context of the struggle for women's equality.[34]

Surveying such rulings handed down by the Indian courts, some analysts place India near the positive end of the free speech spectrum. India's laws, says one Western legal scholar, are not overly broad but narrowly tailored and "limited to seditious intentions, or words that promote ill-will between groups, and therefore do not suppress more speech than is necessary."[35] Such a conclusion seems to be based on the final outcomes of certain landmark cases that have wound their way through the system and resulted in progressive rulings by higher courts. Unlike in the United States, however these rulings have not been consolidated into clear and rigorous tests against which the constitutionality of free speech restrictions are to be judged.[36] Furthermore, the justice system is tainted by corruption at the lower levels and overwhelmed with the sheer numbers of cases: at least 32 million cases are pending in the lower courts, with 56,000 pending before the Supreme Court.[37]

Even if India's courts ultimately tend toward protecting free speech, then, the old adage about justice delayed applies. Individuals who are gratuitously accused under India's insult laws can be denied justice for a prolonged period. This makes insult laws a ready weapon for harassment and censorship, prone to abuse. "The process is the punishment," says Geeta Seshu, a media freedom activist. One victim she tried to help was Shirin

Dalvi, a Mumbai newspaper editor who was hounded for publishing a picture of the cover of *Charlie Hebdo* bearing a caricature of Prophet Muhammad to accompany a story about the killings in Paris. Dalvi was summoned to five different police stations where complaints had been lodged, Seshu says. A practicing Muslim, Dalvi clearly had no intention to cause offense. She apologized as soon as readers objected to the republication of the cover. Seshu was hopeful that the courts would eventually quash the charges, but the damage had already been done: Dalvi lost her job and was forced to go into hiding, due to threats of violence. Her newspaper had to close down and a career she had built over 20 years was in jeopardy.[38]

The ease with which opportunists can game the legal system also explains the gap between election laws and election practice. The Election Commission has been criticized for its failure to regulate hate speech during campaigns, although, to be fair, the job may simply be too large for any institution to cope with. When it sees clear breaches, the Election Commission typically adopts a two-pronged response. Since such speech usually involves a statutory violation, it first lodges a complaint with the police to initiate criminal proceedings. In addition to the Penal Code, the commission may invoke the Representation of the People Act of 1951, which prohibits the practice of urging voters to choose on the grounds of "religion, race caste, community or language," or influencing the vote through "the use of, or appeal to religious symbols." Persons in violation of this act may be disqualified from running for or taking up a parliamentary seat.[39] However, the process of charging and prosecuting offenders could take several years, and is partly at the mercy of uncooperative state governments.

In addition to filing police reports, therefore, the Election Commission independently serves notice that the candidate has violated the Model Code of Conduct. This second prong began as a voluntary mechanism, but it has been endorsed in Supreme Court pronouncements. The code leads with statements on communalism. "No party or candidate shall include in any activity which may aggravate existing differences or create mutual hatred or cause tension between different castes and communities, religious, or linguistic," it says in its first paragraph. Point 3 of the code reads, "There shall be no appeal to caste or communal feelings for securing votes. Mosques, Churches, Temples, or other places of worship shall not be used as forum for election propaganda."[41]

Responding through the Model Code of Conduct has an immediacy that the Penal Code lacks, notes the former chief election commissioner of India, S. Y. Quraishi.[40] Applying the code, the Election Commission can direct political parties not to field a candidate who has used communal speeches, or to impose a gag order on the candidate during the remainder of his or her campaign. The moral authority of the Election Commission is not negligible, since parties do not want to appear too irresponsible. One limitation of the Election Commission's regulation of political activity is that it applies only to the period after elections are called. The Model Code of Conduct does cover election manifestos regardless of when they are released, on the ground that these are clearly intended for electoral purposes. But the Election Commission is powerless to regulate speeches and other communications in between polls—which is most of the time.[42]

The law has never been India's only protection against sectarian politics. India's irreducible diversity provides another powerful check. In the past, major parties and candidates took it for granted that national leaders had to accommodate India's diversity to hold power at the center. This had been the case with BJP's previous tenure, under Prime Minister Vajpayee. Many party leaders interpreted its crushing defeat in 2009 as a rejection of its turn toward more a hard-line Hindu nationalist position. According to this conventional wisdom, a polarizing figure like Modi would be incapable of generating the kind of broad-based support that a national party needed.[43]

Congress leaders continued to make this claim as the 2014 polls approached, with rising desperation and diminishing credibility. Modi remained uncompromising. Instead of reaching out to minorities, he played the mathematics of the first-past-the-post electoral system, consolidating the BJP's base and securing a decisive Hindu majoritarian verdict.[44] His achievement required an ideological reframing of Indian secularism and democracy away from minority rights toward majoritarian power; away from Hindu eclecticism toward Hindutva fundamentalism. Hate spin was critical for this enterprise.

Hate Speech on the Road to 2014

It would be hard to find a hate spin factory that has been more systematic and productive than the Sangh Parivar. Its hate speech was not merely the result of loose cannons. Even when it appeared that its people were losing their heads, there was method to the madness. The Hindu Right cultivated anti-Muslim hate in order to marginalize, and in some cases even disenfranchise, members of the country's largest religious minority. Perhaps even more importantly, the BJP understood that conjuring up a reviled outgroup was the easiest way to unite a Hindu majority divided by caste, class, and language.

Key Themes in Hindutva Hate Speech

One illustrative case involved a Muslim-bashing video titled *Bharat Ki Pukar* (translated as "the call of India"). The BJP circulated this compact disc before the 2007 assembly elections in the key state of Uttar Pradesh. The video employed several well-worn hate speech motifs to depict Muslims as a threat to survival against which the BJP offered salvation. It opened with a voiceover of "Mother India" warning that the country was on the brink of ruin: "By using terrorists, spreading fear and dividing us, Pakistan wants to break India into pieces. ... Now, ordinary people of India have to think, do they want slavery again or Ram Rajya in their independent India."[45]

"Ram Rajya" translates as the Kingdom of Ram. The BJP says that the term merely denotes good governance, but in the context of an election campaign, it is a thinly disguised emotive Hindutva clarion call.[46] The video also included such lines as, "The other parties, they are all agents of the Muslims." The impending Muslim takeover, the video threatened, would mean the closure of all schools and colleges. "What will open are madrasas from where fatwas will be issued to drive Hindus out from this country, enslave them—because they want to rule over here, they want to make India into Pakistan."

The video featured various portrayals of Muslim subterfuge. In one scene, a Muslim man (identified by his skullcap) plants a bomb under a car. Another vignette showed the two sons of a Muslim butcher concealing their identities to trick a Hindu farmer into selling them his cow. A fifty-second-long clip of a buffalo being slaughtered follows. The theme of Muslim deceit continued with the story of a young man who lures a Hindu girl away from her home before revealing his true identity as a Muslim. He gives her to an older man, to be wed. She is dragged away screaming, as her husband-to-be laughs, "When Hindu girls get ensnared by us, they scream and shout but sadly there is no one to listen to them and we have great fun." A later scene showed a Muslim woman declaring it her duty to produce more children. This was followed by what looked like a news clip, in which a Hindu woman said: "Hindus will produce two children and Muslims will marry five times and produce thirty-five pups and make this country into an Islamic state." Near the end of the video, a Hindu social worker urged viewers to mount a new independence struggle and "take an oath to drive those traitors out of the country." The video ends with images of the BJP flag, party leaders, the Babri Mosque being demolished, and so on.

The tropes contained in *Bharat Ki Pukar* were repeated in the 2014 general election campaign. BJP propaganda equates its Muslim opponents with traitorous Pakistanis whose terrorist acts threaten national security. It is not just high-profile, big-city targets that are supposedly at risk. At the village level, Muslims violate the sanctity of cows and the honor of women. Without the BJP's leadership, Muslims would overwhelm Hindus by being more duplicitous and more fecund, voters are told.

The fact that none of this is true is immaterial to the Hindu Right. Consider the claims about Muslim men, their several wives and multitudes of children. There is no evidence that, controlling for income, Muslims have a higher fertility rate than Hindus. The Sangh Parivar's followers nevertheless believe that Muslims, currently 14 percent of the Indian population, are to be feared as a would-be dominant majority. A people renowned for its mathematical prowess thus indulged in creative arithmetic license, concluding that Hindus would become a minority in their own country. If the Sangh Parivar could get away with such fictions, they could perhaps get away with anything. Hence the "love jihad."

Love Jihad and the Muzaffarnagar Riots

The "love jihad" is a bizarre myth about a Muslim campaign to conquer Hindus by stealing their girls, one heart at a time. The story goes that a handsome young man appears in the community and woos away a Hindu girl with his seductive charms and promises of a better life. He has been schooled in a madrassah, but possesses the wherewithal for modern courtship, like a motorcycle and a mobile phone. Only after she has run off with him does he reveal himself as a Muslim, either forcing her to convert or selling her off into slavery.

Like all good propaganda, there is a molehill of fact somewhere within this mountain of fiction. Love often does blossom between young men and women whose matches are deemed unsuitable. Sheer probability dictates that most of these scandalous liaisons involve Hindu couples of different castes or classes; relatively few are interreligious. Some of the couples elope; some are forcibly, even fatally, separated—including through the infamous practice of "honor killings."[47] India does also suffer from the entirely separate problem of human trafficking. One ploy of the modern slave trade in South Asia involves con men appearing before the parents of eligible daughters, proposing marriage with substantial dowries, and then turning over their new brides to brothels in the big cities or the Gulf States. As for the mobile phone, the association with Muslims may ring true, for mobile shops in some parts of the country are owned mainly by landless Muslim men (who, through such enterprise, may also accumulate enough savings to buy motorbikes).[48]

It is apparently easier to blame a mythical love jihad conspiracy than to confront uglier truths—that the obsession with social status sometimes turns young romance into needless tragedy; or that poverty and ignorance makes families easy prey for dowry-bearing human traffickers. Whatever the social psychology behind it, the myth of love jihad became a widely held belief ripe for electoral exploitation in the run-up to the 2014 election. BJP operatives played an active role in its cultivation.

One simple tactic in promoting the myth was to print posters and newspaper advertisements listing a hotline number to call if you feared that a family member might be a victim of a love jihadist. The ads depicted a handsome, bearded young man riding a motorcycle, with a happy girl behind him. Its creativity and simplicity would do any ad agency proud. Instead of trying to prove the existence of a disease, it advertised the cure. The underlying message: if the people in authority need to launch a hotline, there must be a genuine social problem. Since the group behind the ad campaign wasn't expecting any phone calls, they didn't need to spend money to engage an Infosys call center; just a man with one phone line, if at all, would do.

The love jihad legend was not just some trivial sideshow in one of the world's most entertaining electoral contests. It played a role in the BJP's most important victory—the campaign for Uttar Pradesh, India's largest state. If it were a country, Uttar Pradesh's 200 million people would compete with Brazil as the fifth most populous in the world; it accounts for 80 out of 543 seats in the Indian parliament. The dilemma for the BJP was that half the state's population identified with so-called backward castes, which solidly backed two other parties, the Bahujan Samaj Party and the Samajwadi Party. In the 2007 state assembly elections, these two parties won more than 303 out of 403 seats, with the BJP securing only 51. To win the general election, the BJP would need to win over the backward castes and unify the Hindu vote. It could not shed its upper-caste image, but it could present itself as the only force capable of protecting Hindus against a Muslim threat. The *Bharat Ki Pukar* video may not have done the trick in 2007, but the strategy would be refined and repeated in the coming years.

In mid-2013, Narendra Modi dispatched one of his closest associates, Amit Shah, to take charge of the BJP's campaign in Uttar Pradesh. Shortly thereafter, in September 2013, communal riots erupted between Muslims and land-owning Hindu Jats in the district of Muzaffarnagar. Fifty-two people were killed and at least fifty thousand Muslims were forced to flee their homes in the country's worst communal riots in a decade.[49] The trigger event was a fight in Kawal village, allegedly over the harassment of a girl, though it could also have been over a motorcycle accident. In any case, three youths died, one Muslim and two Jats. Kawal at the time had a reputation as a "harmonious and business-friendly" village, where Muslims and Hindus lived apart but in economic codependence.[50] Ordinarily, the fracas would have fizzled out, but provocateurs seized upon the incident. Everything from that point on bore the hallmarks of the engineered mass violence that is part of the rhythm of Indian politics. A crowd of thousands turned up for the cremation of the two Jat youths, after which they entered the Muslim colony of Kawal on tractors and motorbikes, looting and vandalizing Muslim houses and shops. The mob shouted such slogans as "Jao Pakistan, warna Kabristan" (go to Pakistan or the graveyard).[51]

Within days, a video was circulating among Hindus, showing two men being beaten to death by a Muslim mob. Although later revealed to be a two-year-old recording from Pakistan, it was passed off as a video of the killing of the two Jat youth. Jat leaders called a major rally on September 7. Some 150,000 people attended, led by politicians and activists from Uttar Pradesh and neighboring states.

Several days of violence followed.[52] Although a district magistrate in Muzaffarnagar ordered politicians to stay away, the temptation proved irresistible for the BJP.[53] Several politicians were charged with inciting the violence, and one BJP parliamentarian was charged with uploading the fake video.[54] A *Frontline* investigative report found that the love jihad conspiracy theory had been installed as a major plank in the BJP platform in rural Uttar Pradesh. Jats interviewed after the riots claimed that they needed to save the honor of their daughters and sisters.[55] A Sangh Parivar leader said in a press statement that the riots came about because society "could no longer bear the 'love jehadists' outraging the modesty and dignity of Hindu women and girls" in Uttar Pradesh.[56] An independent fact-finding team that visited the area two months later found Jats convinced that Muslims were determined to reduce Hindus to a minority in their country. "It was remarkable that these comments were repeated in almost the same words by all the Jats we met irrespective of the distance that separated their villages. This is probably indicative of a well-organized campaign over a period of time towards communalizing the atmosphere in the entire area," the report said.[57]

The next step for the BJP was to turn the events of Muzaffarnagar into a defining moment for its election campaign—just as Modi had done with the Gujarat pogrom through his Hindu pride tour ahead of 2002 state elections. Amit Shah arranged for some 450 minivans to traverse Uttar Pradesh with Modi's message in pictures, video, and music, as well as a network of local workers organized along the lines of consumer marketing companies' outreach to rural communities.[58] In one rally, Shah said that the elections were about "revenge" and "honour": "This election is about voting out the government that protects and gives compensation to those who killed Jats."[59] The statement betrayed cynical disregard for the fact that Muslim deaths outnumbered Hindu death by more than two to one, and that most of the resulting refugees were Muslim, many of whom were made to sign agreements not to return to their homes in return for financial aid.[60]

The Election Commission took the unprecedented step of banning Shah from campaigning in the state for violating the Model Code of Conduct. But when Shah promised to abide by the Code and not use "abusive or derogatory language," the ban was lifted.[61] To former chief election commissioner S. Y. Quraishi, the commission's action and the politician's reasonable response demonstrates the moral authority of the Model Code. Unfortunately, as Quraishi acknowledged, Shah soon reverted to similar language.[62] Uttar Pradesh responded by giving the BJP its sweetest victory. Of the BJP's net gain of 166 seats in the general election, more than one-third came from the state. Modi handsomely rewarded Shah's stewardship after the election, installing the forty-nine-year-old as the president of the BJP.

The Modi Touch

Throughout the 2014 election campaign, Modi's surrogates continued to spew hate. In the state of Bihar, for example, BJP leader Giriraj Singh was censured by the Election Commission for "highly inflammatory" remarks involving cow slaughter. He also said that people opposed to Modi were "Pakistan-parasht" (pro-Pakistan) and should head there.[63] Singh won his parliamentary seat and resumed his rhetoric of hate.

The most recalcitrant purveyor of hate speech among Sangh Parivar leaders was Praveen Togadia, international president of the Vishva Hindu Parishad. Undeterred by repeated criminal charges going back more than a decade, Togadia again showed his contempt for law and morality. He advised a neighborhood gathering of the various ways they could evict a Muslim businessman who had recently bought a house in a Hindu area in Gujarat, and how they could prevent such sales in the future. Just as Muslims were fighting the army in Kashmir, he said, "Where we have a majority, we should be brave enough to take the law into our hands and frighten them."[64] Modi waited a few days before chiding Togadia, with whom he had fallen out several years earlier: "I disapprove any such irresponsible statement & appeal to those making them to kindly refrain from doing

so. Petty statements by those claiming to be BJP's well-wishers are deviat-
ing the campaign from the issues of development & good governance," he
tweeted.[65] Notably, his statement made no reference to the gravity of Togadia's hate speech against minorities. His main grievance seemed to be that
it distracted from the BJP's current messaging.

In the final week of the campaign, on May 5, Modi appeared at a rally
in the Uttar Pradesh district of Faizabad, adjacent to Ayodhya. Behind the
podium was a giant portrait of Lord Rama. Its strategic placement ensured
that every television camera trained on Modi would also capture Rama's
beatific visage hovering behind him. "Faizabad should allow the lotus to
bloom in the land of Shri Ram," Modi said. Although he did not refer to the
controversial Rama temple project, the backdrop also carried an image of
a temple. Other speakers, including the candidate for the area Lalu Singh,
promised that the BJP would build the temple in Ayodhya.[66] As the candidate, Singh was served notice for violating the ban on religious symbols
contained in the Model Code of Conduct.[67] Given that the campaign period
was drawing to a close, Singh treated the admonishment lightly, remarking
that he would seek legal advice.

While hate speech and communal appeals are nothing new in Indian
politics, the BJP's brazen contempt for the rules in the 2014 campaign was
striking. Politicians, including Modi, openly dared the authorities to take
action against them.[68] One commentator likened the Election Commission
to "an old schoolmaster who keeps ranting while kids continue with their
pranks."[69] While the institution enjoyed wide latitude, its emphasis on due
process allowed appeals and counteraccusations to stall its work.

Unscrupulous politicians also know that the commission's findings are
no match for the verdict of public opinion—in an election, nothing succeeds like success. BJP strategists were willing to write off any loss of support
among Indians—Hindus as well as minorities—who agreed with the Election Commission that the party's use of hate speech was unacceptable. The
party probably made the simple electoral calculation that the gains from
chauvinistic appeals, especially in Uttar Pradesh, would outweigh the loss
of minority and liberal votes. The latter could be mitigated by emphasizing Modi's economic agenda. Indeed, many Muslims were prepared to support him for that reason. Crucially, around 2010, India's powerful business
groups and the media they owned were giving up on the Congress Party
and were beginning to turn to Modi as their next great hope. Bequeathed
with both funds and media support, the RSS and the BJP were brimming
with confidence.

The peculiar logic of polarized sectarian politics enables a kind of rhetorical alchemy: what appears to neutral observers as setbacks and embarrassments are magically transformed into strengths in the eyes of the party faithful. Thus, BJP politicians routinely cited the Election Commission's interventions as evidence of a secular system that was intent on unfairly obstructing the true will of the people. Criticism by liberal journalists and academics helped cast the BJP as victims of a political conspiracy. The fiercer the opposition to the BJP, the more obvious it appeared to its constituency that it needed an uncompromising strongman like Modi.

The Battleground of History

The Sangh Parivar's politics of intolerance and exclusion, most clearly manifested in its rampant use of hate speech in the run-up to the 2014 polls, have been pursued with equal resolve through a parallel campaign away from the electoral process. Instead of focusing on contemporary themes like terrorists from Pakistan or the love jihadi down the street, the propaganda in this campaign touts heroes and villains from centuries and millennia past. Its goal is to rewrite Indian history to match Hindutva ideology.

Of course, every open society debates its past in the light of current ideological battles. What is striking about the Sangh Parivar, though, is the force with which it has attempted to impose its own version of Indian history. Unable to win arguments on the basis of historical facts, the movement simply asserts the inviolability of Hindu feelings. While hate speech is the stock in trade of the Sangh Parivar's rabble-rousing politicians, its assault on history relies on offense-taking. Evidence-based historical research is no match for enraged mobs, especially when these mobs are supported by laws designed to protect their sensibilities. Thus, tantrums triumph over truth.

The campaign's point man is Dinanath Batra, the head of the educational arm of the RSS. Since the BJP's 2014 victory, Batra, who had previously been entrusted with the task of revising history textbooks when the BJP first came to power in 1999, has been in ascendance once again. The rewriting of India's history has become a major Hindutva priority, notes Amartya Sen, because it serves "the dual purpose of playing a role in providing a common basis for the diverse memberships of the Sangh Parivar, and of helping to get fresh recruits to Hindu political activism, especially from the diaspora."[70] Promoting cultural pride in Hindu identity is an important way to appeal to the majority of Hindus who are not necessarily hard-core supporters of the Sangh Parivar, he adds.[71]

Myths Versus History

Romila Thapar, one of the world's most distinguished historians of India, is all too familiar with the Sangh Parivar's mission and methods. She was one of a handful of historians whose textbooks were attacked in the 1970s.[72] In 2003, when she was given a chair at the US Library of Congress, her appointment was pilloried by Hindutva supporters who labeled her as Marxist and anti-Indian. Now an emeritus professor at Jawaharlal Nehru University in Delhi, Thapar continues to speak up for academic freedom and against censorship of academic history.

Over tea in her Delhi home, Thapar elaborates on the centrality of history to the Hindutva project. First, the idea of India as a Hindu homeland and of Hindus as the primary citizens of India requires unquestioned acceptance of a simplistic periodization of Indian history—one that harks back to a golden age of Hinduism as the inspiration for the India of today. The Hindu period is supposed to have been followed by the dark age of Muslim rule, brought by invaders from outside India, and then British colonialism. Ironically, Hindutva periodization is based on colonial historiography—except that in the British version, colonialism marks the high point of Indian history.

"The 'Hindu period' and the 'Muslim period'—we never had that kind of periodization in any historical writing prior to the coming of the British," she tells me. "And to say that there was constant antagonism between the two without investigating the reasons for either antagonism or peaceful coexistence, as the case may be, is not exactly a historical approach." In challenging colonial interpretations of India's past and showing that their ethnic and religious categorization was a construct in support of colonial policy, modern historians like Thapar were also undercutting both religious nationalisms. "If you make a proper historical analysis, then in effect both Hindu and Muslim nationalism are weakened; they don't have a historical basis for cultivating hostile identities or making religion the prime cause of all activity."

Accordingly, Hindutva supporters take offense when historians point out, for example, that caste antagonisms have been at least as important as interreligious divides to India's history. This was one of the inconvenient truths that got Thapar's textbook censored: she had said that the shudras, a subordinate caste, were not treated well by the upper castes. Critics felt that she had failed to highlight the subjugation of Hindus by Muslims in the medieval period.

Second, Hindutva history involves a kind of streamlining to render Hinduism more amenable to political mobilization. "Hinduism in practice and belief was essentially the juxtaposition of multiple sects—where you could choose your deity, your form of worship, decide which temple you want to go to, decide the language of worship, and so on," Thapar notes. Hinduism was organized very differently from Christianity in Europe or Islam in the Middle East, in that these other faiths could refer to a historical founder, a single sacred book, and hierarchical religious institutions. "That did not happen in Hinduism. Anyone is free to teach and create his own sect. And if he has a following, he has a following. And this has been going on right through the subcontinent with its uncountable sects," she points out.[73]

When Hindu nationalists needed to galvanize Hindus across the subcontinent, she says, they found it useful to adopt some of the features of the Judeo-Christian tradition that were amenable to mobilization. Since Hinduism lacks a historical founder, Hindutva ideology elevates the heroic figure of Lord Rama to preeminent status in the Hindu pantheon, based on dubious scriptural evidence. Claiming Ayodhya as his birthplace serves this larger purpose. And although there is no single sacred book in Hinduism, the BJP has floated the idea of according that status to the Bhagavad Gita; it was probably no coincidence that Modi presented a copy to Barack Obama at the White House.[74]

Cow protection—a movement with origins in the religious nationalism of the late nineteenth century—can be read as another attempt to fundamentalize Hinduism. The movement has recently experienced a resurgence, with more states extending their bans on cow slaughter. Pure Hindus, the Hindutva movement needs to say, would never kill cows. Therefore, statements that Aryans of the Vedic period consumed beef—as stated in Thapar's censored 1970s textbook—would have to be condemned as almost blasphemous. Proponents of Hindutva mythology prefer nineteenth-century Orientalist scholarship that plants the roots of Hindu identity in the glorious Vedic civilization of some three thousand years ago, when the Vedas, the oldest Hindu scriptures, were composed. The political need to refer to a pure tradition explains why Hindutva supporters take offense when research about their supposed golden age does not conform to their idealized picture of it.

This zealous streamlining of Hinduism's internal diversity provides simple ideas and symbols around which Hindu support can rally. An especially shrewd aspect of the Hindutva movement is that by defining itself as a national ideology, Hinduness, it does not actually need to reform Hinduism, or require that Hindus change their practices or pledge allegiance to one religious leader over another. There is still no pope or ayatollah; Hindutva does not require the head of state to be the head of the faith. When we recall how much blood has been spilled in power struggles *within* world religions—between Catholic and Protestant, Sunni and Shia—we begin to appreciate the genius of Hindutva mobilization. It focuses on presenting a unified symbolic front against external threats while continuing to allow diversity to flourish within.

Attacks on Academic History

During the BJP's first stint in power, the American academic James Laine's *Shivaji: The Hindu King in Muslim India* became a target. First published in New York, it was released in India by the New Delhi branch of Oxford University Press in 2003. Shivaji, the subject of Laine's study, was a famous seventeenth-century warrior who carved out a Maratha kingdom during the Mughal period. Laine's biography was critical of how the story of a cultural hero was later appropriated and reshaped by those seeking a symbol of Hindu strength standing up to Muslim invaders.[75] The book included the widely accepted fact that Shivaji was greatly influenced by his mother, and mentioned contemporary rumors, such as the following: "The repressed awareness that Shivaji had an absentee father is also revealed by the fact that Maharashtrians tell jokes naughtily suggesting that his guardian Dadaji Konddev was his biological father."[76]

Although Laine did not claim that these stories were true, a group of Indian scholars asked the publisher to withdraw the book, claiming that it had cast baseless aspersions on Shivaji. Oxford University Press (India) expressed regret for the offending statement and instructed all its Indian offices to withdraw all copies of the book from circulation immediately.

The proverbial train, however, had left the station. The following month, in December 2003, Shiv Sena, a far-right political party in the state of Maharashtra, sprang into action. Its thugs attacked a professor of Sanskrit whom Laine had thanked in his acknowledgments. The following day, Shiv Sena visited the Bhandarkar Oriental Research Institute (BORI) in Pune for the same reason, but left without harming anyone. In early January 2004, however, another right-wing Maratha group, the Sambhaji Brigade, attacked BORI. The goons ransacked the library, destroying thousands of books and priceless manuscripts. Ten days later, Maharashtra banned the book under Section 95 of the Criminal Procedure Code.

The state also filed a complaint (in the form of a First Information Report) against Laine, the publisher, and the printer for allegedly breaching various sections of the Penal Code, including Section 153A. Police arrested one of the owners of the printing press. At first, Prime Minister Vajpayee criticized the ban. By March, however, with elections looming, the prime minister climbed aboard the bandwagon, saying that Laine's experience should serve as a warning to foreigners not to take liberties with India's national pride.[77] According to court documents, the Bombay High Court suggested a pragmatic resolution: the author might wish to withdraw the allegedly objectionable portion from his book, simply to put an end to the controversy. Laine, in the meantime, had already faxed an apology after the attack on the Sanskrit professor, and expressed his anguish at the incident in a subsequent interview.[78] He may have agreed to compromise, but the Maharashtra government demurred.

The case finally ended up in the Indian Supreme Court, which quashed the criminal proceedings in April 2007. It invoked a principle that had been set out in a 1997 case: since Section 153A refers to friction "between different" groups, it requires that at least two communities be involved. Merely upsetting one group without reference to another cannot be a violation of that section.[79] Furthermore, the intentions of the author, the intended audience, and the context of the expression had to be taken into account. The court was satisfied that Laine was engaged in "purely a scholarly pursuit." It said, "One cannot rely on strongly worded and isolated passages for proving the charge nor indeed can one take a sentence here and a sentence there and connect them by a meticulous process of inferential reasoning."[80] The Bombay High Court duly lifted the book ban in 2007. The Supreme Court turned down an appeal from Maharashtra in July 2010, stating that the ban could not stand since the case against Laine had already been quashed.[81]

What should have been a victory for intellectual freedom had a hollow ring. The Supreme Court ruling did not diminish the Sangh Parivar's desire to sterilize its ideological environment. Nor did it stiffen the resolve of book publishers or academic institutions to publish works that might offend members of the Hindu Right.

In parallel with the assault on Laine's *Shivaji*, the Sangh Parivar rolled out a scandalously successful campaign to get the University of Delhi to censor an eminent literary scholar's essay on the *Ramayana*. A. K. Ramanujan's article "Three Hundred Ramayanas" highlighted the existence of various versions of the *Ramayana*. The article has been widely recognized as the work of a great lover of the epic. His translations had done much to win Indian mythology new admirers in the English-speaking world.[82]

The essay was added to the reading list of a Delhi University course in 2005. Complaints started surfacing in 2008. When the university stood firm, activists entered the history department head's office, vandalized it, and roughed him up. A group headed by Batra filed a civil suit, as a result of which in 2010 the Supreme Court directed the university to form an expert committee to study the matter and make a recommendation to its Academic Council. Of the four historians appointed to the committee, three endorsed Ramanujan's scholarship and saw nothing controversial about the article. Nevertheless, the Academic Council decided in late 2011 that the essay be dropped from the reading list.

The previous year, ruling on the *Shivaji* case, the Supreme Court had said that a publication's impact had to be judged by the "standards of reasonable, strong-minded, firm and courageous men, and not those of weak and vacillating minds, nor of those who scent danger in every hostile point of view."[83] This appeared to make no impression on the academics, who agreed with the lone expert on the review committee that a combination of ill-equipped teachers and impressionable minds meant that the essay could cause offense. Celebrating the censorship of the article—written by a fellow Hindu, it should be noted—Batra said: "It was a conspiracy hatched on the part of Christian Missionaries and their fellow travellers to demean our gods and goddesses. It has been thrashed." Supporters would be mobilized to keep a close watch over the university syllabus, he added.[84]

Around the same time, another challenge to academic freedom was working its way through the legal system. In February 2010, Batra initiated legal action against the American academic Wendy Doniger over her book *The Hindus: An Alternative History*. The book was first published in the United States by Viking Penguin in 2009 and then released by Penguin India in 2010. Batra claimed that the book was "a shallow, distorted and non-serious presentation of Hinduism," "riddled with heresies and factual inaccuracies," and highly offensive.[85]

Doniger, a professor of the history of religions at the University of Chicago Divinity School, made claims—for instance, that the *Ramayana* is a work of fiction—that were within the mainstream of Indian scholarship. Opponents, however, claimed the work to be hurtful to the feelings of millions of Hindus. Writing in the *New York Times*, Pankaj Mishra noted that fanatics would correctly perceive Doniger's focus on "the fluid existential identities and commodious metaphysic of practiced Indian religion as a threat to their project of a culturally homogeneous and militant nation-state."[86]

The campaign against Doniger's book presents a reality check to well-meaning liberals who believe that showing more respect for religion would appease offense-takers. Batra's original lawsuit alleged, among other things, that the book defames the revered nineteenth-century Hindu monk Swami Vivekananda by saying that he had asked for beef. Doniger has pointed out that Batra did not claim that the passage is false, since it is well documented.

"The objection is simply that repeating that statement in the book defamed Vivekananda," she explained. Their quarrel, therefore, was not over the need for civility—at least, as this virtue is understood in a secular society. Instead, Batra appeared to be claiming that scholars had no business interpreting religious traditions and texts.

Penguin India fought the case for four years before approaching Batra for a settlement. In early 2014, it agreed to cease publication and promised to pulp all remaining copies, although this proved unnecessary as the book had sold out. Penguin said it stood by its original decision to publish *The Hindus*, but claimed that Section 295A of the Penal Code made it "increasingly difficult for any Indian publisher to uphold international standards of free expression without deliberately placing itself outside the law."[87] In a *New York Review of Books* essay, Doniger echoed her publisher's position that India's overbroad laws were to blame. With the wrong judge, you could be convicted under these laws, she opined. "It's hard to imagine how you could write about any subject as sensitive as religion or history without outraging someone; such a rule would mean the end of creative and original scholarly thought," she said. "Any new idea offends people who are committed to the old idea, which is to say, most people. Even in the hands of someone as intellectually challenged as Batra, Article 295A is a weapon of mass cultural destruction."[88]

Many liberals were not as charitable toward Penguin, criticizing it for cowardice. Lawrence Liang of the Bangalore-based Alternative Law Forum issued a legal notice, dripping with sarcasm, stating that since Penguin was "mutating into a chicken" and not interested in exercising its rights as owners of the work, it should allow anyone else to copy, reproduce, and circulate it in India.[89] In a commentary in *Frontline*, the prominent historian and lawyer A. G. Noorani said the publisher and the author were "wildly wrong" to think that the courts would have ruled against them. There was no precedent of a historical work like Doniger's being suppressed either under Section 295A or through a civil suit, Noorani explained. Batra had won "by simply brandishing a toy gun."[90] In Noorani's eyes, Penguin Books India preempted justice when it surrendered to Batra.

There is, of course, a more straightforward explanation of Penguin's behavior. Penguin admitted defeat not because it misunderstood the letter and spirit of the law, but because it correctly appraised the sorry state of India's rule of law. Regardless of what the courts decided, the publisher would have to deal with street justice. It had "a moral responsibility to protect our employees against threats and harassment where we can," Penguin said.[91]

Pratap Bahnu Mehta, a social scientist who heads the distinguished Centre for Policy Research in Delhi, fears that the vitality of Hindu piety is being overwhelmed by an invented communal identity focused on a history of oppression. "It is an identity constituted by a sense of injury, a sense of always having been on the losing side, of being a victimized innocent."[92] For the Hindutva movement, though, the revising of history is long overdue. Gujarat's RSS spokesman, Pradip Jain, says independent India must make up for the lost years of the "in-between period" when Mahatma Gandhi and Jawaharlal Nehru allowed its glorious past to be diluted. They had acted like the new owners of a house who, upon moving in, inexplicably allow the previous owner's décor to remain intact, complete with photos of his ancestors. "I would replace it with my own grandfather's pictures," says Jain.

A Year Later

Faced with the realities of governing, candidates who campaign as extremists often become moderates in power. But two years after Modi's arrival in Delhi, there are few signs of moderation in Hindutva hate spin. Modi handed education and culture to the dogmatic RSS, as a reward for its support in the campaign.[93] The movement is steadily asserting its power over the prime minister, says the historian Ramachandra Guha. All in all, the transition from "campaign Modi to governance Modi" has not been a smooth one.[94] If anything, the rhetoric of intolerance appears to have been ratcheted up, and in some cases gone well beyond mere words, erupting in violent attacks on minorities. For example, BJP MP Yogi Adityanath spearheaded a "ghar wapsi" (homecoming) campaign to convert Muslims and Christians by force to Hinduism.[95] Although politicians like Adityanath are tarnishing Modi's international reputation, it is difficult for him to restrain them, since their platform of religious nationalism got him elected. "It's not a remote control thing that you can switch on and off as you please," notes the journalist Varghese K. George.[96]

Modi's other key platform—economic revitalization—looked shaky. With little to show for its grandiose election claims, the BJP failed in its first major electoral tests after coming to power: it was beaten badly in elections in Delhi and Bihar in 2015.[97] In the absence of strong economic results, identity politics may continue to be the cheapest way to win support. Midway through his first term, the prime minister had yet to go out of his way to reassure minorities that their status was secure.

The main restraint on the Hindutva agenda may be the country's sheer ungovernability—an obstacle that has thwarted Indian leaders' most progressive intentions, and may do the same to Modi's Hindu nationalism. Everything, from India's federal system to its irrepressible argumentative tradition, conspires against totalizing visions. The courts and the quasi-judicial commissions provide additional structural safeguards, says the constitutional lawyer Bhairav Acharya.[98] In addition, other state imperatives, especially national security, may kick in. After a spate of widely publicized attacks on Christians, including the brutal rape of an elderly nun, the former navy chief Sushil Kumar made a telling intervention: India could not afford to pollute its secular environment to such an extent that it compromised its multiethnic armed forces. "The armed forces have always been considered in India as the strongest pillar of our society, and the reason is simply that we are a secular armed force," he said. "Now to allow such a virus to percolate into the armed forces is a very dangerous thing."[99]

Most of the prime minister's rhetoric has focused on the economy and foreign affairs. At the same time, Modi continues to say and do enough to encourage his core constituency on the Hindu Right that the dream of Hindutva is still alive. His divisive rhetoric is striking for its economy. He does not have to say much. Thanks to decades of Hindutva hate propaganda, the ongoing campaign to rewrite Indian history, and the pogroms of Muzaffarnagar and Gujarat, Modi's adulatory audience can fill in any blanks he leaves with readily accessible mental flashcards. In one of his first parliamentary speeches as prime minister, Modi referred, in passing, to the need to shed "1,200 years of slave mentality."[100] His audience required no further elaboration. They knew that negating twelve centuries of history meant transcending not just British colonialism but also India's Muslim heritage. Here was Modi's vision of India's tryst with destiny: a glorious Hindu civilization, foreign invasions, minorities who demand more and more, and a strong leader prepared to teach those invaders a lesson.

5 Indonesia: Democracy Tested amid Rising Intolerance

Outgoing Indonesian president Susilo Bambang Yudhoyono was in his element. It was August 2014, at the Sixth Global Forum of the United Nations Alliance of Civilizations, held on the enchanting island of Bali. President Yudhoyono delivered the keynote opening address to an international audience in a vast convention hall. Many nodded approvingly as he spoke of the need for dialogue, tolerance, and harmony with god, nature, and humankind. These themes were perfectly in tune with the mandate of the Alliance of Civilizations, which was conceived to build bridges between Islamic and Western societies after the Al Qaeda attacks on the United States and the ensuing wars in Afghanistan and Iraq. As the country with the world's largest Muslim population, Indonesia's position in any such ideological debate matters a great deal. Yudhoyono spoke reassuringly of Indonesia's tradition of openness:

> Because of our strategic location, situated in the historic trade and maritime route between the Pacific and Indian Oceans, the people of this archipelago have always been exposed to the intense cross-currents of world civilizations. In a process that spanned centuries, the Islamic, Hindu, Buddhist, Sinic and Western civilizations have merged with local cultures to become part of our rich heritage as a nation. Thus, in Indonesia, there is no fundamental clash of civilizations. Instead, in general, there is a harmonious confluence of civilizations, which together form the heart and soul of Indonesia. And significantly, in the twenty-first century, Indonesia has also demonstrated that Islam, democracy, and modernity can coexist in harmony.[1]

The president's words reflected Indonesia's aspiration to be a model Muslim democracy—a hope shared by many well-wishers near and far. Since the fall of the authoritarian Suharto regime in 1998, Indonesia has democratized at a dramatic pace. On the Freedom House index, the country's political rights score has improved from 7 (the worst possible rating) to 2.[2] Having had four government turnovers through peaceful elections, the republic has consolidated its democracy, which has come to be accepted as what scholars of comparative politics call "the only game in town."[3] Religious nationalists enjoy the freedom to participate in that game, and Indonesia's 140 million voters have the choice to support them—or not. Since 1999, Indonesians have consistently rejected the offer of an exclusive Islamic state. The combined vote share of Indonesia's five main Islamic parties has hovered at around one-third.[4]

Indonesia has not, however, been immune from sectarian conflict. Between 1997 and 2001, at least 19,000 Indonesians were killed and around 1.3 million displaced in ethnic violence. Some of this was the dystopian by-product of democratization and decentralization, which resulted in increased competition between local actors banking on varied communal and political identities to build power at the provincial and district levels.[5] Indonesia has also had to confront global terrorism. In 2002, a jihadist bombing in Bali killed 131 Australians, Europeans, and Americans, as well as scores of Indonesians. With foreign investments and tourism at stake, Indonesia boosted its antiterrorism capacity significantly.

The authorities have been less attentive to a growing culture of hatred and violence against purely local targets.[6] That lack of action is a worry, says Sidney Jones, a leading authority on conflict in Indonesia. "The biggest issue for Indonesian democracy is not terrorism, but intolerance, which is moving from the radical fringe into the mainstream," she says.[7] When the country's human rights record came up for Universal Periodic Review by the United Nations Human Rights Council in 2012, the state's failure to protect religious minorities was heavily criticized.[8] In some districts of Indonesia, absolutist Muslim groups have obstructed perfectly legal plans to build churches for years. Minorities within the Muslim community, particularly the Ahmadiyah sect and Shia Muslims, have been hit particularly hard. Blasphemy laws have played into the hands of intolerant groups. Although infrequently enforced, these laws have served to embolden hardliners in their hate spin campaigns.

In this chapter I dissect the forces of intolerance within Indonesian Islam, looking behind major hate spin episodes to locate the interests of various actors. I place these recent events in the historical context of the unsettled relationship between religion and politics in Indonesia. I also analyze the legal framework within which Indonesian hate spin operates, especially the country's problematic Blasphemy Law. Like India, Indonesia has well-intentioned laws against offense that are exploited by the intolerant. Combined with unevenly enforced prohibitions against incitement, these laws add up to a double threat for minorities.

In contrast to India's Sangh Parivar network and its Hindutva ideology, Indonesia's majoritarian intolerance is not driven by a cohesive movement following a clear doctrine. Instead, there is an ecosystem of organizations and interest groups—political parties, militant gangs, government agencies, and the main Muslim clerical body—whose uncoordinated actions cultivate an environment that is conducive to hate. Indonesian presidents may not have directly benefited from hate spin and its violent effects. They have come to power despite, rather than because of, antidemocratic intolerance. But even as government officials take pride in Indonesia's "harmonious confluence of civilizations," they cannot claim to have done enough to secure an equal place for minorities within the world's third-largest democracy.

Religion in Indonesian Democracy

The vast archipelago of Indonesia is home to almost as many Muslims as the five largest Arab states combined. They make up some 87 percent of a population exceeding 250 million. Christians account for another 10 percent, and Hindus, 1.5 percent. There are also adherents to Buddhism and Confucianism among its small ethnic Chinese population. Around 20 million Indonesians practice faiths associated with various traditional beliefs.[9] Given the size of the Muslim population, it is not surprising that Islam has always influenced Indonesian nationalism. What successive generations of political scientists have found more remarkable about the Indonesian story is Islam's relatively muted role in politics compared with, say, Iran or Egypt. Commentators regularly hold up Indonesia as a positive example to counter sweeping claims about Islam's incompatibility with secular democracy.[10]

Historians have suggested a number of reasons why exclusive Islamic visions of nationhood, though perpetually in circulation, have never consumed Indonesia's state-building project. One is cultural. As President Yudhoyono pointed out in his Alliance of Civilizations speech, Southeast Asia has always been a crossroads of multiple cultural influences. Any purist tendencies were also moderated by the dominant Javanese community, who preferred to lace their Islam with traditional beliefs and practices.[11] Islam in Indonesia was never wedded to any powerful empire capable of imposing a standardized faith. Instead, in the precolonial era, the archipelago was organized into mercantile city-states, inland kingdoms, and tribal areas. As the cultural anthropologist Robert Hefner notes, "There were always different Muslim rulers, diverse religious associations, and alternative ideas as to how to be Muslim."[12]

Nevertheless, the temptation to harness the power of political Islam has been strong. Indonesia's first president, Sukarno, meant for Islam to have preeminence. The Jakarta Charter, the draft preamble to the 1945 constitution, contained a clause requiring Muslims to observe religious law (sharia). After intense debate and negotiation, Indonesians opted instead for a constitution with a secular national justice system and no special status for the religion of the vast majority of its citizens.[13] This decision was less a recognition of the religious freedom of individual citizens than a concession to the paramount need for territorial integrity. Non-Muslims form majorities in certain parts of Indonesia—Bali is predominantly Hindu, while provinces such as Papua and North Sulawesi are mainly Christian—and these areas might have seceded had Jakarta imposed Islam on them.[14]

Under the national ideology of Pancasila, the state officially acknowledged Catholics, Protestants, Hindus, and Buddhists, as well as Muslims. Their sacred days were declared public holidays. Later, Confucianism was added to the list. Pancasila's first principle is the belief in one God, curiously making Indonesia officially monotheistic, but not Islamic. Schools are required to provide religious instruction for every student according to his or her own faith.[15]

But just as the secular nationalisms of the founding fathers of the American and Indian republics never totally extinguished some citizens' cravings for a narrower national identity based on religion, Pancasila has had to contend with Islamist conceptions of the Indonesian state. A "sharia state was always an historical possibility," says Mirjam Künkler, a scholar of religion and politics.[16] Throughout its postindependence history, some have called for Indonesia to become an Islamic state, with Islamic law binding on Muslims. Significantly, though, these advocates for an Islamic Indonesia have had to share public airtime with secularists and Muslim intellectuals and community leaders firmly supportive of religious pluralism. "Although conservative scholars were unhappy with the new cacophony, the result was not a narrowing of the Muslim political voice but its enrichment," argues Hefner.[17]

The biggest concentration of secularists identified with the political left, which meant that they were in the firing line, literally, when the military and Muslim groups massacred communists in 1965. Any dividend for Muslim parties was swiftly stripped away by Suharto's military-backed New Order regime, which immediately began repressing independent political activity. Suharto's tight grip on power kept the lid on political Islam even when Indonesia experienced a strong religious resurgence in the late 1970s and early 1980s—a phenomenon that coincided with the Iranian

Revolution and was aided by a successful mass literacy program that facilitated religious instruction. Like Hosni Mubarak in Egypt, Suharto kept political Islam on the margins. In the final twelve years of his presidency, however, he decided to harness the power of antidemocratic elements within organized Islam, courting groups happy to support his authoritarian regime in exchange for access to power. From 1996, as democratic opposition grew and Suharto became more desperate, his lieutenants resorted to virulently anti-Christian and anti-Chinese rhetoric to split political opponents along ethnic and religious divides.[18] These moves not only resulted in extreme violence, but also degraded the culture of tolerance and inclusivity that Indonesia's new democracy would need for the long term.

Muslim Organizations in Democratic Indonesia

In post-Suharto Indonesia, a diverse array of organizations vie for power and influence over what might loosely be called the Islamic public sphere. Democratization has had important consequences for hard-line religious groups. On the one hand, Indonesia's new openness has allowed such groups freer play. On the other, they cannot dream of monopolizing the pulpit. They must constantly do battle with Indonesians who do not share their views. These include Indonesians who believe in "social Islam" or what Hefner calls "Civil Islam," a worldview that rejects both the false ideal of an Islamic state and the negation of religion's role in public affairs. Their middle path "passes by way of a public religion that makes itself heard through independent associations, spirited public dialogue, and the demonstrated decency of believers."[19]

As a result, while religiosity is clearly on the rise, it is not always expressed in intolerant or exclusive ways. As I noted in chapter 2, the strength of religious identification may have no bearing one way or another on a group's commitment to secular democracy—just as, for example, the Anglican Church in the United Kingdom does more to protect the rights of religious minorities than does the secular English Defense League. Similarly, in Indonesia, socially conservative and purist tendencies do not automatically express themselves in intolerance toward out-groups. Conversely, the most antidemocratic and exclusionary Muslim groups are not necessarily the most sincerely devout or socially representative.

The most violent groups include the Al Qaeda–linked jihadi organization Jemaah Islamiyah (JI), which was responsible for post-2001 terrorist bombings in Bali and Jakarta. While JI may have since weakened, other violent Islamist groups have emerged, targeting local Christians in particular. They believe that Jews and Christians are the natural enemies of Islam.

They also claim to defend Muslims from aggressive evangelical activity by Protestant missionaries.[20]

One prominent hate group is the militant Front Pembela Islam (FPI, the Islamic Defenders Front). No organization illustrates more clearly the roots of hate spin in political opportunism rather than religious conviction. FPI did not emerge from any radical madrassah or a campaign for a global caliphate. It grew out of the secular state apparatus. It was convened and trained by the army to counter antigovernment protestors—mainly students and middle-class citizens—a few months after Suharto stepped down and handed the presidency to his deputy, B. J. Habibie. FPI used mob power to counter people power. Unlike the out-and-out terrorists, FPI doesn't use firearms or bombs—"their weapons of choice are sticks and clubs, better for intimidation and bashing up property."[21]

Having mastered its trade, FPI was not about to wind up its thug-for-hire enterprise when the military's political dominance waned. Togged in black uniforms and armed with bamboo spears, FPI militants continued to find patrons—including officials and security agencies—who needed to play the reactionary Muslim card.[22] Following attacks on Christians by JI members in Central Sulawesi in 2005, the police even commissioned the FPI chief to go on a speaking tour of the province. "The police were operating on the assumption that if young men could be turned into moralist thugs, this was at least better than turning terrorist," Sidney Jones notes.[23]

FPI is explicitly antidemocracy, arguing that political openness transforms Indonesians into infidels. The International Crisis Group calls FPI "extreme moralists," but their behavior is explained better by money than by morals. "The FPI has carved out a niche for itself in the political landscape by intentionally prising open social tensions and instigating moral panics through which it has sought to situate itself as a broker; as a kind of morality racketeer," says the political scientist Ian Wilson, who has studied the group closely.[24]

Other hate groups do not engage in violence directly, but instead promote intolerant views that encourage extremists and justify discrimination. One of the most insidious is Hizbut Tahrir Indonesia (HTI, Indonesia Party of Liberation). This radical utopian group reaches out to the educated middle class in other Muslim organizations, universities, and the ranks of government, promoting its vision of a worldwide caliphate. Like JI and FPI, HTI members deem electoral democracy illegitimate, since it venerates manmade laws. While officially renouncing violence, they advocate intolerance and hostility against non-Muslims as well as against Islamic groups that they consider deviant. HTI has become skilled at "persuading otherwise moderate Muslims that the Islamist position on a given issue is one that all Muslims must accept as Islamic."[25]

The most influential purveyor of intolerance, though, is the Majelis Ulama Indonesia (MUI, Indonesian Ulema Council), made up of Islamic scholars. Founded by Suharto in 1975 as the authorized voice of Indonesian Muslims, MUI declared its independence from government after his fall. It discourages Indonesians from adopting a relaxed live-and-let-live accommodation toward their increasingly cosmopolitan milieu and instead demands stricter adherence with its proliferating precepts. This helps justify MUI's existence—and adds to its bottom line. MUI controls halal certification, a major source of its revenue. The growing popularity of halal cosmetics, for example, benefits both Muslim entrepreneurs and MUI. MUI's religious edicts or fatwas are not legally binding, but they have been used to justify intolerant acts. Hate spin agents regularly refer to a 2005 MUI statement against secularism, pluralism, and liberalism—with the mischievous acronym SiPiLis likening these values to a venereal disease.[26]

The main buffers against extreme tendencies within the Islamic public sphere are two mass organizations, Nahdlatul Ulama and Muhammadiyah. There is also the much smaller Jaringan Islam Liberal and other loose networks of urban intellectuals, inspired by the "pembaruan" or renewal movement of the late public intellectual Nurcholish Madjid, who emphasized intellectual freedom and openness.[27] Nahdlatul Ulama (NU), founded in 1926 and now claiming some 50 million members, is the country's largest Islamic organization, and probably the largest Sunni Muslim group in the world. Active in the independence struggle, it later retreated from politics, deciding that its religious cause would be better served by focusing on culture and education. The goal was to create a Muslim civil society, infused with the values of tolerance and participation, to counterbalance a state that was increasingly seen as illegitimate.

The late long-serving leader of NU, Abdurrahman Wahid, became Indonesia's first democratically elected president. NU has a traditionalist bent, in the sense that it upholds the culturally open, syncretic attitudes that have long prevailed at the grassroots against the encroachment of more doctrinaire approaches to Islam. It was founded in reaction to Muhammadiyah, which is now the second-largest national Muslim organization. Dating from 1912, Muhammadiyah attempted to modernize Indonesian Islam by ridding it of syncretic practices. It has a more purist outlook, which may be taken to extremes by some members who then join hard-line groups. But its emphasis on individual learning and interpretation, as opposed to blind adherence to scholars' teachings, has kept the organization open to dialogue and strictly opposed to violence.

Indonesia also possesses a range of Muslim-based political parties, the largest and most influential of which is the Partai Keadilan Sejahtera (PKS, Prosperous Justice Party). It promotes itself as a moderate party that does not seek to establish an Islamic state. Although it once emphasized sharia, it now focuses on an anticorruption and conservative-values agenda. Originally inspired by Egypt's Muslim Brotherhood, it shifted its gaze to Turkey's ruling AKP party.[28] The oldest Islamic party in Indonesia is the Partai Persatuan Pembangunan (PPP, United Development Party), which has campaigned for sharia. Partai Kebangkitan Bangsa (PKB, National Awakening Party) and Partai Amanat Nasional (PAN, National Mandate Party) are more moderate Muslim-based parties. PKB was set up as the political vehicle of Nahdlatul Ulama leader Abdurrahman Wahid.

One of the paradoxes of Indonesian democracy is Muslim-based parties' failure at the polls, despite the obvious public appetite for a greater role for religion in public life. Many observers have greeted the Islamist parties' lackluster performance as a triumph for secular democratic values. But the election results obscure a more complex picture. One key reason that Islamic political parties have been unable to capitalize on Indonesians' more religious outlook is that secular parties have themselves responded to social trends by increasing their use of Islamic symbols and rhetoric.[29] More conservative Muslim officials have emerged within the senior ranks of government, promoting their values at the expense of freedom of expression and the rights of religious minorities. During Yudhoyono's second term, four such cabinet ministers were on the central board of MUI, which also benefited from increased government funding. Thinking of Indonesian politics in terms of a neat secular/religious binary can therefore be misleading, notes the political scientist Robin Bush. A secular, non-Islamist state in Indonesia has, as a result of rational political calculation, pursued a conservative, antipluralist agenda.[30]

At the grassroots, religious intolerance is institutionalized in a government agency called Bakor Pakem. This is the Badan Koordinasi Pengawas Aliran Kepercayaan Masyarakat, or the Coordinating Board for Monitoring Mystical Beliefs in Society. Coming under the intelligence division of the public prosecutor's office, it has branches in every province and regency. Its investigations target beliefs and practices that hard-liners consider harmful.[31] Agencies like Bakor Pakem, together with opportunistic politicians, the clerics of MUI, the vigilante thugs of FPI, and various other hate groups have made hate spin part of the culture of democratic Indonesia.

The discourse of pluralism and tolerance, despite its deep foundations in Indonesian society, is losing ground to more absolutist and exclusive religious norms. "The incremental legitimation of orthodoxy in Muslim societies around the world—an illustration of underlying social and attitudinal change—has not bypassed Indonesia," says Donald Emmerson, a leading scholar of Indonesian politics.

The Legal Environment

Indonesian hate spin operates in a mixed legal environment where progressive features coexist with anachronistic laws. The pro-democratic "Reformasi" movement that brought down Suharto in May 1998 infected even the legislators who had been handpicked by him. Barely six months after Suharto's fall, they voted in favor of ratifying all United Nations human rights instruments.[32] Press licensing and other restrictions were lifted during this euphoric reform period, allowing the flowering of critical media.[33] As part of amendments passed in 2000, freedom of expression was enshrined in Article 28F of the Constitution: "Every person shall have the right to communicate and to obtain information for the purpose of the development of his/her self and social environment, and shall have the right to seek, obtain, possess, store, process and convey information by employing all available types of channels."[34]

From 2004, however, there were clear signs that liberalization would have to confront a conservative pushback. A draft antipornography bill that had contained fairly standard and uncontroversial wording was suddenly broadened to regulate "porno-action"—anything that conservatives deemed indecent. The new wording would ensnare popular entertainment, traditional art, public behavior, and women's clothing that did not conform to standards of propriety set by uncompromising Muslim clerics.[35] A full-blown "culture war" ensued, pitting Muslim conservatives against a wide range of civil society actors, including women's groups and cultural organizations.[36] At least four provinces—including mainly Hindu Bali and Christian North Sulawesi—opposed the proposed legislation because of its cultural bias. By the time the bill was passed in 2008, it was clear that it would be basically unenforceable.[37]

The pornography debate was ultimately a proxy for the larger question of who should get to define the culture of the new Indonesia. The verdict was indeterminate. On the one hand, the conservatives' success in pushing through a patently problematic bill demonstrated their perceived power in the eyes of political elites. On the other hand, the antipornography law ended up being largely ignored, showing that mainstream segments of Muslim society as well as influential non-Muslim minorities would not allow hard-line conservatives to interfere too much with their way of life. The hard-liners probably overreached when they tried to whip up national indignation against everything from nude paintings to "dangdut" shows— a popular genre of music and dance. If the hate spin agents had picked targets that lacked mass appeal, they might have faced less resistance. They found the easy scapegoats they were looking for in the form of unpopular religious minorities. The hard-liners didn't even need to fashion new legislative weapons. Indonesia's decades-old Blasphemy Law was at hand, ready to be brandished for hate spin campaigns.

Religious Freedom and the Blasphemy Law

The retrograde Blasphemy Law, coupled with the special legal status given to certain faiths, has created ideal conditions for inflicting hate spin on religious minorities. The laws are exploited as instruments of oppression by hate groups claiming to represent the dominant Sunni Muslim orthodoxy. As in India, Indonesia's laws prohibiting religious insult enable hate spin agents to commandeer the coercive machinery of the state against targeted communities. Indonesia's discriminatory state policies also have indirect utility. Nonstate actors try to justify their incitement to vigilante violence by citing the Blasphemy Law as well as opinions of officials labeling certain minorities as deviant.

Indonesia's 1945 Constitution guarantees all persons the freedom of worship according to his or her own religion and belief. The 1999 Human Rights Law (39/1999) reaffirmed the freedom of religion, and 2001 constitutional amendments reinforced it. Article 28E of the Constitution upholds the right to choose and practice the religion of one's choice and to believe and express one's faith according to conscience. Article 28J, however, allows the state to restrict the exercise of religious freedom on certain grounds. This is partly in line with Article 18 of the International Covenant on Civil and Political Rights, which allows limitations necessary "to protect public safety, order, health, or morals or the fundamental rights and freedoms of others." The Indonesian version, however, accepts an additional justification for restricting religious freedom: "religious values." In other words, the state can suppress some people's religious expression if it is deemed offensive to the religious values of others—which is, of course, the opposite of what is usually understood as religious freedom.

This large loophole allowed Indonesia's Blasphemy Law to survive into the twenty-first century.[38] Adopted by presidential decree in 1965, the

Blasphemy Law prohibits in Article 1 any acts and interpretations that deviate from the basic teachings of a religion. It applies explicitly to the six religions "embraced by the people of Indonesia." The teachings and practices of any of the six named faiths (say, Protestantism) would not be deemed as a blasphemous deviation from one of the others (say, Catholicism). Nor does the law prohibit religions clearly distinguished from the six recognized faiths, such as Judaism.[39] The impact therefore falls mainly on communities that practice alternative forms of Islam, such as the Ahmadiyah sect. Under Article 2 of the law, violators will first be instructed to stop their activities. Failure to comply can result in the banning or dissolution of the group and five years' imprisonment (Article 3). Article 4 could be used against adherents of traditional belief systems: it disallows the expression of views intended to discourage others from adhering to any monotheistic religion.

This highly illiberal piece of legislation was overlooked during the frenzied post-Suharto Reformasi period. This was partly because the law had not been actively used, but also because communication law reform in Indonesia followed a pattern typical of transitional democracies: structural impediments to media industries tend to be removed first, with restrictions on content fixed later, if at all.[40] When the repressive potential of the Blasphemy Law became clearer, various groups called for its abolition.[41] Critics argued that the law is incompatible with constitutional guarantees and violates the International Covenant on Civil and Political Rights, which Indonesia ratified in 2006. They pointed out that it puts the state in the untenable position of having to identify a religion's fundamentals, against which deviance is to be ascertained. The Constitutional Court nevertheless upheld the statute in 2010. The court cited the aforementioned Article 28J of the Constitution, adding that the act remained "very necessary" to prevent misleading practices and to ensure religious harmony and the maintenance of public order.[42]

Another piece of legislation that serves a purpose similar to the Blasphemy Law is Article 156A of the Indonesian Criminal Code, which prohibits deliberate and public expressions that abuse or stain a religion that is adhered to in Indonesia. Religious offense is also dealt with under Article 28 of Law 11/2008 on Electronic Information and Transactions. This section covers anyone who "who knowingly and without authority disseminates information aimed at inflicting hatred or dissension on individuals and/or certain groups" based on ethnicity, religion, or race. It was used to imprison a self-declared atheist, Alexander Aan, for posting provocative links about Islam on Facebook.[43]

Far from preserving harmony and order, these laws provide an opportunity for hate spin, which has in turn generated discrimination and outright violence against religious minorities and nonbelievers. On paper, Indonesian law contains protections against such harms. Law No. 40/2008 on the Elimination of Racial and Ethnic Discrimination, for instance, forbids incitement to hatred. Article 156 of the Criminal Code provides for up to four years' imprisonment for expressions of hatred against racial, religious, and other groups. But a pattern of selective enforcement creates a situation in which the law usually sides with riotous mobs over vulnerable minorities.

Anti-Christian Hate

Hard-line groups have gone to war against what they call the "Christianization" of Indonesia. They point to vigorous proselytizing by some missionaries and evangelical groups, as well as to the perceived growth of Christians' influence among political and business elites. As is so often the case with fear campaigns, this one extrapolates from a sliver of truth. Protestant evangelicals, both American-based and homegrown, are active in Indonesia, especially in the West Java areas that surround Jakarta. Some of them have an explicit mission to convert Muslims to Christianity. Their more controversial tactics include publishing pamphlets with Arabic script on their covers, making them look like Islamic literature at first glance.[44] A particularly assertive group, Yayasan Mahanaim, allegedly formed a human cross in front of a mosque in Bekasi, just east of Jakarta, supposedly to cleanse the area.[45] Such an aggressive approach to proselytization makes many Indonesians deeply uncomfortable. Islamist groups have attempted to inflate this understandable unease into reactions of extreme offendedness. The fallout has punished individuals and groups in the region who have nothing to do with the admittedly provocative acts of a small number of evangelicals.

One resulting case of hate spin involved a sculpture, "Three Beauties," by the Balinese artist Nyoman Nuarta.[46] The seventeen-meter-tall statue, erected in Bekasi in 2007, depicted three women in the traditional dress of the Sundanese community, the dominant and largely Muslim ethnic group in West Java. It was in keeping with the cultural and nonreligious themes of Nyoman Nuarta's body of work. For three years, the bronze and copper statue graced the front of an upmarket residential complex. In early 2010, however, Islamist groups began proclaiming that the sculpture was another Christian provocation. They said that the women in the statue actually represented the Virgin Mary—or, perhaps, the Holy Trinity.[47] To complete its makeover into an injustice symbol, agitators also claimed that the statue had been placed on a historically important site where Muslim resistance fighters had fallen in the battle against the Dutch. In a May 14, 2010, mass demonstration against Christianization, protestors spray-painted the statue's base and tried to wrap it up with cloth. When they petitioned the Bekasi mayor to remove the sculpture, he acquiesced, apparently because he lacked a strong Muslim political base and felt vulnerable to charges that he was being too sympathetic to Christians. The owners dismantled the sculpture and trucked it off to another city.[48]

The most sustained and serious anti-Christian hate spin, though, has been deployed against church construction. Many congregations' building plans have encountered bureaucratic resistance, and some have faced physical attack.[49] One target is the Batak Protestant community (Huria Kristen Batak Protestan) in Bekasi. This ethnic-based denomination has not sought to convert Muslims, but has nevertheless been accused of pushing for the Christianization of Indonesia. Bataks make up one of the larger immigrant communities in Bekasi, so the animosity they face from the local Betawis is probably more socioeconomic and xenophobic than religious. In 2007, one of their congregations, Filadelfia, bought a plot of land for the purpose of erecting a church. The community, comprising around 130 families, had previously held services in congregants' homes. Despite complying with relevant regulations, their plans were blocked by the local authorities. A similar fate befell the Indonesian Christian (GKI) Yasmin Church in Bogor. What is remarkable about the Filadelfia and Yasmin disputes is that both congregations successfully took their cases to the Supreme Court; both won their appeals on paper—but not on the ground, where intransigent officials continued to stand in their way. The Indonesian government took no steps to enforce the court's decisions.[50] In protest, the two churches have taken to conducting joint open-air services in the heart of Jakarta every two weeks, across the road from the presidential palace.[51]

Leaders of these two Christian congregations do not regard Islam as such to be the problem.[52] To emphasize the point, they routinely give a prominent place to representatives from mainstream Muslim organizations such as Nahdlatul Ulama in their Sunday services. Rather, they see themselves as victims of local officials who either are Islamists or need the political support of Islamists. Furthermore, for the right price, even hard-liners are prepared to soften their resistance. The very groups that publicly justify their intolerance on religious grounds have privately solicited protection money from their victims, promising that this would end opposition to their houses of worship. While many other churches appear to have opted for this pragmatic solution, the Filadelfia and Yasmin churches have decided to claim Pancasila's promise of religious freedom. Encouraged by the Supreme Court decisions in their favor, they believe they have a duty to persist in a principled struggle. "Paying these groups would solve our problem, but it won't address the fundamental issue, which is to defend our Constitution," says Yasmin's spokesman, Bonar Sigalingging. "We are convinced we must stand up for our rights as citizens of the Republic of Indonesia."[53]

Indonesian scholars of religion and politics say bad laws are partly to blame for the churches' plight. The main administrative stumbling block for the Filadelfia congregation is Joint Regulation 8/9 of the Home Affairs and Religious Affairs Ministries. The regulation says that proposals to build a house of worship must be endorsed by sixty community members of different religions as well as heads of the district religious affairs office and the multifaith religious harmony forum (Forum Kerukunan Umat Beragama, FKUB). The process was meant to reduce conflict, but has backfired. By creating an avenue for religious leaders and local communities to vet a group's application to build a place of worship, the state has abrogated its responsibility to protect minority rights.

Zoning and other technical regulations are required, concedes Ihsan Ali-Fauzi, the director of the Center for the Study of Religion and Democracy at Paramadina University. "But these are decisions that should be taken in the somber chambers of deliberation, not deliberated on the street," he says.[54] In at least two cases he has examined, the 2006 regulation subverted norms of interfaith cooperation that communities had evolved independently. For example, in Ende and Ambon, Muslims and Christians had a tradition of working together to build their mosques and churches: the Christians might contribute a pillar for a mosque construction project, and the Muslims would return the favor when the church needed help. The new, centrally imposed approval system undermines this tradition by allowing local officials to block projects if they fear offending intolerant sections of the community. In the Filadelfia case, the congregants succeeded in collecting the requisite sixty signatures from community members, but the application stalled at the district's religious affairs office.

Of the multitude of studies produced on the repression of Christians in Indonesia, none has found evidence of some inevitable friction between antagonistic religions, or a fundamental incompatibility between Christianity and a majority-Muslim nation-state.[55] All point the finger at sins of commission and omission by identifiable actors: violent hate groups and their ideological cheerleaders, and state authorities that are failing to uphold the rule of law. With the right legal reforms and a commitment by government at all levels to enforce the laws, there is no reason that Indonesia cannot fulfill its responsibility to protect its law-abiding Christians.

The Persecution of Deviance

Minority groups within Indonesia's Muslim population have also experienced persecution while the state looks the other way. According to Franz Magnis-Suseno, a Jesuit Catholic priest and philosopher who has lived in Indonesia for almost fifty years, these Muslim minorities face the brunt of Indonesia's intolerance. He points out that mainstream Muslim theology has always recognized other religions such as Christianity and is not "insulted" by their existence or their forms of worship.[56] Therefore, he contends, most Muslim Indonesians do not find the notion that Christians should be recognized as full citizens controversial. But that is not the case with the Ahmadiyah sect or Shia Muslims. "Only a relatively small number of enlightened Muslims recognize their right to full religious freedom," Magnis-Suseno observes.[57]

Anti-Ahmadiyah Hatred

The Ahmadiyah community has been the most openly and consistently abused. Ahmadiyah is a movement that emerged among India's Muslims in the 1880s, arriving in Indonesia in the 1920s. It claims to have up to 400,000 members, although the Ministry of Religion puts the number at a fraction of this, between 50,000 and 80,000.[58] Mainstream groups denounce Ahmadiyah as heretical mainly because of its belief that the Prophet Muhammad was not the final recipient of divine revelation; its founder Ahmad claimed to have received a revelation that he was the Messiah. "Most of the Muslim community sees such 'sects' as direct challenges to their beliefs, as destabilizing their religion from within, and as unfaithfulness directly in the face of God's revealed religion," Magnis-Suseno says.[59] Bambang Harymurty, publisher of *Tempo*, agrees that prejudice against Ahmadiyah is widespread. "Even educated people are taken in by lies, that Ahmadiyah have a different Quran, and so on."[60] After 2000, emergent extreme moralist groups like the Islamic Defenders Front, FPI, targeted Ahmadiyah for special attention. In 2005, MUI—as part of a barrage of intolerant fatwas it fired off that year—proclaimed that Ahmadiyah should be outlawed.[61]

The government, at best, neglected to provide security to these vulnerable citizens. At worst, officials actively encouraged a culture of intolerance. In 2005, the Ahmadis were forced to appeal for police protection after their annual conference in Bogor was attacked. The city authorities responded in a style all too familiar in countries with weak rule of law: they sided with the more numerous aggressors against the outnumbered victims who were deemed to have provoked the majority. When the authorities told the Ahmadis to shut down their headquarters in Bogor, the FPI decided to enforce the ruling with a mob of three thousand. After the Ahmadis were evacuated, the crowd proceeded to plunder and burn homes and other buildings. No arrests were made.[62] From then on, Ahmadiyah centers experienced regular attacks. In some localities, mobs drove Ahmadis from their homes. One community was evicted from Mataram, West Nusa Tenggara, in 2005; more than a hundred of them remained internally displaced ten years later.[63]

The year 2008 marked a tipping point. In April, the antideviancy government agency Bakor Pakem came out in favor of a national ban on Ahmadiyah activities, repeating a recommendation of the previous year.[64] In response, concerned liberals held a peaceful rally in support of Pancasila and religious freedom. The June 1 rally in central Jakarta was organized by the National Alliance for Freedom of Religion and Faith, an umbrella group for more than seventy organizations. It included Ahmadis.

At least four hundred men from FPI and other radical groups stormed the rally at the National Monument. Armed with clubs and spiked bamboo sticks and shouting abuse at Ahmadiyah, they assaulted the demonstrators, injuring around seventy people. One of the organizers, Mohamad Guntur Romli of the Liberal Islam Network, recalls how unprepared they were for the brazenness of the attack. This was not some remote location, but rather one of the nation's most stately sites, fringed by the presidential palace and government buildings. That same morning at that very spot, a Pancasila event organized by a political party took place under a heavy police watch. By the afternoon, the police were conspicuously absent as FPI thugs descended on the civil society rally. Guntur spent the next four days in hospital being treated for injuries.[65]

Public opinion was sufficiently outraged to cause the government to react—albeit with a classic illustration of how not to deal with hate spin and mob violence. It decided to prioritize order over law, by siding with intolerant groups who had chosen to take violent offense at law-abiding minorities. On June 9, 2008, eight days after the attack, the Minister of Religious Affairs, the Minister of Home Affairs, and the Attorney General issued a Joint Decree warning followers of Ahmadiyah against propagating their religious beliefs for as long as they claimed to be believers of Islam. The officials acted under the authority of the Blasphemy Law. Their Joint Decree did not outlaw Ahmadiyah outright. Moreover, the decree warned against vigilante action against the Ahmadis. It nevertheless amounted to an official declaration that Ahmadis did not have the same rights as the followers of other religions.[66]

If the Joint Decree was an attempt to appease orthodox Muslims and restore peace, it failed miserably. Offense-taking, in the hate spin playbook, does not seek conciliation, but rather the political advantage that can be milked from a heightened state of indignation. It should come as no surprise, then, that the government's concession to the absolutists only emboldened them. The central government's move also encouraged several local authorities to issue bans on the group's activities.[67] Government ministers, local officials and hate groups fed off one another. Anti-Ahmadiyah hate spin escalated in intensity. In October 2010, the minister of religion, Suryadharma Ali, opined that it would be a good idea to ban Ahmadiyah altogether. By 2011, around half of Indonesia's thirty-three provinces had done exactly that.[68]

For most mainstream Muslims, bans on Ahmadiyah are probably just symbolic. But in localities where violations of religious freedom were already routine, such official declarations reached not only receptive ears but also willing hands, eager to translate theological abstractions into bloody violence. On February 6, 2011, three Ahmadis in the Cikeusik district of the province of Banten were attacked and killed in the ugliest anti-Ahmadiyah incident to date.[69]

For many years, local religious leaders had been unhappy with the missionary work of Ismail Suparman, the Ahmadiyah representative in Cikeusik. His house was the center of Ahmadiyah activities in the district. Ten months before the attack, in April 2010, the village chief delivered a speech saying that Ahmadiyah should be disbanded. From September to November 2010, Suparman was summoned to a series of meetings—first with the village chief, then with district officials, Bakor Pakem and an anti-Ahmadiyah group—asking him to renounce Ahmadiyah. Suparman refused, but agreed to obey the Joint Decree against propagating Ahmadiyah teachings. This did not satisfy the hard-liners. In January 2011, they reached out to an influential cleric, Ujang Muhammad Arif, who sent out text messages calling on Muslims to destroy the Ahmadis in Cikeusik.[70]

Having set the date for the dissolution of Ahmadiyah, the activists called on nearby communities to join their cause. Word of the impending attack reached the Ahmadis. They notified the police, the military and security officials four days before the attack. On February 5, police evacuated Suparman, his wife and child, and another Ahmadiyah leader. They were housed in the police station, keeping them out of harm's way. On the morning of

February 6, however, seventeen Ahmadi men arrived at Suparman's house to protect it. They were led by Deden Sudjana, the Ahmadiyah's national security chief. They ignored police advice to leave.[71]

A mob of between 1,000 and 1,500 people descended on the house, as police and army personnel looked on. Video of the violence, later circulated via the Internet, shows the attack in grisly detail.[72] Young men—many wearing Islamic skullcaps and a few wielding foot-long machetes—enter the compound shouting "Allahu Akbar," as a few policemen make feeble attempts to usher them away. The attack starts with stones being pelted into the house. When the Ahmadis fling the stones back at the attackers, the mob rushes in. The video next shows the curled-up, half-naked, and bloodied bodies of victims on the bare ground outside. Attackers take turns beating these unconscious and possibly dead bodies with long wooden sticks, once with so much force that the stick cracks and splinters.

It is natural to want to categorize such images of inhumanity as animal-like and unthinking. Unfortunately, the facts do not provide such refuge. "To say that the Cikeusik murders were premeditated would be an understatement," says the writer and artist Bramantyo Prijosusilo.[73] As the above account makes clear, Cikeusik Muslims' final solution of their Ahmadiyah problem had been in the works for months. Nationally, the deliberate cultivation of hate had been going on for even longer. "The fate of Indonesian Ahmadis had been sealed years before, when Islamic Defenders Front (FPI) leaders began calling for their killing," Prijosusilo points out. The National Commission of Human Rights, Komnas HAM, warned as early as 2006 that the fatwas against Ahmadiyah amounted to hate speech. One national FPI leader, Sobri Lubis, was seen on a YouTube video, screaming at a congregation in Indonesian, "Kill! Kill! Kill! Kill Ahmadiyah!" Prijosusilo notes that news media discussed this video years before the Cikeusik murders. The Indonesian authorities ignored the threat despite the existence of laws banning the incitement of religious hatred. One common excuse made for government inaction in such cases is a lack of policing capacity. This is a real limitation in a vast archipelagic nation with some spots that are 3,000 kilometers away from the capital. Cikeusik, however, is not such a place. It may be small and provincial but—barely a four-hour drive on toll roads from Jakarta—it is not beyond the reach of even the short arm of the law.

Government ministers—whose inflammatory statements had contributed to the culture of hate and impunity—made excuses for the Cikeusik violence or even appeared to condone it. President Yudhoyono did not publicly reprimand his ministers.[74] The authorities' callous disregard for an unpopular religious minority was on full display in the criminal prosecution of the killers. Twelve individuals, including teachers and students of local Islamic schools, were charged for the violence against the Ahmadis, which, to emphasize, had been recorded on multiple phones. But public prosecutors demanded only five to seven months imprisonment for the twelve. The court issued jail sentences of three to six months. Thanks to time already served, the twelve walked free within fifteen days of their sentencing. The court did level an incitement charge against one of the protagonists, but, astonishingly, the accused was Deden Sudjana, the Ahmadiyah head of security, who was seriously wounded in the incident. The indictment called for an outrageous six-year jail term; the court imposed a six-month sentence.[75] One month after the three Ahmadis were killed, the governor of Banten issued a prohibition of the Ahmadiyah congregation's activities in his province.[76]

Targeting Shias

The Sunni–Shia divide, present in many Muslim societies, offers Indonesian hate spin agents another opportunity for mobilization. One long-running case on the island of Madura illustrates how a family feud can escalate into religious conflict. It ended with a Shia cleric, Tajul Muluk, receiving a four-year prison sentence for blasphemy under Article 156A of the Indonesian Criminal Code. More than a hundred members of his congregation were subsequently evicted from their homes.

Tajul Muluk came from a family following Indonesia's dominant Sunni tradition, but became a Shia as an adult. According to news reports, the trouble started in 2004. Tajul's Sunni brother, Rois al-Hukama, proposed marriage to a woman named Halima, who declined. Rois then discovered that Halima had agreed to marry a young Shia man. The matchmaker had been none other than Rois's Shia cleric brother, Tajul. The infuriated Rois began agitating against his brother's Shia community.[77] In 2006, forty Sunni clerics and four police officers signed a statement condemning Shia Islam as heretical and urging the authorities to act against the Shia for blasphemy. The local chapter of the Indonesian Ulema Council adopted a fatwa prohibiting the practice and the spread of Shia teachings. Although it lacked a legal basis, the fatwa was used to justify anti-Shia attacks.

Islamist militants in Madura escalated their campaign in 2011, burning Shia Muslims' houses, a place of worship, and the madrassah. Only one militant was charged for the arson attack. The police's idea of a solution was to advise Tajul Muluk and another Shia cleric to leave the village. The chief prosecutor of the regency, a member of Bakor Pakem, pressed for a ban on Tajul's teachings and initiated the blasphemy proceedings. Tajul's original sentence of two years' imprisonment, meted out by the district court, was doubled by a higher court on appeal. The Surabaya High Court said Tajul deserved an increased sentence for causing disharmony among Muslims. Local authorities such as the Sampang Regent supported the anti-Shia groups' demands that the exiled Shias not be allowed back unless they converted to Sunni Islam. Unable to work on their farms, the victims were forced into unemployment or low-paying jobs.[78]

A Consolidated Democracy of Uncertain Quality

Indonesia is a much younger democracy than either the United States or India. Its institutions are less established and its prospects harder to discern. Optimists can point to its record of peaceful, competitive elections, consistently won by parties at the secular end of the spectrum. Pessimists observe the kinds of events described in this chapter and know that not all is well. The young democracy may already be too entrenched to fail, but its democratic values are partially developed at best. In addition to the episodic violence, survey data indicate rising religious intolerance among the general population. The strong opposition to the broadly worded antipornography bill showed that most Indonesians will not let go of their hard-won media freedoms and their right to assemble, tweet, and post at will. But many are not yet sold on the idea of sharing such rights with unpopular minority groups.

The roots of Indonesia's religious hardening are complex. The fiercest critics of "SiPiLis" sound as if their goal is to convert Indonesia into an Islamic caliphate ruled by sharia and free of deviants. The most detailed studies of religion and politics in Indonesia, though, reveal less straightforward agendas. Consider the agitation for sharia. John Bowen, an anthropologist, has found that the trend is really about "an Indonesia in the process of redefining and relegitimizing its institutions, not an Indonesia captured by a uniform national religious frenzy."[79] Elites use sharia as an accessible sign of authenticity and autonomy, Bowen says. Hate spin, too, has a symbolic function. The biggest post-Reformasi campaign of righteous indignation produced new legislation against pornography and "porno-action," but after achieving that symbolic victory, hard-liners did not really exploit the law to cleanse Indonesia of everything they deemed indecent. This was also true of the protests against the *Innocence of Muslims* YouTube trailer, discussed in chapter 3. A series of protests culminated in a demonstration by thousands outside the US embassy, organized by the Prosperous Justice Party, PKS.[80] The controversy died down shortly after Google took the trailer off YouTube in Indonesia; it did not revive even though the full movie later became available to Indonesians on the site.

Even the hate spin against Ahmadis and Shias may be largely symbolic, notwithstanding its occasional escalation into very real violence. Most of the anti-Ahmadiyah regulations have not been enforced, notes the legal scholar Melissa Crouch in her detailed nationwide study.[81] Mary McCoy, who studies political rhetoric, argues that unpopular religious minorities fulfill a useful "fantasy function" for absolutists who are trying to sell the idea of a pure and perfectly cohesive community.[82] Such cohesion, McCoy points out, is an "unsustainable illusion," especially in a country as large and diverse as Indonesia.[83] So, the purveyors of intolerance need scapegoats for the failure to realize a pure society. Paradoxically, blaming deviants is an effective way to continue selling the fiction that a cohesive community is possible one day. McCoy says this intolerant streak in Indonesian political rhetoric is rooted in certain master metaphors developed during Suharto's era, which framed the community as a "body and container that must be protected from external invasion and internal disintegration."[84] The real agenda, of course, is the consolidation of power by constructing an imagined enemy—just as Hindu nationalists have done in India.

While one cannot predict where these trends will take Indonesia, it is possible to identify the main factors that will either pull it toward or push it away from a future of pluralism and tolerance. I've already discussed one in some detail: Indonesia needs constitutional provisions, statutes, and regulations to match its vision of equality. These need to take into account the presence of groups eager to exploit any technical loophole or symbolic signal that they can treat as a green light to inflict discrimination and violence against vulnerable communities. Although most international discussions about hate speech have focused on speech laws, the Indonesian case shows the importance of legislation supporting the freedom of religion and belief. The unequal distribution of this right, as well as the right given to the majority to take offense at the religious expression of minorities, is behind much of Indonesia's hate spin.

Two other factors loom large: civil society and political leadership. These have the ability to either nurture habits of tolerance, or push Indonesia deeper down the path toward religious polarization and conflict. The direction each will take is unclear. But in general, we see civil society weakening as a buffer against intolerance, while the political commitment to pluralism seems to be mostly a matter of individual calculation and personality.

Civil Society's Fading Light

Compared with India, Indonesia possesses a more intellectually vibrant, firmly institutionalized, and well-organized liberal-secular tradition within its majority faith. The two dominant Muslim organizations, Nahdlatul Ulama (NU) and Muhammadiyah, have a tradition of supporting inclusive and secular democracy. NU, in particular, has evolved a pragmatic attitude of openness toward diverse cultural and intellectual sources, as well as an awareness of its responsibilities as the majority community for peaceful conflict resolution.[85] It is a decentralized movement, subject to the whims of local leaders who may not be equally open minded. But some NU groups have been at the forefront of protecting Christian churches against violence.

Leaders of these movements have shown Indonesians that it is possible to debate and counter hard-line absolutists self-confidently, in both theological and secular language. A prominent case in point is the late NU leader Abdurrahman Wahid, popularly known as Gus Dur. Elected as president of Indonesia in 1999, he championed an open and tolerant brand of Islam. Opposing the antipornography bill, he commented that, based on the drafters' standards, even the Quran would have to be banned. Hardliners were incensed, of course, but they could not persuasively dismiss Gus Dur's statements as the views of an enemy of Islam. Former Muhammadiyah leader Amien Rais has made similarly unequivocal remarks about the value of pluralism and the need to interpret the Quran in the light of modern conditions. The Quran, he has said, is "a source of law, a source of moral and ethical principles," but "not a book of law": "If the Quran is considered a book of law, Muslims will become the most wretched people in the world."[86]

The strength of Indonesia's Muslim civil society organizations is partly due to Indonesians' healthy distrust of centralized political power and its potentially corrupting influence on religion. In Dutch colonial times, the founders of Quranic schools and other Muslim groups decided it was best to plant roots far from the centers of political power. Suharto's excesses cemented this distrust.[87] He also did Indonesia the favor of providing state patronage for civil Islam, actively supporting the development of liberal interpretations of the religion. Into this space entered major thinkers with a background in both traditional Islamic education and training in modern philosophy and theology. The scholar Harun Nasution established a rationalist, interpretive, and critical approach to Islamic studies. Products of that approach, such as the public intellectual Nurcholish Madjid, helped perpetuate a dynamic and inclusive form of Islamic thinking. Their doctrines were sufficiently robust and appealing to resist the incursion of less tolerant teachings from abroad. Mirjam Künkler writes that the result of all this was "a new hegemonic discourse that prioritizes religious pluralism, a rationalist hermeneutic in approaching the religious texts, and the defense of democratic norms and processes."[88]

Civil Islam is nevertheless not immune to what some have called the conservative turn in mainstream Indonesian Islam since the early years of the 2000s.[89] Within NU and Muhammadiyah, conservatives and absolutists have been gaining ground over progressives and liberals. Abdurrahman Wahid's death in 2009 left NU without a comparable champion of pluralist values. His successor as NU chairman, Hasyim Muzadi, spoke up against the Joint Decree on Ahmadiyah in 2005, but by 2011 he too was calling for the sect to be expelled from Islam.[90] Donald Emmerson observes a similar trend in Muhammadiyah. Ahmad Syafi'i Ma'arif, who headed Muhammadiyah from 1998 to 2005, willingly took the risk of challenging violent manifestations of intolerance within the Muslim community, Emmerson says. "In contrast, his successor Din Syamsuddin was inclined to respond to such incidents by reminding the public of his personal participation in interfaith dialogues held in Indonesia and around the world." Syamsuddin also served as vice-chair and then chair of the ulema council, MUI, at a time when compliance with orthodoxy was prized over freedom of thought and interpretation.[91] The leading Muslim reformist intellectual in late twenty-century Indonesia, Nurcholish Madjid, died in 2005. "As of 2015 he had not been replaced by any Indonesian Muslim intellectual of comparable scholarship, readership, and reformist conviction," Emmerson notes.

A Political Failure

On the surface, Indonesia's government continues to uphold its multifaith tradition. When appropriate—like when burnishing Indonesia's brand as a model Muslim democracy—the president brackets his speeches not only with the Islamic greeting "Assalamu'alaikum," but also with the Hindu "Om Swastyastu" and "Om Shanti Shanti Shanti Om," and the Jewish "Shalom." Such niceties, however, are peripheral to the challenge that Indonesian democracy faces. Interfaith dialogues like the 2014 Alliance of Civilizations forum in Bali are often "little more than feel-good talk-fests that do not grapple with real problems," the International Crisis Group notes.[92] What civilization most needs from the Indonesian state is the fortitude to stand up to intolerant speech and action. "The state lacks the courage to do its duty and thereby indirectly encourages popular violence and the impunity of intolerant groups and organizations," says the Catholic priest Magnis-Suseno.[93]

Like many large countries, Indonesia is frequently let down by a police force that is short on professionalism. In some areas, the police have a symbiotic relationship with the protection racket operated by moralist militias. When FPI thugs complain about immoral activity, this provides police officers "the opportunity to give forewarning to businesses on the FPI hit list, which can pay for police protection, strengthen their own security, or make the FPI an offer."[94] In many other cases, the police simply find it easier to side with might rather than right.

Political leaders and government officials are similarly guilty of either active collusion with hate groups or amoral utilitarian calculations that find minority rights not worth the expense of political capital. Many Indonesian analysts blame Susilo Bambang Yudhoyono's presidency (2004–2014) for failing to moderate—or actually promoting—the conservative turn in Indonesian Islam. His government inserted itself into religious matters in ways that actively encouraged and even institutionalized intolerance. Within the first year of his presidency, Yudhoyono accepted MUI's invitation to open its national congress. His speech in July 2005 boosted the council's prestige and self-confidence. He said he and his government opened its "hearts and minds" to the recommendations of MUI and Islamic scholars. "We want to place MUI in a central role in matters regarding the Islamic faith," he added.[95] Yudhoyono made these comments at the same congress where MUI issued its fatwa against liberalism, pluralism, and secularism.

His government revived the official antideviancy agency Bakor Pakem—a Suharto creation that had become moribund after Reformasi—in response to MUI's 2005 anti-Ahmadiyah edict.[96] This effectively provided MUI with a permanent partner within government. Yudhoyono also appointed religious conservatives to key ministries and failed to correct them when they engaged in hate speech. His government made the mistake of trying to adjudicate theological disputes and assuage religious feelings at the expense of upholding the rule of law. The 2006 regulation on building houses of worship and the 2008 Joint Decree on Ahmadiyah were classic cases. The social scientist Abdul Malik Gismar, who has traversed the country in the course of his work on Indonesia's democracy index, is convinced that these two regulations have done immeasurable damage. "They never solve the problem; they create the problem."[97]

Analysts cite a number of factors behind Yudhoyono's indulgence toward Islamists. One is that he had to swim with the tide of a Muslim majority that had become more conservative. Although the Islamist parties seemed incapable of winning power, they were not without influence.

The president's ruling coalition included the Muslim-based United Development Party, PPP. Yudhoyono may have felt obligated to offer the position of minister of religious affairs to the PPP chairman, Suryadharma Ali, who became notorious for using the office to issue intolerant statements and rulings. In a political culture that has come to expect piety in its public servants, individual politicians and officials also fear being embarrassed and harassed by allegations that they are not religious enough—a threat that Islamists are adept at exploiting. "They use religious symbols very effectively," says Endy Bayuni, a veteran journalist and cofounder of the International Association of Religion Journalists. "If you are seen as anti-Islam, it can be dangerous."[98]

Another factor was Yudhoyono's personal temperament and philosophy of government. He was famous for skirting confrontation and controversy, to the point of inaction. When forced to make a decision, he preferred to strike a balance between opposing sides. "Whenever the winner takes all, it's harmful, there will be losers, and losers generally like to hit back, and if that then gets out of control, then it can be terrible," he explained in an interview with academics after he stepped down. "Ya, I must admit that I *love* to maintain balance, yes, the balance in life, in our country."[99] This approach may have been based on an accurate perception of his country as deeply divided, and a paternalistic desire to mediate between conflicting interests. But it meant minority rights were not regarded as sacrosanct. As the scholars who interviewed him realized, "the prospect of a particular decision leading to 'clashes' carried, for him, the same weight as the Constitution's guarantee of religious freedom."[100]

All this suggests that a different kind of presidency might put up a stiffer resistance to the forces of intolerance. Yudhoyono's successor offered hope. Jakarta governor Joko Widodo, popularly known as Jokowi, ran for the presidency in 2014 promising more decisive and effective governance. While governor, he won a highly publicized showdown with the militant FPI. He had instituted a merit-based system in appointing subdistrict heads, as a result of which a female Christian civil servant was put in charge of a predominantly Muslim part of Jakarta. When FPI instigated a petition against her, Jokowi stood firm and the ruckus eventually died down.[101] "The fears proved unfounded," notes Bayuni.[102]

Then, campaigning for the presidency, Jokowi had to deal with attacks on his deputy governor, Basuki Tjahaja Purnama, an ethnic Chinese and Christian. Basuki was in line to take over the governorship if Jokowi became president. Islamists said that a vote for Jokowi was thus a vote for a Chinese

Christian governor of the nation's capital. Jokowi stood by Basuki, saying that the law on succession was clear. Jokowi was not above the need to show his piety. His pilgrimage to Mecca during the hiatus in campaigning, just prior to polling day, was probably intended to lay to rest doubts about his personal religious convictions.[103] He made clear, however, that he intended to arrest the trend toward religious intolerance. His platform identified "intolerance and crisis in the nation's character" as one of the three main challenges facing the republic.

After his victory, he and his Religious Affairs Minister Lukman Hakim Saifuddin promised to draft a law on religious tolerance to protect religious minorities. Through his appointments and public pronouncements he has raised the status of Nahdlatul Ulama relative to its hard-line opponents. The US Commission on International Religious Freedom acknowledged "a different, more inclusive tone" in his government's statements.[104]

The new Jakarta governor, Basuki, has also been a breath of fresh air. Non-Muslim elites in Indonesia are especially wary of being branded as anti-Islam. Early in his tenure as governor, Basuki defied this convention by requesting that FPI be banned after a string of violent incidents in the city. Although he was unsuccessful, he has demonstrated that hard-liners are not untouchable. He followed this up with a bold defense of Ahmadiyah.

Jokowi and Basuki have helped challenge the conventional wisdom that confronting hard-line Muslim groups amounts to political suicide.[105] "The myth that they can mobilize the majority of voters is now less credible," says Bambang Harymurty, publisher of *Tempo*. The struggle against the forces of intolerance, though, is far from over. One clear indicator can be found outside the presidential palace. More than a year into the Jokowi presidency, the Filadelfia and Yasmin Protestant congregations were still conducting their twice-monthly services in the open air. The government had yet to find a way to clear the local obstacles preventing them from building houses of worship.

Indonesia's democratic development is a success story but, like India, it is a country torn between opposing visions of nationhood. "The mere existence of a democratic political system is no guarantee of religious tolerance," notes Donald Emmerson. "Cultures and climates of opinion and the leaders who influence them can and do move independently of the liberal norms that democracies are supposed to uphold. And those norms themselves can be, or become, illiberal." Indonesians like Mohamad Guntur Romli of the Liberal Islam Network believe that the basis for religious tolerance is already in the republic's foundations. "If we go back to our Constitution, our dream is Pancasila; it guarantees freedom of expression, freedom of religion, a plural society," he says. These were the values he wanted to defend when he led the march in support of Ahmadiyah in 2008, only to be physically beaten and see his elected officials side with the forces of intolerance. Indonesia's identity, like its economy, is still emerging and fragile, he realizes. "Who is the Indonesian? Muslim? Javanese? Like Americans and the West? Or Arab? The discussion is not over. Maybe our problem here is that we have different dreams."[106]

Today, Alabama's cities are places of pilgrimage where Americans contemplate some of the country's most notorious incidents of racism as well as some of its most inspiring civil rights victories. For decades, African Americans were lynched with impunity in Alabama and the rest of the South. In 1963, a bomb placed by the Ku Klux Klan ripped through a Birmingham church, killing four African American girls. The same year, the governor placed himself at the doors of the state university as television cameras rolled, to tell the world that racial desegregation was not welcome. But Alabama also witnessed more positive moments. It was where Rosa Parks's act of defiance on board a public bus in 1955 spurred a boycott and a regional movement; and where a young preacher, Martin Luther King Jr., fashioned a civil disobedience campaign that eventually generated the 1964 Civil Rights Act and the 1965 Voting Rights Act.

Fifty years later, these memories made Alabama a focus for national nostalgia. Readers of *USA Today* named the state capital, Montgomery, America's "Best Historic City" in 2014.[1] In early 2015, Americans from all over the country arrived to relive the drama of the Selma to Montgomery voting rights march. For those not inclined to make the trek, Hollywood served up its own recreation, *Selma*, complete with an Oscar-winning gospel-rap anthem, "Glory." Not to be outdone, Barack Obama stood before the Edmund Pettus Bridge and delivered one of the most stirring speeches of his presidency. He recalled how marchers had confronted police there in a "contest to determine the meaning of America," and that, thanks to them, "the idea of a just America and a fair America, an inclusive America, and a generous America—that idea ultimately triumphed."[2]

It has been said that those who forget the past are doomed to repeat it; but recent events in Alabama suggest that the memory of past injustices cannot totally forestall the rehashing of prejudice and hate. Thus, in 2014, the state's legislators approved a referendum for voters to decide on an amendment to the state's constitution, called "American and Alabama Laws for Alabama Courts." The measure's innocuous title masked a years-long exercise in minority bashing through legislation. The amendment's sponsors told voters that the law was needed to defend the state from an existential threat—Muslims, whose religion compelled them to impose the tyranny of sharia law wherever they went. Placed on the ballot during the midterm elections that November, the proposition passed easily, with more than 72 percent voting in its favor.[3]

Islamophobia has taken root within a sizeable section of American society. In mid-2014, around 40 percent of Americans reported feeling "cold" toward Islam (compared with 17 percent feeling that way toward Catholics and 10 percent toward Jews).[4] Roughly the same proportion favor the profiling of Arab and Muslim Americans by law enforcement agencies.[5] The irony that these views were circulating even as the nation celebrated the fiftieth anniversary of a movement for minority rights was not lost on one Muslim Alabaman I spoke with. Had ethnic prejudice simply found a new target, I asked him? "Americans will always need a nigger," he smiled ruefully.

Some level of antipathy among Americans toward Muslims is to be expected, of course, after the trauma of the terror attacks of September 11, 2001. Long before that, there was the Iranian hostage crisis of 1979–81, perpetrated by an Islamic theocracy whose leader, Ayatollah Khomeini, came to power describing the United States as the Great Satan. More recently, the atrocities of the so-called Islamic State (IS) have strained cosmopolitan tolerance to breaking point. Even more than the beheading of captives in Syria and Iraq, IS attacks on "soft targets" in the United States and Europe have induced a siege mentality, as reflected in the support for presidential hopeful Donald Trump's declaration that the United States should close its borders to all Muslims until the authorities could figure out what to do about Islamic radicals. A significant minority of Americans surveyed—and a majority of Republicans—favored his idea, despite its disregard for the US Constitution as well as common sense.[6]

The ground sentiments that Trump cynically exploited cannot be explained by jihadist terrorism alone. Six months after 9/11, the proportion of Americans who said that Islam is more likely than other faiths to encourage violence was 25 percent. A decade later, in 2011, it was 35 percent. The percentage with favorable views of Islam fell from 41 percent in 2005 to 30 percent in 2010.[7] Oddly enough, therefore, anti-Muslim feeling increased during the lull period between 9/11 and the emergence of IS.

Hatewatch groups attribute this rise to a misinformation campaign engineered by a small but identifiable group of agitators on the political right. This group forms "a well-funded, well-organized fringe movement" pushing "discriminatory policies against a segment of American society by intentionally spreading lies while taking advantage of moments of public anxiety and fear," says a report by the Center for American Progress, a progressive policy institute.[8] While these hate spin agents are beneficiaries of preexisting stereotypes, the accentuation and politicization of these attitudes—turning ignorance into fear and fear into policy proposals—depends on their active machinations. The manufacture of offense and offendedness by far-right pundits and think tanks is so systematic and self-interested that analysts of intolerance have dubbed them the "Islamophobia industry."[9] The term "Islamophobia" refers to an unfounded fear of Muslims that operates at the individual, psychological level, but that can also be institutionalized as a set of policies and practices.[10]

The 2016 presidential campaign showcased the Islamophobia industry's success in gaining access to the mainstream of national politics. One example is misinformation expert Frank Gaffney and his Center for Security Policy, a prolific source of anti-Muslim propaganda. Among other claims, the extremist think tank and its founder have called Barack Obama the first Muslim president of the United States and stated that the Muslim Brotherhood has penetrated the American public school system. When Trump called for a ban on Muslim arrivals, he cited a Center for Security Policy poll, debunked by experts, showing an alarming degree of support for violence among Muslims.[11] Trump's rival for the Republican ticket, Ted Cruz, had deeper ties to the Islamophobia network and named Frank Gaffney to his national security team.[12]

Of course, those parlaying paranoia into political advantage would argue that a fear of Muslims is entirely rational. For an expert perspective on objective threats to peaceful coexistence in the United States, I turned to the Southern Poverty Law Center (SPLC), an independent watchdog organization. Located just across the road from the Civil Rights Memorial in Montgomery, Alabama, the nonprofit was founded in 1971 to counter hate and bigotry. Initially, the white supremacist Ku Klux Klan kept SPLC's hands full—as late as 1983, Klansmen torched its offices—but in the late 1990s the center widened its investigative work to cover all hate groups. In February 2015, I found Mark Potok putting the finishing touches to the latest issue of SPLC's *Intelligence Report*, containing the results of its annual survey of hate groups in the country. As a newspaper journalist in the early 1990s, Potok had covered the deadly confrontation between authorities and the Branch Davidian Christian sect in Waco, Texas. He also covered the revenge attack in Oklahoma City two years later by Timothy McVeigh, which killed 168 people in the worst act of domestic terrorism prior to 9/11. Potok joined SPLC in 1997 and has been monitoring hate groups full time since then.

Hate against Muslims has shown a significant rise, he tells me. "I think we are entering a very bad moment."[13] But, that begs the chicken-and-egg question. Which came first: anti-Muslim hate propagated through Christian talk radio, Fox News, and dubious think tanks; or, extreme anti-American sentiment that Muslims radicals are inciting through social media and mosques? Put another way, which is the bigger threat to American democracy today, Islamophobia or Islamic extremism? Potok answers without hesitation, "I think Islamophobia is a bigger danger in this country." This is not France, he points out. Muslim Americans form a small and relatively well-integrated minority, and they are no more likely than other groups to engage in hate crimes or political violence.

For many people outside the United States, the country's democratic journey is an inspiration. Parallel to that road, though, has been a virtually uninterrupted stream of intolerance, directed at one minority community after another. Famously, the economic rise of the United States depended on ideologies of hate that dehumanized Africans and Native Americans, the better to rob them of their labor and land. Chinese, Japanese, Jews, Irish, Catholics, and gays have taken turns at being targets of gross prejudice, discrimination, and violence. Today, though, the merchants of Islamophobia are the preeminent practitioners of hate spin in the United States. They have manufactured indignation at the building of Muslim places of worship, the adoption of school textbooks containing respectful explanations of the religion, and the alleged encroachment of Muslim law. In this chapter I examine their motivations and methods. First, though, I look at how religion, democracy, and free speech relate to one another in the American political system.

The First Amendment and the Culture Wars

There are similarities between the United States, India, and Indonesia. In each, the giving and taking of religious offense has emerged as a potent political weapon. The policy battlegrounds are also similar: the writing of history textbooks and the siting of places of worship can be as controversial in the United States as they are in India or Indonesia. As with many other areas of social and political life, however, the United States also represents a giant exception. Its unique constitutional take on religious offense means that American hate spin exponents navigate a legal terrain very different from their counterparts elsewhere. No other democracy is as convinced—both in its law and its political culture—that hate speech can be largely left to the marketplace of ideas to resolve. In American constitutional doctrine, the state has no business using its power to take sides in peaceful public debates between people who display civic virtues and those who are outright bigots.

Outsiders often perceive the US position as a product of an idolization of free speech and individual rights, and a callous disregard for sacred community values. This caricature misunderstands American secularism, which should not be confused with, say, French-style *laïcité* or what some call have called secular fundamentalism. It is worth recalling that the First Amendment to the US Constitution does not protect freedom of expression alone. Its opening clauses—"Congress shall make no law respecting an establishment of religion, or prohibiting the free exercise thereof"—embody two fundamental principles regarding religion. The portion known as the Establishment Clause prevents the state from adopting an official religion or singling out any one religion or sect for special treatment. The Free Exercise Clause bans the government from interfering with people's right to practice or express their religious beliefs. The country's religious minorities are therefore in the globally unique position of having to endure vicious insult with practically no protection from the state, while simultaneously being guaranteed that they will be safe from official oppression and discrimination.

These founding principles have not ended debates about the separation between church and state. Policies on polygamy, school prayer, abortion and same-sex marriage have required the US Supreme Court to make controversial judgments balancing different rights and interests. The question of where to draw these lines continues to generate some of the country's most polarizing political debates. In Alabama, for example, the state's chief justice Roy Moore was sacked over his refusal to comply with a federal order, based on the Establishment Clause, that he remove a monument to the Ten Commandments he had commissioned for the judicial building. Eric Johnston, the lawyer who drafted the state's Amendment One to protect Alabamans from sharia, has spent decades resisting what he sees as the US Supreme Court's antireligious interventions. In the view of Christian conservatives like Johnston, the Supreme Court has privileged the Establishment Clause over the Free Exercise Clause, thus allowing a secular worldview to trample on Americans' religious freedoms.[14]

These contemporary tensions are deeply rooted in American history. In the seventeenth and eighteenth centuries, Europeans sailed to the New World in search of religious refuge as much as economic opportunity. When the founding fathers of the United States decided to keep their newly constituted government at an arm's length from religious authority, it was not because of any conversion to some post-religious multicultural ideal or a vision of interfaith peace and understanding. Instead, a double distrust—both of one another's sects and of government—convinced them never to allow the state to be captured by any religious group. The desire to check tyranny, as much as any positive appreciation of diversity, undergirded the First Amendment's religion clauses. This background helps explain the republic's sometimes-paradoxical relationship with religion. The country has been capable of great popular intolerance toward religious minorities, but also affords them a degree of legal protection rarely matched elsewhere.

Like India and Indonesia, American democracy has careened between two compelling visions of nationhood. Primers on the United States tend to stress just one of them, the constitutional order that some have called "civil religion." While readily declaring that the United States is "under God," this perspective emphasizes that it is also "one nation"—diverse, equal, and inclusive. This narrative points out, for example, that Thomas Jefferson owned an English translation of the Quran—so keen was he to understand an alien civilization that could not be excluded if Americans were going to be serious about building a society on universal principles of civil rights.[15] When State Department officials lead delegations from Muslim countries on tours of the nation's capital, they point to the mural on the interior of the dome of the nineteenth-century Library of Congress building, on which a ring of twelve figures representing the main contributors to Western civilization includes one labeled "ISLAM."

This spirit of openness emanates from an idea of nationhood that is anchored not in history or culture, but in transcendent political values. The US Constitution, as the ultimate expression of the will of the people, is the final word. "The principles of our Constitution unite all of us as a nation," intones the government's twelve-minute film introducing US history and civics for immigrants. The film acknowledges that American democracy was not born perfect and remains a work in progress, a matter for ongoing debate. But, in this liberal-secular view, the direction of the constitutional order is clear: "over time, its promise of freedom has included more and more people," it says. "Many groups of people were denied certain freedoms in the past, but have gained equality through amendments to the US Constitution. It took seventy-five years and a Civil War to end slavery. And it was another hundred years until laws were passed to make it illegal to discriminate against people based on race, color, religion, sex, or national origin." The only advice in this video that impinges on immigrants' cultural identity is, "Learn English." It is not race or religious tradition, but rather "common civic values that make us all Americans."[16]

This transcendental ideal is expressed with such inspiring eloquence that it is easy to overlook the competing paradigm—a more exclusive and intolerant religious nationalism rooted more explicitly in the white and Christian roots of the United States. This countercurrent has been part of the republic's history from the start, ebbing and flowing, but always there. With the possible exception of a liberal consensus in the first two decades after World War II, religious nationalism has remained a steady feature of American life.[17] In 1992, presidential hopeful Patrick Buchanan trumpeted this worldview as a keynote speaker at the Republic National Convention. Highlighting the chasm between Republicans and Democrats on abortion, gay rights, and school prayer, his rousing battle cry came to be known simply as the Culture War Speech. "Friends, this election is about more than who gets what. It is about who we are," he said. "It is about what we believe and what we stand for as Americans. There is a religious war going on in this country. It is a cultural war, as critical to the kind of nation we shall be as the Cold War itself. For this war is for the soul of America."[18]

By then, though, the Culture Wars strategy was at least twenty years old. Richard Nixon's 1968 and 1972 presidential campaigns successfully used cultural appeals to win over the white Christian majority.[19] Nixon played the race, religion, and patriotism cards to trump social class in mobilizing voters. This strategy would become central to the Republican Party. "By consciously polarizing the American electorate along cultural lines, the Republican Party sought to minimize the salience of economic issues and draw working-class whites into a coalition that in actuality catered to the interests of the country's elites," argues the political scientist Scott Hibbard. "It was this type of right-wing populism that informed the culture wars of the 1990s."[20]

Then, there were the epic events of September 11, 2001. Once shorn of inconvenient details—like the role US foreign policy played in the genesis of Al Qaeda and the radicalization of Osama bin Laden—the event fit elegantly into the master narrative of a Christian nation whose values were under attack by evil nonbelievers abroad and traitorous liberals at home.

In 2008, it looked as if the pendulum was swinging back. Barack Obama entered the White House speaking the old familiar language of civil religion once again, appearing to vindicate the self-correcting quality of functioning democracies. By then, though, American society had become too deeply polarized for Obama to unite. Religious nationalism flourished in the movement known as the Tea Party, alarming even many conservative

Republicans. The historian Robert Horwitz distinguishes the Tea Party's "antiestablishment conservatism" from previous mainstream Republican values. The Tea Party's uncompromising dogmatism and its stress on "faith over facts" is a radical effort to "overturn settled law, norms, and institutions."[21] This tendency dominated the 2016 Republican primaries. Ted Cruz was deeply committed to Tea Party positions. In comparison, Donald Trump was hardly a true believer, but the fact that he chose to hitch his campaign to those same forces attests to the religious nationalists' success in changing the terms of the national conversation. Most worryingly, the Tea Party's brand of conservatism has infused politics with a sense of "victimhood, resentment, and anger about the perceived loss of individual autonomy," eating away at a culture of tolerance and inclusivity.[22] The Tea Party is thus the inheritor of the "paranoid style" in American politics, which the late historian Richard Hofstadter identified when trying to explain how the nation could have been so spellbound by the irrational reactionary rants of Senators Joseph McCarthy and Barry Goldwater in the 1950s and 1960s.[23]

Hofstadter's "paranoid style" thesis remains relevant today, but it is incomplete. Hofstadter focused on the social psychology underlying American political culture and its final expression in structural outcomes. What he missed, notes Robert Horwitz, was the middle level of analysis: how and why certain institutions channel and mobilize that fear and anger in a conservative direction. Horwitz highlights the active role played by "long-established networks of right-wing money, idea-generating political organizations, and mass media."[24] The same dynamics can be seen behind the manufacture of paranoia toward Islam.

The Cultivation of Islamophobia

In Birmingham, Alabama, seventy-six-year-old Larry Houck represents the face of anti-Islamic grassroots activism. Houck is a small-businessman in the real estate line, who drives a Toyota truck with a bumper sticker that reads "Get US out of the United Nations." A diligent student of Islamophobia ideologues, he heads the local chapter of the radical anti-Islam network, ACT! for America. He was seized by the cause around 2010, in the course of reading more and more books—fourteen in total, he says—about the threat that Islam poses to the United States and Europe. "Right now, there is a war going on," he tells me over coffee at a Starbucks off Interstate 65 in Alabama.[25]

Houck is simultaneously alarmed and energized by the fact that most of his fellow Americans do not share his sense of dread, and he works hard to awaken them to the reality as he sees it. In his view, Muslims plan to use sharia to eventually take over the West. Sharia, as Houck understands it, is a totalitarian system that enslaves women and governs every part of life. When Muslims claim that theirs is a religion of peace, non-Muslims must realize that the Quranic doctrine of *taqiyya* allows Muslims to deceive nonbelievers. When Muslims are in control, he adds, non-Muslim women will be told to cover themselves up, as they already do in France. Islam will eventually take over Europe, Houck predicts, because Muslim men can take four wives, resulting in a higher birth rate. There are already no-go zones across Europe; European mayors have denied their existence, but they can be located online, he says. Islam has already devastated India, taking over more than half of the land, he adds. According to Houck, President Obama has infiltrated Washington, D.C., with the Muslim Brotherhood. And so on.

Houck and other activists like him are the cottage manufacturers within the Islamophobia industry. To anyone, Muslim or not, who has had access to reliable facts about the religion, the picture of Islam they try to sell would be dismissed as belonging to the lunatic fringe. If you listen to the wider political conversation, however, you realize that their views have a familiar ring, echoing ideas being bandied about by pundits and politicians who have a national presence. Like Hindutva rhetoric in India, the tropes of the US Islamophobia network have grand narratives with recycled themes and factoids, which through sheer repetition have taken on the authority of common sense.

The good news is that this is "not a vast right-wing conspiracy," according to the Center for American Progress (CAP).[26] The Islamophobia campaign could be effectively pushed back with robust counter-speech and naming-and-shaming, says Yasmine Taeb, a civil rights lawyer who coauthored CAP's 2015 Islamophobia report.[27] Hate-watch groups like CAP identify half a dozen self-styled, mutually referencing experts generating most of the anti-Islam propaganda in the United States. These individuals work through ten key organizations whose core business is to sow hatred against Islam. Between 2001 and 2012, these groups received a total of almost $57 million from eight major donors, according to CAP.[28] Employing slightly different yardsticks, the Council on American–Islamic Relations (CAIR) counted at least thirty-seven groups in the "inner core" of the Islamophobia network, with access to almost $120 million in revenues between 2008 and 2011.[29]

Misinformation is disseminated through sympathetic politicians and preachers. The Islamophobia industry's media reach is considerable. It can generally count on Fox News and the *Washington Times* to reports its views uncritically. Nationally syndicated radio talk show hosts Rush Limbaugh, Sean Hannity, Glenn Beck, and Mike Savage routinely propagate Islamo-phobic viewpoints. The core groups and individuals also operate their own platforms, notably the Jihad Watch (www.jihadwatch.org) and Middle East Forum (www.meforum.org) websites. These are not amateurish produc-tions. Rich in content and optimized for search engines, their pages are rou-tinely listed near the top of Google searches for information about Islam. (For example, MEforum's skewed entry was the top item, ahead of even Wikipedia, when I tried Googling "taqiyya" in Hong Kong.[30])

While American Islamophobia feeds off the war on terror, it does not necessarily help the cause. When American troops and counterterrorism personnel combat Muslim militants abroad, they need to work alongside Muslim allies and among Muslim civilians. Domestically, most tipoffs about suspicious activities among Muslims come from Muslim Americans. From a hard-nosed security perspective, therefore, the United States cannot afford to be perceived by Muslims as being at war with Islam. This probably explains why even President George W. Bush, not known for a nuanced view of the world, took pains to declare his high regard for the majority of Muslims and their faith. The Bush Administration's insistence that Islam was not the enemy may explain why, after its post-9/11 spike, hate crimes and negativity toward the religion briefly declined.

The Islamophobia network has a broader agenda than combating terror-ism. Some of the most committed fearmongers are animated by the Israeli–Palestinian conflict. "The vast majority of the individuals and groups spewing anti-Muslim rhetoric in the United States are the ideological patrons of the Israeli state and its policies against the Palestinians," notes Nathan Lean, author of the 2012 book, *The Islamophobia Industry*. "In some cases, as that of the Clarion Fund, which has produced three or four anti-Muslim films, they are directly engaged with Israel."[31] Demonizing Mus-lims is obviously one of the most effective ways to ensure that American citizens and their elected representatives never permit the US government to depart from its pro-Israel position to pursue justice for Palestinians.

An outer ring of supporting organizations with different missions add to Islamophobia's firepower (and financial resources). These varied groups on the religious Right bring diverse motivations to the fight against Islam. Some evangelicals feel a messianic zeal to defeat what they see as a false religion. For most, however, this religious mandate is probably outweighed by the frustration and anxiety that conservatives have long felt about social trends in their country—the same trends that Buchanan condemned in his Culture War speech. The ever-wider application of individual rights has led to conservative defeats on hot-button issues, most recently on same-sex marriage. Meanwhile, immigration has changed the complexion of the country; white Americans will make up less than half the population in a few decades. "White people are going to lose their majority for the first time since the Europeans arrived. That is a huge thing," notes Potok.[32] "It's changing everyday life for people where they live. How do we transition to a truly multicultural country in which no one group predominates for the very first time in our history? I think it's a very rough ride." The image and rhetoric of a conservative white Christian president in the form of George W. Bush seemed to help cushion that ride, but Barack Obama's presence in the White House offered no such sensory comfort.

Muslims make up less than 1 percent of the US population, which is perhaps why they are useful scapegoats for Americans' cultural anxiety.[33] Latinos, in contrast, have enough electoral clout to require politicians to frame the immigration debate as a problem with illegal aliens instead of a cultural issue. Conservatives seeking office also need to be careful in what they say about sexual minorities, who now have enough support in the media to strike back at homophobic politicians. Indeed, by late 2014, some media commentators were declaring an end to, or at least a shift in the tide of, the Culture Wars. "For a younger generation of voters, the old right-wing nostrums about the 'sanctity of life' and the 'sanctity of marriage' have lost their power, revealed as intrusions on human freedom," the *New York Times* wrote in an editorial.[34] Around the same time, a *Politico* commentator claimed that Republicans had lost the Culture War: "Indeed, on issue after cultural issue, Republican positions poll miserably, especially with younger voters."[35] The Muslim American population, as the scholar Saeed Khan argues, is "one of the only remaining communities in America that is the object of derision and lacks social and political capital."[36] The taking of offense against mosques, textbooks, and Muslim traditions can be seen within this wider context.

Opposition to Mosques

The Islamophobia industry's breakout performance came in 2009–10, when a local Muslim businessman decided to build a community center in Lower Manhattan. The center would include a much-needed prayer hall for the thousands of Muslims living and working in the area. Opponents of the plan labeled it the "Mosque at Ground Zero," condemning it as an affront to the memory of the 3,000 lives lost to Muslim terrorists at the World Trade Center a few blocks away. The controversy was a test for America's rule of law (which it passed) and its culture of tolerance (which emerged somewhat bruised).

For middle-of-the-road politicians, the most common response was to express support for diversity, including Muslims' freedom to worship, while also suggesting that the particular choice of location for the building may have been unwise and insensitive. The site, however, was not initially perceived as objectionable. When the Park51 project, also known as Cordoba House, was first announced, the subsequent outrage was not foreseen. "In December 2009, the Cordoba House was not seen as a scandalous project, but rather as a non-controversial, safe and legal undertaking, and furthermore as a positive initiative for relations between different religious communities," notes the political scientist Nadia Marzouki.[37] In the first article on the plan in the *New York Times*, political and religious leaders were quoted as responding positively.[38]

The cordial response was not surprising, given the actual facts of the case. The developer, Sharif el-Gamal, wanted to address a crying need for prayer space in the neighborhood. Rather than build a dedicated mosque, he conceived of it as a multipurpose community facility, open to all faiths. He drew inspiration from a Jewish community center on the Upper West Side where he had taught his children how to swim. As had been the case for so many other New Yorkers, 9/11 had been a life-changing experience for el-Gamal; he had volunteered at Ground Zero, spending two days handing out water to emergency crews and victims. The Sufi Muslim imam he appointed, Feisal Raum, was well known for his promotion of interreligious peace. Even the conservative political commentator Laura Ingraham welcomed the project when she hosted a segment on Fox News about it. Interviewing Raum's wife Daisy Khan, Ingraham said that she had not found many people who had a problem with the idea. "I like what you're trying to do," she said on air.[39]

Offense had to be manufactured, largely by hate spin agents from outside the local community. On December 21, 2009—almost two weeks after the first report in the *New York Times*—the virulently anti-Muslim blogger Pamela Geller attacked the Park51 plan. Next came Robert Spencer, director of the Jihad Watch organization and one of the sextet of leading misinformation experts identified by CAP. By May 2010, Islamophobia agents had mounted a full-blown campaign against the center. They built their opposition on a series of extreme allegations. That these allegations were almost entirely false should come as no surprise at this point: hate spin never lets the facts get in the way of righteous indignation.

The philosopher Martha Nussbaum's analysis of the controversy systematically debunks the falsehoods, which start with the name itself.[40] The "Mosque at Ground Zero" was no such thing; rather, it was planned as a community center with a Muslim prayer hall. Ground Zero is three blocks away, and not visible from the site. Even if the facility had been a mosque, it would not be a concept alien to Lower Manhattan. There was already a mosque on Warren Street nearby, and the abandoned building where the center was to be built was already being used as a temporary Muslim prayer venue. Nor did protesters apply their sensitivity about Ground Zero's sacredness consistently: a betting facility and two strip clubs, New York Dolls and Pussycat Lounge, were both located closer to the site than the planned Park51 site. And of course there was no basis in fact for the idea that the place would somehow be used to celebrate or inculcate the kind of extremist thinking behind the 9/11 attacks. Both el-Gamal and the imam he appointed "are moderates who strongly condemn radical Islam in all its forms, and they have guaranteed that such opinions will have no place in the proposed center," Nussbaum notes.[41]

None of these details could pierce through the wall of generalized prejudice promoted by members of the Islamophobia network. Some Muslims had murdered New Yorkers, so Muslims could not be treated like everyone else. On June 6, 2010, a demonstration organized by Stop Islamization of America took place in Lower Manhattan. The sponsoring organization was new, having been created by Geller and Spencer in the model of an equivalent organization in Europe. The demonstration attracted speakers with a wide variety of grievances and goals. "Opposition to the Islamic cultural center's construction became an opportunity to defend a range of causes as disparate as the rights of Copts in Egypt, the rights of Muslims to leave the faith or convert to another religion, Israel's security and the survival of Christianity in the Western world," says Marzouki.[42] With midterm elections just five months away, politicians entered the debate. Rival Republican contenders for the state governorship, Rick Lazio and Carl Paladino, engaged "in a contest of one-upmanship, continuously escalating their condemnation of the Islamic cultural center."[43] Paladino, the eventual winner of the Republican primary, promised that he would, if elected, use his powers of eminent domain to "stop this mosque and make the site a war memorial instead of a monument to those who attacked our country."[44]

In contrast, citizens entrusted with representing the local community's interests continued to support Cordoba House. On May 25, 2010, the Lower Manhattan Community Board voted in favor of the project by a large margin. Then, on July 13, the city's Landmarks Preservations Commission unanimously refused to cede to protesters' demands that the building site be given landmark status, which would have blocked the redevelopment plans. Politicians who felt no need to pander to the religious Right were equally firm in their backing. Michael Bloomberg, who had been elected to his third and final term as mayor in 2009, voiced his unequivocal support, both for religious freedom and the property rights of the site owners. The district's politically secure congressman, Democrat Jerrold Nadler, joined him. Andrew Cuomo, who was running an uncontested campaign for the Democratic governor's ticket, also spoke up for diversity and tolerance.[45]

The United States' steadfast commitment to religious freedom and property rights ensured that the legal disputes were eventually resolved in favor of Park51. Even so, however, many moderate commentators continued to point out that, even if Muslims had a legal right to practice their faith and build a mosque in the vicinity of the 9/11 site, they should have acknowledged the special sensitivities associated with the area and moved the project elsewhere. Such views—assuming they aren't rooted in prejudice themselves—smack of a tendency among multicultural-minded liberals to make excuses for the intolerant, due to their instinct to empathize with the perspectives of others. They assume good faith on the part of hate spin exponents—as if assuaging reasonable-sounding concerns about the location of Park51 would unlock opponents' hearts and allow their inner pluralists to emerge.

The Murfreesboro Mosque

It is not hard to test the theory that a mosque project would have a warmer reception if it were located a respectful distance from Ground Zero. One just needs to travel to the city of Murfreesboro, Tennessee, about eight hundred miles southwest of Manhattan. Around the same time that Park51 was being conceived, Murfreesboro's Muslims were looking to build a new mosque. They were following events in Manhattan with interest, but never expected that they would be victims of the same intolerance. "In New York, you had a reason to oppose the plan," Murfreesboro's imam, Ossama Bahloul, says. "Here, what is your reason?"[46] In hindsight, they realize that key players in the national campaign against Islam looked at Murfreesboro as a growth opportunity. Says Saleh Sbenaty, a mosque board member, "This is the buckle of the Bible Belt. They think they can continue their campaign here."[47]

Murfreesboro's Muslim community comprises about 250 families and 500 students, many of them enrolled at Middle Tennessee State University (MTSU). They used to worship at a small mosque downtown, but had outgrown it: during Friday prayers, the congregation spilled out onto the pavement and parking lot. In 2009, community leaders found, on the outskirts of town and at a reasonable price, a nondescript plot of land where they could build a larger mosque. Members of the community responded immediately to the appeal for donations—on a single Friday, they contributed $300,000, enabling the board to pay for the land in full.[48]

The first hint of trouble appeared in January 2010. On a sign erected to indicate the site of the proposed Islamic Center of Murfreesboro, someone spray-painted the words "NOT WELCOME." "We didn't think much of it, as we had no experience of Islamophobia," recalls Sbenaty, who has lived in Tennessee since the 1990s and works as an MTSU engineering professor. By the middle of 2010, however—simultaneous with the Park51 protests—the hate spin circus had come to town with its usual tricks, from legal challenges to fearmongering and personal attacks. "We were bullied, we were harassed, we had arson, we had bomb threats, we had lawsuits," says Sbenaty.

After the county's planning authority approved the site plans, opponents voiced their unhappiness at the county's board of commissioners meeting in June. In July, they marched in the hundreds to deliver a petition to the county courthouse, demanding that approval for construction be withdrawn. In September, they began their court challenges, filing a lawsuit against county officials, allegedly for violating the state's open meetings law. In May 2012, a judge ruled that officials did not give adequate notice of their meeting, which stopped construction in its tracks. Federal prosecutors came to the rescue with a discrimination lawsuit, as a result of which a federal court enabled the new mosque to open in time for the holy fasting month of Ramadan that August. Other higher courts also protected the rights of the Murfreesboro Muslims. In 2013, a state appeals court overturned the earlier judge's decision against the county's approval. The mosque's opponents tried to appeal, but the Tennessee Supreme Court declined to hear the case. The US Supreme Court decided likewise in 2014.[49]

During this time, Murfreesboro's Muslim community also had to endure more personal attacks. "They hired people to investigate us," says Ossama, the mosque's imam. He holds a PhD in comparative religion from Cairo's prestigious Al-Azhar University, engages in interfaith dialogue, and is deeply respectful of the US constitutional order. But the county's newspaper, the *Rutherford Reader*, published advertisements accusing the imam of being a Muslim Brotherhood radical. Laurie Cardoza Moore, a Nashville-based pro-Israel activist who was a spokesperson for the protesters, falsely claimed on CNN's *Anderson Cooper 360°* that Ossama's previous mosque in Texas was under investigation for terrorism-related activities. To the program's credit, reporters did some quick fact-checking, after which Cooper debunked the claim.

As in Manhattan, the 2010 midterm primaries figured into the campaign. Tennessee lieutenant-governor Ron Ramsey, gunning for the Republican nomination for the gubernatorial elections, was among those promoting anti-Muslim views in the midst of the Murfreesboro debate. Lou Ann Zelenik, a Tea Party Republican vying for a seat in Congress, was another. In 2010, and even more shrilly in 2012, Zelenik tried to use her rabid opposition to the mosque to distinguish herself from her conservative rival in the Republican primaries.[50] Her anti-Islam stance drew the support of a sympathetic multimillionaire backer.[51] Whether or not the issue itself was a vote winner in its own right, is unclear—neither Ramsey nor Zelenik succeeded in their bids—but Islamophobia certainly earned the candidates media attention and raised their profiles. "They know we are a small community and it is difficult for us to defend ourselves," Ossama says.

"There is some kind of injustice about allowing some group to say whatever they want to say," Sbenaty muses. "Is it freedom of expression to intentionally hurt and intimidate? They just throw mud, and even if it doesn't stick, it leaves a mark." Despite these misgivings about the American marketplace of ideas, the mosque leaders were convinced that the best policy was to remain accessible and engaged. They threw open all meetings, allowing critics to drop by without prior notice and observe their practices. "We assured individuals that our door is always open, and that we will stand with you against radicals," says Sbenaty. When they received specific allegations, they invited law enforcement agencies to investigate.

Their trust in the American system was vindicated. Thanks to the US Constitution and most Americans' sense of fairness, the Muslim community of Murfreesboro ultimately won their battle to worship at a new mosque. The collateral damage from this and the Park51 disputes, however, has been significant—both incidents produced a rash of anti-Muslim propaganda, which captured media attention, energized activists, and put ideological opponents on the defensive. This may have been the hate spin agents' goal all along. "They don't care whether the mosque exists or not," notes Ossama. Their larger purpose was to exploit the controversy to communicate key Islamophobic talking points.

One such message, printed on signs in the July 2010 protest, said, "Islam is not a religion." This was a legal strategy as much as an political slogan. A house of worship was the only authorized nonresidential use of the site that the Murfreesboro Muslims had purchased. If Islam isn't a religion, a mosque isn't a house of worship, and one could not be built there. There was, of course, never any chance that the authorities would accept that argument. Judges dismissed the claim, and just in case, the federal government filed a legal brief affirming the seemingly obvious point that Islam is a religion.[52] But beyond the Murfreesboro dispute, casting doubt on Islam's status as a world religion is also part of the Islamophobia network's wider agenda. Doing so makes room for the claim that Islam is really a violent political ideology, and that discriminating against Muslims does not violate the principle of religious freedom.

Challenging Books

In late 2013, Larry Houck of ACT! for America petitioned the Alabama State Board of Education, objecting to its proposed selection of social studies textbooks. The offending volumes—published by such mainstream houses as Pearson, McGraw Hill, and Houghton Mifflin—were in keeping with the secular, multicultural approach to teaching children about other religions. The textbooks described Islam's contributions to the world and the common values that it shares with other faiths. Houck, however, alleged that these materials were examples of the "infiltration of Islamic falsehoods and deceptions into our nation's school textbooks."[53]

The intervention was neither as intimidating as the mosque dispute just up I-65 in Tennessee, nor as successful as the sharia-blocking constitutional amendment that was being drafted in Alabama. Houck's lobbying delayed, but did not alter, the school board's decision. Nevertheless, the Alabama textbook dispute is worth a closer look. It is an example of the Islamophobia network's grassroots activism, designed to turn administrative processes at the local level into opportunities to engage in hate propaganda through campaigns of righteous indignation.

ACT! for America is a single-issue citizens action network founded in 2007 by a leading Islamophobia peddler, Brigitte Gabriel. The organization aims to do with the anti-Islam cause what the National Rifle Association has done with gun rights—influence legislation and electoral contests and become a pillar of the Republican Party. As a relatively new organization, it was able to borrow from the religious Right's established repertoire of contention. The book challenge has long been a classic item on that repertoire. It is part of the religious Right's decades-old battle "to shape what children learn by controlling their access to books in school libraries and curricula, and the content of their textbooks," notes the progressive think tank, People For the American Way (PFAW).[54] Conservatives have tried to keep school libraries and curricula uncontaminated by books containing open-minded discussions of sexuality, race, and history, or by fiction with supernatural themes, like *Harry Potter*.[55]

The religious Right's desire to control what children read is not surprising, given its concerns about values and education. Besides, the process of selecting library books and school textbooks presents political opportunities for the manufacture of righteous indignation. These openings are highly decentralized, since education in the United States is a local matter. Book challenges thus allow the religious Right to think cosmically and act locally.

In 1982, the US Supreme Court weighed in to ensure that students' free speech rights are not shortchanged by local authorities who stray beyond their educational mandates when making decisions about library books. The court opined that the First Amendment implies a right to receive information and ideas, and "students may not be regarded as closed-circuit recipients of only that which the State chooses to communicate."[56] The justices were ruling in favor of a group of students who challenged their school board's decision to remove from the school library certain books that it considered "anti-American, anti-Christian, anti-Semitic and just plain filthy."[57] The court said that a school board wanting to remove library books should assess them solely on educational suitability.

On the other hand, local authorities cannot simply ignore the opinions of ideologically driven pressure groups. School boards and public libraries have had to establish transparent procedures for selecting materials and handling complaints. These forums and protocols allow conservatives to influence, and in some cases control, what children read in public schools and libraries. This is nowhere close to the situation in India, where groups have derived a de facto right to be offended from laws prohibiting the wounding of religious feelings. But there is enough of an opening for hate spin agents to exploit.

ACT! for America entered the textbook wars in earnest in 2011, launching a detailed guide for its activists.[58] Its report on thirty-eight commonly used textbooks alleged that they contained historical inaccuracies and theoretical misrepresentations that, together, painted too rosy a picture of Islam. "More often than not, the typical treatment of Islam amounts more to indoctrination than to education," it said.[59] In Alabama, ACT! for America was alerted to the opportunity for a textbook challenge by Eagle Forum, a more established religious Right group. Eagle Forum was founded in 1972 to counter the feminist movement and continues to champion traditional social values. It began working with the Islamophobia network in 2009 or so.[60] Houck says a member of the Eagle Forum asked him to lead a textbook challenge on the Islamic front.

After locating the titles in the local university library, Houck and half a dozen helpers worked "day and night" scouring through them. They identified sixteen books containing information about Islam that made them "very dangerous."[61] Introducing himself to the school board as a "lay expert in the study of political Islam and its brutal, barbaric, and anti-constitutional Sharia law," Houck warned of the "infiltration of Islamic falsehoods and deceptions into our nation's school textbooks."[62]

In his letter to the Alabama's State Board of Education in December 2013, Houck wrote, "Islam was spread by the sword in most every case. The Muslims have killed millions in their 1,400-year history and enslaved millions more."[63] His review of a Pearson title for eighth graders, *My World History*, said that it was "laced with lies, deception, propaganda, and indoctrination about Islam." He criticized the book for not teaching children that 7 percent of Muslim's obligatory charitable giving is used to fund holy war; that one-half of the Quran teaches Muslims to slay or subjugate nonbelievers; that sharia allows men to beat their wives; and so on.

Noting that forty-four pages were devoted to Islam and only fourteen to Christianity, Houck said that *My World History* "serves as a powerful influence to convert school children to Islam one day."[64] He later told the press that he wanted to warn Americans that there was a nonviolent jihad going on in the United States, perpetrated by influencing textbook publishers. The protesters also said that some statements in the book offended Christianity. "Jesus is presented as a man who decided to preach to people about his 'ideas.' No mention of his virgin birth or of his deity as the Son of God. This is offensive and an insult to the Holy Bible scriptures," read one review sent to school board members.[65]

Ordinarily, the State Board of Education relies on the recommendations of its twenty-three-member Textbook Selection Committee, which is made up mainly of teachers and subject-area experts. In this case, however, the board postponed its vote by a month to consider the complaints from Houck's group. In January 2014, the board approved the list by a 5–2 vote. The only one of the twelve books dropped was a title that was accidentally duplicated.

Houck was bitterly disappointed when the State Board of Education stood by the professional decisions of its educators. He called the board's dismissive treatment of his appeal a "bad joke." He felt that his research went over the members' heads—showing how much more work needs to be done to wake up Americans to the threat of Islamization.[66] Having lost the battle at the state level, the campaigners vowed to approach the state's more than 130 city and county school districts, whose committees and boards are free to omit books on the state's recommended list. At this stage, Eagle Forum activists took over.

Such pressure may affect the future decisions of publishers, school boards, and libraries that want to avoid controversy. The American Library Association has warned of this harmful side effect of persistent book challenges. "In these cases," the association says, "material may not be published at all or may not be purchased by a bookstore, library, or school district."[67]

The Islamophobia network's textbook campaign amounts to an assault on the very idea of multicultural religious education—to promote greater mutual understanding, respect, and reciprocity among different religious communities in secular, pluralist societies—as well as the role schools play in support of those efforts. Such education usually emphasizes shared values and the common ground of various belief systems, without privileging any of them. It is one of the solutions most commonly suggested for the global problem of religious conflict. Unfortunately, religious hard-liners with exclusive visions consider the multicultural approach a betrayal and a threat.

Houck was undoubtedly committed to his assigned task of removing offending textbooks from Alabama's schools. As with all hate spin, though, the campaign's mission as interpreted by a foot soldier like him may not be what its leaders really have in mind. Their hidden agenda was to cultivate Islamophobia. That objective can be achieved even if the targeted books emerge unscathed. "Organizing a protest of a textbook that they claim 'promotes jihad' may not accomplish its stated goal, but might still succeed in stoking fear and resentment against Muslim Americans in that community," PFAW says. The same is true of the next example of hate spin we'll look at. The campaign for anti-sharia laws was, on its surface, a pointless safeguard against a nonexistent threat; but it nonetheless served as an effective vehicle for anti-Muslim propaganda.

Targeting Sharia

The Islamophobia network has called sharia "the preeminent totalitarian threat of our time."[68] Its campaign against sharia is a particularly sophisticated form of hate spin, whipping up moral panics over what independent legal experts say is an imaginary threat. Ted Cruz, on the road to the US Senate in 2012, was among the politicians who lent his voice to the cause, calling sharia an "enormous problem."[69] That year, the Republican National Convention adopted the cause in its platform.[70]

The campaign's success can be measured in part by the number of states—eleven as of early 2016—that have changed their laws or constitutions to protect against sharia. The campaign's real effect may be even wider. More than twenty other states have debated the need for a legislative or constitutional ban on sharia. Although they ultimately rejected the idea, the debates themselves may have succeeded in changing the way Americans think and talk about Islam. Putting sharia on trial in legislatures and in the press mainstreams pejorative rhetoric about Muslims, and adds to the perception that the threat of Islam is real—and, of course, that the Islamophobia experts are worth funding.[71]

Oklahoma was one of the first states to legislate against sharia. State Question 755—the "Save Our State Amendment"—sought to introduce language into the state's constitution that would insulate the courts from the influence of Islamic law. The amendment would require courts to uphold and adhere to American laws, including, if necessary, the laws of other states, as long as those laws did not include sharia. "The courts shall not look to the legal precepts of other nations or cultures. Specifically, the courts shall not consider international law or Sharia Law," it read.[72] In May 2010, a resolution to put SQ 755 before the voters was adopted by the Oklahoma House of Representatives by a 91–2 vote, and in the Senate by a 41–2 margin. That November, more than 70 percent of voters supported the proposition. The wording of the amendment clearly violated the First Amendment's Establishment Clause, which prohibits discrimination among religions. The head of the Oklahoma chapter of the Council on American–Islamic Relations duly challenged the legality of SQ 755. A federal district court, followed by the federal court of appeals, agreed that the measure was unconstitutional.

The law reformers did not give up. To get around the Establishment Clause, they simply substituted the religious bias with a national one, proposing that American laws should be insulated from un-American influences. The main political entrepreneur behind this more successful anti-sharia franchise is the lawyer David Yerushalmi, a former resident of a Jewish settlement in the Israeli-occupied West Bank.[73] His work in the United States has earned him a place in CAP's rogues' gallery of "misinformation experts" in the Islamophobia network.[74] The Anti-Defamation League, the leading American Jewish civil rights organization, says Yerushalmi has "a record of anti-Muslim, anti-immigrant and anti-black bigotry."[75]

Although he has no formal training in the subject, Yerushalmi has become convinced that observing Islamic law is akin to sedition. In 2009,

Yerushalmi found a way to operationalize his paranoia. He developed a model statute to be disseminated to right-wing groups across the country. He worked closely with Frank Gaffney, who provided the connections to neoconservatives among former and serving officials, security analysts, and political activists.[76] Gaffney's Center for Security Policy has produced voluminous reports that supposedly provide justifications for the campaign. Their book, *Shariah: The Threat to America* (downloadable for free at shariahthethreat.com), likens US government policy toward Islam to 1970s-era détente with the Soviet Union, a policy they consider equally misguided. The report rejected "the policies of coexistence, accommodation, and submission," which it believed underestimated the Islamic threat as being confined to violent extremism. The enemy, it clarifies, is "not just al Qaeda, but also a significant percentage of the hundreds of millions of Muslims who are dedicated to the imposition of shariah on us by violence or by stealth."[77] Yerushalmi's response to this imaginary threat, the "American Laws for American Courts" template legislation, does not explicitly mention sharia, but its preamble and supporting literature makes clear that sharia is its main obsession.[78] In 2011–2012, Arizona, Kansas, Louisiana, and Tennessee passed bills with language credited to Yerushalmi.[79]

Meanwhile, in Alabama, Eric Johnston took up the cause. Since the 1980s, he had been working on countering what he saw as the loss of religiosity and Judeo-Christian influence in the United States.[80] A large framed copy of the Bill of Rights hangs alongside biblical verses and portraits of Ronald Reagan in his law office in a business park on the outskirts of Birmingham. In 2015, Johnston would be actively involved in Alabama's legislative campaign to resist the US Supreme Court's historic ruling on gay marriage. In 2014, however, his main triumph was the adoption of Amendment One to the state's constitution. Johnston had offered his services to legislators after witnessing Republican senator Gerald Allen fail to pass an anti-sharia bill in 2011.[81] Modeled on the Oklahoma law, Allen's bill never progressed because of the specific mention of sharia. In response, Johnston drafted a constitutional amendment that would "prohibit the application of foreign law in violation of rights guaranteed natural citizens by the United States and Alabama Constitutions."[82] In 2013, pressed for time at the end of a late-night session, the Alabama legislature approved with no debate a ballot measure that would enable the electorate to vote on the amendment.[83] An overwhelming majority of voters passed the resolution when it was placed on the ballot in the November 2014 midterm elections, with more than 72 percent voting yes.[84]

Alabama's small Muslim community felt powerless in the face of this tide of Islamophobia. Ashfaq Taufique, the president of the Birmingham Islamic Society, gave several interviews trying to explain that sharia posed no threat to Alabamans. His outreach was nothing new. The society's centers had for years thrown open its doors to visitors and worked regularly on interfaith community projects. Within these more progressive circles, Muslims, Christians, and Jews participate in one another's functions and forums. Like the Muslims in Murfreesboro, Tennessee, those in Birmingham, Alabama, had been accepted by their neighbors and made to feel at ease in their surroundings, even after 9/11. This made the anti-sharia legislation all the more of a shock. To Ashfaq, who had emigrated from Pakistan two decades earlier, the dynamics are reminiscent of geopolitics in South Asia. Just as Pakistan and India use each other as bogeymen, Islam is the "other" in American political culture, it seems to him.[85]

Muslim Americans were not alone in trying to resist the wave of anti-sharia legislative activity. Many other individuals and organizations recognized it for what it was—"a thinly concealed attempt to inflame anti-Muslim attitudes," in the words of a report by New York University's Brennan Center for Justice.[86] Both religious and legal experts pointed out that sharia was a nonexistent threat. There is no evidence of US courts being seduced by real or imagined sharia, or of any Muslim group attempting to introduce it. Proponents of anti-sharia laws have not cited a single case in which the US justice system has resolved a dispute by relying on Islamic law. There is no danger of the country's freedoms being corrupted by contact with foreign legal systems. American courts have well-established and uncontroversial rules governing how they cite laws from abroad, experts note.[87]

The American Bar Association (ABA) felt concerned enough to adopt a resolution against "blanket prohibitions" that stopped courts from using foreign or international law, or the "entire body of law or doctrine of a particular religion."[88] The ABA argued that while it might be proper to regulate specific practices of a particular religion, "initiatives that target an entire religion or stigmatize an entire religious community, such as those explicitly aimed at 'Sharia law,' are inconsistent with some of the core principles and ideals of American jurisprudence." The ABA cited the example of Mormonism: "Thus, while the Supreme Court upheld the conviction of a Mormon on a polygamy charge in 1898 (at a time when polygamy was an accepted tenet of Mormonism), the law in question did not embody a broader 'anti-Mormon' legislative initiative, but rather one aimed at specified conduct that was deemed socially harmful."[89]

Christian groups are among those who have spoken up against the anti-sharia hysteria. The most notable voice was Randy Brinson, the head of the conservative Christian Coalition of Alabama and a prominent Republican. He felt the initiative sent the wrong message about Alabama. "Other cultures would see us as bigoted and unsympathetic to their cultures," he told me later.[90] The amendment's proponents were exploiting people's fears and built-in biases, he said. Although committed to the cause of shoring up the country's traditional Christian values, Brinson could see that the existing legal system could take care of itself without anti-sharia legislation. "We don't need it any more than we need a constitutional amendment to hunt and fish," he said. Appearing on the *Daily Show*'s segment lampooning Amendment One, Brinson pointed out that even Christianity could be adversely affected by such laws, since Jesus and the Bible were foreign imports.

Eric Johnston is unmoved by such criticisms. His amendment, he says, did not introduce any substantive new rights or restrictions. It merely gives "guidance" that, while not necessary now, could be required in the future, as the US Muslim population grows. Judges needed a warning not to be swayed by lawyers who might use religious arguments when representing Muslim clients, he says. Although he claims that there exists a "a compendium of several hundred" such cases, he states that the amendment is mainly a "prophylactic" in anticipation of a looming problem. "The unique aspect of sharia law compared to, say, Protestantism or Catholicism or Judaism, is that there is a political and legal component to it. And that tends to come into conflict with the freedoms that people enjoy under the Constitution of Alabama and of the United States," Johnston says. "We live in a world now where news is immediate across the globe. And that brings us to a more homogeneous people; we become more and more alike. If we want to maintain our separate existence and our separate identity, we have to maintain our laws and protect them."[91]

Adapting to Exceptional Conditions

Before leaving the United States, we should pause to reflect on how hate spin operates in the exceptional context of the First Amendment. First, the country clearly allows a level of hate speech that would be subject to criminal sanction or at least civil defamation suits in other democracies. In recent years, some politicians have called Muslims "enemies of America," likened them to Nazis, suggested that they be removed from the US military and denied their freedom of speech, and asked for mosques to be banned or burned down.[92] Commentators and legal analysts the world over have criticized the lack of legal protection against hate speech in the United States. From the perspective of critical race theory, First Amendment doctrine's vision of a marketplace of ideas is not sensitive enough to the structural inequalities that limit minorities' participation.

The Murfreesboro controversy shows the unfairness of that marketplace. Volunteers in a small community with no prior experience in political lobbying suddenly found themselves having to confront the well-oiled misinformation machinery of national hate groups. Although local politicians led the assault in Murfreesboro, the campaign drew supporting fire from Islamophobia salespersons fresh from the "Mosque at Ground Zero" campaign, where they had cut their teeth fighting heavyweights like New York City mayor Michael Bloomberg. "You're talking about big-name outsiders," says Saleh Sbenaty. "When the issue of Park51 quieted down, they moved their fight over here." The community had not budgeted for this kind of contingency. "We did not expect this at all."[93]

Second, though, that same First Amendment places a ceiling on how much harm hate spin can inflict on religious communities. The Establishment Clause and especially the Free Exercise Clause provide strong protections for religious minorities. Despite vocal popular opposition to mosque building, even Muslims in the Bible Belt have been able to count on the courts to protect their rights to express and practice their faith. "The Constitution was on our side," says Ossama Bahloul. Besides, Islamophobes don't represent the majority of Americans, he adds. "That's why this mosque exists."[94]

As for anti-sharia laws, overtly discriminatory versions have either been struck down by the courts or are likely to be when challenged. Alabama's Amendment One, by its architect's admission, is a piece of legislation that has no effect on the law. Book challenges are often successfully resisted by public bodies and professional associations that, informed by First Amendment doctrine, do not recognize offense as a compelling justification for censorship. What makes hate spin so pernicious, though, is that even when attempts to suppress a book, minority practice, or building project are thwarted, the claims that hate propagandists make along the way may still achieve the objective of vilifying the target community and heightening the level of fear. Over time—as Donald Trump demonstrated in the 2016 presidential race—such discourse can pollute the center of the public sphere, corroding the civic values on which American democracy is built.

Speaking in March 2015 at Selma, Alabama, Barack Obama paid tribute to the marchers who confronted racist authorities half a century earlier:

"Because of what they did, the doors of opportunity swung open not just for black folks, but for every American. Women marched through those doors. Latinos marched through those doors. Asian Americans, gay Americans, Americans with disabilities—they all came through those doors."[95] For Muslims in the United States, that history must seem bittersweet, offering both the promise of an America that grows steadily more inclusive, and the despair that, after all this time, equal dignity is not guaranteed but must still be fought for.

One of the most common ways that purveyors of hate defame an entire group is to refer to Muslims as terrorists. When Muslims object to this gross stereotype, the hatemongers—but also many liberals who are trying to be helpful—reply that peace-loving Muslims should speak up more forcefully against the murderous violence regularly perpetrated in their religion's name. They claim that Muslims need to be more visible in taking owner-ship of the problem, and that only then will others realize that the terrorists are a tiny, unrepresentative minority.

One problem with this suggestion is that even when "moderate" Mus-lims speak out, they do not necessarily get airtime for their messages of peace. In fact, Muslim groups have repeatedly denounced terrorism and the death cult of the so-called Islamic State, IS. In September 2014, more than 120 Muslim leaders and scholars from around the world issued a point-by-point rebuttal of IS claims that its ideology was based on the Quran.[1] In Britain, one hundred Sunni and Shia imams came together to produce a YouTube video decreeing IS illegitimate and not representative of Islam.[2] Such statements, though, are never the end of the matter. A religious com-munity trying to protect its identity against extremists is engaged in a battle of images and symbols in a media terrain that it does not control. It is not enough to find effective spokesmen; the spokesmen also need the mass media's cooperation. Unfortunately, a hundred respected preachers inton-ing Quranic verses of peace will not receive as much news coverage as a fringe militant beheading a Western citizen in the name of his God.

Such selective attention is sometimes willful. Fox News, in the United States, is clearly intent on portraying Muslims as silent bystanders in the fight against IS, in line with the network's larger agenda of persuading Americans that they are in the midst of a religious war. In one episode of her show, Greta Van Susteren got swept away by Fox's own misinformation and issued a challenge: "So here's my offer. I will give any Muslim leader of national or international stature the platform right here, *On the Record* [the name of her show], to condemn Islamic extremism and to make a call to arms of every Muslim leader of every mosque to do the same. Condemn Islamic extremism."[3]

The Council on American-Islamic Relations (CAIR) immediately volunteered, but was rebuffed. Two weeks later, CAIR released its own video pointing out that it had repeatedly voiced the American Muslim community's condemnation of religious extremism and terrorism. Each time, it said, its statements were sent to more than 170 Fox News email addresses. "Time after time, we hear Fox hosts and commentators calling for Muslim leaders to speak out, asking where the Muslim condemnations of terrorism and religious extremism are," said CAIR's national executive director Nihad Awad. "That's a good question. Where are those condemnations? The answer? Those condemnations are in the in-boxes of Fox staffers."[4]

This exchange raises themes that are central to the concerns of this chapter. How a society responds to hate spin depends on not only its laws, but also its social norms—in particular, whether people consider bigotry to be socially acceptable or something to fight against, how comfortable they are with ideas and beliefs that are different, and whether their sense of national belonging is based on inclusive democratic values or an exclusive cultural identity. For example, the ineffectualness of Islamist parties in Indonesia compared with, say, Egypt, cannot be explained without some reference to the moderating influence of Indonesia's two Muslim mass organizations. Similarly, despite far stricter laws in India, hate speech is more routine in its general elections than in US presidential campaigns, where prevailing social norms of civility and tolerance ensured a strong mainstream reaction against Donald Trump's anti-Muslim rhetoric, even from within his own party. India itself is not without its own resistance to hate spin. In 2014, Hindu hard-liners agitated against a Bollywood comedy, *PK*, whose main message parallels this book—that entrepreneurial middlemen are exploiting people's religious needs for their own gain. Taking offense at the film's satirical depictions of Hindu idolatry, the protesters demanded a ban, organized a boycott, and vandalized cinemas. Cinemagoers ignored them and made *PK* the highest grossing film in Indian movie history.[5]

In this chapter I examine the role of nonstate actors in shaping societies' responses to hate spin. Along with government and the law, these players— secular and religious civil society groups, news organizations, and social media platforms, for example—are essential parts of any effort to build democracies that are respectful of religious differences. But, like state policy, media and civil society organizations are also often part of the problem, facilitating, encouraging, or even generating hate spin.

The Mixed Media Landscape

Hate spin episodes are almost always media events—spectacles designed for performance through news media. How they actually play out depends partly on decisions made by the media. Editors exercise a gatekeeping function that involves determining which ideas and interests should enter the public sphere from the cacophony of voices vying for admission.[6] Journalists also have an exposure or watchdog role. They can try to reveal what the public should know, but elites prefer to keep covered up. Watchdog journalism is in a position to expose hate spin's double deception: the untruths contained in its propaganda and the hidden, self-serving motives behind it.

Societies' dependence on professional journalists and news organizations to fulfill these roles has been reduced significantly by the Internet, which allows anyone to speak directly to the public. Even so, the death of gatekeeping at the hands of the World Wide Web—like the death of journalism itself—has been grossly exaggerated. In many societies, print and broadcast news media still have greater reach than the Internet. Even in countries where most people consume their media online, audiences tend to gravitate to incumbent news organizations' Internet platforms, where traditional journalistic judgments still apply, more or less. As the social theorist Manuel Castells notes, "Most socialized communication is still processed through the mass media, and the most popular information Web sites are those of mainstream media, given the importance of branding in the source of the message."[7] A handful of elite editors can no longer silence dissonant voices, but they still have considerable say over which of those voices are considered important and worthy of more attention. The fact that anyone can get his fifteen seconds of fame on the Internet does not mean that everyone will end up equally famous. In the din, audiences still rely on media cues. Socially responsible journalism is therefore essential for "informing society about contentious societal issues in a balanced manner" and "preventing individuals from falling prey to promises of easy solutions and extremist rhetoric," says Frank La Rue, the former United Nations Special Rapporteur on freedom of expression.[8]

How the media choose to use this power in relation to hate spin varies greatly. The ideals of truth seeking, accuracy, and objectivity resonate among journalists around the world.[9] But beyond this broad generalization, we find great variety in how they position themselves in relation to powerful interests and pressing social problems. Based on a major international survey of journalists in eighteen countries (including Indonesia and the United States, though not India), Thomas Hanitzsch identifies four distinct characterizations of the profession's function in society. In its "populist disseminator" role, journalism focuses on trying to attract a broad audience, taking cues from the public without trying actively to guide it. The "detached watchdog" role places more emphasis on helping audiences make informed political decisions, for which it tries to stay independent and skeptical of elites. The "critical change agent" takes the watchdog role a step further: it is more interventionist in trying to effect social change by setting the agenda and influencing public opinion. Finally, the journalist as "opportunist facilitator" partners with elites, serves as their cheerleader, and champions their causes. Hanitzsch found all four role perceptions in every country he studied, although the relative strengths varied in each. The detached watchdog norm dominates in Western democracies, while more than half of journalists in Indonesia and China identify with the opportunist facilitator perspective. On the other hand, journalists in countries undergoing major social changes, such as Indonesia and Turkey, are much more likely to see themselves in the activist, critical change agent role than their counterparts in stable Western democracies.[10]

The existence of differing interpretations of journalism's role is not inconsistent with democratic theories of the press. No single media type can serve democracy's multiple communication needs.[11] Therefore, according to such media scholars as James Curran and the late C. Edwin Baker, media systems should be judged by the diversity of the whole as much as by the quality of their individual parts.[12] A diverse media system would include different and complementary organizational forms. In the same vein, UNESCO identifies "pluralism" as one goal of media development. The agency says that countries need "viable public, private, and community media sectors" to allow for "a wide range of social, political, and cultural values, opinions, information, and interests."[13]

Privately owned commercial news organizations—journalism's main home—have historically excelled at building up the financial strength to withstand government pressure. These, however, tend to be biased toward the corporate interests of their owners and advertisers. Independent, public service broadcasters (PSBs), such as Britain's BBC, are therefore an important supplement. While financially dependent on the state, their charters can require them to provide a common space for national deliberation, ensuring that all relevant voices are heard and all interests represented, regardless of their market value. The community media sector, or, more broadly speaking, "alternative media," includes the vehicles of civil society organizations, social movements, and subcultural groups.[14] Usually small and sometimes informal and amateurish, community media are compatible with theories of radical democracy, which recognize that multiple counter-publics are needed for marginalized groups to develop "alternative styles of political behavior and alternative norms of public speech," away from the hegemonic influence of dominant interests.[15]

Anywhere in the world, therefore, we should expect to see the news media relate in multiple and contradictory ways to the elite propagators of hate and the intolerant publics they cultivate. Some media will actively combat such forces, while others passively reflect the negative trends. And some will eagerly facilitate the downward spiral, partnering with elites who advocate intolerance. Societies may need to restrict the most extreme of these media. But the more pertinent question to ask is whether bad media are being neutralized by better media, and if not, why not.

Facilitators of Hate

In the Rwandan genocide, not even the term "incitement" can capture the degree of involvement of the notorious broadcaster, RTLM: "The radio station did not incite genocide so much as organise it, notably by identifying targets, broadcasting vehicle number-plates, refuges where potential victims were hiding, and so on."[16] Thankfully, RTLM is a rare exception. It is not uncommon, however, to find activist and partisan media serving as echo chambers for hate spin agents. The *Fear, Inc.* study of the US Islamophobia network identifies several mass media outlets that amplify the fear and misinformation about Muslims being generated by a small number of anti-Islam activists.[17] Fox News heads the list, bringing its alarmist views to around 40 million Americans per month.[18] The network goes beyond leaning to the right in its opinions and interpretations. It also purveys patent falsehoods that appeal to its conservative, Christian, Republican, older demographic.[19] The result is the well-documented "Fox News effect": its regular viewers are more likely than the general public to hold erroneous beliefs about proven facts at the heart of various contested issues. Fox viewers, for instance, were more likely that members of the general public to believe false rumors about the so-called Mosque at Ground Zero project.[20] In an early 2011 survey by the Public Religion Research Institute, one-third of Fox News followers said they believed that American Muslims wanted to establish sharia in the United States, compared with less than 10 percent of respondents who most trusted public television.[21]

The satirist Stephen Colbert has captured Fox's style of news in his neol-
ogism, "truthiness"—referring to the appeal of statements that feel right
to a certain audience, even though they are not true.[22] Colbert's observa-
tion, that some people have a strong preference for "truthy" messages over
what's actually true, is supported by research into what behavioral scientists
call a "confirmation bias" or "congeniality bias."[23] Reviewing this literature,
Christopher Mooney suggests that Fox's diet of self-affirming information
appeals to viewers committed to defending their preexisting views, such
as those connected to core values that they believe to be under threat.[24]
Similar research is lacking in most other countries, but the US pattern may
be generalizable: in societies where conservatives feel that social values are
eroding fast, there may be a market demand for news media that prioritize
affirmation over accuracy. These could become ready conduits for the misinformation of hate spin.

The American Islamophobia network can also count on the Christian
Broadcasting Network, which reaches a narrower constituency but sometimes broadcasts programs with more extreme views, and to a more captive
audience. The country's most popular syndicated talk-show hosts—Rush
Limbaugh, Sean Hannity, Mike Savage, Glenn Beck, and Mark Levin—all
lace their conservative messages with doses of anti-Muslim propaganda
when convenient.[25]

In other countries, hate spin is similarly amplified by a range of ideologically sympathetic media. In Indonesia, the weekly magazine *Sabili* served as
a platform for radical Islamic writers to spout intolerant views. It was one of
the country's most popular magazines before it declined into oblivion after
2005. *Media Dakwah*, the magazine of the extreme-conservative Indonesian
Islamic Da'wa Council, has opposed secularism, portrayed liberal thinkers
as agents of the United States and Israel, and spread paranoia that Islam in
Indonesia is being overrun by Christianity.[26] Voice of al-Islam, a website set
up by a militant who had trained with violent jihadis, was a key instigator
of hate against Christian evangelical activity in Bekasi, outside Jakarta.[27]
The extremist militant group Laskar Jihad, active in the early 2000s, developed a range of media platforms—including a website, print publications
and radio programs—advocating violent jihad against Christians.[28]

Public Service Media

Democracies provide freedom for media that champion narrow causes and
interests, even those that seem shocking and destructive. The centrifugal
effect of such media needs to be counteracted by others with the mandate and the resources to serve the overarching public interest. While many

news organizations claim to adopt that mission voluntarily, the question is whether they should be subjected to external oversight. Since the dawn of radio and television, the conventional wisdom in democracies is that content regulation of free-to-air broadcasters is not incompatible with the principle of media freedom. Their use of scarce public airwaves justifies a role for such public bodies as the Federal Communications Commission in the United States and Ofcom in the United Kingdom. In this sector, therefore, it is reasonable to expect a licensing authority to withdraw or suspend broadcasting permits of stations that promote hate—even if they do not cross the legal threshold of incitement to violence and genocide.

Most Western democracies have embraced the concept of public service broadcasters. These institutions, typified by the BBC, are publicly funded but insulated from government interference. They are usually charged with the explicit responsibility to serve as trusted spaces for national conciliation and dialogue across cultural and ideological divides.[29] The Charter of the Australian Broadcasting Corporation, for example, requires its services to take account of "the multicultural character of the Australian community."[30] In line with this, its editorial standards require its programs to present "a diversity of perspectives so that, over time, no significant strand of thought or belief within the community is knowingly excluded or disproportionately represented."[31] Freed from the need to pander to either political elites or public opinion, PSBs may be better placed than commercial media to protect multiculturalism against a rising tide of intolerance.

Unfortunately, the PSB sector has been steadily weakening. Although its role as conciliator is more important than ever, the policymaking window of opportunity for establishing strong PSBs has long passed. Practically all of the world's independent PSBs were developed in liberal democracies in the first half of the twentieth century, when there was an elite consensus that the power of new radio and television technologies had to be used for the social good while at the same time remaining free from day-to-day government control. Decades later, cable, satellite, and Internet technologies ended the era of scarce bandwidth, and with it the main economic argument for a nonmarket approach in national broadcast policy. The ascendance of neoliberal ideology has further undermined the principle of strong public-sector media.

Therefore, the many countries that opened their broadcasting industries to competition from the 1990s onward did not try to establish strong PSBs. India, Russia, and Malaysia retained their government-controlled broadcasters alongside aggressively commercial channels. Indonesia and South Africa tried to turn their government broadcasters into independent PSBs as part of their democratic reforms, but the process has been slow. The Philippines, following the US example, left television almost entirely in the hands of private owners. In most countries, therefore, much of the burden of countering hate falls not on the public sector but on professional journalists working in commercial news organizations.

Blunting Journalistic Independence

Unlike public service broadcasters, commercial news media rarely have an explicit corporate mission to promote tolerance. When editors want to speak up for vulnerable minorities and expose the political machinations behind hate spin, they may find corporate interests standing in their way. In India, the tireless efforts of investigative journalists and human rights activists have accumulated damning evidence of Narendra Modi's complicity in the 2002 Gujarat pogrom. Yet, as Modi rose through the BJP ranks, India's mainstream media did not live up to its reputation for dressing down those in power. The businesses that own most of the national newspapers and television news stations came to see Modi's decisive leadership as the answer for India's economic woes. "Prior to 2009–2010, nobody ever spoke of him as a national candidate," says Siddharth Vardarajan, the former editor of the *Hindu*. "Suddenly you have Modi emerging as a person around whom the entire business community gravitates; the media also emerges as a cheerleader."[32]

The problem goes beyond the political economy of media—this is not just about greedy owners wanting to protect their pecuniary interests. Journalists and their media organizations need to build a relationship of trust with the community they serve by speaking up for it and reflecting its values and interests. They can earn a loyal base of followers when they bravely expose corrupt politicians and businessmen on the public's behalf, or when they play a leading role in a revolution or independence movement. In stories involving minority rights, however, watchdog journalism may need to direct its fiercely independent gaze toward the community that it counts as its core public. The very qualities that the public prizes when applied outward—independence and moral courage in fighting for the weak—are resented when turned inward, against the majority community itself. Yet, that is precisely what a plural democracy requires of the press when majoritarian forces threaten the human rights of religious minorities, immigrants, and other defenseless groups.

This dilemma helps to explain the somewhat muted response of Indonesia's press to violations against Ahmadiyah and Shia minorities. The news media—like politicians—are wary of being labeled anti-Islamic, which experience says they will be if they are too critical of hard-liners. *Kompas*, the country's largest newspaper, is especially allergic to this risk, as it was founded by Catholic Indonesians. Thoughtful editors the world over will privately admit that the public can be as threatening to freedom and democracy as government and business are. But this dilemma is one that rarely figures in professional or scholarly discussions about journalism and democracy, which tend to assume that majority opinion is altogether more benign than the evidence suggests. While the values of individual journalists can turn them into passionate defenders of minority rights, most are unlikely to deviate greatly from the cultures and norms of their societies. Thus, surveys in Indonesia have revealed views among journalists that mirror national attitudes: they are resistant to any nexus between religious and political power, but are sympathetic to religious arguments that justify discrimination against minority sects. While more than four-fifths of journalists surveyed did not think religious leaders should influence voting, almost two-thirds supported a ban of Ahmadiyah.[33]

In the United States—whose press has come under the microscope more than in any other country—a classic study by the sociologist Herbert Gans observed that the elite American media upheld certain enduring values, such as moderatism and a public-spirited form of democracy.[34] Such values may encourage American journalists to stand up for the rights of minorities against the intolerance of the Tea Party and other extreme voices. At the same time, Gans identified an America-first ethnocentricism as another enduring value of the press, particularly when stories have an international dimension. The succession of military encounters that the United States has had with Muslim-majority states over the past few decades must make it difficult for its journalists to think of American Muslims as just another minority group. And that's on top of the historic prejudices that Edward Said analyzed in *Orientalism* and *Covering Islam*.[35]

Ethnocentricism sometimes seeps into respected mainstream journalists' copy. In the midst of the Park51 controversy in 2010, the syndicated *New York Times* columnist Thomas Friedman penned a strong defense of the project, arguing that it was a powerful statement of the inclusion and openness that makes the United States attractive to anyone who wants to live in an inventive and creative environment. The column was reviled by the protesters—but was itself not free of the kind of biases at the heart of the controversy. Friedman took issue with the stated intention of Imam Feisal Abdul Rauf, a US citizen, to use the center to help "bridge and heal a divide" between Muslims and others. "Personally, if I had $100 million to build a mosque that promotes interfaith tolerance, I would not build it in

Manhattan. I'd build it in Saudi Arabia or Pakistan," Friedman opined. "You can study Islam at virtually any American university, but you can't even build a one-room church in Saudi Arabia."[36]

If Friedman were consistent in his moral reasoning—that global obligations take priority over the national—he would also have had to advise his colleagues at the *New York Times* to stop critiquing the dysfunctions of the United States and to focus instead on countries that are in much greater need of all the news that's fit to print. In effect, the columnist was treating the imam as a member of the Muslim world first, and as an American second (if at all). This would not be considered acceptable if applied to most other groups in the United States. Friedman thus buys into and recycles the same double standards about Muslim identity that underlie Islamophobia.

Exploiting News Judgment

Even with the best of intentions, journalists can find their work exploited by hate spin agents. Sociologists of media have observed that the news media have no choice but to routinize their operations if they wish to produce newspapers or news bulletins within tight deadlines. The standard processes often become ritualistic, nudging out critical self-reflection. The most important and universal of these routines is the exercise of news judgment—the rules of thumb that journalists all over the world use to decide what story angles are most likely to interest their mass audience. Thus, the news lens zooms in on events that have impact, contain conflict, and are unusual, current, and close by. It also helps if the names involved are already prominent, or if the story has an emotional or "human interest" aspect. These criteria for "newsworthiness" have been codified in journalism textbooks, but anthropologists suggest that they may have been hardwired in humans since preliterate times, as a quick way to survey the environment for threats and opportunities.[37] It is certainly remarkable that they transcend cultural differences between societies: when given the freedom to choose, journalists everywhere bank on these same criteria for predicting whether the public will be drawn to their stories.

The code is no secret. It has been learned and applied by the public relations industry to design promotional messages with a higher probability of being picked up as "news." This is what the trade calls "earned media"—publicity that journalists accept as newsworthy, as opposed to paid advertising or using one's own communication channels. In more economically advanced markets, public relations workers generally outnumber reporters, which means that more man-hours are devoted to crafting the messages of paying clients than deconstructing and fact-checking them for the public, as the *Guardian* journalist Nick Davies documented in *Flat Earth News*, his devastating critique of the British press.[38] This manipulation is not inherently evil. When a humanitarian crisis fails to score highly on rich countries' newsworthiness charts because it is far away and drawn out, one can hardly fault an international aid agency for engaging a Hollywood star to serve as an attention-grabbing goodwill ambassador. Similarly, a local authority that finds a creative way to generate free headlines around an otherwise boring health education campaign probably deserves kudos for efficient use of its publicity budget. Indeed, time-pressed newsrooms are usually grateful for such prefabricated media events and well-crafted hand-outs, as it saves them the trouble of searching for a newsy angle. Despite the profession's self-image as being highly skeptical of overeager sources, in practice the press has a symbiotic relationship with public relations.

Hate spin, like PR, has cracked the news code and learned how to exploit media routines. Hate propagandists design made-for-media pseudo-events that attract more press attention than they deserve. Performances of offense and offendedness are choreographed with news values in mind; they are "mediatized" public crises.[39] A large and unruly mob or extreme violence easily meets the criteria of unusualness. The prominence score can be ramped up by burning globally recognized symbols like an effigy of a US president, the American flag, or a holy book, or by denouncing a household name like Google. When covering religion, the uncritical application of news judgment results in small, extreme groups and their spokesmen earning more publicity than those who are numerically more representative of the religion. Through the distorting lens of media routines, minor players can thus attain a disproportionately large presence in the public mind.

Terry Jones, a once obscure Florida pastor, understood this logic well. In 2010, he declared an International Burn a Quran Day to coincide with the anniversary of the September 11, 2001, terror attacks on the United States. First the national media, and then international outlets, picked up the story, propelling a marginal figure with minimal influence into a global anti-Muslim icon. He did not succeed in drumming up support for his stunt—and did not himself carry it out that year, after the Obama administration counseled him against it. But then, the plan was never to reduce the number of Qurans in circulation by two hundred. It was to provoke a reaction. "We more than accomplished our goal; we never imagined we would get such media attention," he told the BBC. "Even though we did not burn the Quran, there was still a wide outbreak of violence which definitely proves our point."[40]

The Terry Jones case is one of countless examples of how sensational events—those that are unusual and sudden—are catapulted to the top of the news agenda by the ritualistic application of news values. The US media allowed this to happen despite knowing full well that Jones was a highly unrepresentative outlier in American Christianity, and that his hateful act was not going to become a trend. In such cases, journalists justify the reporting of dubious views by recourse to another deeply entrenched professional ritual—objectivity. As a sacred touchstone of many journalists, objectivity has its positive aspects. The principle urges them to stay disinterested, consider all other relevant perspectives, and build their stories on empirical evidence. In an age when the media are powerful institutions in themselves, objectivity is one of the main restraints on the abuse of that power. However, like news judgment, objectivity is often implemented as an unthinking shortcut. Without the time to assess the veracity and value of competing claims, the "objective" reporter contents himself with accurately quoting authority figures and, for balance, their prominent opponents.[41] The result is a kind of "he said, she said" stenography that fails to enlighten the audience. The ritualistic application of objectivity can result in giving undue weight to extreme points of view, regardless of their merit.[42]

Days before the proposed Quran-burning event, the Poynter Institute ethicist Kelly McBride asked if the media had erred by giving it any attention in the first place. Editors should think carefully about the harm they could cause by amplifying an act designed to fuel conflict, she argued.[43] Similarly, in his report to the UN General Assembly in 2012, Frank La Rue cited this episode as an example of the need for media to exercise more caution in their reporting on extremists.[44] That being said, it is easier to urge care than to specify what careful reporting of such events would look like. Suppressing the news altogether may not have been the wisest option, either. Had the US media blacked out Terry Jones, Muslims might have objected: it would have appeared that the American media was all too happy to highlight cases of Muslim intolerance, while trying to cover up the existence of Christian extremism. Journalists have a duty to document offensive points of view, as McBride notes: "When we ignore acts of hate, no one has the opportunity to react, to condemn them, or to proclaim a different belief system."

Mark Potok, the former investigative journalist whose work with the Southern Poverty Law Center I discuss in chapter 6, is convinced of the need to subject extremists to the glare of publicity. He notes that media adopted the opposite strategy of "quarantine" in the 1960s, against the

American Nazi Party. Jewish agencies appealed to media organizations to deny the fascists any coverage. This seemed a feasible idea back when the news was controlled by a small number of gatekeepers, but it failed even then: The Nazi Party upped the ante with more and more outrageous stunts that became harder to ignore.[45] The best answer to this dilemma, Potok is convinced, is to provide more probing—and "not stupid"—coverage of intolerant groups. Unfortunately, at a time when budgets for independent reporting have been slashed in the United States and are not necessarily growing even in booming media markets, many hate spin agents can count on news media for a free ride.

Ethical Responses

The journalistic dilemmas highlighted above are not meant to fill readers with despair. Media that are committed to social responsibility can—and do—take steps to ensure that they do not become unwitting instruments of hate spin agents. Even if they cannot solve the problem, they can at least avoid exacerbating it. At minimum, they can deny a regular platform to columnists who show signs of becoming opinion leaders for intolerant segments of society—a tendency that is particularly pronounced in Turkey, for example.[46] Most industry codes of practice and self-regulatory systems, such as independent press councils, already promote respect for diversity. Most of these recommend building diverse and representative newsrooms to help sensitize editors to the biases and blind spots that often result in unfair coverage of minority issues. They also typically caution against the use of stereotypes. The concise code of practice of the International Federation of Journalists (IFJ) devotes one of its nine points to the problem of discrimination: "The journalist shall be aware of the danger of discrimination being furthered by the media, and shall do the utmost to avoid facilitating such discrimination based on, among other things, race, sex, sexual orientation, language, religion, political or other opinions, and national or social origins."[47] Similarly, the US Society of Professional Journalists' code states that journalists should "examine their own cultural values and avoid imposing those values on others" and "avoid stereotyping by race, gender, age, religion, ethnicity, geography, sexual orientation, disability, physical appearance or social status."[48]

Professional codes also urge media to apply their standards of newsworthiness and objectivity more judiciously. The Committee of Concerned Journalists states that journalism "must keep the news comprehensive and proportional"; they should avoid "inflating events for sensation, neglecting others, stereotyping, or being disproportionately negative."[49] Both the

BBC and Reuters, accustomed to the challenges of working across cultural boundaries, instruct their journalists that fairness in coverage does not mean giving equal space for fringe groups.[50] The BBC tells its journalists to provide "due weight" instead.

Several organizations have developed guides and training programs focused specifically on covering religion.[51] They urge journalists to report intolerance in context. For example, stories should not misrepresent an extreme preacher as a spokesman for the entire community, and should take pains to include countering views from more mainstream leaders.

A more ambitious reform agenda has been promoted by advocates of "peace journalism," a movement attempting to develop the media's positive potential in conflict resolution and peace building. Peace journalism training sensitizes media professionals to their mostly unconscious use of frames—the inevitable selectivity in the detail and context they choose to include in their stories, which affects how the audience thinks about the reported event. Conflict, for example, is usually reported through a "war frame," with a focus on combatants, violence, and who's winning and losing—much like sports journalism. The recommended "peace frame" would instead highlight the ordinary and long-term victims of any armed conflict and advocate conflict resolution and reconciliation. Health reporting offers a template, as it focuses not only on reporting the battle against a particular disease, but also on educating the public about the roots of the problem and the various cures and prevention measures.[52] The peace journalism approach would help to limit the impact of hate spin by building a public resistant to messages of intolerance and division.

One salutary example of a peace journalism project comes from Ambon, Indonesia, where the persistence of deadly Muslim–Christian conflict finally persuaded newspapers representing the two different communities to try to create a common space for reconciliation.[53] Another was in Northern Ireland in the late 1990s. Previously, the nationalist, Catholic *Irish News* and the unionist, Protestant *News Letter* had reported on a highly contentious annual parade "like politicians in their forceful and colourful use of rhetoric, and in the strategic use they made of particular frames or arguments."[54] In 1997 and 1998, the newspapers took the conciliatory step of publishing joint editorials urging compromise on the conflict over the parade. The news stories within the same newspapers, however, quickly reverted to their traditional, partisan framing of the dispute, showing how resilient these habits can be. Furthermore, peace journalism may be implementable only after other elites in the society are in the mood for conflict resolution, which was the case in Ambon. Mainstream media—and, even less so, partisan media—are unlikely to blaze the trail toward reconciliation.[55]

Peace journalism can be seen as part of the "interventionist" school of journalism practice, which challenges the dominant norm of the journalist as a neutral and disinterested observer.[56] Partly for this reason, it has only a small following. Peace journalism's emphasis on downgrading the news value of conflict also limits its appeal. This does not mean, though, that members of the news media are not interested in or capable of raising their ethical standards. In the Terry Jones case, some news organizations ticked all the right boxes. For example, a lengthy Associated Press (AP) report emphasized that Jones was the leader of a small congregation and, for the most part, seen locally as "a fringe character who doesn't deserve special attention." The AP also reported that mainstream churches in the city had come out together in force with other faith groups to express their solidarity with Muslims.[57] Thomas Kent, who was at the time the editor overseeing ethical standards at the AP, says that the agency understands that hate speech poses special problems. "Conscientious journalists believe that coverage of hate speech issues shouldn't consist simply of repeating it, or quoting an equal amount of hate on the other side," he says. "Stories need to analyze what gives rise to hate speech, and to fact-check the claims of haters. Intolerant voices in a community should be balanced by tolerant voices that may exist as well."[58] Hate speech does not always need to be reported, he adds. "Our news agency believes that speech and actions designed simply to provoke and offend are not inherently worthy of coverage, and we should not be a conveyor belt for them."[59]

A 2012 IFJ report has recommended further work in developing ethical guidelines for reporting on race, migration, and religion. The study found that poor examples of media coverage tended to involve "labelling, selective use of data, generalizing incidents, negative stereotyping, giving one side of a story, using derogatory words, mixing facts and views, absence of fact checking, and miss-matching of the content of the text and headlines, images, and sound." Conversely, good coverage was built on "in-depth reporting, providing background information, explaining legal contexts, considering the impact, giving a voice to the voiceless, showing respect, raising awareness about diversity, avoiding stereotypes, taking a stand on discrimination, moving beyond the event, and minimizing harm."[60]

Clearly, journalists regularly breach their self-professed ethical principles. It is doubtful that most are even aware that the IFJ code exists, let alone know what it says about discrimination. The point, though, is that such statements generated from within the profession offer openings for conversations about the media's ethical responsibilities in dealing with intolerance.

Making journalism hate-spin-ready doesn't require reinventing the profession. It is more about a return to principled basics. Many journalists already subscribe to certain normative values that have a strong affinity with the idea of protecting minority rights against majoritarian power. For example, they think of their professional role as being "to comfort the afflicted and to afflict the comfortable." The Pulitzer Prize–winning cartoonists Gary Trudeau and Steve Sack have cited this principle to explain why they did not agree with the satire of *Charlie Hebdo* and *Jyllands-Posten*: the publications were "punching down" at disadvantaged minorities instead of "punching up," as Trudeau put it.[61]

If journalists have not done as much as they can to combat hate spin, it may be because they have failed to grasp its importance. My basic objective in this book, therefore, has been to name the problem, thus enabling us to see more clearly what we are dealing with when we encounter religious offense and offendedness. Religious rage is not a set of irrational behaviors to be described like some chemical reaction—the video that "sparked" protests, and so on—but the product of calculated moves by sophisticated political entrepreneurs whose identities, motives, and machinations are waiting to be investigated and exposed by enterprising reporters. In the same way that journalists scoff at peers who are taken in by corporate and government spin and find satisfaction in revealing unvarnished truths, they should treat the deconstruction of hate spin as a matter of professional pride.

Crowdsourced Hate Spin

When news media first started experimenting with the Internet in the late 1990s, many journalists were enamored of its potential to enable greater public participation in their enterprise. The journalism of the lecture would be replaced by the journalism of the conversation, said the online journalism pioneer Dan Gillmor.[62] The romance quickly evaporated.[63] There were conversations aplenty, but many resembled a bar near closing time more than the civilized café or salon that democrats envisioned. It turned out that many of "the people formerly known as the audience," as one popular Internet-age expression called them, felt no desire to realize the promise of a digital public sphere.[64] On news sites, many of the comments posted beneath articles were not just irrelevant but also abusive.

There is a silver lining to this development: the Internet has pushed such views out of the closet, where they can be challenged openly. But this optimistic view of the Internet as a marketplace assumes that such speech merely mirrors existing levels of intolerance in the wider society.

In fact, intolerant elements may be disproportionately vocal. "The abusive groups, which are a small fraction, are known to be hyperactive on digital platforms," says A. S. Panneerselvan, the readers' editor of the *Hindu*.[65] This imbalance can then exacerbate the problem by winning more converts. It can also result in an erosion of civility in public spaces, as it becomes more normal to express hitherto private bigotry. This is a trend Panneerselvan sees in India: "This narrow-minded element that was so far camouflaged by societal niceties is getting play through the anonymity of social media. We are talking about an ugly side that is rearing its head."[66]

Toxic speech may so pollute a forum that it becomes inhospitable for the conduct of civil discourse, resulting in more reasonable voices withdrawing from the conversation. This outcome may be the result of the well-documented process of a "spiral of silence," whereby people keep their views to themselves for fear of social exclusion by what they perceive to be a majority with an opposing view—a perception that may be wrong but is nonetheless intensified as more and more people decide to stay silent.[67] Self-exclusion may also be the result of direct harassment and personal attacks, which may grow unbearable even if it is clear that they come from a small minority.

Although a thorough accounting is impossible, the Internet—even the parts of it managed by more socially responsible news organizations—has almost certainly proved to be a net benefit for hate propagandists, since gatekeeping for online sites is usually less strict than for their print or broadcast media parents. In many settings, intolerant groups are clearly using hate speech in a deliberate and orchestrated strategy to nudge out public intellectuals and other commentators who oppose them. Such "trolling" raises the cost of participating in online debates. The wider effect is to erode the public's right to receive the full range of relevant viewpoints it needs for popular self-government—a right that is at the heart of the democratic value of freedom of expression.

Many journalists and media commentators are disappointed that the vaunted principle of democratic citizen participation, which was supposed to have been facilitated by the Internet, has come to this: name-calling and the venting of spleen. According to a study of 104 news organizations from 63 countries conducted by the news publishers association WAN-IFRA, editors were frustrated with the way comments sections were being abused by readers, but were uncertain about how to respond. Around three-quarters of sites provide guidelines, and most of these say that hate speech is not welcome. However, the study noted, "few have proactive measures to tackle it and most are not educating their readers and commenters on this issue."[68] Just as an intelligent discussion with engaged readers can enhance the image of a news brand, idiotic and extreme speech can taint it. News media, no less than individuals, are judged by the company they keep.

For these reasons, it is in the interests of the owners and editors of online forums to police civic norms voluntarily, even as they resist government censorship of offensive speech. And yet, despite the compelling arguments for a more active approach to managing online forums, hate speech continues to be allowed to seep in.

Publishers are unlikely to ban comments altogether, since increased reader engagement makes a site more attractive to advertisers. The challenge, therefore, is to exercise more editorial control over comment sections. Anonymity is believed to be a major culprit, emboldening people to share extreme and vulgar views. Many news sites now require some form of registration, not necessarily with real names. This allows administrators to lock out those with a history of posting inappropriate comments. For determined purveyors of hate speech, however, registration and moderation are merely minor inconveniences, easily dodged through multiple accounts and other tricks.

In traditional print media, editors read every letter being considered for publication in a newspaper; submissions are printed only after a positive decision—and usually some editing. According to the WAN-IFRA study, journalists know that this would be the ideal way to manage online comments as well, but their sheer volume makes this impractical. Instead of "pre-moderation"—the online jargon for editing before publication—most news organizations therefore opt for some form of post-moderation. The most passive version relies on readers to flag problematic comments, which are then assessed by an editor. The most active form involves editors reading every post soon after it appears on the site. The writer of the original article may be encouraged to post replies, to steer the conversation in constructive directions. Many news organizations do a mix of both, tracking comments more closely for stories that touch on controversial or sensitive issues. Other coping mechanisms include outsourcing comment moderation to specialized third-party companies. A few preemptively close the comments for particular articles, having learned from experience that certain topics almost never generate productive online debate.

The difficulties of moderating news media's discussion sections are just one part of a much wider problem on the Internet. Social media platforms present a separate set of problems, and their operating logic is quite different from that of the news media. As I note in chapter 3, most social media platforms prefer to see themselves as common carriers who should, on principle, exercise minimal editorial control over the content they host.

As a result, hate propagandists enjoy much more latitude on such platforms than they do on news media sites.

An evolving consensus absolves Internet intermediaries from legal responsibility for content they have not produced or modified. Digital rights activists have moreover declared that Internet intermediaries have no responsibility to proactively monitor the content posted on their sites.[69] But given the clear role of social media and online forums in proliferating shockingly antisocial speech, online hate continues to be the subject of intense research and policy debate. Researchers are investigating not only the prevalence of online hate speech, but also how hate messages are received: whether, on balance, they spread and intensify intolerance, or whether they provoke a counter-reaction that strengthens society's resolve to protect the rights of vulnerable communities. If the latter, pushing trolls underground and giving society a false sense of security could do more harm than good.

Nor do we know enough about how online hate relates to the wider ecosystem of intolerance—whether it is a key driver, or merely a symptom. While online hate is more visible than other forms of intolerance, the danger is that policymakers mistake salience for impact. There is nothing to suggest that online hate speech is more powerful than, say, an incendiary sermon at a mosque, a call to arms on Christian talk radio, or a door-to-door rumor campaign. Even hundreds of individual tweets are unlikely to be as influential as the bigoted views of a political or religious leader who is quoted uncritically in a national newspaper or news channel.

Even in the absence of hard data and formal regulations, companies responsible for online forums and platforms can't go wrong by investing more in timely post-moderation, guided by transparent standards consistent with international human rights norms. Their commitments should be followed through with conscientious implementation—for example, by hiring enough staff members who know local languages and cultures to do their jobs effectively. It is hardly acceptable for Western intermediaries doing business in non-English-speaking markets—such as Facebook in Myanmar—to claim that the language barrier prevents them from checking if their own standards are being breached.

Responses from Civil Society

The term "civil society" refers to a realm distinct from the state, the economy, and private households.[70] It comprises voluntary associations, religious organizations, cultural groups, trade unions, social movement organizations, and so on. It is similar to what public policy discourse refers to as the "people sector," as distinct from the public and private sectors. The concept of civil society has strong normative connotations. Civil society is where people build social capital and engage in intermediate forms of civic participation that fill the gaps left by formal political institutions. When society requires collective responses to address major problems, and when state action is feared to be too coercive or clumsy, civil society frequently offers the best solution. Such is the case with the issue of religious intolerance.

Of course, voluntary associations, religious institutions, and the like are also among the main generators of hate spin, and there is no guarantee that the more civic-minded segments of the people sector will win the day. Nevertheless, civil society organizations have designed some of the most creative projects to push back against hate spin and build a culture of tolerance. What follows is a sampling from around the world. The examples include responses to misogyny, racism, and other forms of hate, since the same tactics can be used against religious intolerance as well.

Hate Speech Monitoring and Early Warning Systems

While social media platforms facilitate the proliferation of hate speech, they are also more amenable to surveillance than offline discourse. A number of projects take advantage of this feature of social media by engaging in monitoring hate speech in real time. When the monitors detect worrisome spikes, responders can snap into action. Hatebase, possibly the largest of these projects, has created an online, location-based repository of hate speech that agencies can use as a predictor for regional violence.[71] Fight Against Hate focuses on the role of social media companies, monitoring how they respond to reports about hate speech. The idea is to hold them accountable for responding to breaches of their stated terms of service.[72]

Mobilizing the Middle Ground

Concern about online hate has spawned media literacy campaigns that aim to raise Internet users' awareness about the problem and encourage them to take a stand against it. The Council of Europe, for example, initiated a No Hate Speech Movement targeting youth, providing resources to be used in national campaigns.[73] In Myanmar, activist blogger Nay Phone Latt launched a "flower speech" campaign, Panzagar, that encourages Internet users to speak up against hate speech. Such efforts are based on the assumption that hate speech is the product of a small but vocal minority, whose disproportionate impact results from the silence of the broad middle ground. Many people dislike hate speech but do not know how to respond; these campaigns provide simple ways for citizens to express their support for tolerance, for instance by changing their Facebook profile photos or signing a pledge. Other campaigns urge citizens to respond in a civil but firm manner to extreme speech, including by reporting abusers to the moderators of forums and social media.

Naming and Shaming

Naming and shaming hardcore hate spin agents may not embarrass them, since they usually wear as a badge of pride that which would appear shameful in liberal eyes. Nevertheless, exposing hatemongers can pressure associated organizations to withdraw support. Women's rights groups in Britain successfully used this tactic to force Facebook to change its terms of service after activists revealed that major corporations' advertisements were appearing on pages with graphic content that demeaned women.[74] In the United States, exposés about the Islamophobia network succeeded in persuading mainstream conservative Republicans to distance themselves from anti-Muslim rhetoric. It also made some foundations and companies more wary of associating with Islamophobes. In Tennessee in 2011, several hotels refused to serve as venues for anti-Muslim events. A Nashville hotel decided to forego an $8,000 deposit in turning away the first national conference dedicated to the sharia "threat." Although news reports said the hotel based its decision on security concerns, Muslims in Tennessee believe that it was reluctant to be associated with hate speech. once it realized what the event was about.

Bureaucratization and Professionalization

Publishing houses, museums, universities, and libraries are among the main targets of manufactured offendedness. Hate spin agents exploit situations where decisions concerning cultural products are left to the discretion of managers behind closed doors. In these gray areas, decision makers can be pressured to yield to community sensitivities and engage in self-censorship. One way to make the targeted organizations more resilient to such campaigns is to subject their processes to clear and transparent guidelines and protocols, which managers on the ground can cite when assailed by complaints. This positive form of bureaucratization is exemplified by the American Library Association, which has many decades of experience dealing with book challenges. The association provides support for librarians facing complaints, including those coming from organized campaigns.[75] It urges librarians to be prepared and to follow the set procedures exactly. Its

Library Bill of Rights states, "Materials should not be proscribed or removed because of partisan or doctrinal disapproval."[76] Such broad statements of professional principle are accompanied by detailed guidelines, not just on how to interpret librarians' responsibilities, but also on formal procedures for dealing with complaints and tips on communicating the library's policies. "Talk about freedom of choice, the library's role in serving all people, and the responsibility of parents to supervise their own children's library use," it advises.[77]

Crowding Out Hate Speech

When the controversial anti-immigrant Dutch parliamentarian Geert Wilders announced his plans to release a film about Islam called *Fitna*, there was no doubt it would be hateful and inflammatory. A large counter-campaign sprang into action, uploading hundreds of homemade videos to YouTube, each tagged "fitna" and "wilders." The effect of this flood of videos was similar to jamming a radio station: at the peak of the controversy, it became more difficult to locate Wilders' actual film through popular search engines upon its release in late March 2008. The Amsterdam-based multimedia company behind the effort urged Dutch citizens to "compete for attention" and express how they felt about intolerance. "Just to let the world (and ourselves) know that allowing confused people to speak does not mean that we agree with what they say. ... Let's smother this Wilders in our apologies. If we work hard enough, no one will be able to find his crap among all the noise we produce."[78]

Hate Spin Deflation

Since power is at least in part a matter of perception, it may be possible to deflate hate propaganda by mocking it. Many anti-hate campaigns bank on this hunch, appropriating the hateful expression, lacing it with a large dose of (usually dark) humor, and flinging it back at the source. One example comes from India in 2009. Members of an ultraconservative Hindu group attacked young women who were drinking in a pub; their leader then threatened action against unmarried couples found dating on Valentine's Day. Outraged liberals set up the Consortium of Pub-Going, Loose, and Forward Women, and then launched a "pink chaddi" campaign: women were urged to mail the Hindu leader pink underwear.[79] Twitter hashtag campaigns that crowd-source ironic ripostes against prejudice fall into the same category. These include #MuslimRage, which emerged in response to a *Newsweek* cover story with that title. An example: "Lost your kid Jihad at the airport. Can't yell for him. #MuslimRage."[80]

Muckraking

Muckraking was an early twentieth-century American press tradition, in which journalists dug up scandals as part of their efforts to fight for progressive reforms. Anti-hate groups with the resources for sustained investigation, such as the Southern Poverty Law Center, have employed the method to discredit vocal proponents of hate speech. Alongside more conventional tactics, SPLC probes hate groups and their leaders in search of cracks that can be exploited to create internal discord. Its successes have included exposing the leader of an anti-Semitic group as having been born a Jew. Revealing that a white supremacist leader had a black girlfriend—or, even better, a black boyfriend—is the kind of scandalous exposé that can trigger a group's disintegration, says Mark Potok.[81] Such intrusions into opponents' private lives may seem distasteful. Perhaps, though, they are legitimate when used against individuals who attack the racial, religious, sexual, and other cherished identities of fellow citizens, and who claim superiority on the basis of supposed cultural purity.

Denial of Status

Most hate spin campaigners crave respectability—a resource that can be denied them even as they continue to enjoy formal democratic freedoms. When the German anti-immigrant group Pegida (Patriotic Europeans Against the Islamisation of the Occident) drew 17,000 people to a Christmas concert outside Dresden's Semper Opera House in December 2014, the building's management turned off the lights to silently signal its disapproval. The event went on, but Pegida was denied the picturesque backdrop of a major city landmark. Dresden's massive Volkswagen factory also went dark. This tactic has followed Pegida's outdoor demonstrations across Germany.[82] In Cologne, church authorities denounced the Pegida marches as un-Christian and turned off the floodlights illuminating the exterior of Cologne Cathedral, Germany's most visited landmark. Authorities did the same at the Brandenburg Gate in Berlin. Opponents of Pegida, understanding that hate groups' freedom of expression does not include a right to unlimited photo opportunities, have thus been able to prevent the group from basking in the reflected glory of Germany's most iconic architecture.

These and other civil society tactics help cultivate norms of respect and civility in the public sphere, not necessarily by extinguishing intolerant expression, but by pushing it out into the fringes. These types of actions cannot, of course, substitute for strong laws. They also have a tendency to preach to the choir. A provocative campaign like the pink chaddi movement is intended mainly as a show of solidarity to steel the spine of urban liberals, with the added benefit of demonstrating that intolerant voices do not speak for all. The anti-*Fitna* campaign was, similarly, an assertion of liberal citizenship.[83] These efforts, while a necessary part of a broader strategy against hate spin, are probably unable to influence the conservative ground, let alone hard-liners. Far more effective would be anti-hate efforts that come from religious communities that speak the hard-liners' own language.

A Role for Faith-Based Groups

Most of the efforts to monitor and resist hate propaganda are led by either secular-liberal groups or organizations representing religious minorities. Such groups, however, are unlikely to have much influence over hate groups' core audience—their conservatively inclined coreligionists. Typically, such constituencies already feel that their country is becoming too secular and liberal, and that their religion's status is being threatened. To them, activists representing secular interests or other religions are symbols of what's going wrong, not people with helpful solutions. They are more likely to listen to faith-based groups from within the same religious community.

This may be the main factor that explains why India's Hindu Right has had more success in pushing the country down the path of exclusionary, intolerant politics than has the Christian Right in the United States or the Muslim Right in Indonesia. Although most of the individuals resisting the Hindutva movement are themselves Hindu, and while many Hindu organizations are not part of the Sangh Parivar, India lacks a national, Hindu-based movement that can counter Sangh Parivar's mobilizational power. This means that Sangh Parivar has been able to present itself as the only vehicle capable of articulating, channeling, and realizing the desires of millions of Hindus who want to take their religious identity more seriously.

The situation in Indonesia is strikingly different. Absolutist Muslim groups preaching exclusivity and intolerance do not dominate, let alone monopolize, the Muslim public sphere. Like Indian Hinduism, Indonesian Islam doesn't only have diverse scholarly influences, but also multiple organizational vehicles. As a result, Indonesian Muslims' bubbling religiosity has flowed in different directions, including toward an enthusiastic embrace of democratic values. Absolutist groups have not been able to speak to and for Muslims more compellingly than the mainstream Nahdlatul Ulama and Muhammadiyah mass movements.

In the United States, similarly, Christian and Jewish organizations have come out strongly against their coreligionists in the Islamophobia industry. Predictably, the most outspoken can be found among the more liberal groups, which have a history of interfaith cooperation and support of human rights. One example is the National Religious Campaign Against Torture (NRCAT), an interfaith coalition established after the Abu Ghraib prison abuse scandal. In 2010, NRCAT joined with other denominational and faith groups to start a national campaign called Shoulder-to-Shoulder, with the specific mission of fighting anti-Muslim bigotry. Tara Morrow, a director of NRCAT and a candidate for ordination in the United Methodist Church, notes the entry of conservative Christians into this space as a promising sign.[84] For example, the New Evangelical Partnership for the Common Good, a splinter group from the religious Right, has adopted Christian–Muslim dialogue as a key part of its agenda.[85]

The pushback against Islamophobia recently achieved a breakthrough in Alabama, when the president of the Christian Coalition of Alabama (CCA), Randy Brinson, emerged as a vocal critic of the anti-sharia ballot measure. Although the state passed Amendment One, he succeeded in inserting an alternative message within conservative discourses.[86] Brinson, a gastroenterologist by profession, has impeccable religious Right credentials. His CCA is one of the state's largest evangelical networks. He also heads Redeem the Vote, a nonprofit he founded to engage young people of faith in the political process. His involvement in the anti-sharia campaign illustrates one of the key points of this book, that religious conviction as such does not determine one's position on the spectrum between pluralism and intolerance. Despite his obvious addiction to politics, Brinson has neither run for office himself nor committed his support to any one politician. He says he prefers to be guided by conscience, and he is contemptuous of elected officials who speak for the religious Right but act in support of tobacco, alcohol, and casino lobbies, contrary to Christian values. "I want to be known as a fair arbiter of the truth," he says of his criticism of the anti-sharia law. "We have to show the true spirit of what makes America great."[87]

NRCAT's Morrow notes that the Christian organizations that counter Islamophobic campaigns do so for a variety of reasons. NRCAT approaches the issue from a human rights perspective. "We're firmly against anything that is at heart anti-Muslim," she says. Other groups come on board because they are uneasy about the potential impact of Islamophobia on their own religious freedom. This argument has been made in conservative media. "If you value your own religious freedom, it is prudent to defend the other guy's religious freedom when it comes under attack," wrote the Princeton law professor Robert P. George, a former chairman of the US Commission on International Religious Freedom. "A precedent established by people in, say, Murfreesboro, Tennessee, who despise Islam and see it as a pernicious force, may prove very handy to people in, say, San Francisco who have a similar attitude toward Catholicism."[88] Writing in the *National Review*, Matthew Schmitz similarly argued that it would be a "great political miscalculation" if conservatives boarded the anti-sharia bandwagon, as it would weaken their position when fighting challenges to their religious liberty. "Anti-Muslim bigots and their public apologists must be vigorously opposed by Americans who recognize the value of a religious voice in the public square and the imperative that all Americans be treated equally under the law, whether they are religious or irreligious, Christian, Muslim, or Jew," he said.[89]

These viewpoints suggest that a broad-based commitment to inclusion and equality may be one of the most effective ways to counter the exclusionary effects of religious hate spin. When the state is prohibited from discriminating among beliefs—which is the effect of the US First Amendment's Establishment Clause—it follows that the line drawn for one religion will be the line for all. Then, it becomes in each religious community's enlightened self-interest to oppose bigotry and defend the rights of all religious groups. Religious conservatives may be personally convinced that theirs is the only path to God, and that others are in the grip of Satan. They are unlikely to deny nonbelievers the right to practice and express their religion, though, since this could mean losing their own. Thus, the unwavering constitutional protection of religious freedom and equality can turn even doctrinaire groups within the majority faith into stakeholders in the rights of minorities to live free of discrimination, hostility, and violence. This is a theme that I pick up in the next, and final, chapter.

Democracies are meant to be self-correcting. By subjecting leaders to constant competitive pressures and allowing citizens to debate and organize around alternatives, democracies are supposed to have a built-in propensity for nonviolent, creative destruction, allowing them to learn from mistakes, adapt, rebuild, and stay stable. If the theory holds, there is reason to hope that the forces of intolerance will not prevail. Good sense will push nations back from the brink of a downward spiral that would otherwise culminate in widespread interreligious violence. Perhaps what Amartya Sen said of famines is also true of genocides: they don't happen in democracies, because massive, murderous injustice can only be sustained in countries where information does not flow freely and where the powerful are not held accountable.

Each of the three mega-democracies discussed in this book offers some reassuring signs of self-correction. In India in 2015, the BJP decisively lost important local elections in Delhi and the state of Bihar. It turns out that Narendra Modi's Hindu nationalist agenda is constrained by tensions within the Sangh Parivar, the countervailing power of the Indian federation's regional parties, and, above all, the challenges of actually delivering on electoral promises and satisfying most of the people most of the time. Indonesia's much younger democracy has also proved to be more resilient than many feared. Voters have repeatedly rejected the Islamist political parties that pose the greatest threat to Indonesia's secular, multireligious system. Joko Widodo's victory in the 2014 presidential election, after staring down hard-line Muslim groups, also demonstrated the limits to the radicals' influence. In the United States, politicians' anti-Muslim rhetoric and other overt displays of bigotry appeal to some groups, but they are usually rebuffed by the majority of citizens.[1]

Even when voters ultimately opt for moderate leaders, however, there is more to a democracy's health than electoral outcomes. We should also consider "democratic quality"—a set of factors that would include a supportive political culture that values "participation and the equal worth and dignity of all citizens," which implies "tolerance of political and social differences, and thus acceptance by groups and individuals that others (including weaker parties and one's adversaries) also have equal rights under law."[2] In each of the three countries studied, sustained campaigns of hate spin have degraded such dimensions of democratic quality. Exclusionary ways of talking about targeted minorities have become normalized in mainstream political discourse, threatening minorities' status as citizens with equal rights to participate in the country's democratic life. In extreme cases—such as the displaced victims of religious violence in India and Indonesia—some citizens have been effectively disenfranchised. For a Christian congregation in Bekasi denied their constitutional right to build a church, or Ahmadis driven out of their homes, there is scant comfort in knowing that the religious extremism victimizing them has not been able to win power at elections.

I would nonetheless argue that faith in democratic systems is justified—but only as long as citizens and states appreciate that achieving prosocial outcomes through democracy is a process that requires ongoing and active commitment. It is not an ontological given. Some of the most formidable opponents of pluralistic democracy profess a deep faith in God, but any political gains they've made stem from an equally strong conviction that God helps those who help themselves. Democrats need to demonstrate a similar combination of trust in theory and appetite for action. They must muster legal, political, social, and cultural resources to do battle with hate spin. In the previous chapter, I dealt with the roles that media and civil society can play in establishing an environment resistant to hate spin. In this chapter I examine the role of the state.

No single type of intervention is sufficient; each has its strengths and weaknesses. Legal solutions appear to promise certainty, but the required democratic checks and balances often mean that they are slow, costly, and cumbersome. If those checks are bypassed, we end up with abuses far worse than the problems that the interventions were meant to address. Social and political responses—by civil society, media, and other influencers—work through voluntary cooperation, moral suasion, and the power of example. They are more flexible and responsive than the law, but are also easier to for purveyors of hate spin to ignore. Legal responses are necessary when there is no room for noncompliance. For example, every citizen, without exception, has the right to be protected against violent hate crimes; incitement to such serious harms calls for a zero tolerance policy. In contrast, a policy goal of maintaining a general tenor of civility and respect for religions does not require extinguishing every instance of vilification. Nonlegal approaches could do the job.

In strategizing responses to hate spin, we also need a mix of upstream and downstream interventions. Upstream policies are preventive measures that try to deal with hate closer to its source, before it swells into an unmanageable flood. But this is a speculative exercise, since most vilification just evaporates if left alone. Upstream actions carry a risk of overkill, unnecessarily stifling provocative speech that may have social value. Downstream interventions are those that wait until harmful effects are already evident or imminent. These reactive moves are less likely to cause collateral damage. On the other hand, they may arrive too late, perhaps succeeding in averting immediate violence but failing to prevent a long-term poisoning of the culture by hateful speech.

In this book I have stressed the distinction between the two sides of hate spin, namely incitement and indignation, or the giving and taking of offense. When the law attempts to salve righteous indignation, it plays into the hands of hate spin agents and encourages a culture of intolerance. Instead of trying to prohibit religious offense or insult, better to nudge it into the fringe without resorting to the force of law. In contrast, democracies must prohibit incitement to hatred, sacrificing freedom of expression when it is abused to bring about discrimination or violence against vulnerable minorities. I'll argue, though, that laws against incitement, while necessary, are not really up to the task. We'll make more headway if we invest in antidiscrimination and equality-enhancing policies, and require states to protect the basic security and other substantive rights of vulnerable groups. These conclusions are based on this book's ground-level studies of religious hate spin at work. I start by synthesizing what we've learned about a political strategy too often mistaken as visceral and irrational.

How Hate Spin Works

The study of unruly politics underwent a paradigm shift when pioneering social movement scholars dragged it from the domain of abnormal psychology some forty years ago. Nonroutine forms of collective action became more intelligible when they were no longer dismissed as symptoms of unbalanced minds.[3] The same goes for the subject of this book. Explosions of righteous indignation and incitement are more than the hysteria of mad mullahs and enraged mobs. When we start treating hate spin as the work of political entrepreneurs, we realize that we are dealing with a sophisticated form of contention—one that is strategic, versatile, and networked.

Strategic Intent

The ostensible goal of hate spin campaigns is to purify society by, say, removing an offending film from the Internet or a heretical sect from a district. Go deeper, and we find that hate spin agents have more strategic, and usually unstated, objectives. They can get mileage from the process of offense-taking regardless of whether the protest's stated short-term goals are achieved. This was observed decades ago, in studies of American movements pushing for bans on alcohol and pornography. The activists were not particularly concerned with either enforcement or compliance, as their goals were more symbolic—to declare their values and get local and national leaders to acknowledge those values at a time of great social change.[4] Similarly, in the contemporary democracies I've featured in this book, the strategic intent of hate spin agents may be to exercise agency more than to excise offense. Thus, hate spin agents' purification goals are never absolute. Agitators turned a blind eye to the various channels through which the object of their outrage—*The Satanic Verses* book or the *Innocence of Muslims* video, for example—could still be accessed in their societies after they triumphantly secured a ban. Furthermore, for every book, film, or event declared to be an intolerable affront, it is not difficult to identify several other violations that are equally qualified for the metaphorical or literal pyre, but are simply ignored.

This strategic aspect of hate spin also explains why its agents are willing to whip up controversies that are bound to increase the visibility of the offending materials—conduct that does not square with their stated goals of shielding their prophets and icons from sacrilegious assault, or their communities from the corrupting exposure to impure ideas. Indeed, popular cultural products are often the targets precisely because their publicity vehicles are easy to hijack. Publishers and producers invest heavily in launch publicity, absorbing much of the outreach cost of a well-timed protest. "Such forms of 'censorship'—calling for the withdrawal of this or that film, book, or newspaper article—are obviously not just silencing tactics; rather they rely, for their political efficacy, on harnessing and mobilizing the public energy of the very artifacts that they appear to be trying to suppress," one study of Indian censorship concludes.[5]

Of course, incitement to genocide is something more than symbolic: Nazi Germany didn't exterminate Jews on an industrial scale just to get attention. Today, the resurgence of anti-Semitic hate speech and violence in

Europe is raising the specter of past horrors. One notorious Danish imam, Abu Bilal Ismail, implored Allah to "destroy the Zionist Jews" in a sermon in a Berlin Mosque: "Count them and kill them to the very last one. Don't spare a single one of them."[6] Hungary's right-wing party, Jobbik, has called on the government to compile a list of Jews who pose a national security threat—a statement that the Simon Wiesenthal Center said had echoes of the "genocidal Nazi regime."[7] The continent's tiny Jewish population has been the target of violent hate crimes, prompting many to emigrate.[8] But despite extreme rhetoric that invites comparisons to the Holocaust, the new anti-Semitism is not really directed at emptying Europe of its Jews. The liberal Israeli paper *Haaretz*, in a series of articles on the future of European Jews, distinguishes recent incidents from the terrors faced by the community in the past.[9] Anti-Semitism in today's Europe seems to be just one convenient and tangential outlet for the extreme populist politics of both radical Muslim migrant organizations and far-right nationalists. As with offense-taking, hate speech directed at Jews today contains a large symbolic element.

The same is true of anti-Muslim hate in Europe, which has been used to unify right-wing groups.[10] And in Indonesia, Muslim radicals' attack on Ahmadiyah betrays a similar symbolic intent. As much as Ahmadiyah is reviled and persecuted, the sect serves a political need because of "the centrality of such targets to the very identity of fundamentalist groups," notes Mary McCoy, a scholar of rhetoric.[11] This explains the insatiable need for a group like Indonesia's Islamic Defenders Front to find people and behaviors to condemn. These groups would be at a loss for words to define themselves if they actually succeeded in eliminating offense. It is as if, to paraphrase Voltaire, if ungodliness didn't exist, it would be necessary to invent it.

"If you want to be a hero, you need a villain," is how the educator Asifkhan Pathan explains anti-Muslim hate in India. "If you want to be a superhero, you need a supervillain. Muslims are not villains but that is the fear that is created."[12] A Muslim who runs a school in the ghetto of Juhapara in Ahmedabad, Pathan witnessed the 2002 Gujarat massacre, which he calls genocide. Nowadays, he has to cope with the challenges of what resembles a state of apartheid, where the school he runs is denied piped water and other municipal services. When he hears the BJP talk of a Hindu *rashtra*, or nation, he knows that some radicals will follow through with killings, forced conversions, and flagrant discriminatory acts. But he also knows that the BJP needs the Muslim bogeyman, for there is no better way to unite Hindus of different sects and castes behind the party. "It is not about religion. If they cannot create a threat among Hindus, they cannot get voted in, and if they don't get voted in, they won't get money and power."

To say that hate spin agents' short-term tactics—censorship or persecution—don't necessarily lead to a Final Solution is not to suggest that we take them any less seriously. The point, rather, is to be conscious of the actual war being waged. A group may achieve its political objectives even if it fails to incite actual violence. For a hate group, the final outcome of a court battle may be less important than the opportunity the legal process offers to harass and malign its victims. Hate spin is, in that sense, verdict-proof. A Supreme Court may uphold a community's right to build a place of worship or a publisher's right to distribute a thousand copies of a scholarly book, but if the hearings provide a national forum for bigotry, the hate spin agent's strategic objective would have been achieved. Similarly, anti-sharia bills don't need to affect a state's legal framework to serve their intended purpose. "A shift in cultural consciousness and discourse is as much a goal of the Islamophobia movement as is its legislative gains," notes the sociologist Haj Yazdiha.[13]

The US Islamophobia network has turned such "lawfare" into an art form. The campaign by the American Freedom Defense Initiative (AFDI) to buy space for anti-Muslim advertisements on buses and in subway stations is, at one level, aimed at disseminating the hate messages contained in the posters. The main objective, though, is to invite a ban from the transport authorities and trigger court proceedings with far greater publicity potential than the ads themselves.[14] Sometimes, the authorities seem to get the upper hand, as when the Washington, DC, Metro decided to ban all issue-oriented ads so that it wouldn't be found guilty of viewpoint discrimination. But this decision was spun to the activists' strategic advantage. It allowed AFDI's Pamela Geller to draw a connection between the Metro ban and her other misinformation campaigns: "This is sharia in America," she declared.[15]

Versatile Methods

Hate spin agents choose from among a range of offense-giving and offense-taking tactics. Whether they use outright hate speech in electoral politics seems to depend more on prevailing social norms than on laws prohibiting incitement. Although I've not attempted to quantify the pattern, hate speech appears more flagrant and prevalent in elections in India than in the United States, despite the wider legal latitude that the First Amendment offers American politicians. US political culture penalizes national politicians who indulge in hate speech more effectively than a panoply of legal provisions restrains their Indian counterparts.

Social norms also help explain the fact that theological disputes are not central to most religious hate spin campaigns. This is curious, considering that religions are ultimately distinguished by doctrinal differences. No matter how hard one works to find common ground, there are details central to Christianity that can be offensive to Muslims, as the former archbishop of Canterbury Rowan Williams has acknowledged.[16] Yet, religious texts are not usually targeted for hate spin in democracies. There is a branch of the New York Public Library close to the 9/11 memorial site, but the rabid campaigners against the "Mosque at Ground Zero" have not demanded that libraries a three-minute walk away from Ground Zero remove the Quran and educational books about Islam from their shelves. Hate spin agents seem to recognize that their displays of indignation must appear reasonable to the wider public.

Because of their pragmatic acceptance of societal norms, hate spin agents prefer injustice symbols that can be framed in secular terms. For example, most cities' building regulations already take into account such subjective factors as cultural congruence and community feedback. Thus, it is relatively easy to present one's resistance to a house of worship in nonreligious language, giving it a veneer of legitimacy. Once this window has been opened, protesters can let fly with hate propaganda that depicts the proposed church or mosque as an alarming threat to the society's way of life.

Different hate spin tactics have different strengths. They are deployed to achieve three related but distinct objectives: a mobilizational effect (rallying followers at the grassroots); publicity for the movement (spreading its message beyond the in-group); and engagement with governing elites. The mobilizational agenda is best fulfilled by highly decentralized campaigns that allow local activists to take the lead. This is generally the case with opposition to houses of worship. In the United States, where public libraries and schools are administered locally, book challenges are another important way for the grassroots to take on responsibilities and contribute to the cause. Thus, book challenges conducted by the anti-Muslim network do more than create an alternate set of facts about Islam, notes Miranda Blue, a researcher with People For the American Way. "ACT! for America has been fostering local leaders through these textbook challenges, starting at the school board level," she says.[17]

On the other hand, the proliferation of library book challenges, sometimes involving famous titles like *Harry Potter* but usually not, also means that they have ceased to become particularly newsworthy—so much so that the American Library Association has had to organize an annual "Banned

Books" week to remind the public that this type of censorship still goes on. Decentralization also means that book controversies rarely draw in politicians at the state or national levels.

For engaging prominent political elites, hate spin agents need different tactics. Legislative and judicial forums serve as ideal arenas. Tabling a bill can guarantee years' worth of opportunities for high-level hate spin, as the US anti-sharia campaign has shown. Debates in legislatures lack the spectacle of street demonstrations, but pay off handsomely in getting elected representatives to echo the core messages of the campaign within an elite political sphere closely watched by media.

The legal and cultural space available to hate spin agents is another factor that influences their choice of tactics. In India and Indonesia, where the legal system offers redress for hurt communal feelings and government agencies are involved in censorship, political entrepreneurs find it easy to target films, concerts, artworks, and scholarly books for righteous indignation. In the United States, the state's adamant refusal under the First Amendment to protect Americans' religious feelings from offense severely restricts the opportunity to demand government censorship. Yet, even in the United States, activists have been creative enough to find institutional spaces, such as school boards and local libraries, where they can press their claims.

Hate spin agents, like other social movement activists, both develop their own tactics and borrow from a repertoire developed by other groups.[18] The technique of the book challenge diffused to the American Islamophobia network from the Evangelical movement, which has used it to oppose the teaching of evolution, for example.[19] This tactic has even spread beyond the US borders. One case involves the award-winning children's book *And Tango Makes Three*, which tells the true story of two male Central Park Zoo penguins that adopted a penguin chick. Its implicit support of alternative families put it at the top of the American Library Association's list of 10 Most Challenged Books in 2006 and 2010.[20] By 2014, conservatives in Singapore had managed to persuade the national library there to destroy its copies of *And Tango Makes Three*—showing what can happen when offense-taking spreads beyond First Amendment territory. Several American conservative organizations such as Focus on the Family have Singapore affiliates through which values and strategies can be exported.

The general approach of manufactured indignation is itself something that can be learned. In India, the "right to be offended" was exercised by Muslims and Christians long before the Hindutva succeeded in manufacturing a collective feeling of hurt. "In recent decades, however, feeling offended was learnt from India's minority groups," says the journalist Varghese K. George. Hindutva hate spin agents cite the Muslim example to spur Hindus to greater heights of offendedness, George says. "They are challenging Hindus: 'Aren't you ashamed that when it happens to Muslims, when it happens to Allah, Muslims stand up and get counted; if you don't stand up, you are surrendering your authority over this land.' That challenge, increasingly, people respond positively to."[21]

Networked and Layered Hate Spin

Hate spin campaigns involve a division of labor. Fringe groups and lone individuals use the most extreme language, but they usually lack the credibility to attract people beyond their core supporters. Activist media targeted at the broader public keeps these more extreme views under wraps, employing "reasonable racism" to attract new converts to the cause.[22] Similarly, leaders of political parties and other politicians vying for national office usually cannot afford to be caught uttering extreme speech. They may use code words whose hateful meaning is clear to an audience in the know, but allow plausible deniability when legal or political sanction threatens. They rely not only on other contemporary speakers around them to fill in the blanks, but also on connections to past speech and events. Orienting one's speech to different historical frames can superimpose an "extra layer of significance" to the discourse, which the audience can interpret using its own background knowledge, as one study of human rights violators in apartheid South Africa has observed.[23] Hate spin agents can thus engage in what is commonly referred to as dog whistling, conveying meanings that are imperceptible to outsiders but heard loud and clear by the intended audience. The effective communication of hate relies not only on that speaker's discrete messages but also on complementary ideas and symbols that are already in the air, thanks to what others are saying and to shared memories.

All the hate spin processes discussed in this book have this distributed, networked quality. In India, Narendra Modi, the prime beneficiary of Hindutva intolerance, did not need to indulge in the direct use of hate speech. That was left to lieutenants like Amit Shah. And even they did not need to be too explicit, as that job could be performed by activists at the grassroots. The BJP embedded its campaign messages within narrative themes assiduously built up over the years, or even over decades. The manufactured threat of sexually predatory, overly fecund Muslims goes back to the early years of the Hindutva movement, as does the idea of re-Hinduizing India—by force, if necessary.[24]

Another core narrative of Hindu nationalists in India is the identification of Muslims with foreign invaders, Pakistanis, or terrorists—themes that conveniently resonate with the global discourse of the Islamic terrorist threat. Such stereotypes enabled BJP campaigners in 2014 to label an area in Uttar Pradesh with a high Muslim population as "a base of terrorists," without any real justification.[25] In a campaign speech in the same must-win state, Modi declared: "Terrorists and criminals are rewarded in this state these days. ... Ten years ago, in Gujarat, there used to be many riots. But now the people of Gujarat know they have to live in peace, to live free from the politics of polarisation. They know they have to take the path of development. And all is calm."[26]

Beneath such seemingly unobjectionable words lurks a chilling ambiguity. Both within the Hindutva movement and among its critics, the conventional wisdom is that Modi's 2002 pogrom in Gujarat was about finally putting Muslims in their place and teaching them a lesson.[27] Other Sangh Parivar leaders have stated this quite explicitly. Modi has never disavowed that interpretation. The closest he has come to expressing regret for 2002 is to say that one would naturally feel sad if a puppy were run over by one's car, regardless of who was at the wheel.[28] When he boasted that Gujaratis now know how to live in peace, and that "all is calm," the audience knew what he really meant.

In Indonesia, hard-line Muslim hate spin lacks the coherent vision that Vinayak Damodar Savarkar provided Hindu nationalists with his Hindutva philosophy. Well before the 2014 elections, it was clear that the Indonesian electorate did not want a Muslim-based party running the country. With no immediate chance of winning the ultimate political contest, hard-line groups have had to experiment with other ways of expanding their power. Some shun electoral politics altogether, stating that democracy is sinful; others try to ally with secular parties. They seem to be united primarily by a mutual interest in appearing relevant, so as to claim more influence and resources. Central to this goal is the construction of a common threat in the form of Christianity, Shia Islam, Ahmadiyah, and atheists. The cumulative effect is a culture of intolerance, discrimination, and violence against minorities.

But, as in India, hate spin in Indonesia has a distributed and historically layered quality that makes it difficult to pin legal culpability on any one institution or individual. The national council of clerics, MUI, mainly profits from the growing halal-certification and Islamic finance markets, but it also tries to enhance its brand by issuing intolerant fatwas. MUI's declarations are reinforced by the state's antideviancy watchdog organization, Bakor Pakem, which similarly tries to justify its existence by whipping up moral panics against supposed deviants. Statements by MUI and Bakor Pakem may not in themselves amount to incitement—MUI has not issued any fatwa as outrageous as Ayatollah Khomeini's instruction to kill Salman Rushdie. However, by narrowing the space for what is considered acceptable expression and practice within Islam, MUI provides more extreme groups like the Islamic Defenders Front (FPI), with all the justification they need to inflict physical violence on perceived deviants. MUI, in turn, benefits from FPI's readiness to mete out earthly retribution rather than await divine justice in the afterlife. The many Indonesians who might otherwise casually brush aside clerics' moral censure now think twice about giving militants any excuse to show their power.

The US Islamophobia network's division of labor has been thoroughly documented by progressive groups.[29] The falsehoods propagated by the core ideologues at the heart of this network are echoed by a coterie of "validators," in the form of hawkish military types and individuals of Middle Eastern descent who are convinced that Islam is evil. The ideologues also work through grassroots activists of single-issue organizations such as ACT! for America and Stop Islamization of America, as well as older religious Right organizations that sympathize with their cause, such as Eagle Forum. Leading figures of the religious Right, such as Franklin Graham and Pat Robertson, amplify Islamophobia rhetoric.

Even so, Islamophobia would remain on the political fringe but for its embrace by elected officials and political leaders. Right-wing politicians at the national and state levels spout anti-Muslim messages through electoral debates, legislative processes, and media appearances. Presidential hopefuls Ted Cruz and Donald Trump made Islamophobic rhetoric part of the national conversation in the run-up to the 2016 elections.[30] Trump lacked the self-restraint required to limit himself to dog whistles, but even though his pronouncements were readily audible as hate speech, they were not as extreme or as frequent as the messages churned out by the core Islamophobia producers like Frank Gaffney and Brigitte Gabriel. If post–2016 America is an altogether less comfortable home for Muslims, it would be due to the combined efforts of multiple actors.

How the Law Should Respond

Societies trying to defend democracy against the forces of intolerance must take into account the strategic, versatile, and networked qualities of hate spin. Their responses need to be equally creative, dynamic, and multi-pronged. No template solution will apply to all societies, since not even new democracies, let alone those with deeply entrenched traditions, can be treated as a blank page.[31] Thus, the United States' exceptionally strong commitment to free speech has to be accepted as a given, just as it would be unthinkable for Indonesia to remove the belief in God as one of the pillars of its republic, or for India to dispense with the group rights that it grants to its major ethnic communities. Nevertheless, some broad principles apply. It can be said with some confidence that offense laws are an extremely poor and often counterproductive way to achieve a culture of respect for religion and belief. At the same time, democracies need strong laws against incitement, and those laws must be evenly and strictly enforced.

The False Promise of Insult Laws

How democracies deal with insult is one of the main litmus tests distinguishing liberal from more traditionally ordered societies. Although this is admittedly a relatively new development in liberty's march, liberal democracies reject religious offense as legitimate grounds for restricting free speech. International human rights norms are clear that the law should step in to protect only real people (not ideas, beliefs, dead prophets, or God) from real harms (not just offended feelings, no matter how deep the sense of indignation). The United Nations Human Rights Committee has stated that, under the International Covenant on Civil and Political Rights, laws must not prohibit displays of disrespect of a religion or other belief system if they do not also amount to incitement. It would not be permissible "for such prohibitions to be used to prevent or punish criticism of religious leaders or commentary on religious doctrine and tenets of faith," the committee says.[32]

Cases of violence by the offended have put mounting pressure on liberal democracies to reconsider their idolization of freedom of expression. Defending liberal principles in peaceful debates is one thing, but the cost escalates when the indignant are prepared to exact bloody revenge.[33] After the execution of *Charlie Hebdo* cartoonists by Muslim gunmen in Paris in January 2015, the most immediate and visible reaction in the West was a massive show of solidarity behind the right to criticize others' beliefs. But interspersed in the phalanx of "*Je suis Charlie*" guardians of democracy were voices expressing doubts about whether freedom of expression should always be prioritized over respect for religions. Perhaps, they said, types of speech that may provoke a violent backlash should be restricted on public order grounds. The European Council on Tolerance and Reconciliation, chaired by former British prime minister Tony Blair, proposed lowering the threshold for government intervention.[34] Its model law for European countries moots the suppression of "group libel," which would include not only incitement to violence but also malicious attempts to vilify the group, such as calling all Muslims terrorists.[35]

There is in fact a good case for treating group libels more seriously. Religious vilification can create cultural barriers that exclude immigrant minorities, especially in countries—like in much of Europe—that have defined their nationhood in ethnolinguistic or religious terms. Western societies may also have a public relations rationale for making some adjustments: their failure to present a position on religion offense that doesn't sound arrogant and Eurocentric can affect the global reception of the values they are trying to export.[36]

It is clear, however, that laws against insult or offense generally backfire badly. In India and Indonesia—not even the worst offenders in this regard—we have seen how powerful political interests abuse religious insult laws. Leaders in these two states have used these laws not only to maintain public order, but also to win political points with religious conservatives. Indonesia's blasphemy law protects mainstream religious orthodoxy from what religious authorities say is heretical, resulting in sustained violations of minority rights. The Indian Penal Code's Section 295A in effect prohibits blasphemous libel, and all major religious communities partake of this official indulgence. Among the critically acclaimed artistic works to which the public has been denied access in all or parts of India are Salman Rushdie's *The Satanic Verses*, Deepa Mehta's *Fire*, and *Jesus Christ Superstar* by Andrew Lloyd Webber and Tim Rice, for offending Muslims, Hindus, and Christians respectively. Over time, a culture of competitive offendedness sets in.

Extending to all communities the equal right to be offended may have intuitive appeal to those who believe that potentially inflammatory religious insult should be kept out of the public sphere; they want it confined to the private spaces of the respective communities for the sake of peaceful coexistence. But no matter how well intentioned, it is naïve to use the law to enforce cultural insulation. The approach assumes that everyone who claims to be a victim of religious insult is acting in good faith, in the sense of having made a sincere attempt to protect oneself from offense, in the spirit of live-and-let-live. The system breaks down when people go out of their way to find or fabricate indignation, which is exactly the case with hate spin.

Consider some of the episodes we have touched on, for instance the Muslim activists who claimed that the "Three Beauties" statue in Bekasi was an intolerable symbol of Christianity's Holy Trinity; or Hindu activists who drove M. F. Husain into exile, condemning his modern painting of a nude Hindu goddess, as if ancient temples depict deities fully clothed; or Islamophobia merchants in the United States who are challenging textbooks for failing to describe Islam as a murderous ideology. All are instances of offense-taking as a weapon, where the offended are the aggressors and those accused of causing offense, the victims. Yet, it can be difficult for secular authorities to contradict religious offense-takers and to tell them that, really, they are making something out of nothing, so they should turn around and go home.[37] Even when the offended parties have no legal leg to stand on, politicians feel political pressure to hand them a crutch. Giving them legal ammunition in addition to political support is foolhardy.

US legal tradition offers an instructive contrast to laws protecting communities from offense. Some Americans may feel that their country grants too much freedom to hurt religious feelings, but they accept it as a given. The Supreme Court's unequivocal stand, that no one can count on government to protect their religious feelings in public debate, encourages religious minorities to channel their hurt into responses other than demands for censorship. For the small Muslim communities in Murfreesboro and Birmingham, this has meant unceasing engagement with their community. Particularly interesting is the case of the Mormon Church—the country's only major homegrown religious institution. Although frequently mocked in the popular media, the Church of Jesus Christ of Latter-Day Saints, as it is formally known, has a policy of not calling for boycotts, knowing that these tend to create more publicity for the offending work. Instead, it urges its members to use such provocations as an opportunity to demonstrate the church's maturity, dignity, and thoughtfulness.[38] In response to the mercilessly satirical Broadway musical *The Book of Mormon*, for example, the church simply issued a statement saying, "The production may attempt to entertain audiences for an evening, but the Book of Mormon as a volume of scripture will change people's lives forever by bringing them closer to Christ."[39]

Limitations of Incitement Laws

While I question the wisdom of legislating against religious offense, my study supports the case for laws prohibiting incitement. No credible free speech argument could justify Indonesian preachers calling on their listeners to kill Ahmadis, or Sangh Parivar activists' instigation of the Muzaffarnagar riots, for example. We shouldn't expect democracies to converge around an identical standard. The United States will continue to apply its exceptionally high threshold of imminent violence, while other societies recognize the need to act against incitement to discrimination as well, in line with international human rights norms. Precise definitions will differ from country to country, and we can expect laws to be refined in the light of experience. What's important here is the general principle: the state has a duty to protect vulnerable groups from expression that would cause them to suffer objective harms.

Laws against incitement are necessary, but they are not sufficient. Legal responses suffer from a number of limitations. The most obvious is that in many states, institutions fail to apply or enforce the laws on the books. Courts are not immune to majoritarian pressures—certainly not in the United States, where many lower-level judicial positions are elected. Even if the judicial system ultimately protects human rights, severe backlogs may mean lengthy periods in which injustice prevails, as is chronically the case in India. The police, meanwhile, may fail to do their jobs because they themselves are steeped in prejudice, or perhaps because they are corrupt or lack resources, as is the case in Indonesia.

Recognizing these problems, the United Nations' 2012 Rabat Plan of Action, discussed in chapter 2, not only spells out the required legislation to address hate speech, but also the necessary improvements in jurisprudence and other policies to make the laws stick. It says that states must ensure that people have access to fair and public hearings by competent, independent, and impartial tribunals; that courts are regularly updated about developments in international standards; and that the police receive training on the prohibition of incitement.[40] The Rabat Plan's laundry list of recommendations is the kind of thing that makes the legal scholar Eric Posner extremely skeptical about the utility of human rights treaties. Even if states in the Global South sincerely wish to reach international human rights standards, he says, the prerequisite institution-building may be too steep a hill to climb, especially when other needs, like poverty reduction, cry out for attention. Hate spin exponents in India, for example, are able to take advantage of enforcement gaps in the country's strict laws against provoking communal tensions. Too frequently, politicians have been able to get away with hate speech. The results of the 2014 election would surely suggest to any unscrupulous Indian politician that an investment in hate speech pays handsome dividends.

But there is another problem in regulating hate speech, one related to the unbridgeable gap between the networked and layered form of hate speech as it is actually practiced and what democracies can effectively regulate. Hate speech laws work best when a speaker (A) sends his message (X) to an audience (B) against a target group (C); where A is in a position to exert a strong, direct, and immediate influence over B; where B is clearly in a position to cause harm to C; and where X contains all the elements that amount to intentional incitement. In addition to having a tendency to cause harm, X should sound extreme, violating "social norms of respect."[41] As we've seen, most systematic and industrialized hate speech does not come in this convenient package. It is a distributed activity conducted by a syndicate, whose hateful meanings are pieced together in the audience's mind, with the most powerful actors keeping their hands clean. Regulating hate speech in this way is like trying to use laws against armed robbery to convict the white collar criminals and market manipulators who caused the 2008 banking crisis. But while financial regulators can try to catch up with sophisticated forms of thievery, it is not possible to broaden the scope of hate speech law without severely restricting the basic freedom of expression that democracy requires.

Free Speech

Freedom of expression is not a sacrosanct right. Its status as a fundamental human right does not foreclose the need to balance it with other vital rights. We can expect democracies to debate where the outer boundaries of free speech should be drawn, and courts to make occasional adjustments. The United States, uniquely permissive toward extreme speech, will probably continue to generate examples of abuse that other democracies would find difficult to abide. For example, the First Amendment wins few fans when it allows the mass export of hate music with explicit white supremacist and anti-Semitic themes, which is a key recruitment vehicle for neo-Nazis.[42] The deliberate baiting of Muslim extremists through stunts like the Prophet Muhammed cartoon contest in Texas in May 2015—condemned by the *New York Times* as "an exercise in bigotry and hatred" and "not really about free speech"—is another example of the kind of abuse that should encourage liberals to review their stance toward free speech laws.[43] When we see harmless mosque volunteers and imams libeled with impunity as supporters of terrorism, it should be clear that there are problems with how the United States has drawn the limits of free speech.

But, we should not assume that a more restrictive regime is necessarily more supportive of minority rights. Often, commentators mistakenly perceive freedom of expression as being in opposition to freedom of religion or belief, as if the enhancement of one must always involve the erosion of the other. "Instead they are mutually dependent and reinforcing," the Rabat Plan of Action stresses. Freedom to exercise or not exercise one's religion or belief can exist only if freedom of expression is respected, it notes. Conversely, free public discourse depends on "respect for the diversity of deep convictions which people may have."[44]

The most serious attacks on the dignity of religious communities are invariably accompanied by the silencing of their members. The groups who are most unwilling to tolerate the coexistence of other beliefs are the ones who tend to demand state censorship or who intimidate minorities into silence. India's Vishva Hindu Parishad (VHP) and Indonesia's Front Pembela Islam (FPI) are classic examples of this phenomenon. Intolerance operatives in the United States like AFDI and ACT! for America, working within a constitutional environment where free speech is sacred, do not overtly call for censorship. But, at a deeper level, they are similar to the likes of VHP and FPI. They use hate propaganda to demonize and, thus, stifle the speech of targeted minorities and their spokesmen, such as the Council on American–Islamic Relations (CAIR). "When people are denied public participation and voice, their issues, experiences and concerns are rendered invisible, and they become more vulnerable to bigotry, prejudice and marginalisation," the Camden Principles (see chapter 2) remind us.[45] Genocides are always preceded by the suppression of speech, as the German poet Heinrich Heine presciently observed when he wrote that the burning of books culminates in the burning of men.

Freedom of expression is also indispensable for the human rights workers, hate-watch groups, and investigative journalists who are combating the forces of intolerance. It is worth recalling that the United States' unique take on defamation was a direct outcome of the civil rights campaign, when public employees were using libel suits to silence accusations against them. The 1964 Supreme Court ruling in *New York Times Co. v. Sullivan*, which overturned one such lawsuit, was intended to make it easier for civil rights campaigners to blow the whistle on abuses by the authorities— showing once again how historically disadvantaged minorities benefit from wider avenues for expression. Today, the Southern Poverty Law Center, for instance, benefits from that tradition when it investigates and exposes scandals within hate groups.[46]

In India, civil rights activists have depended on the country's freedoms to challenge the BJP narrative about the Gujarat pogrom. "Advocacy requires systematic and thorough documentation," says Cedric Prakash, a

Jesuit priest in Ahmedabad who is part of Citizens for Justice and Peace (CJP), which was formed to pursue justice for Gujarat victims. "We are convinced that unless we put the facts on the table, nothing is going to change. It's the only weapon that groups like us have, who are in a very miniscule minority."

CJP founder Teesta Setalvad has endured years of targeted intimidation and harassment for her dogged campaign to bring Modi and his lieutenants to justice. She believes it would be even worse if India did not have the freedoms that it has. "We need to be as free as we are, but we also need to recognize that this freedom is available for some and not for others," she says. The problem in India, she says, is that dominant groups have the liberty to incite hate with impunity, while their victims are being silenced. "The issue is not simply freedom, but how do we apply this freedom, to whom, where, and how. Are we equally nondiscriminatory in the application of these laws?"[47] Restricting free speech across the board usually handicaps the weak even more than it does the powerful. Wherever democracies choose to draw the outer limits of freedom of expression, that line needs to be sensitive to power—the structural inequalities in the marketplace of ideas that make it harder for historically disadvantaged groups to be heard.

From Speech to Equality

One of the most common myths about regulating religious offense and incitement is the intuitively appealing idea that the more seriously a society treats religion, the more strictly it would police speech. States like India, rightly mindful of their history of communal violence, therefore apply lower legal thresholds for state intervention than Western democracies. It is as if they set their cooling thermostats at a lower setting, to cut off offensive speech when it causes discomfort, rather than waiting for it to grow into red-hot incitement. Described this way, a policy of prohibiting religious offense—including wounding of religious feelings, religious insult, defamation of religion, blasphemy, and the like—appears to be a responsible response in a world weary of the dangers of human diversity.

The problem with this view is that it imagines offense and incitement to be simply different points on a single scale of extreme speech, differing only in degree. The myth evaporates when we study how prohibitions are applied in India, Indonesia, and many other countries where insult laws and incitement laws coexist. Sticking with the thermostat metaphor we would expect that, in jurisdictions where relatively mild cases of offended feelings trigger police action, the state would also respond—and much more forcefully—to full-blown incitement to violence. Yet, this is not the case. Again and again, we see individuals being prosecuted or books being censored for wounding religious feelings, while others are allowed to incite mob violence with total impunity. It turns out that offense and incitement are not just different degrees of extreme speech. They differ in kind and are measured on different scales, reflecting distinct norms. Offense, being inherently subjective, is usually gauged by how much indignation is expressed. Authorities treat the volume of protest as an indicator of impending disorder or a loss of support for those in power. They measure incitement, on the other hand, by the threat posed to a victimized group's security and equality. Incitement, with its tangible effects, is much more amenable to objective testing by independent courts.

Because they are measured on different scales, a strict policing of insult can, and frequently does, coexist with a lax attitude toward incitement. Hate spin agents take advantage of the over-regulation of offense to engineer campaigns of righteous indignation, while at the same time exploiting under-regulation of incitement to indulge in vilification. The coexistence of over- and under-regulation appears paradoxical—until we view it through the lens of power. Then, the pattern becomes clear. A government punishes offense to appease powerful groups that threaten to withdraw their political support or to take their unhappiness to the streets. But the same government may permit or even directly engage in incitement when the targets of hatred are weak.

The net result is a legal environment in which dominant groups can protect their religious identities from criticism while indulging with impunity in hate speech that harms others. Weaker groups, on the other hand, must endure vilification that pushes them further out to the margins, while refraining from expressing their own identities and values. The human rights approach tries to avoid these injustices by protecting speech that offends while prohibiting speech that incites.

Redefining the Problem

Although laws prohibiting incitement are necessary, they are rarely sufficient. Even passionate defenders of the human rights standard harbor growing doubts about their effectiveness. Agnes Callamard, one of the leading authorities on freedom of expression around the world, suggests that the time has come for some honest stocktaking. "Have these legal instruments produced any tangible positive results over people's rights to equality and intercultural, interreligious understanding?" she asks of Europe's proliferation of hate speech regulation. "In my view, the sooner we recognize, and acknowledge clearly the limits of the criminalization or civil law responses, the sooner will we be able to identify alternative responses and devote energy, time, and funds where they are most needed."[48]

The worst cases of hate spin—which combine manufactured indignation and incitement to persecute minorities—demand a broader approach than simply addressing speech. We need policies that specifically further the cause of equal rights. As we have seen, laws prohibiting offense and incitement are likely to become tools of repression when they are superimposed on a system that does not protect equality. In such societies, the power to define offense is not fairly distributed. Communities that are deprived of the freedom of religion and belief then find their practices deemed offensive to dominant groups, and they become targets of hate.

In contrast, in a society with strong antidiscrimination laws, hate speech may not be able to inflict much harm. If we look narrowly at hate speech laws, the United States can seem heartless in its refusal to protect religious communities from vicious attacks on their cherished beliefs. But there is more to the First Amendment than its Free Speech Clause: it doggedly protects religious freedom through the Free Exercise Clause and the Establishment Clause. Free speech means that the opponents of a proposed mosque can demonstrate their hostility far more freely in the United States than in many other countries. But freedom of religion means that, after all is said and done, Muslims in the United States can have far greater confidence than Christians in Indonesia that the authorities will stand up to the mob and allow them to build their house of worship.

Or take the issue of religious dress. In June 2014, the European Court of Human Rights found no fault in the French government's ban on full-face coverings in public places, which had been challenged by a Muslim woman living in the country.[49] Meanwhile, a young Muslim woman in the United States was suing the fashion retailer Abercrombie & Fitch for denying her a job because she wore a headscarf. Her case was taken up by the Equal Employment Opportunity Commission, a government agency. In 2015, the US Supreme Court ruled 8–1 in her favor, allowing her to claim damages for the company's breach of the Civil Rights Act of 1964, which prohibits religious discrimination in hiring decisions.[50] American courts' nonchalance toward most religious insult should not be confused with indifference toward the rights of religious minorities.

When a state protects people's freedom of religion and belief without exception or discrimination, religious minorities have much less to fear and resent when they are on the receiving end of offensive speech. Taking this more holistic view, effective antidiscrimination policies may be able to compensate for a community's exposure to vilification of its identity. While the latter remains cause for concern, we can be more realistic in crafting policy, abandoning futile attempts at watertight, legally enforceable solutions, and instead focusing on civic and political responses that nudge hate speech out of the mainstream. In many cases, this is all minorities are asking for: a clear signal that wanton disrespect is not welcome in the center of the public square, even if it is impossible and even undesirable to root out entirely at the margins. Uncompromising legal interventions can be directed instead at upholding the democratic value of equality against unfair discrimination based on religion or other markers of identity.

Scholars and activists combating the problem of religious intolerance only rarely discuss the potential of antidiscrimination law in limiting the effects of hate speech. Policy debates gravitate instead toward the regulation of expression—perhaps because we live in an age of communication, where depictions of intolerance seize our attention more than structural inequality. Yet, defending the rights of religious communities against unfair discrimination will do far more for their long-term welfare than trying to protect them from insult. Arguably, the outrage expressed against the provocations of the *Jyllands-Posten* and *Charlie Hebdo* cartoons, for example, was fueled more by the injustice of discrimination against Muslim immigrants in Europe than by the disrespect shown toward the Prophet.

When religious minorities can be confident in an equality-protecting constitutional order, they have a greater incentive to adapt to the dominant political values. In the United States some minorities, like the Amish, have decided to opt out. But most US religious minorities have been willing to undergo the kind of accommodation that the religion scholar Eric Michael Mazur has called "Americanization." Such adaptation carries a cost, including acknowledging the supreme authority of the secular state over worldly matters and accepting norms of pluralism and civility, but it eventually brings the benefit of full acceptance into the American family.[51]

The Muslims of Murfreesboro and Birmingham in America's Deep South fall squarely within that tradition. The flagpoles outside the mosques are as tall as their spires, and, following the custom of American church buildings, they fly the Stars and Stripes. For Murfreesboro's imam, Ossama Bahloul, such shows of allegiance are more than cosmetic. In a TEDx Talk in Nashville after the mosque dispute had ended, Bahloul spoke of his unbroken faith in mainstream American society and in the US Constitution. Some decisions of the local authorities in Rutherford County went against the mosque project, but religious freedom ultimately prevailed. He recalled his wonderment as someone from the Middle East, sitting in an American courtroom for the first time, watching attorneys representing the United States of America fighting Rutherford County on the Muslims' behalf.[52] This sort of firm state action in defense of equality is the most effective antidote to hate propaganda, and the best way to encourage aggrieved minorities to remain within the law.

Mainstream Muslims in the United States can look hopefully to the country's track record of embracing one previously loathed minority after another—blacks, Irish, Jews, Catholics and so on—as a source of inspiration. To Corey Saylor of the Council on American–Islamic Relations, the experience of Japanese Americans is especially inspiring. Severely discriminated against when Japan was at war with the United States, they won acceptance in a matter of decades. "Yes, it's difficult, but I am very confident that ultimately Islam will be viewed as just another boring religion in the landscape of America."[53]

Toward an Assertive Pluralism

In this book I have cautioned against an overreliance on the law to regulate offensive expression and develop a culture of tolerance. As I stressed in chapter 7, neutralizing religious intolerance requires the involvement of socially responsible media, progressive civil society organizations, and a public resistant to the guiles of provocateurs. Too often, though, the prescriptions stop there—and governments are let off the hook. When discussing what to do about hate propaganda, many analysts operate with the binary categories of protected speech and criminalized speech, ignoring other public policy options.[54] Even if a particular hate campaign cannot be banned, that does not justify the government leaders washing their hands of the problem. At the very minimum, the state must fulfill its fundamental duty to provide security for its citizens. No amount of philosophical squabbling over the definition and regulation of hate speech should obscure a government's straightforward obligation to protect people from actual hate crimes and the kind of mob violence that continues to terrorize vulnerable groups around the world. States need to protect groups at risk of harm, through antidiscrimination policies and by upholding the rule of law.

Countries that are prepared to undergo constitutional reforms can also consider architectures that reduce the incentives for political contenders to manufacture group-based hatred. Religiosity, as such, is not a problem for democracy. The problem emerges only when politics become organized along religious lines, and when exclusive religious loyalties are converted into a political resource. At that point, matters of faith become intractably divisive and destructive. To counter this tendency, electoral systems can be designed to require politicians to appeal to different cultural groups, thus limiting the viability of exclusionary politics.[55] Indonesia provides a positive example of this approach. Its dramatic decentralization has not resulted in destructive, Yugoslav-style ethnic politics, in part because parties that want to contest local elections are required to have some national presence, which discourages them from appealing solely to local ethnic identities.[56] Neighboring Singapore's electoral system requires political parties to field multiethnic slates if they want to win power, making the equivalent of a BJP government—lacking even one member of parliament from the country's largest minority group—a constitutional impossibility.

Some may criticize such structural fixes as constraining choice on both the demand and supply sides of the electoral marketplace. Yet, every democracy tweaks its system to address major risks of national disintegration, even if it means diluting the principle of one person, one vote. Geographic regions are commonly granted representation disproportionate to their population size. For instance, California's 37 million residents and Wyoming's half-million get an equal 2-percent say in the make-up of the US Senate. It should not be unthinkable for countries to adjust their electoral systems to recognize the risks of identity politics, just as they have done so to avert regional secessionism.

States have other instruments at their disposal. They can dispense or withhold patronage and wield tremendous symbolic and administrative powers. The Canadian federal government gives out millions of dollars a year for projects that support its multiculturalism agenda.[57] In addition, much more substantial investments have already been made "to increase minority participation in Canada's major institutions by bringing diversity into these institutions as a natural, normal, and positive component of decision-making, resource allocation, and the setting of priorities," as one report notes.[58] The United States is more laissez-faire than Canada in its approach to diversity, but its First Amendment ban on viewpoint discrimination in regulating public discourse has not stopped the state from taking substantive positions on issues like racism and intolerance, as Robert Post, the dean of Yale Law School, points out. The US government regularly affirms the principles of equality and toleration. "Consider our stamps and monuments. Consider the ongoing expression of American government officials about issues of race and toleration. Consider the rules and regulations that the American state imposes on the army, on government institutions, on contractors, and so on," Post notes. "No one should confuse the American state with a neutral state."[59]

Since government leaders, even in liberal democracies, do have the latitude to take a firm political and administrative stand against religious intolerance, there is really no excuse for them not to do so. Free speech laws may stop them from censoring or punishing hate speech in the public sphere, but that shouldn't deter officials from engaging in counter-speech. An assertive pluralism would require leaders of democracies to defend to the death their citizens' right to speak—but also to proclaim their vigorous disagreement with what is spoken when the speech promotes intolerance. Governments that fail to take this action will appear callous in their disregard for people's religious identities. This was the political failure at the heart of the *Jyllands-Posten* Prophet Muhammad cartoon controversy of 2005. Events might have turned out quite differently had Danish prime minister Anders Fogh Rasmussen responded positively to the first request for a meeting from the envoys of Muslim countries.[60] By concentrating on legal and constitutional matters, he failed to use the political space available to him.[61]

Such lapses are particularly serious in societies with weak rule of law. The absence of clear signals from the executive branch can translate into lax policing of abuses. In Indonesia, the security expert Sidney Jones faults the Susilo Bambang Yudhoyono administration (2004–2014) for failing to use its "bully pulpit" to speak out firmly against intolerance.[62] On the contrary, it allowed radical preachers to spread their messages at state schools, for example. Although there are limits to the central government's power in a republic that has become highly decentralized, an Indonesian president and his ministers still have a variety of tools at their disposal to promote a culture of tolerance and keep hard-liners on the margins of public life, she notes.

The main reasons for such failures of democratic leadership are fairly obvious. In some situations, as epitomized by Narendra Modi and the BJP, the forces of intolerance have captured power. They are the problem, and can't be expected to offer solutions. In other cases, such as with Yudhoyono, Barack Obama, and Aung San Suu Kyi, leaders may feel hemmed in by public opinion and unable to expend political capital on constituencies with limited electoral clout.

Their conundrum reflects the dilemma at the heart of hate spin. The title of this book refers to hate spin as a threat to democracy. It is also a threat *from* democracy. Not democracy as it should be understood, but a deformed version that elevates the popular will above the rights of the individual. This is the democratic vote minus democratic values, dazzling in its empowerment of the many, but blind to the injustices suffered by the few.

Democratic societies require publics who are not just aware of their right to choose their government, but also educated in other essential requirements of democratic life, including the values of tolerance and mutual respect. These values have little chance of flowering in societies where the rot of fear and hatred of the "other" has already set in. There, the very institutions—families, schools, religious organizations, and media—that we hope will instill the right values may themselves be promoting bigotry.

It doesn't help that purveyors of religious intolerance are usually convinced of the moral superiority of their ideological wares. After all, human groups have been able to generate rules for social existence long before the arrival of modern human rights. When facing contemporary social challenges, it seems natural and proper to look to a community's received wisdom, which often draws from religious thought. It is not surprising, therefore, that many citizens find the "rule of identity" more appealing than culture-negating rule of law.

The fatal flaw in this thinking is its failure to account for the irrefutable fact of human diversity. To some, that diversity is human civilization's most glorious characteristic; to others, the need to accommodate difference is one of the curses of globalization. Denying it, though, is not an option. Even societies that appear homogeneous from the outside never are; preserving the myth of homogeneity eventually involves injustice and relies on force. When societies try to rely on traditional community standards for resolving differences, they are erroneously conflating community and nation. A nation is not a community; it is a "marketplace of communities," as Post puts it, with each community having its "own particular ways of distinguishing decency from indecency, critique from hatred."[63]

Faced with this heterogeneity, it is tempting to try to base national identity and norms on the shared values of different communities. Indeed, one of the goals of a sound civic education should be to reveal to children this common ground. But, in resolving disputes between communities, appeals to shared traditional values can only go so far. No community would be satisfied with limiting the expression of its values to some lowest common denominator. Some beliefs and practices considered essential to one community will be incommensurate with others' beliefs and practices.

The question that remains, then, is what to do about these irreducible differences. Compromises are inevitable, and unless we are prepared to live with grave injustice and risk violent conflict, these have to be negotiated through a system that is compatible with the reality of diversity. Blood and belonging cannot outrank law. This is why nations need a constitutional order compatible with modern human rights, protecting the fundamental civil and political rights of every individual, including his or her freedom of expression, religion, and belief. A human rights framework may reflect the cultural preferences of the secular West, as some critics have alleged. But, as yet, we have not found a better way to reconcile and regulate tensions over religious speech in a heterogeneous world.[64]

More traditional modes of thinking prevail in many countries, including in Western democracies. On-going convulsions in European societies seem to be partly due to the way many of them have understood national identity—in terms of characteristics like blood, ethnicity, and religion, which most new immigrants and refugees do not share.[65] In countries that are already polarized around religious identity, breaking the cycle requires morally courageous leaders who are capable of prying open their people's minds to the possibility of unity in diversity: leaders in the mold of Mahatma Gandhi, Martin Luther King Jr., and Nelson Mandela. But even Gandhi could never eradicate sectarianism, and indeed was killed by it, as was King. South Africa did not even wait for Mandela to die before sliding into an ugly xenophobia. Charismatic, unifying leaders can kick-start a virtuous circle, but without constant renewal and institutionalization, their legacy will be short-lived.

A legal framework protecting people's liberty and equality must be reinforced by civic values that are sensitive to the reality of diversity. This involves cultivating what Martha Nussbaum calls a sympathetic imagination, or the inner eyes that allow one to see others as full human beings, with their own dreams and fears.[66] It also requires that people recognize that they are "diversely different," as Amartya Sen puts it.[67] People don't just differ along religious lines. They also have racial, linguistic, national, regional, class, caste, vocational, gender, and generational identities, plus loyalties to different localities, schools, pop celebrities, and football teams. This may appear to complicate the task of building social solidarities but the opposite is true. Being diversely different means that there are always connections that can be activated between members of seemingly antagonistic communities. But hate spin agents specialize in getting people to overlook these ties and to treat one salient, emotive marker of identity as supreme, simply because this is more convenient for mobilization.[68] People's basic instincts are thus used "to crowd out the freedom to think."[69]

The project of assertive pluralism demands a clarity of purpose that can compete with hate propagandists' simple myth of us-versus-them. Liberals prefer not to silence every voice of intolerance, even though this is how the intolerant prefer to deal with their ideological opponents. But liberal tolerance doesn't need to descend into a debilitating moral relativism. An assertive pluralism can be built on the well-founded position that a multicultural, equality-protecting constitutional order is superior to ways of organizing nation-states that privilege one religious or cultural identity over all others. Proponents of an exclusive and absolutist vision of society have simply got it wrong.

Assertive pluralism does not negate people's religious identities, but it does insist that people should not deny the diversity around them. It does not challenge a religion's legitimate place in the public life of a democracy, or trivialize its believers' need for respect. But it resists strenuously the position that such legitimacy and respect should be the preserve of just one religion, and denied to unpopular beliefs. No human being, let alone a whole society, can be fully defined by one overarching identity. But this is the confidence trick that political entrepreneurs play on hundreds of millions of citizens, always to enhance their own power. In hate spin, these opportunists have found a strategy that is formidably effective—but one that can still be countered, with enough conviction and vigilance.

Notes

Preface

1. Anil Netto, "Forum on Secular Law Disrupted," *Inter Press Service News Agency*, May 15, 2006, http://www.ipsnews.net/2006/05/rights-malaysia-forum-on-secular -law-disrupted.

Chapter 1

1. "Political Leadership Key to Implementing Zero-Tolerance Policy towards Anti-Semitism in Hungary, Say OSCE Officials during Joint Visit," Organization for Security and Co-operation in Europe, Office for Democratic Institutions and Human Rights, Press Release, June 19, 2015, http://www.osce.org/odihr/165361.

2. Leonid Bershidsky, "Russia Tries Cracking Down on Opera," *Bloomberg View*, March 10, 2015, http://www.bloombergview.com/articles/2015-03-10/russia-tries -cracking-down-on-opera; "Russian Theater Director Fired over Wagner Opera," *Salon*, March 29, 2015, http://www.salon.com/2015/03/29/russian_theater_director _fired_over_wagner_opera.

3. Ishak Ibrahim, "Tales of Blasphemy in Egypt," Atlantic Council website, April 23, 2015, http://www.atlanticcouncil.org/blogs/egyptsource/tales-of-blasphemy-in -egypt; "Teacher, Students Released on Bail for 'Contempt of Religion' after ISIS Video," *Daily News Egypt*, June 9, 2015, http://www.dailynewsegypt.com/2015/ 06/09/teacher-students-released-on-bail-for-contempt-of-religion-after-isis-video.

4. "Furious Oyedepo Asks Church To Kill Anyone Who Looks Like an 'Islamic Demon,'" *Nigerian Bulletin*, January 4, 2015, http://www.nigerianbulletin.com/ threads/furious-oyedepo-asks-church-to-kill-anyone-who-looks-like-an-islamic -demon.106001/.

5. Bruce Douglas, "Attack on 11-Year-Old in Rio Highlights Fears of Rising Religious Intolerance," *The Guardian*, June 19, 2015, http://www.theguardian.com/world/ 2015/jun/19/candomble-brazil-rio-de-janeiro-evangelical.

6. "Texas Shooting: Two Gunmen Shot Dead Outside Muhammad Exhibition—Rolling Coverage," *The Guardian*, May 4, 2015, http://www.theguardian.com/us-news/live/2015/may/04/two-gunmen-shot-dead-in-texas-outside-muhammad-cartoon-exhibition-rolling-coverage.

7. Julian Hattem, "DC Metro Bans 'Issue' Ads after Muhammad Cartoon Request," *The Hill*, May 28, 2015, http://thehill.com/policy/national-security/243351-dc-metro-limits-ads-after-request-for-muhammad-cartoon.

8. Sarah Kaplan, "The Serene-Looking Buddhist Monk Accused of Inciting Burma's Sectarian Violence," *Washington Post*, May 27, 2015, https://www.washingtonpost.com/news/morning-mix/wp/2015/05/27/the-burmese-bin-laden-fueling-the-rohingya-migrant-crisis-in-southeast-asia/; "Myanmar: The Politics of Rakhine State," International Crisis Group, *Asia Report*, October 22, 2014, http://www.crisisgroup.org/~/media/Files/asia/south-east-asia/burma-myanmar/261-myanmar-the-politics-of-rakhine-state.pdf.

9. "Myanmar Parliament Rails at UN Chief's Comments over Rohingya," UNHCR: The UN Refugee Agency, *Refugees Daily*, November 16, 2014, http://www.unhcr.org/cgi-bin/texis/vtx/refdaily?pass=52fc6fbd5&id=5469ad148.

10. Vanessa Paige Chelvan, "Amos Yee's Appeal to Overturn Conviction and Jail Term Dismissed," *Channel News Asia*, October 9, 2015, http://www.channelnewsasia.com/news/singapore/amos-yee-s-appeal-to/2176608.html.

11. Amanda Hodge, "Losing Their Religion," *The Australian*, December 5, 2015, http://at.theaustralian.com.au/link/881e0fd23a54aad01d6633927dc7e6a5?domain=theaustralian.com.au.

12. Pal Ahluwalia and Toby Miller, "The Politics of Free Speech," *Social Identities: Journal for the Study of Race, Nation and Culture* 18 (2012): 628.

13. UN General Assembly, *International Covenant on Civil and Political Rights*, United Nations, Treaty Series, vol. 999, December 16, 1966.

14. Garry Trudeau, "The Abuse of Satire," *The Atlantic*, April 11, 2015, http://www.theatlantic.com/international/archive/2015/04/the-abuse-of-satire/390312.

15. Miklos Haraszti, "Foreword: Hate Speech and the Coming Death of the International Standard before It Was Born (Complaints of a Watchdog)," in *The Content and Context of Hate Speech: Rethinking Regulation and Responses*, ed. Michael Herz and Peter Molnar (New York: Cambridge University Press, 2012), xvi.

16. Anealia Safdar and Phil Rees, "Myanmar's 'Muslim-Free' Election," *Aljazeera*, October 29, 2015, http://www.aljazeera.com/indepth/features/2015/10/myanmar-muslim-free-election-151024182312301.html.

17. Sheryl Gay Stolberg, "Obama Strongly Backs Islam Center near 9/11 Site," *New York Times*, August 13, 2010, http://www.nytimes.com/2010/08/14/us/politics/14obama.html.

18. "Statement by the President on the Occasion of Ramadan," The White House, August 11, 2010, https://www.whitehouse.gov/the-press-office/2010/08/11/statement-president-occasion-ramadan.

19. Karen Tumulty and Michael D. Shear, "Obama: Backing Muslims' Right to Build NYC Mosque Is Not an Endorsement," *Washington Post*, August 15, 2010, http://www.washingtonpost.com/wp-dyn/content/article/2010/08/14/AR2010081401796.html.

20. Martha C. Nussbaum, *The New Religious Intolerance: Overcoming the Politics of Fear in an Anxious Age* (Cambridge, MA: Belknap Press, 2012), 214.

21. Gardiner Harris, "Obama, in Mosque Visit, Denounces Anti-Muslim Bias," *New York Times*, February 3, 2016, http://www.nytimes.com/2016/02/04/us/politics/obama-muslims-baltimore-mosque.html.

22. "Global Religious Diversity: Half of the Most Religiously Diverse Countries Are in Asia-Pacific Region," Pew Research Center, April 4, 2014, http://www.pewforum.org/2014/04/04/global-religious-diversity/.

23. For example: Gilbert Ramsay and Sarah Victoria Marsden, "Radical Distinctions: A Comparative Study of Two Jihadist Speeches," *Critical Studies on Terrorism* 6 (2013): 392–409.

24. For example: Naomi Sakr, "Enriching or Impoverishing Discourse on Rights? Talk about Freedom of Expression on Arab Television," *Middle East Journal of Culture & Communication* 3 (2010): 101–119.

25. Ivan Hare and James Weinstein, eds., *Extreme Speech and Democracy* (New York: Oxford University Press, 2011); Michael Herz and Peter Molnar, eds., *The Content and Context of Hate Speech: Rethinking Regulation and Responses* (New York: Cambridge University Press, 2011); Lorenz Langer, *Religious Offense and Human Rights: The Implications of Defamation of Religions* (Cambridge: Cambridge University Press, 2014).

26. Eric Posner, *The Twilight of Human Rights Law* (Oxford: Oxford University Press, 2014), 144.

27. Larry Diamond, "Thinking About Hybrid Regimes," *Journal of Democracy* 13 (2002): 21–35; Philippe C. Schmitter and Terry Lynn Karl, "What Democracy Is ... and Is Not," *Journal of Democracy* 2 (1991): 75–88; Andreas Schedler, "What Is Democratic Consolidation?" *Journal of Democracy* 9 (1998): 91–107; Guillermo O'Donnell and Philippe C. Schmitter, *Transitions from Authoritarian Rule: Tentative Conclusions about Uncertain Democracies* (Baltimore: Johns Hopkins University Press, 2013); Juan

José Linz and Alfred Stepan, *Problems of Democratic Transition and Consolidation* (Baltimore: Johns Hopkins University Press, 1996).

28. Samuel Issacharoff, *Fragile Democracies* (New York: Cambridge University Press, 2015).

29. Timothy Samuel Shah, Alfred Stepan, and Monica Duffy Toft, eds., *Rethinking Religion and World Affairs* (New York: Oxford University Press, 2012); Alfred Stepan and Charles Taylor, eds., *Boundaries of Toleration* (New York: Columbia University Press, 2014).

30. Sidney Tarrow, *Power in Movement: Social Movements and Contentious Politics*, 2nd ed. (Cambridge: Cambridge University Press, 1998), 4–5.

31. Sidney Tarrow, "Transnational Politics: Contention and Institutions in International Politics," in *Annual Review of Political Science* 4 (2001): 1–20.

32. William A. Gamson, *The Strategy of Social Protests*, 2nd ed. (Belmont, CA: Wadsworth, 1990).

33. Robert D. Benford and David A. Snow, "Framing Processes and Social Movements: An Overview and Assessment," *Annual Review of Sociology* 26 (2000): 611–639.

34. William A. Gamson, "Injustice Frames," in *The Wiley-Blackwell Encyclopedia of Social and Political Movements*, ed. David A. Snow et al. (Oxford: Blackwell Publishing Ltd, 2013), doi: 10.1002/9780470674871.wbespm110.

35. Thomas Olesen, *Global Injustice Symbols and Social Movements* (New York: Palgrave Macmillan, 2015); Thomas Olesen, "From National Event to Transnational Injustice Symbol: The Three Phases of the Muhammad Cartoon Controversy," in *Dynamics of Political Violence: A Process-Oriented Perspective on Radicalization and the Escalation of Political Conflict*, ed. Lorenzo Bosi, Charles Demetriou, and Stefan Malthaner (Farnham, UK: Ashgate, 2014), 217–236; Thomas Olesen, "Transnational Injustice Symbols and Communities: The Case of Al-Qaeda and the Guantanamo Bay Detention Camp," *Current Sociology* 59 (2011): 717–734.

36. Doug McAdam, Sidney Tarrow, and Charles Tilly, *Dynamics of Contention* (Cambridge: Cambridge University Press, 2001).

37. Elisabeth Noelle-Neumann, "The Spiral of Silence: A Theory of Public Opinion," *Journal of Communication* 24 (1974): 43–51.

38. William Hart et al., "Feeling Validated versus Being Correct: A Meta-Analysis of Selective Exposure to Information," *Psychological Bulletin* 135 (2009): 555–588.

39. Amartya Sen, *The Idea of Justice* (London: Penguin Books, 2009).

40. Michael Waltman and John Haas, *The Communication of Hate* (New York: Peter Lang, 2011).

41. Anne Weber, *Manual on Hate Speech* (Strasbourg: Council of Europe Publishing, 2009), 3.

42. Alexander Tsesis, *Destructive Messages: How Hate Speech Paves the Way For Harmful Social Movements* (New York: New York University Press, 2002), 1.

43. Waltman and Haas, *The Communication of Hate*.

44. Susan Benesch, "Words as Weapons," *World Policy Journal* 29 (2012): 11.

45. Jeffrey Goldberg, "Is It Time for the Jews to Leave Europe?" *Atlantic*, April 2015, http://www.theatlantic.com/magazine/archive/2015/04/is-it-time-for-the-jews-to -leave-europe/386279.

46. Amy Chua, *World on Fire: How Exporting Free Market Democracy Breeds Ethnic Hatred and Global Instability* (New York: Doubleday, 2003).

47. Cees J. Hamelink, *Media and Conflict: Escalating Evil* (Boulder, CO: Paradigm Publishers, 2011), 21.

48. Rita Kirk Whillock, "The Use of Hate as a Stratagem for Achieving Social and Political Goals," in *Hate Speech*, ed. Rita Kirk Whillock and David Slayden (Thousand Oaks, CA: Sage Publications, 1995), 32.

49. Tsesis, *Destructive Messages*, 26.

50. Priscilla Marie Meddaugh and Jack Kay, "Hate Speech or 'Reasonable Racism?' The Other in Stormfront," *Journal of Mass Media Ethics* 24 (2009): 254.

51. "Al-Qaida Leader Calls for Holy War on US and Israel over Anti-Islamic Film," *The Guardian*, October 13, 2012, http://www.theguardian.co.uk/world/2012/oct/13/ al-qaida-leader-holy-war-us.

52. Brooks Barnes, "Man Tied to Anti-Islam Film Denies Probation Charges," *New York Times*, October 11, 2012, http://www.nytimes.com/2012/10/11/us/man-tied-to -anti-islam-film-denies-probation-violations.html.

53. "Editorial: 'Muslim Rage' is Lazy Shorthand for a Complex Story," *Observer*, September 23, 2012, http://www.guardian.co.uk/commentisfree/2012/sep/23/editorial -muslim-protests.

54. Salil Tripathi, *Offense: The Hindu Case* (London: Seagull Books, 2009), 12.

55. Paul R. Brass, *Theft of an Idol: Text and Context in the Representation of Collective Violence* (Princeton, NJ: Princeton University Press, 1997).

56. Ibid., 14.

57. "Crime Against Humanity," Concerned Citizens Tribunal—Gujarat 2002 (Mumbai: Anil Dharkar for Citizens for Justice and Peace, 2002), http://www .sabrang.com/tribunal/tribunal1.pdf.

58. R. B. Sreekumar, interview by author, April 23, 2015; Nivedita Menon, "Gujarat Genocide—the State, Law and Subversion: R B Sreekumar," *Kafila*, February 27, 2012, http://kafila.org/2012/02/27/gujarat-genocide-the-state-law-and-subversion-r -b-sreekumar/.

59. Harsh Mander, "Cry, the Beloved Country," *Outlook*, March 19, 2002, http:// www.outlookindia.com/article/cry-the-beloved-country/214944.

60. Harsh Mander, interview by author, April 23, 2015.

61. Brass, *Theft of an Idol*, 267.

62. Fahad Desmukh, "Pakistani Artists Say Their Country's YouTube Ban Is about Politics, Not Religion," *PRI*, February 28, 2014, http://www.pri.org/stories/ 2014-02-28/pakistani-artists-say-their-countrys-youtube-ban-about-politics-not -religion; Lois Parshley, "Meet the Woman behind Pakistan's First Hackathon," *Wired*, May 15, 2013, http://www.wired.com/2013/05/pakistans-first-hackathon.

63. "Saad Aziz Confesses to Sabeen's Murder for Holding Valentine's Day Rally," *Express Tribune*, May 22, 2015, http://tribune.com.pk/story/890555/saad-aziz -confesses-to-sabeens-murder-for-holding-valentines-day-rally; Imtiaz Ali, "Sabeen's Murder Investigation Inches Forward as Suspicion Falls on Religious Extremists," April 30, 2015, http://www.dawn.com/news/1179007.

64. Veengas Yasmeen, discussion with author, July 27, 2015.

65. Raza Rumi, "Sabeen Mahmud, Martyr for Free Speech," *New York Times*, April 29, 2015, http://www.nytimes.com/2015/04/30/opinion/sabeen-mahmud-martyr -for-free-speech.html; Aqil Shah, "There Will Be Blood," *Foreign Affairs*, May 2, 2015, https://www.foreignaffairs.com/articles/pakistan/2015-05-02/there-will-be-blood.

66. Saad Hammadi, "Third Atheist Blogger Killed in Bangladesh Knife Attack," *Guardian*, May 12, 2015, http://www.theguardian.com/world/2015/may/12/third -atheist-blogger-killed-in-bangladesh-after-knife-attack.

67. Sabir Mustafa, "Bangladesh Bloggers: Clear Pattern to Killings," *BBC News*, May 12, 2015, http://www.bbc.com/news/world-asia-32708975.

68. Ain o Salish Kendra, "Bangladesh: Situation of Bloggers and Online Activists," unpublished report, 2015.

69. "Facts, Narratives and Sensationalism," *Shunyastan*, November 27, 2015, http:// shunyastan.org/2015/11/27/blogger.

70. Francisco Panizza, "Introduction: Populism and the Mirror of Democracy," in *Populism and the Mirror of Democracy*, ed. Francisco Panizza (London: Verso, 2005), 1–31.

71. Tarrow, *Power in Movement*, 5.

72. Joseph Stiglitz, *Globalization and Its Discontents* (New York: Penguin, 2003); Jeffrey D. Sachs, *Common Wealth: Economics for a Crowded Planet* (New York: Penguin, 2008).

73. Nussbaum, *The New Religious Intolerance*, 21.

74. Ibid., 24.

Chapter 2

1. Frank La Rue, *Report of the Special Rapporteur on the Promotion and Protection of the Right to Freedom of Opinion and Expression*, United Nations General Assembly, September 7, 2012, A/67/357, 20.

2. UN General Assembly, *International Covenant on Civil and Political Rights*, December 16, 1966, United Nations, Treaty Series, vol. 999.

3. Eric Posner, *The Twilight of Human Rights Law* (Oxford: Oxford University Press, 2014).

4. "United Nations Charter," United Nations, October 24, 1945.

5. UN General Assembly, *Universal Declaration of Human Rights*, December 10, 1948.

6. UN General Assembly, *International Covenant on Civil and Political Rights*.

7. La Rue, *Report of the Special Rapporteur*, 2012.

8. Ivan Hare, "Extreme Speech Under International and Regional Human Rights Standards," in *Extreme Speech and Democracy*, ed. Ivan Hare and James Weinstein (Oxford: Oxford University Press, 2009), 66.

9. Tarlach McGonagle, "A Survey and Critical Analysis of Council of Europe Strategies for Countering 'Hate Speech,'" in *The Content and Context of Hate Speech: Rethinking Regulation and Responses*, ed. Michael Herz and Peter Molnar (Cambridge: Cambridge University Press, 2012), 456–498.

10. Article 19, *The Camden Principles on Freedom of Expression and Equality* (London: Article 19, 2009), http://www.article19.org/data/files/pdfs/standards/the-camden -principles-on-freedom-of-expression-and-equality.pdf; United Nations Office of the High Commissioner for Human Rights, "Rabat Plan of Action on the Prohibition of Advocacy of National, Racial or Religious Hatred That Constitutes Incitement to Discrimination, Hostility or Violence" (conclusions and recommendations emanating from the four regional expert workshops, organized by the OHCRR in 2011 and adopted by experts in Rabat, Morocco, October 5, 2012).

11. UN General Assembly, *International Covenant on Civil and Political Rights*.

12. Organization of American States, *American Convention on Human Rights*, November 22, 1969.

13. Council of Europe, "European Convention for the Protection of Human Rights and Fundamental Freedoms, as amended by Protocols Nos. 11 and 14," November 4, 1950, http://www.refworld.org/docid/3ae6b3b04.html.

14. La Rue, *Report of the Special Rapporteur*, 2012, 11.

15. Ibid., 15.

16. Article 19, *The Camden Principles*, 10.

17. Article 19, "Towards an Interpretation of Article 20 of the ICCPR: Thresholds for the Prohibition of Incitement to Hatred," A Study Prepared for the Regional Expert Meeting on Article 20, Organized by the Office of the High Commissioner for Human Rights, Vienna, February 8–9, 2010.

18. Article 19, *The Camden Principles*, 10.

19. La Rue, *Report of the Special Rapporteur*, 2012, 13–14.

20. Ibid., 15.

21. United Nations Human Rights Committee, General Comment no. 34, International Covenant on Civil and Political Rights—Article 19: Freedoms of Opinion and Expression, September 12, 2011, CCPR/C/GC/34, 11.

22. United Nations Office of the High Commissioner for Human Rights, "Rabat Plan of Action," 3.

23. La Rue, *Report of the Special Rapporteur*, 2012.

24. Toby Mendel, "Does International Law Provide for Consistent Rules on Hate Speech?" in *The Content and Context of Hate Speech: Rethinking Regulation and Responses*, ed. Michael Herz and Peter Molnar (New York: Cambridge University Press, 2012), 417–429.

25. Article 19, "Broadcasting Genocide: Censorship, Propaganda and State-Sponsored Violence in Rwanda 1990-1994," Article 19, 1996, http://www.article19.org/pdfs/publications/rwanda-broadcasting-genocide.pdf.

26. Asma Jahangir and Doudou Diène, *Report of the Special Rapporteur on Freedom of Religion or Belief, and the Special Rapporteur on Contemporary Forms of Racism, Racial Discrimination, Xenophobia and Related Intolerance*, United Nations Human Rights Council, September 20, 2006, A/HRC/2/3.

27. Ibid., 14.

28. Ibid., 15.

29. *Handyside v. The United Kingdom*, 5493/72, Council of Europe: European Court of Human Rights, November 4, 1976.

30. Helmi Noman, "In the Name of God: Faith-Based Internet Censorship in Majority Muslim Countries," OpenNet Initiative, August 1, 2011, http://opennet.net/sites/opennet.net/files/ONI_NameofGod_1_08_2011.pdf.

31. The First Amendment also doesn't protect "fighting words" (usually referring to face-to-face personal abuse that is inherently likely to provoke a violent reaction) or intimidation through "true threats." See http://www.firstamendmentcenter.org. These types of speech fall outside the hate speech definition and are not discussed here.

32. Michel Rosenfeld, "Hate Speech in Constitutional Jurisprudence: A Comparative Analysis," in *The Content and Context of Hate Speech*, ed. Michael Herz and Peter Molnar (New York: Cambridge University Press, 2012), 242–289.

33. *I.A. v. Turkey*, 42571/98, Council of Europe: European Court of Human Rights, September 13, 2005.

34. German Criminal Code, Section 130, http://www.gesetze-im-internet.de/englisch_stgb/englisch_stgb.html.

35. Phillip I. Blumberg, *Repressive Jurisprudence in the Early American Republic* (Cambridge: Cambridge University Press, 2010).

36. Rosenfeld, "Hate Speech in Constitutional Jurisprudence," 264.

37. Anne Weber, *Manual on Hate Speech* (Strasbourg: Council of Europe Publishing, 2009).

38. "Obscenity," Legal Information Institute, Cornell University Law School, 2009, https://www.law.cornell.edu/wex/obscenity.

39. Jo-Anne Prud'homme, *The Impact of Blasphemy Laws on Human Rights* (Washington, DC: Freedom House, 2010), http://www.freedomhouse.org/sites/default/files/Policing_Belief_Full.pdf.

40. Canadian Criminal Code, Section 318(4), http://laws-lois.justice.gc.ca/eng/acts/c-46/FullText.html.

41. United Nations General Assembly, "Declaration on the Elimination of All Forms of Intolerance and of Discrimination Based on Religion or Belief," November 25, 1981, A/RES/36/55, http://www.un.org/documents/ga/res/36/a36r055.htm.

42. Article 19, "Broadcasting Genocide."

43. Indian Penal Code, Section 153A(1).

44. *Robert Faurisson v. France*, Communication No. 550/1993, United Nations Human Rights Committee, UN Doc. CCPR/C/58/D/550/1993(1996).

45. Article 19, *The Camden Principles*.

46. *Karataş v. Turkey*, Application no. 23168/94, Council of Europe: European Court of Human Rights, July 8, 1999.

47. Cindy Tham, "Sin Chew Reporter Released after One Day under ISA Detention," *Nut Graph*, September 13, 2008, http://www.thenutgraph.com/sin-chew-reporter -released-after-one-day-under-isa-detention.

48. *Jersild v. Denmark*, 36/1993/431/510, Council of Europe: European Court of Human Rights, August 22, 1994.

49. *Surek v. Turkey*, Application no. 26682/95, Council of Europe: European Court of Human Rights, July 8, 1999.

50. La Rue, Frank. *Report of the Special Rapporteur*, 14.

51. Pakistan Penal Code, Articles 295 and 295A.

52. Prud'homme, *The Impact of Blasphemy Laws*.

53. Mark Potok, interview by author, February 20, 2015.

54. Peter Molnar, "Interview with Robert Post," in *The Content and Context of Hate Speech*, ed. Michael Herz and Peter Molnar (New York: Cambridge University Press, 2012), 31.

55. Heyman, Steven J. "Hate Speech, Public Discourse, and the First Amendment." In *Extreme Speech and Democracy*, ed. Ivan Hare and James Weinstein (Oxford: Oxford University Press, 2009), 165.

56. *R.A.V. v. City of St Paul* (No. 90–7675) 505 US 377 (1992).

57. *Brandenburg v. Ohio*, 395 US 444 (1969).

58. *Yates v. United States*, 354 US 298 (1957).

59. Molnar, "Interview with Robert Post," 21–22.

60. Ronald Dworkin, "Foreword," in *Extreme Speech and Democracy*, ed. Ivan Hare and James Weinstein (Oxford: Oxford University Press, 2009), viii.

61. Kyu Ho Youm, interview by author, July 11, 2015.

62. *New York Times Co. v. Sullivan*, 376 US 254 (1964).

63. Alexander Tsesis, *Destructive Messages: How Hate Speech Paves the Way for Harmful Social Movements* (New York: New York University Press, 2002), 207.

64. Frederick Schauer, "Uncoupling Free Speech," in *The Price We Pay: The Case against Racist Speech, Hate Propaganda, and Pornography*, ed. Laura Lederer and Richard Delgado (New York: Farrar, Straus and Giroux, 1995), 265.

65. Eric Michael Mazur, *The Americanization of Religious Minorities: Confronting the Constitutional Order* (Baltimore: Johns Hopkins University Press, 1999).

66. Jeremy Waldron, "Hate Speech and Political Legitimacy," in *The Content and Context of Hate Speech: Rethinking Regulation and Responses*, ed. Michael Herz and Peter Molnar (New York: Cambridge University Press, 2012), 336.

67. Ibid., 339.

68. Molnar, "Interview with Robert Post."

69. Organization of the Islamic Conference (OIC), *Cairo Declaration on Human Rights in Islam*, August 5, 1990.

70. Organization of the Islamic Conference, "First OIC Observatory Report on Islamophobia," Presented to the 35th Council of Foreign Ministers, Kampala, Uganda, June 18–20, 2008, 2.

71. United Nations Human Rights Council, "Combating Defamation of Religions," Resolution 7/19, March 27, 2008, http://ap.ohchr.org/documents/E/HRC/resolutions/A_HRC_RES_7_19.pdf.

72. "Resolutions on Defamation of Religions Do Not Belong at United Nations, Organizations Say," Freedom House, November 10, 2009, https://freedomhouse.org/article/resolutions-defamation-religions-do-not-belong-united-nations-organizations-say.

73. Jahangir and Diène, *Report of the Special Rapporteurs*.

74. Lorenz Langer, *Religious Offense and Human Rights: The Implications of Defamation of Religions* (Cambridge: Cambridge University Press, 2014).

75. Ibid.

76. United Nations General Assembly, Resolution 66/168: Elimination of All Forms of Intolerance and of Discrimination Based on Religion or Belief, A/RES/66/168, December 19, 2011.

77. Langer, *Religious Offense and Human Rights*.

78. Ibid., 378.

79. Ibid., 360.

80. David Kaye, "Expression, Opinion and Religious Freedoms" (keynote speech at the "Expression, Opinion and Religious Freedoms in Asia" regional consultation, Jakarta, Indonesia, June 3, 2015).

81. Mark Lilla, "The Return of Political Theology," in *The Rule of Law and the Rule of God*, ed. Simeon O. Ilesanmi, Win-Chiat Lee, and J. Wilson Parker (New York: Palgrave Macmillan, 2014), 15–29.

82. Scott M. Thomas, "Outwitting the Developed Countries? Existential Insecurity and the Global Resurgence of Religion," *Journal of International Affairs* 61 (2007): 21.

83. Pippa Norris and Ronald Inglehart, *Sacred and Secular: Religion and Politics Worldwide* (Cambridge University Press, 2004).

84. Bryan S. Turner, "Religion in a Post-Secular Society," in *The New Blackwell Companion to the Sociology of Religion*, ed. Bryan S. Turner (Chichester, UK: Blackwell, 2010), 649–667.

85. Thomas, "Outwitting the Developed Countries?"

86. José Casanova, "Religion Challenging the Myth of Secular Democracy," in *Religion in the 21st Century: Challenges and Transformations*, ed. Lisbet Christoffersen et al. (Farnham, UK: Ashgate, 2013), 25.

87. Ibid., 26.

88. Mazur, *The Americanization of Religious Minorities*.

89. Jonathan Fox, "World Separation of Religion and State into the 21st Century," *Comparative Political Studies* 39 (2006): 537–569; Jonathan Fox and Deborah Flores, "Religions, Constitutions, and the State: A Cross-National Study," *The Journal of Politics* 71 (2009): 1499–1513.

90. Grace Davie, "Resacralization," in *The New Blackwell Companion to the Sociology of Religion*, ed. Bryan S. Turner (Chichester, UK: Blackwell, 2010), 160–177.

91. Alfred Stepan, "Religion, Democracy, and the 'Twin Tolerations,'" in *World Religions and Democracy*, ed. Larry Diamond, Mark F. Plattner, and Philip J. Costopoulos (Baltimore: Johns Hopkins University Press, 2005), 5.

92. Lilla, "The Return of Political Theology," 16–17.

93. Langer, *Religious Offense and Human Rights*.

94. Jeffrey Haynes, "Introduction," in *Routledge Handbook of Religion and Politics*, ed. Jeffrey Haynes (Abingdon, UK: Routledge, 2009), 1–7.

95. William Schweiker, "Monotheistic Faith and the Cosmopolitan Conscience," in *The Rule of Law and the Rule of God*, ed. Simeon O. Ilesanmi, Win-Chiat Lee, and J. Wilson Parker (New York: Palgrave Macmillan, 2014), 41.

96. Samuel P. Huntington, *The Clash of Civilizations and the Remaking of World Order* (New York: Simon & Schuster, 1996).

97. Graeme Wood, "What ISIS Really Wants," *Atlantic*, March 2015.

98. Jonathan Fox, *Religion, Civilization, and Civil War: 1945 Through the New Millennium* (Lanham, MD: Lexington Books, 2005).

99. Norris and Inglehart, *Sacred and Secular*.

100. Jonathan Fox, "Integrating Religion into IR Theory," in *Routledge Handbook of Religion and Politics*, ed. Jeffrey Haynes (Abingdon: Routledge, 2009), 273–292.

101. Pew Research Center, "The Global Religious Landscape" (Washington, DC: Pew Research Center's Forum on Religion & Public Life, December 2012).

102. Abdul Malik Gismar, interview by author, June 4, 2015.

103. Andrea Teti and Andrea Mura, "Islam and Islamism," in *Routledge Handbook of Religion and Politics*, ed. Jeffrey Haynes (Abingdon: Routledge, 2009), 92–110; Akeel Bilgrami, "The Clash within Civilizations," *Daedalus* 132 (2003): 88–93.

104. Shaheen Sardar Ali, "'Systemically Closed, Cognitively Open'? A Critical Analysis of Transformative Processes in Islamic Law and Muslim State Practice," in *Religion in the 21st Century: Challenges and Transformations*, ed. Lisbet Christoffersen et al. (Farnham, UK: Ashgate, 2013), 119.

105. "The Myanmar Daily Show," *The Daily Show* (Comedy Central, November 13, 2015), https://youtu.be/vX-KwOVL-Y8.

106. Stepan, "Religion, Democracy, and the 'Twin Tolerations,'" 10.

107. Schweiker, "Monotheistic Faith and the Cosmopolitan Conscience," 36.

108. Langer, *Religious Offense and Human Rights*, 340.

109. John Anderson, "Religion and Democratisation," in *Routledge Handbook of Religion and Politics*, ed. Jeffrey Haynes (Abingdon, UK: Routledge, 2009), 208.

110. Ibid., 202.

111. Genevieve Zubrzykci, "Religion and Nationalism: A Critical Re-Examination," in *The New Blackwell Companion to the Sociology of Religion*, ed. Bryan S. Turner (Chichester, UK: Blackwell, 2010), 606.

Chapter 3

1. Alexei Oreskovic, "Exclusive: YouTube Hits 4 Billion Daily Video Views," *Reuters*, January 23, 2012, http://www.reuters.com/article/us-google-youtube -idUSTRE80M0TS20120123.

2. Benjamin Ducol, "A Radical Sociability: In Defense of an Online/Offline Multidimensional Approach to Radicalization," in *Social Networks, Terrorism and Counter-Terrorism: Radical and Connected*, ed. Martin Bouchard (Abingdon, UK: Routledge, 2015), 82–104; Ramón Spaaij and Mark S. Hamm, "Key Issues and Research Agendas in Lone Wolf Terrorism," *Studies in Conflict & Terrorism* 38 (2015): 167–178.

3. "Violent Islamist Extremism, the Internet, and the Homegrown Terrorist Threat." Majority and Minority Staff Report. Washington, DC: United States Senate Committee on Homeland Security and Governmental Affairs, May 8, 2008.

4. Ali Wajahit, Eli Clifton, Matthew Duss, Lee Fang, Scott Keyes, and Faiz Shakir. *Fear, Inc.: The Roots of the Islamophobia Network in America.* Washington, DC: Center for American Progress, 2011.

5. Wajahit et al., *Fear, Inc.*, 90.

6. "Myanmar: 'Buddha Bar' Guilty Verdict Another Blow to Freedom of Expression," Amnesty International, March 17, 2015, https://www.amnesty.org/en/latest/news/2015/03/myanmar-buddha-bar-verdict-a-blow-to-freedom-of-expression.

7. Roger Silverstone, *Media and Morality: On the Rise of the Mediapolis* (Cambridge: Polity, 2007), 13.

8. Margaret Bald, *Banned Books: Literature Suppressed on Religious Grounds* (New York: Facts On File, 2006).

9. Gayatri C. Spivak, "Reading *The Satanic Verses*," *Third Text* 4 (1990): 41–60.

10. Geoffrey Robertson, "Looking Back at Salman Rushdie's *The Satanic Verses*," *Guardian*, September 14, 2012.

11. Quoted in Mehdi Mozzafari, "The Rushdie Affair: Blasphemy as a New Form of International Conflict and Crisis," *Terrorism and Political Violence* 2 (1990): 416–417.

12. Ibid.

13. Sohail Inayatullah, "Understanding the Postmodern World: Why Khomeini Wants Rushdie Dead," *Third Text* 4 (1990), 96.

14. Alice Jones, "Salman Rushdie: We're All Too Offended Now," *Independent*, August 11, 2013, http://www.independent.co.uk/arts-entertainment/books/news/salman-rushdie-were-all-too-offended-now-8755930.html.

15. Signe Engelbreth Larsen, "Towards the Blasphemous Self: Constructing Societal Identity in Danish Debates on the Blasphemy Provision in the Twentieth and Twenty-First Centuries." *Journal of Ethnic and Migration Studies* 40 (2014): 194–211.

16. Ibid.

17. Ibid., 202, emphasis in the original.

18. Ibid., 195.

19. "After Van Gogh," *Economist*, November 11, 2004, http://www.economist.com/node/3379357.

20. Lorenz Langer, *Religious Offense and Human Rights: The Implications of Defamation of Religions* (Cambridge: Cambridge University Press, 2014), 37.

21. Quoted in Stephanie Lagouette, "The Cartoon Controversy in Context: Analyzing the Decisions Not to Prosecute under Danish Law," *Brooklyn Journal of International Law* 33 (2008): 382.

22. The Organisation of the Islamic Conference was renamed the Organization of Islamic Cooperation in 2011.

23. "Countries at the Crossroads: Egypt," Freedom House, 2005, https://freedomhouse.org/report/countries-crossroads/2005/egypt.

24. Khairi Abaza, *Political Islam and Regime Survival in Egypt*. Policy Focus #51. Washington, DC: The Washington Institute for Near East Policy, January 2006.

25. Mushahid Ali Munshi Asmat Ali, interview by author, January 19, 2015.

26. Michael Moynihan, "The Repentant Radical," *Daily Beast*, September 17, 2013, http://www.thedailybeast.com/articles/2013/09/17/ahmed-akkari-repents-violent-opposition-to-danish-cartoons-lampooning-islam.html.

27. Lindsay Wise, "Amr Khaled vs Yusuf Al Qaradawi: The Danish Cartoon Controversy and the Clash of Two Islamic TV Titans," *Transnational Broadcasting Studies*, 16 (2006), http://stuff.jworld.ch/al-jazeera/19%20Vertiefungstext%2010.pdf.

28. Shawn Powers, "Examining the Danish Cartoon Affair: Mediatized Cross-Cultural Tensions?" *Media, War & Conflict* 1 (2008): 339–359; Naomi Sakr, "Enriching or Impoverishing Discourse on Rights? Talk about Freedom of Expression on Arab Television," *Middle East Journal of Culture & Communication* 3 (2010): 101–119.

29. Teguh Santosa, interview by author, November 8, 2013.

30. Moynihan, "The Repentant Radical."

31. Sergei F. Kovaleski and Brooks Barnes, "From Man Who Insulted Muhammad, No Regret," *New York Times*, November 25, 2012.

32. Ibid.

33. Lauren Markoe, "Jewish Groups Say Conspiracy Theory over Anti-Islam Film Won't Die," *Huffington Post*, September 30, 2012, http://www.huffingtonpost.com/2012/09/30/jews-backed-innocence-of-muslims-conspiracy-theory_n_1924548.html.

34. Daniel L. Byman, "Terrorism in North Africa: Before and After Benghazi," *Brookings Institution*, July 10, 2013, http://www.brookings.edu/research/testimony/2013/07/10-terrorism-north-africa-before-after-benghazi-byman.

35. William Branigin, "Obama Urges Fla. Pastor to Call off Koran Burning," *Washington Post*, September 9, 2010, http://www.washingtonpost.com/wp-dyn/content/article/2010/09/09/AR2010090903014.html.

36. Byron Tau, "Obama Administration Airs Ads in Pakistan, Condemning Anti-Islam Film," *Politico*, September 20, 2012, http://social.politico.com/politico44/2012/09/obama-administration-airs-ads-in-pakistan-condemning-136174.html.

37. "Community Guidelines," YouTube, accessed June 1, 2013, http://www.youtube.com/yt/policyandsafety/communityguidelines.html.

38. "Transparency Report, July to December 2012," Google, 2013, http://www.google.com/transparencyreport/removals/government/notes/?hl=en#period=Y2012H2.

39. Faheem Hussain, interview by author, March 22, 2015.

40. "Response to Media Queries on the Film 'Innocence of Muslims,'" Singapore Ministry of Home Affairs, September 14, 2012, accessed June 1, 2013, http://www.mha.gov.sg.

41. "Don't Let Quarrels, Unrest Elsewhere Affect S'pore: PM Lee," *Straits Times*, September 16, 2012, https://www.singaporeunited.sg/CEPAPP/Pages/NewsRoom.aspx?refid={9A74D745-51AC-496F-B7A4-259775B53BC0}.

42. "Statement on the Blocking of Access to the Film 'Innocence of Muslims,'" Singapore Ministry of Home Affairs, September 19, 2012, accessed June 1, 2013, http://www.mha.gov.sg.

43. "*Zoolander* Upsets Singapore Censors," *CNN.com*, February 8, 2002, http://edition.cnn.com/2002/SHOWBIZ/Movies/02/08/singapore.zoolander/index.html.

44. Eric Posner, "The World Doesn't Love the First Amendment," *Slate.com*, September 25, 2012, http://www.slate.com/articles/news_and_politics/jurisprudence/2012/09/the_vile_anti_muslim_video_and_the_first_amendment_does_the_u_s_overvalue_free_speech_.html.

45. Michael Weiss, "Guilt and the 'Innocence of Muslims.'" *World Affairs*, September 2013.

46. Emad Mekay, "The Muhammad Movie: Look Who Fanned the Flames," *Columbia Journalism Review*, January 7, 2013.

47. Dwayne R. Winseck, "Intermediary Responsibility," in *International Encyclopedia of Digital Communication and Society*, ed. Robin Mansell and Peng Hwa Ang (Oxford: Wiley-Blackwell, 2015). DOI: 10.1002/9781118767771.wbiedcs143.

48. Zee, "Newsweek in 1995: Why the Internet Will Fail," *Next Web*, February 27, 2010, http://thenextweb.com/shareables/2010/02/27/newsweek-1995-buy-books-newspapers-straight-intenet-uh.

49. Winseck, "Intermediary Responsibility."

50. Uta Kohl, "Google: The Rise and Rise of Online Intermediaries in the Governance of the Internet and beyond (Part 2)," *International Journal of Law and Information Technology* 21 (2013): 232.

51. "Company Overview," Google Company, accessed November 2, 2015, http://www.google.com/about/company.

52. Thomas L. Friedman, "Is Google God?" *New York Times*, June 29, 2003, http://www.nytimes.com/2003/06/29/opinion/is-google-god.html.

53. "GoogleMonitor.com Launches Today," GoogleMonitor.com, January 27, 2010, http://www.googlemonitor.com/wp-content/uploads/2010/01/1-27-10-GoogleMonitor.com-release.pdf.

54. Benoit Frydman and Isabel Rorive, "Fighting Nazi and Anti-Semitic Material on the Internet: The Yahoo! Case and Its Global Implications" (paper presented at the conference Hate and Terrorist Speech on the Internet: The Global Implications of the Yahoo! Ruling in France, Cardozo Law School, February 11, 2002).

55. Joel R. Reidenberg, "Yahoo and Democracy on the Internet," *Jurimetrics* 42 (2002): 261.

56. Ibid., 263.

57. John P. Barlow, "A Declaration of the Independence of Cyberspace" (e-mail circular, February 8, 1996), http://w2.eff.org/Censorship/Internet_censorship_bills/barlow_0296.declaration.

58. Mathias Reimann, "Introduction: The Yahoo! Case and Conflict of Laws in the Cyberage." *Michigan Journal of International Law* 24 (2003): 663–672.

59. Jon Henley, "Yahoo! Agrees to Ban Auctions of Nazi Memorabilia," *Guardian*, January 4, 2001, http://www.theguardian.com/technology/2001/jan/04/internetnews.media.

60. "Carriage of Lithium Batteries," International Air Transport Association, Position Paper, October 8, 2014, http://www.iata.org/policy/Documents/lithium-batteries-position-paper.pdf.

61. Frank La Rue, *Report of the Special Rapporteur on the Promotion and Protection of the Right to Freedom of Opinion and Expression*, United Nations General Assembly, August 10, 2011, A/66/290.

62. Rishi Jaitly, "Intermediary Liability and the Future of the Internet in India," Google Public Policy Blog, October 14, 2007.

63. Kohl, "Google: The Rise and Rise of Online Intermediaries," 192.

64. Ibid., 195.

65. Cynthia Wong and James X. Dempsey, *The Media and Liability for Content on the Internet* (London: Open Society Foundations, 2011).

66. Kohl, "Google: The Rise and Rise of Online Intermediaries," 193.

67. Rachel Whetstone, "Our Approach to Free Expression and Controversial Content," Google Official Blog, March 9, 2012, http://googleblog.blogspot.sg/2012/03/our-approach-to-free-expression-and.html.

68. "Government Requests to Remove Content," Google Transparency Report, http://www.google.com/transparencyreport/removals/government.

69. Jeffrey Rosen, "Google's Gatekeepers," *New York Times Magazine*, November 28, 2008.

70. http://globalnetworkinitiative.org/principles/index.php.

71. Stephen John Stedman, "Spoiler Problems in Peace Processes," *International Security* 22 (1997): 5–53.

72. Rebecca MacKinnon and Ethan Zuckerman, "Don't Feed the Trolls," *Index on Censorship* 41 (2012): 18.

73. Ibid.

74. Mary Douglas, *Purity and Danger: An Analysis of Concepts of Pollution and Taboo* (London: Routledge & Kegan Paul, 1966).

75. Joseph R. Gusfield, *Symbolic Crusade: Status Politics and the American Temperance Movement* (Urbana: University of Illinois Press, 1963).

Chapter 4

1. "Religion," Office of the Registrar General and Census Commissioner, India, 2001, accessed March 1, 2015, http://censusindia.gov.in/Census_And_You/religion.aspx.

2. Pew Research Center, "Indians Reflect on Their Country & the World," March 31, 2014, http://www.pewglobal.org/2014/03/31/chapter-1-indians-in-a-sour-mood.

3. "India: Statement on 2014 General Elections," People's Alliance for Democracy and Secularism, May 24, 2014, http://sacw.net/article8763.html.

4. "Crime Against Humanity," Concerned Citizens Tribunal—Gujarat 2002 (Mumbai: Anil Dharkar for Citizens for Justice and Peace, 2002), http://www.sabrang.com/tribunal/tribunal1.pdf; Paul R. Brass, *The Production of Hindu-Muslim Violence in Contemporary India* (Seattle: University of Washington Press, 2003).

5. "The Original Sin of November 1984," *The Hindu*, November 1, 2012. http://www.thehindu.com/opinion/editorial/the-original-sin-of-november-1984/article4051648.ece.

6. Romila Thapar, "Secularism, History, and Contemporary Politics in India," in *The Crisis of Secularism in India*, ed. Anuradha Dingwaney Needham and Rajeswari Sunder Rajan (Durham, NC: Duke University Press, 2007), 191–207.

7. Aishwary Kumar, *Radical Equality: Ambedkar, Gandhi, and the Risk of Democracy* (Stanford, CA: Stanford University Press, 2015), 2.

8. Paul R. Brass, *Theft of an Idol: Text and Context in the Representation of Collective Violence* (Princeton, NJ: Princeton University Press, 1997), 281.

9. Zahir Janmohamed, interview by author, December 9, 2015. See also Zahir Janmohamed, "Gujarat: A Tale of Two Cities," *The Hindu*, May 25, 2015.

10. Pradip Jain, interview by author, April 25, 2015.

11. Rajeswari Sunder Rajan and Anuradha Dingwaney Needham, "Introduction," in *The Crisis of Secularism in India*, ed. Rajeswari Sunder Rajan and Anuradha Dingwaney Needham (Durham, NC: Duke University Press, 2007), 1–44.

12. Amrita Basu, "The Long March from Ayodhya: Democracy and Violence in India," in *Pluralism and Democracy in India: Debating the Hindu Right*, ed. Wendy Doniger and Martha C. Nussbaum (New York: Oxford University Press, 2015), 153–173.

13. "Babri Demolition Planned; Advani, P V Narasimha Rao Knew of Plot: Cobrapost Sting," *Times of India*, April 4, 2014, http://timesofindia.indiatimes.com/india/Babri-demolition-planned-Advani-P-V-Narasimha-Rao-knew-of-plot-Cobrapost-sting/articleshow/33202922.cms.

14. Varghese K. George, "India: A Hindutva Variant of Neo-Liberalism," *The Hindu*, April 4, 2014.

15. Diptendra Raychaudhuri, "Elections 2014: RSS Swallows the Great Indian Media," *Mainstream Weekly* 52 (May 17, 2014), http://www.mainstreamweekly.net/article4925.html.

16. George, "India: A Hindutva Variant of Neo-Liberalism."

17. Ibid.

18. Diptendra Raychaudhuri, "Elections 2014."

19. Dinesh Narayanan, "RSS 3.0," *Caravan*, May 1, 2014.

20. Angana Chatterji, Lise McKean, and Abha Sur, *Genocide in Gujarat: The Sangh Parivar, Narendra Modi, and the Government of Gujarat* (Coalition Against Genocide, March 2, 2005), 14. See also: Kamal Mitra Chenoy et al., "Ethnic Cleansing in

Ahmedabad: A Preliminary Report by the SAHMAT Fact Finding Team to Ahmedabad, 10–11th March 2002," *Outlook*, March 22, 2002; Human Rights Watch, *We Have No Orders to Save You: State Participation and Complicity in Communal Violence in Gujarat* (New York: Human Rights Watch, April 30, 2002).

21. Freedom House, "Freedom in the World 2015—Discarding Democracy: Return to the Iron Fist" (Washington, DC: Freedom House, 2015), https://freedomhouse.org/report/freedom-world-2015/discarding-democracy-return-iron-fist.

22. Nicole McLaughlin, "Spectrum of Defamation of Religion Laws and the Possibility of a Universal International Standard," *Loyola of Los Angeles International and Comparative Law Review* 32 (2010): 395–426.

23. Scott W. Hibbard, *Religious Politics and Secular States: Egypt, India, and the United States* (Baltimore: Johns Hopkins University Press, 2010); Sumit Ganguly, "The Crisis of Indian Secularism," *Journal of Democracy* 14 (2003): 11–25; Thapar, "Secularism, History, and Contemporary Politics in India"; Rajan and Needham, "Introduction."

24. Robert L. Hardgrave, "India: The Dilemmas of Diversity," *Journal of Democracy* 4 (1993): 54–68.

25. Ibid.

26. Bhairav Acharya, interview by author, April 22, 2015.

27. Neeti Nair, "Beyond the 'Communal' 1920s: The Problem of Intention, Legislative Pragmatism, and the Making of Section 295A of the Indian Penal Code," *Indian Economic and Social History Review* 50 (2013): 319.

28. Bhairav Acharya, comments at "Freedom of Expression in a Digital Age" conference, The Centre for Internet & Society, Delhi, April 21, 2015.

29. Acharya, interview by author.

30. Nair, "Beyond the 'Communal' 1920s."

31. *Gopal Vinayak Godse v. Union of India and Ors* on August 6, 1969 (AIR 1971 Bom 56).

32. *Ramesh s/o Chotalal Dalal v. Union of India and Ors* on February 16, 1988 (1 SCC 668).

33. *Anand Patwardhan v. Union of India and Ors* on July 19, 1996 (AIR 1997 Bom 25).

34. *Sujato Bhadra v. State of West Bengal* on September 22, 2005 (3 CALLT 436 HC).

35. McLaughlin, "Spectrum of Defamation of Religion Laws," 425.

36. Acharya, interview by author.

37. Freedom House, "Freedom in the World 2013," Washington, DC: Freedom House, 2013, https://freedomhouse.org/report/freedom-world/2013/india #.VRV83UayxA9.

38. Geeta Seshu, interview by author, April 22, 2015.

39. "Handbook for Candidates," Election Commission of India, 1998, Reprint 1999.

40. Shahabuddin Y. Quraishi, interview by author, May 18, 2015.

41. "Model Code of Conduct for the Guidance of Political Parties and Candidates," Election Commission of India, 2014.

42. Saurav Datta, "Why It Is Open Season for Hate Speech in India's Elections," *Index on Censorship*, April 28, 2014.

43. M. K. Venu, "Modi and the Numbers Game," *The Hindu*, June 12, 2013.

44. G. Sampath, "Mandate 2014: Triumph of the Spin," *Mint*, May 20, 2014.

45. "What the BJP's Election Campaign CD 'Bharat Ki Pukar' Presents—Excerpts from the Transcript," *The Hindu*, April 7, 2007.

46. Krishna Pokharel and Paul Beckett, "Ayodhya, the Battle for India's Soul: Chapter Four," *The Wall Street Journal*, India Real Time blog, December 6, 2012, http://blogs.wsj.com/indiarealtime/2012/12/06/ayodhya-the-battle-for-indias-soul-chapter-four.

47. Mohan Rao et al., "Communalism and the Role of the State: An Investigation into the Communal Violence in Muzaffarnagar and Its Aftermath," *Economic & Political Weekly*, December 2013.

48. Ajoy Ashirwad Mahaprashasta, "The Riot Route," *Frontline*, October 4, 2013.

49. Rao et al., "Communalism and the Role of the State."

50. Mahaprashasta, "The Riot Route."

51. "Muzaffarnagar Violence: Death Toll Mounts to 28; 4 BJP MLAs, Cong Leader Booked," *Times of India*, September 9, 2013, http://timesofindia.indiatimes.com/india/Muzaffarnagar-violence-Death-toll-mounts-to-28-4-BJP-MLAs-Cong-leader-booked/articleshow/22431800.cms.

52. "Muzaffarnagar: Tales of Death and Despair in India's Riot-Hit Town," *BBC News*, September 25, 2013, http://www.bbc.com/news/world-asia-india-24172537.

53. Jason Burke, "Muzaffarnagar Riots: Politicians Banned over Fears of Spreading Violence," *The Guardian*, September 9, 2013, http://www.theguardian.com/world/2013/sep/09/muzaffarnagar-india-riots-politicians-banned.

54. *Mohd. Haroon and Ors. v. Union of India* on March 26, 2014 (5 SCC 252); "Didn't Ask Police to Go Slow on Controlling Muzaffarnagar Riots: Azam Khan," *Hindustan*

Times, September 18, 2013, http://www.hindustantimes.com/india/didn-t-ask-police
-to-go-slow-on-controlling-muzaffarnagar-riots-azam-khan/story-
kLQhA6JKMJgv3lc1gIylrN.html; Press Trust of India, "Authorities Seek Video Con-
ferencing of Som, Rana in Riots Case," *Business Standard India,* October 2, 2013,
http://www.business-standard.com/article/pti-stories/authorities-seek-video
-conferencing-of-som-rana-in-riots-case-113100200543_1.html.

55. Mahaprashasta, "The Riot Route."

56. Ibid.

57. Rao et al., "Communalism and the Role of the State," 7.

58. Ratan Mani Lal, "Decoding Amit Shah's Campaign: How He Conquered Uttar
Pradesh," *Firstpost,* May 23, 2014.

59. Annirudha Ghosal, "Amit Shah is Charge-Sheeted in Election 'Hate Speech'
Case," *Indian Express,* September 11, 2014, http://indianexpress.com/article/india/
politics/amit-shah-chargesheetd-for-objectionable-speech-during-ls-polls/.

60. Rao et al., "Communalism and the Role of the State."

61. Shyamantha Asokan, "Election Commission Lifts Campaign Ban on Amit
Shah," *Reuters,* April 18, 2014, http://in.reuters.com/article/2014/04/18/uk-india
-election-shah-idINKBN0D402Y20140418.

62. Quraishi, interview by author.

63. "General Elections to Lok Sabha, 2014," Election Commission of India letter to
Government of Bihar, No. 464/JH-HP/2014, April 22, 2014, http://eci.nic.in/eci
_main1/current/CI_22042014.pdf; "FIR Filed against Giriraj Singh, Gadkari," *The
Hindu,* April 20, 2014, http://www.thehindu.com/news/national/fir-filed-against
-giriraj-singh-gadkari/article5931366.ece.

64. Aakar Patel, "Pravin Togadia's Real Estate Advice," *Live Mint,* April 23, 2014.
http://www.livemint.com/Leisure/FBAlnPEVlDBqxZSCWHHUoO/Pravin-Togadias
-real-estate-advice.html.

65. "Shiv Sena Leader Kadam Shares Stage with Modi, Makes Hate Speech against
Muslims," *India Today,* April 22, 2014, http://indiatoday.intoday.in/story/shiv-sena
-leader-ramdas-kadam-hate-speech-against-muslims-narendra-modi/1/357009.html.

66. Sachchidanand Shukla, "Faizabad: Modi Invokes Ram but Mum on Temple, EC
Seeks Report on Speech," *Hindustan Times,* May 6, 2014, http://www.hindustantimes.
com/india-news/modi-invokes-ram-to-seek-votes-in-faizabad-ec-seeks-report-on
-speech/article1-1215684.aspx.

67. "Faizabad's BJP Candidate Served Notice for Placing Lord Rama's Photo," *Web
India 123,* March 27, 2014, http://news.webindia123.com/news/Articles/India/
20140505/2387523.html.

68. Pankaj Sharma and Rohit Joshi, "Is Election Commission Losing Much of its Sheen?" *DNA*, May 6, 2014, http://www.dnaindia.com/india/report-is-election-commission-losing-much-of-its-sheen-1985766.

69. Archana Dalmia, "Jekyll and Hyde Syndrome Spells Danger for Nation," *New Indian Express*, May 11, 2014, http://www.newindianexpress.com/columns/Jekyll-and-Hyde-Syndrome-Spells-Danger-for-Nation/2014/05/11/article2217530.ece.

70. Amartya Sen, *The Argumentative Indian: Writings on Indian History, Culture and Identity* (New York: Penguin, 2005), 63.

71. Amartya Sen, "The Politics of History," in *Pluralism and Democracy in India: Debating the Hindu Right*, ed. Wendy Doniger and Martha C. Nussbaum (New York: Oxford University Press, 2015), 21–34.

72. Thapar, "The Crisis of Secularism in India."

73. Romila Thapar, interview by author, April 22, 2015.

74. "Narendra Modi Gifts Bhagavad Gita to Obama," *Indian Express*, September 30, 2014, http://indianexpress.com/article/india/india-others/narendra-modi-gifts-bhagavad-gita-to-obama/; Tarique Anwar, "Unacceptable and Stupid: Scholars Pour Scorn on Sushma Swaraj's Plan to Make Gita the National Book," *Firstpost*, December 11, 2014.

75. Richard H. Davis, "Book Review," *Shivaji: Hindu King in Islamic India*, by James W. Laine, *Journal of the American Academy of Religion* 72 (2004): 1047.

76. James W. Laine, *Shivaji: Hindu King in Islamic India* (Oxford: Oxford University Press, 2003), 93.

77. Davis, "Book Review."

78. *State Of Maharashtra and Ors. v. Sangharaj Damodar Rupawate and Ors* on July 9, 2010 (5 Bom CR646).

79. *Bilal Ahmed Kaloo v. State of Andhra Pradesh* on August 6, 1997 (7 SCC 431).

80. *Manzar Sayeed Khan v. State of Maharashtra & Anr* on April 5, 2007 (Appeal (crl.) 491 of 2007).

81. V. Venkatesan, "Blow to a Ban," *Frontline*, August 31, 2010, http://www.frontline.in/static/html/fl2716/stories/20100813271604100.htm.

82. Ramachandra Guha, "Life with a Duchess," in *Patriots & Partisans* (London: Penguin Books, 2013), 280–293.

83. Samanwaya Rautray, "'Reasonable Reader' Test for Book Bans," *Telegraph India*, July 12, 2010, http://www.telegraphindia.com/1100713/jsp/nation/story_12677500.jsp.

84. Ajoy Ashirwad Mahaprashasta, "The Rule of Unreason," *Frontline* 28 (November 5–18, 2011).

85. Stephen Prothero, "India's Fundamentalists Triumph In Case Over Wendy Doniger's *The Hindus*," *Huffington Post*, February 26, 2014, http://www .huffingtonpost.com/stephen-prothero/wendy-doniger-the-hindus_b_4858720 .html?ir=India; Jason Burke, "Outcry as Penguin India pulps 'alternative' history of Hindus," *The Guardian*, February 13, 2014, http://www.theguardian.com/ world/2014/feb/13/indian-conservatives-penguin-hindus-book.

86. Pankaj Mishra, "Another Incarnation," *New York Times Book Review*, April 24, 2009.

87. "Penguin India's Statement on 'The Hindus' by Wendy Doniger," Penguin India, February 2014, http://www.penguinbooksindia.com/en/node/4090.html.

88. Wendy Doniger, "India: Censorship by the Batra Brigade," *New York Review of Books*, May 8, 2014.

89. Lawrence Liang, "Legal Notice for Violation of Rights of Readers," February 14, 2014, https://www.documentcloud.org/documents/1018093-notice-to-penguin-by -alternative-law-forum.html.

90. A. G. Noorani, "Penguin & the Parivar," *Frontline*, April 4, 2014.

91. "Penguin India's Statement."

92. Pratap Bhanu Mehta, "Hinduism and Self-Rule," in *World Religions and Democracy*, ed. Larry Diamond, Marc F. Plattner, and Philip J. Costopoulos (Baltimore: Johns Hopkins University Press and the National Endowment for Democracy, 2005), 65.

93. Ramachandra Guha, "A Play in Five Acts—Narendra Modi and the RSS," *Telegraph India*, December 12, 2015.

94. Varghese K. George, interview by author.

95. FP Politics, "RSS Won't Back Down: Yogi Adityanath Amps up Rhetoric despite Modi's Rebuke," *Firstpost*, December 16, 2014, http://www.firstpost.com/politics/rss -wont-back-down-yogi-adityanath-amps-up-rhetoric-despite-modis-rebuke-1851749 .html.

96. Varghese K. George, interview by author.

97. "Brushing off the BJP," *Economist*, February 9, 2015, http://www.economist .com/news/asia/21642616-getting-brush.

98. Acharya, interview by author.

99. "'Fear Among Christians Can Hit Armed Forces': Ex-Navy Chief Echoes Julio Ribeiro," The Buck Stops Here, NDTV, March 31, 2015, http://www.ndtv.com/video/

player/the-buck-stops-here/fear-among-christians-can-hit-armed-forces-ex-navy
-chief-echoes-julio-ribeiro/361856.

100. Debobrat Ghose, "1,200 Years of Servitude: PM Modi Offers Food for Thought," *Firstpost,* June 13, 2014, http://www.firstpost.com/politics/1200-years-of-servitude-pm-modi-offers-food-for-thought-1567805.html.

Chapter 5

1. Susilo Bambang Yudhoyono, "Keynote Speech by President of the Republic of Indonesia" (Sixth Global Forum of the United Nations Alliance of Civilizations, Nusa Dua, Bali, Indonesia, August 29, 2014).

2. Freedom House, "Freedom in the World: Indonesia 2015," Freedom House, 2015, https://freedomhouse.org/report/freedom-world/2015/indonesia.

3. Juan José Linz and Alfred Stepan, *Problems of Democratic Transition and Consolidation* (Baltimore: Johns Hopkins University Press, 1996).

4. Alexander R. Arifianto, "Unpacking the Results of the 2014 Indonesian Legislative Election," *ISEAS Perspective,* no. 24 (April 17, 2014).

5. Edward Aspinall, "How Indonesia Survived," in *Democracy and Islam in Indonesia,* ed. Mirjam Künkler and Alfred Stepan (New York: Columbia University Press, 2013), 144.

6. Human Rights Watch, "Indonesia: Religious Minorities Targets of Rising Violence," Human Rights Watch, February 28, 2013.

7. Sidney Jones, "Indonesian Government Approaches to Radical Islam Since 1998," in *Democracy and Islam in Indonesia,* ed. Mirjam Künkler and Alfred Stepan (New York: Columbia University Press, 2013), 125.

8. United Nations General Assembly, *Summary Prepared by the Office of the High Commissioner for Human Rights in Accordance with Paragraph 5 of the Annex to Human Rights Council Resolution 16/21—Indonesia,* March 9, 2012, A/HRC/WG.6/13/IDN/3.

9. US Department of State, *International Religious Freedom Report for 2013—Indonesia* (Washington, DC: US Department of State, Bureau of Democracy, Human Rights and Labor, 2014).

10. Alfred Stepan, "Religion, Democracy, and the 'Twin Tolerations,'" in *World Religions and Democracy,* ed. Larry Diamond, Marc F. Plattner, and Philip J. Costopoulos (Baltimore: Johns Hopkins University Press, 2005), 3–23.

11. Robert W. Hefner, *Civil Islam: Muslims and Democratization in Indonesia* (Princeton, NJ: Princeton University Press, 2000).

12. Ibid., 14.

13. Mirjam Künkler, "How Pluralist Democracy Became the Consensual Discourse Among Secular and Nonsecular Muslims in Indonesia," in *Democracy and Islam in Indonesia*, ed. Mirjam Künkler and Alfred Stepan (New York: Columbia University Press, 2013), 53–72; Aspinall, "How Indonesia Survived."

14. Alfred Stepan and Mirjam Künkler, "An Interview with Amien Rais," *Journal of International Affairs* 61 (2007): 205–216.

15. Ibid.

16. Künkler, "How Pluralist Democracy Became the Consensual Discourse."

17. Hefner, *Civil Islam*, 217.

18. Hefner, *Civil Islam*; Edward Aspinall, *Opposing Suharto: Compromise, Resistance, and Regime Change in Indonesia* (Stanford, CA.: Stanford University Press, 2005).

19. Hefner, *Civil Islam*, 218.

20. Sidney Jones, "Briefing for the New President: The Terrorist Threat in Indonesia and Southeast Asia," *International Crisis Group*, June 25, 2008.

21. "Indonesia: 'Christianisation' and Intolerance," Policy Briefing No. 114 (Jakarta/ Brussels, International Crisis Group, November 24, 2010), 15.

22. Jones, "Indonesian Government Approaches to Radical Islam Since 1998."

23. Ibid., 120.

24. Ian Wilson, "Resisting Democracy: Front Pembela Islam and Indonesia's 2014 Elections," *ISEAS Perspective*, no. 10 (February 24, 2014).

25. R. William Liddle et al., "Indonesian Democracy," in *Democracy and Islam in Indonesia*, ed. Mirjam Künkler and Alfred Stepan (New York: Columbia University Press, 2013), 24–50.

26. Jan Woischnik and Philipp Muller, "Islamic Parties and Democracy in Indonesia," *Konrad Adenauer–Stiftung International Reports*, no. 10 (2013): 59–79.

27. Martin Van Bruinessen, "What Happened to the Smiling Face of Indonesian Islam? Muslim Intellectualism and the Conservative Turn in Post-Suharto Indonesia," RSIS Working Paper Series (Singapore: S. Rajaratnam School of International Studies, January 6, 2011).

28. Woischnik and Muller, "Islamic Parties and Democracy in Indonesia."

29. Ibid.

30. Robin Bush, "Religious Politics and Minority Rights during the Yudhoyono Presidency," in *The Yudhoyono Presidency: Indonesia's Decade of Stability and Stagnation*, ed. Edward Aspinall, Marcus Mietzner, and Dirk Tomsa (Singapore: Institute of Southeast Asian Studies, 2015), 239–257.

31. "Indonesia: Shia Cleric Convicted of Blasphemy," Human Rights Watch, July 12, 2012, http://www.hrw.org/news/2012/07/12/indonesia-shia-cleric-convicted-blasphemy.

32. Patrick Ziegenhain, *The Indonesian Parliament and Democratization* (Singapore: Institute of Southeast Asian Studies, 2008).

33. Article 19 and Aliansi Jurnalis Independen, *Freedom of Expression and the Media in Indonesia,* December 2005.

34. The 1945 Constitution of the Republic of Indonesia, http://www.embassyofindonesia.org/wordpress/wp-content/uploads/2014/03/IndonesianConstitution.pdf.

35. Pam Allen, "Challenging Diversity?: Indonesia's Anti-Pornography Bill," *Asian Studies Review* 31 (2007): 101–115.

36. Endy M. Bayuni, "Porn Bill Debate Exposes Culture War Fault Lines," *The Jakarta Post*, March 27, 2006.

37. Abdul Khalik, "Porn Law a 'Dead Document,'" *The Jakarta Post*, November 4, 2008, http://www.thejakartapost.com/news/2008/11/04/porn-law-a-039dead-document039.html.

38. The Blasphemy Law's full title is Law No. 1/PNPS/1965 Concerning the Prevention of Religious Abuse and/or Defamation.

39. Equal Rights Trust, *Stakeholder Submission to the Universal Periodic Review of the Republic of Indonesia* (submitted to the UN Human Rights Council, 2011).

40. Toby Mendel, interview by author, August 28, 2014.

41. Article 19, "Indonesia: Human Rights NGOs Argue 'Defamation of Religions' Law Contravenes Freedom of Expression, Freedom of Religion and Equality In Legal Brief to Constitutional Court" (press release, March 23, 2010).

42. Melissa Crouch, "Judicial Review and Religious Freedom: The Case of Indonesian Ahmadis," *Sydney Law Review* 34 (2012): 545–572; Nisa Nurun, "Constitutional Court Rejects Judicial Review of Religious Defamation Law," *The Wahd Institute Monthly Report on Religious Issues*, April 29, 2010, 1–3.

43. "Atheist Alexander Aan Gets of Prison." *The Jakarta Post*, January 31, 2014, http://www.thejakartapost.com/news/2014/01/31/atheist-alexander-aan-gets-prison.html.

44. International Crisis Group, *Indonesia: "Christianisation" and Intolerance.*

45. Ibid.

46. Hasyim Widhiarto, "'Three Ladies' Removal Irks Harapan Indah Residents," *The Jakarta Post*, June 21, 2010, http://www.thejakartapost.com/news/2010/06/21/%E2%80%98three-ladies%E2%80%99-removal-irks-harapan-indah-residents.html.

47. Hasyim Widhiarto, "Noted Sculptor Questions Logic behind Religious Blasphemy Accusations," *The Jakarta Post*, June 20, 2010, http://www.thejakartapost.com/news/2010/06/20/noted-sculptor-questions-logic-behind-religious-blasphemy-accusations.html.

48. International Crisis Group, *Indonesia: "Christianisation" and Intolerance*.

49. Ihsan Ali-Fauzi et al., *Disputed Churches in Jakarta*, ed. Tim Lindsey and Melissa Crouch (Jakarta: Pusat Studi Agama dan Demokrasi, Paramadina Foundation, Reprint, 2014).

50. US Department of State, *International Religious Freedom Report for 2013—Indonesia*.

51. Dewanti A. Wardhani, "Another Churchless Christmas for GKI Yasmin, HKBP Filadelfia," *The Jakarta Post*, December 26, 2015, http://www.thejakartapost.com/news/2015/12/26/another-churchless-christmas-gki-yasmin-hkbp-filadelfia.html.

52. Edwin Lubis and Bonar Sigalingging, interview by author, February 14, 2016.

53. Sigalingging, interview by author.

54. Ihsan Ali-Fauzi, interview by author, June 4, 2015.

55. CHRD, *Indonesia: Submission to the UN Universal Periodic Review. Thirteenth Session of the UPR Working Group of the Human Rights Council*, Malang, Indonesia: Center for Human Rights and Democracy, Faculty of Law, University of Brawijaya, Indonesia, May 2012; Kikue Hamayotsu, "The Limits of Civil Society in Democratic Indonesia: Media Freedom and Religious Intolerance," *Journal of Contemporary Asia* 43 (2013): 658–677; United Nations General Assembly, *Report of the Working Group on the Universal Periodic Review—Indonesia*, Human Rights Council, July 5, 2012, A/HRC/21/7.

56. Franz Magnis-Suseno, "Christian and Muslim Minorities in Indonesia," in *Democracy and Islam in Indonesia*, ed. Mirjam Künkler and Alfred Stepan (New York: Columbia University Press, 2013), 82.

57. Ibid., 84.

58. Crouch, "Judicial Review and Religious Freedom."

59. Magnis-Suseno, "Christian and Muslim Minorities," 82–83.

60. Bambang Harymurty, interview by author, August 28, 2014.

61. "MUI Fatwa Feeds Flames of Clerics' Hate Speech," *Jakarta Post*, January 17, 2011, http://www.thejakartapost.com/news/2011/01/17/mui-fatwa-feeds-flames-clerics%E2%80%99-hate-speech.html.

62. Muhammad As'ad, "Ahmadiyah and the Freedom of Religion in Indonesia," *Journal of Indonesian Islam* 3 (2009): 390–413.

63. United States Commission on International Religious Freedom, *USCIRF Annual Report 2015—Tier 2: Indonesia*, May 1, 2015.

64. As'ad, "Ahmadiyah and the Freedom of Religion in Indonesia."

65. Mohamad Guntur Romli, interview by author, February 27, 2014.

66. "Indonesia: Reverse Ban on Ahmadiyah Sect," Human Rights Watch, June 10, 2008, http://www.hrw.org/en/news/2008/06/09/indonesia-reverse-ban-ahmadiyah -sect.

67. Crouch, "Judicial Review and Religious Freedom."

68. Mary E. McCoy, "Purifying Islam in Post-Authoritarian Indonesia: Corporatist Metaphors and the Rise of Religious Intolerance," *Rhetoric & Public Affairs* 16 (2013): 275–315.

69. Julian Millie, "One Year after the Cikeusik Tragedy," *Inside Indonesia*, no. 107 (January–March 2012).

70. Rizal Panggabean, and Ihsan Ali-Fauzi, *Policing Religious Conflicts in Indonesia*. Translated by Natalia Laskowska. Jakarta, Indonesia: Center for the Study of Religion and Democracy (PUSAD), Paramadina Foundation, 2015.

71. Ibid.

72. "Anti Ahmadiyah Violence In Cikeusik, Indonesia," YouTube video, July 11, 2011, https://www.youtube.com/watch?v=r4cBG9lut0A.

73. Bramantyo Prijosusilo, "A Year after the Murders in Cikeusik, Why Is the Govt Going Soft on Hard-Liners?" *Jakarta Globe*, February 6, 2012.

74. Bush, "Religious Politics."

75. Kathy Quiano, "Indonesia under Fire for Light Sentences in Islamic Sect Attack," *CNN.com*, July 28, 2011, http://www.cnn.com/2011/WORLD/asiapcf/07/28/ indonesia.sentences/.

76. Banten Governor Regulation No. 5 of 2011.

77. Dedy Prianto, "Akhir Cerita Asmara Halima, Rois Dan Tajul Muluk," *OkeZone. com*, August 30, 2012, http://news.okezone.com/read/2012/08/30/337/682508/akhir -cerita-asmara-halima-rois-dan-tajul-muluk.

78. "Indonesia: Release Tajul Muluk, Resolve Situation of Evicted Shi'a Community in East Java," Amnesty International, June 16, 2014, http://www.amnesty.org.au/ news/comments/34816; "Indonesia: Shia Cleric Convicted of Blasphemy"; "Isu Syiah Sampang Jadi Komoditas Politik Pilkada," *Tempo*, May 7, 2013, http://nasional .tempo.co/read/news/2013/05/07/078478574/isu-syiah-sampang-jadi-komoditas -politik-pilkada; "Secuil Hari Di Pengungsian Syiah." *Tempo*, July 10, 2014, http://

ramadan.tempo.co/read/news/2014/07/10/155592104/secuil-hari-di-pengungsian
-syiah.

79. John Bowen, "Contours of Sharia in Indonesia," in *Democracy and Islam in Indonesia*, ed. Mirjam Künkler and Alfred Stepan (New York: Columbia University Press, 2013), 167.

80. "Tifatul Pastikan 'Innocence of Muslims' Terblokir," *KOMPAS.com*, September 18, 2012, http://nasional.kompas.com/read/2012/09/18/16531067/Tifatul.Pastikan .Innocence.of.Muslims.Terblokir.

81. Crouch, "Judicial Review and Religious Freedom."

82. McCoy, "Purifying Islam," 295.

83. Ibid., 294.

84. Ibid., 279.

85. Magnis-Suseno, "Christian and Muslim Minorities."

86. Stepan and Künkler, "An Interview with Amien Rais," 205–206.

87. Hefner, *Civil Islam*.

88. Künkler, "How Pluralist Democracy Became the Consensual Discourse," 70.

89. Van Bruinessen, "What Happened to the Smiling Face of Indonesian Islam."

90. McCoy, "Purifying Islam."

91. Donald Emmerson, interview by author, August 14, 2015.

92. International Crisis Group, *Indonesia:"Christianisation" and Intolerance*.

93. Magnis-Suseno, "Christian and Muslim Minorities," 85.

94. International Crisis Group, *Indonesia:"Christianisation" and Intolerance*, 6.

95. Quoted in "Indonesia: Implications of the Ahmadiyah Decree," *Asia Briefing* no. 78 (Jakarta/Brussels: International Crisis Group, July 7, 2008), 8.

96. Ibid.

97. Abdul Malik Gismar, interview by author, June 4, 2015.

98. Endy Bayuni, interview by author, August 26, 2014.

99. Quoted in Edward Aspinall, Marcus Mietzner, and Dirk Tomsa, "The Moderating President: Yudhoyono's Decade in Power," in *The Yudhoyono Presidency: Indonesia's Decade of Stability and Stagnation*, ed. Edward Aspinall, Marcus Mietzner, and Dirk Tomsa (Singapore: Institute of Southeast Asian Studies, 2015), 13.

100. Ibid., 12.

101. Lenny Tristia Tambun and Bayu Marhaenjati, "Protests Target Female Non-Muslim Chief," *Jakarta Globe*, August 29, 2013, http://jakartaglobe.beritasatu.com/news/protests-target-female-non-muslim-chief.

102. Endy Bayuni, personal communication, August 26, 2014.

103. Alphonse F. La Porta, "Indonesia's Presidential Election: Will Democracy Survive?" *CSIS PacNet*, no. 55 (July 15, 2014), http://csis.org/publication/pacnet-55-indonesias-presidential-election-will-democracy-survive.

104. *USCIRF Annual Report 2015*.

105. Ihsan Ali-Fauzi and Ben Hillman, "Confronting Intolerance: New Hope for Indonesia's Religious Minorities," *East Asia Forum* 7 (January–March 2015), http://www.paramadina-pusad.or.id/publikasi/kolom/confronting-intolerance-new-hope-for-indonesias-religious-minorities.html.

106. Mohamed Guntur Romli, interview by author, February 27, 2014.

Chapter 6

1. Amber Sutton, "Montgomery Wins USA Today Travel's 10 Best Contest, Named Best Historic City in America," *AL.com*, April 30, 2014, http://www.al.com/news/montgomery/index.ssf/2014/04/montgomery_wins_usa_today_trav.html.

2. Barack Obama, "Remarks by the President at the 50th Anniversary of the Selma to Montgomery Marches," Edmund Pettus Bridge, Selma, Alabama, March 7, 2015, https://www.whitehouse.gov/the-press-office/2015/03/07/remarks-president-50th-anniversary-selma-montgomery-marches.

3. "Alabama Election Results," *New York Times*, December 17, 2014, http://elections.nytimes.com/2014/alabama-elections.

4. "How Americans Feel About Religious Groups," Pew Research Center, July 16, 2014.

5. Mary Wisniewski, "American Opinion of Arabs, Muslims Is Getting Worse: Poll," *Reuters*, July 29. 2014, http://www.reuters.com/article/2014/07/29/us-usa-muslims-poll-idUSKBN0FY1ZR20140729.

6. Janet Hook and Patrick O'Connor, "Donald Trump's Plan on Muslims Is Opposed by Most Americans; GOP Is Split, WSJ/NBC Poll Finds," *Wall Street Journal*, December 10, 2015, http://www.wsj.com/articles/wsj-nbc-poll-finds-majority-opposes-trump-plan-to-ban-muslims-1449784927; John McCormick, "Bloomberg Politics Poll: Nearly Two-Thirds of Likely GOP Primary Voters Back Trump's Muslim Ban," *Bloomberg*, December 10, 2015, http://www.bloomberg.com/politics/articles/2015-12-09/bloomberg-politics-poll-trump-muslim-ban-proposal.

7. Andrew Kohut et al., "Continuing Divide in Views of Islam and Violence" (Washington, DC: The Pew Research Center for The People & The Press, March 9, 2011); Andrew Kohut et al., "NYC Mosque Opposed, Muslims' Right to Build Mosques Favored—Public Remains Conflicted Over Islam" (Washington, DC: The Pew Research Center, August 24, 2010).

8. Matthew Duss et al., *Fear, Inc. 2.0* (Washington, DC: Center for American Progress, 2015), 2.

9. Nathan Lean, *The Islamophobia Industry: How the Right Manufactures Fear of Muslims* (Chicago: University of Chicago Press, 2012).

10. Haj Yazdiha, "Law as Movement Strategy: How the Islamophobia Movement Institutionalizes Fear Through Legislation," *Social Movement Studies* 13 (2014): 267–274.

11. Lauren Carroll and Louis Jacobson. "Trump Cites Shaky Survey in Call to Ban Muslims from Entering US," *Politifact*, December 9, 2015, http://www.politifact.com/truth-o-meter/statements/2015/dec/09/donald-trump/trump-cites-shaky-survey-call-ban-muslims-entering; Philip Bump, "Donald Trump's Call to Ban Muslim Immigrants Is Based on a Very Shoddy Poll," *The Washington Post*, December 7, 2015, https://www.washingtonpost.com/news/the-fix/wp/2015/12/07/donald-trumps-call-to-ban-muslims-from-coming-to-the-u-s-has-a-very-bad-poll-at-its-center.

12. Alan Rappeport, "Ted Cruz Faulted for Adviser With Anti-Islam Views," *The New York Times*, March 17, 2016, http://www.nytimes.com/politics/first-draft/2016/03/17/ted-cruz-faulted-for-advisor-with-anti-islam-views.

13. Mark Potok, interview by author, February 20, 2015.

14. Eric Johnston, interview by author, February 19, 2015.

15. Denise A. Spellberg, *Thomas Jefferson's Qur'an: Islam and the Founders* (New York: Alfred A. Knopf, 2013).

16. U.S. Citizenship and Immigration Services, "A Promise of Freedom: An Introduction to U.S. History and Civics for Immigrants," undated, accessed July 23, 2015, http://www.uscis.gov/citizenship/learners/study-test/study-materials-civics-test/promise-freedom-introduction-us-history-and-civics-immigrants.

17. Scott W. Hibbard, *Religious Politics and Secular States: Egypt, India, and the United States* (Baltimore: Johns Hopkins University Press, 2010).

18. Patrick J. Buchanan, "Address to the Republican National Convention," Republican National Convention 1992, Houston, Texas, August 17, 1992.

19. Scott W. Hibbard, *Religious Politics and Secular States: Egypt, India, and the United States* (Baltimore: Johns Hopkins University Press, 2010).

20. Ibid., 208.

21. Robert B. Horwitz, *America's Right: Anti-Establishment Conservatism from Goldwater to the Tea Party* (Cambridge: Polity, 2010), 10.

22. Ibid., 200.

23. Richard Hofstadter, *The Paranoid Style in American Politics, and Other Essays* (New York: Knopf, 1965).

24. Horwitz, *America's Right*, 200.

25. Larry Houck, interview by author, February 21, 2015.

26. Ali Wajahit et al., *Fear, Inc.: The Roots of the Islamophobia Network in America* (Washington, DC: Center for American Progress, 2011).

27. Yasmine Taeb, interview by author, March 9, 2015.

28. Duss et al., *Fear, Inc. 2.0.*

29. CAIR, *Legislating Fear: Islamophobia and Its Impact on the United States* (Washington, DC: Council on American-Islamic Relations, 2013).

30. Search conducted March 11, 2015, using google.com.hk. Using google.com, the top entry was another anti-Islam website, www.thereligionofpeace.com.

31. Nathan Lean, interview by author, January 16, 2015.

32. Potok, interview by author.

33. Saeed A. Khan, "Sharia Law, Islamophobia and the U.S. Constitution: New Tectonic Plates of the Culture Wars," *University of Maryland Law Journal of Race, Religion, Gender and Class* 12, (2012): 123–139.

34. The Editorial Board, "The Tide of the Culture War Shifts," *New York Times*, September 28, 2014, http://www.nytimes.com/2014/09/29/opinion/the-tide-of-the -culture-war-shifts.html.

35. Bill Scher, "How Republicans Lost the Culture War," *Politico Magazine*, October 12, 2014, http://www.politico.com/magazine/story/2014/10/how-republicans-lost -the-culture-war-111822.html.

36. Khan, "Sharia Law," 129.

37. Nadia Marzouki, "Moral Offense versus Religious Freedom," *Revue Francaise de Science Politique (English)* 61, no. 5 (2011): 4.

38. Ralph Blumenthal and Sharaf Mowjood, "Muslim Prayers Fuel Spiritual Rebuilding Project by Ground Zero," *New York Times*, December 8, 2009, http://www .nytimes.com/2009/12/09/nyregion/09mosque.html.

39. Quoted in Justin Elliott, "How the 'Ground Zero Mosque' Fear Mongering Began," *Salon*, August 16, 2010, http://www.salon.com/2010/08/16/ground_zero _mosque_origins/.

40. Martha C. Nussbaum, *The New Religious Intolerance: Overcoming the Politics of Fear in an Anxious Age* (Cambridge, MA: Belknap Press, 2012).

41. Ibid.

42. Marzouki, "Moral Offense," 6.

43. Ibid.

44. Ibid., 7.

45. Ibid.

46. Ossama Bahloul, interview by author, February 22, 2015.

47. Saleh Sbenaty, interview by author, February 22, 2015.

48. Ibid.

49. Chris Echegaray, "Murfreesboro Mosque Plan Ignites Backlash," *Tennessean*, June 17, 2010, http://archive.tennessean.com/article/20100617/NEWS06/6170326/ Murfreesboro-mosque-plan-ignites-backlash; Travis Loller, "Planned US Mosque Draws Opponents, Supporters," *Associated Press Newswires*, July 15, 2010, 09:49 a.m. edition; Travis Loller, "Judge's Ruling Stops Construction of Tennessee Mosque, Finding Public Didn't Get Enough Notice," *Associated Press Newswires*, May 30, 2012, 6:40 a.m. edition; Robbie Brown and Christine Hauser, "After Attacks and Threats, Tennessee Mosque Opens," *New York Times Blog*, August 10, 2012, http://thelede .blogs.nytimes.com/2012/08/10/after-attacks-and-threats-tennessee-mosque-opens/.

50. Guy Jordan, "The Politics of (Mere) Presence: The Islamic Center of Murfrees-boro, Tennessee," Conversations: An Online Journal of the Center for the Study of Material and Visual Cultures of Religion (2014), http://mavcor.yale.edu/ conversations/essays/politics-mere-presence-islamic-center-murfreesboro-tennessee; Tim Murphy, "The Craziest GOP House Race of the Year," *Mother Jones*, July 30, 2012, http://www.motherjones.com/politics/2012/07/lou-ann-zelenik-congress.

51. CAIR, *Legislating Fear*, 37.

52. Ibid.

53. Larry Houck, "Address to the Alabama State Board of Education" (notes pro-vided to the author by Houck).

54. PFAW, *Book Wars: The Right's Campaign to Censor Literature, History, and Science* (Washington, DC: People for the American Way, 2014).

55. Ibid.; PFAW, *Texas Textbooks: What Happened, What It Means, and What We Can Do About It* (Washington, DC: People For the American Way, 2010), http://www .pfaw.org/sites/default/files/rww-in-focus-textbooks.pdf.

56. Quoted in Claire Mullally, "Banned Books," First Amendment Center Website, September 13, 2002, http://www.firstamendmentcenter.org/banned-books.

57. Ibid.

58. ACT! for America, *Education or Indoctrination? The Treatment of Islam in 6th through 12th Grade Assessment Textbooks*, ACT! for America Education, 2011, http:// www.actforamerica.org/downloads/Full_Report_version_7.31.12.pdf.

59. Ibid., 31.

60. Wajahit et al. *Fear, Inc.*

61. Larry Houck, interview by author, February 21, 2015.

62. Houck, "Address to the Alabama State Board of Education."

63. Quoted in Evan Belanger, "Fear of Pro-Islamic Bias Delays State Board's Adoption of New Social Studies Books," *AL.com*, December 12, 2013, http://blog.al.com/ wire/2013/12/fear_of_pro-islam_bias_stalls.html.

64. Larry Houck, "Review of *My World History*" (submitted to Alabama State Board of Education, undated).

65. Quoted in Evan Belanger, "Are These Pro-Islamic Books? State Board Delays Vote on Textbooks after Bias Concerns Raised," *AL.com*, December 12, 2013, http:// blog.al.com/wire/2013/12/are_these_books_pro-islamic_st.html.

66. Houck, interview by author.

67. Robert P. Boyle, *Books Challenged or Banned 2013–2014* (Chicago: American Library Association, 2014), https://www.ila.org/content/documents/bbw_2014_short .pdf.

68. Center for Security Policy, *Shariah: The Threat to America* (Washington, DC: Center for Security Policy, 2010).

69. Tim Murphy, "The Texas GOP Just Nominated a Gay-Hating Conspiracy Theorist for US Senate," *Mother Jones*, August 1, 2012, http://www.motherjones.com/ mojo/2012/08/ted-cruz-texas-senate-conspiracy-theories.

70. Ryan Reilly, "GOP Platform Takes Hard Stance Against Imaginary Sharia Threat," *Talking Points Memo*, August 21, 2012, http://talkingpointsmemo.com/livewire/gop -platform-takes-hard-stance-against-imaginary-sharia-threat.

71. Katherine Lemons and Joshua Takano Chambers-Letson, "Rule of Law: Sharia Panic and the US Constitution in the House of Representatives," *Cultural Studies* 28

(2014): 1048–1077; Philip Bump, "How Sharia Law Became Embedded in Our Political Debate," *The Washington Post*, January 8, 2016; Yazdiha, "Law as Movement Strategy."

72. Carlo A. Pedrioli, "Constructing the Other: U.S. Muslims, Anti-Sharia Law, and the Constitutional Consequences of Volatile Intercultural Rhetoric," *Southern California Interdisciplinary Law Journal* 22 (2012): 78.

73. Andrea Elliott, "The Man Behind the Anti-Shariah Movement," *New York Times*, July 30, 2011.

74. Duss et al., *Fear, Inc. 2.0.*

75. Anti-Defamation League, "David Yerushalmi: A Driving Force Behind Anti-Sharia Efforts in the U.S.," January 13, 2012, http://www.adl.org/assets/pdf/civil-rights/david-yerushalmi-2012-1-11-v1.pdf.

76. Elliott, "The Man Behind the Anti-Shariah Movement."

77. Center for Security Policy, *Shariah*, 172.

78. David Yerushalmi, *CLE Course on Draft Uniform Act: American Laws for American Courts*, Law Offices of David Yerushalmi, P.C., November 7, 2012.

79. CAIR, *Legislating Fear.*

80. Johnston, interview by author.

81. Alabama Senate Bill 62.

82. Quoted in Kay Campbell, "Amendment One to Outlaw 'Foreign Law' in Alabama? Not Such a Good Idea, Some Christians Say," *AL.com*, October 30, 2011, http://www.al.com/news/huntsville/index.ssf/2014/10/how_will_you_vote_on_amendment.html.

83. "Late-Night Passage Puts Constitutional Amendment to Voters; Spells Out Foreign Law Protections," *Associated Press*, May 22, 2013.

84. "Alabama Election Results," *New York Times*.

85. Ashfaq Taufique, interview by author, February 21, 2015.

86. Faiza Patel, Matthew Duss, and Amos Toh, *Foreign Law Bans: Legal Uncertainties and Practical Problems*, (Washington, DC: Center for American Progress, 2013), http://www.brennancenter.org/sites/default/files/publications/ForeignLawBans.pdf.

87. Paul Horwitz, "Amendment One Is Useless, Costly, and Wrong," *AL.com*, October 30, 2014.

88. "Resolution 113A," American Bar Association, August 8–9, 2011.

89. Ibid., 4.

90. Randy Brinson, interview by author, February 20, 2015.

91. Johnston, interview by author.

92. CAIR, *Legislating Fear*, 75–78.

93. Sbenaty, interview by author.

94. Bahloul, interview by author.

95. Obama, "Remarks by the President at the 50th Anniversary of the Selma to Montgomery Marches."

Chapter 7

1. Lauren Markoe, "Muslim Scholars Tell Islamic State: You Don't Understand Islam," *Religion News Service*, September 24, 2014, http://www.religionnews.com/2014/09/24/100-plus-muslims-scholars-refute-isis-ideology/.

2. "British Imams Condemn ISIS," ImamsOnline.com, July 11, 2014, https://www.youtube.com/watch?v=KKjAt6lIlgY.

3. Greta Van Susteren, "My Offer to Muslim Leaders—Come on 'On the Record' and Condemn Islamic Extremism," *On the Record with Greta Van Susteren*, October 6, 2014.

4. "CAIR Video Calls Out Fox News' Faux 'Condemn Islamic Extremism' Challenge to Muslim Leaders," Council on American–Islamic Relations, November 13, 2014.

5. Phil Hoad, "Aamir Khan's Religious Satire PK Becomes India's Most Successful Film," *Guardian*, January 7, 2015, http://www.theguardian.com/film/2015/jan/07/global-box-office-pk-the-hobbit-big-hero-6-unbroken.

6. Maxwell McCombs and Tamara Bell, "The Agenda-Setting Role of Mass Communication," in *An Integrated Approach to Communication Theory and Research*, ed. Michael B. Salwen and Don W. Stacks (Mahwah, NJ: Lawrence Erlbaum, 1996), 93–110; Pippa Norris and Sina Odugbemi, "Evaluating Media Performance," in *Public Sentinel: News Media & Governance Reform*, ed. Pippa Norris (Washington, DC: World Bank Publications, 2010), 3–30.

7. Manuel Castells, "A Network Theory of Power," *International Journal of Communication* 5 (2011): 780–781.

8. Frank La Rue, *Report of the Special Rapporteur on the Promotion and Protection of the Right to Freedom of Opinion and Expression*, United Nations General Assembly, August 10, 2011, A/66/290, 20.

9. Thomas Hanitzsch, Patrick Lee Plaisance, and Elizabeth A. Skewes, "Universals and Differences in Global Journalism Ethics," in *Global Media Ethics: Problems and Perspectives*, ed. Stephen J. A. Ward (Chichester, UK: Wiley-Blackwell, 2013), 30–49.

10. Thomas Hanitzsch, "Populist Disseminators, Detached Watchdogs, Critical Change Agents and Opportunist Facilitators: Professional Milieus, the Journalistic Field and Autonomy in 18 Countries," *The International Communication Gazette* 73 (2011): 477–494.

11. Margaret Scammell and Holli A. Semetko, "The Media and Democracy," in *The Media, Journalism and Democracy*, ed. Margaret Scammell and Holli A. Semetko (Burlington, UK: Ashgate, 2000), xi–xlix.

12. James Curran, "What Democracy Requires of the Media," in *The Institutions of American Democracy: The Press*, ed. Geneva Overholser and Kathleen Hall Jamieson (New York: Oxford University Press, 2005), 120–140; C. Edwin Baker, *Media, Markets, and Democracy* (Cambridge: Cambridge University Press, 2002).

13. Courtney C. Radsch, ed., *World Trends in Freedom of Expression and Media Development* (Paris: United Nations Educational, Scientific and Cultural Organization, 2014), 18.

14. Chris Atton, *Alternative Media* (London: Sage Publications, 2002); John D. H. Downing, *Radical Media: Rebellious Communication and Social Movements* (Thousand Oaks, CA: Sage, 2001); Marisol Sandoval and Christian Fuchs, "Towards a Critical Theory of Alternative Media," *Telematics and Informatics* 27 (2010): 141–150.

15. Nancy Fraser, "Rethinking the Public Sphere: A Contribution to the Critique of Actually Existing Democracy," in *Habermas and the Public Sphere*, ed. Craig Calhoun (Cambridge, MA: MIT Press, 1992), 116.

16. Article 19, *Broadcasting Genocide: Censorship, Propaganda and State-Sponsored Violence in Rwanda 1990–1994* (London: Article 19, 1996), 106.

17. Ali Wajahit et al., *Fear, Inc.: The Roots of the Islamophobia Network in America* (Washington, DC: Center for American Progress, 2011).

18. Jesse Holcomb and Amy Mitchell, "Cable: By the Numbers," *State of the News Media 2013* (Washington, DC: Pew Research Center, 2013).

19. "Partisanship and Cable News Audiences," Pew Research Center, October 30, 2009.

20. Erik Nisbet and Kelly Garrett, "Fox News Contributes to Spread of Rumors about Proposed NYC Mosque," Columbus, Ohio: Ohio State University, October 14, 2010.

21. Public Religion Research Institute, "Survey: Majority Say Congressional Hearings on Alleged Extremism in American Muslim Community 'Good Idea,'" *PublicReligion.org*, February 16, 2011, http://publicreligion.org/research/2011/02/

majority-say-congressional-hearings-on-alleged-extremism-in-american-muslim-community-'good-idea'.

22. "2006 Word of the Year," *Merriam-Webster Online Dictionary*, http://www.merriam-webster.com/word-of-the-year/2006-word-of-the-year.htm.

23. William Hart et al., "Feeling Validated versus Being Correct: A Meta-Analysis of Selective Exposure to Information," *Psychological Bulletin* 135 (2009): 555–588.

24. Chris Mooney, *The Republican Brain: The Science of Why They Deny Science—and Reality* (Hoboken, NJ: John Wiley & Sons, 2012).

25. Wajahit et al., *Fear, Inc.*

26. Martin Van Bruinessen, "What Happened to the Smiling Face of Indonesian Islam? Muslim Intellectualism and the Conservative Turn in Post-Suharto Indonesia," *RSIS Working Paper Series* (Singapore: S. Rajaratnam School of International Studies, January 6, 2011); Akh Muzakki, "Contested Islam: Examining the Material Base of Islamic Discourse in New Order Indonesia," *Graduate Journal of Asia-Pacific Studies* 6 (2010): 71–88.

27. International Crisis Group, "Indonesia: 'Christianisation' and Intolerance," *Asia Briefing*, November 24, 2010.

28. Merlyna Lim, "Islamic Radicalism and Anti-Americanism in Indonesia: The Role of the Internet," *Policy Studies* 18 (Washington, DC: East–West Center Washington, 2005). http://scholarspace.manoa.hawaii.edu/bitstream/handle/10125/3520/PS018.pdf?sequence=1.

29. James Curran, "Rethinking Media and Democracy," in *Mass Media and Society*, ed. James Curran and Michael Gurevitch (London: Arnold, 2000), 120–154.

30. "About the ABC: Legislative Framework," Australian Broadcasting Corporation, accessed November 5, 2015, http://about.abc.net.au/how-the-abc-is-run/what-guides-us/legislative-framework/.

31. Australian Broadcasting Corporation, *Editorial Policies: Principles and Standards*, 2011, updated 2015.

32. Siddharth Vardarajan, remarks at Mumbai Press Club forum, "The Elephant in the Room: The Crisis in Journalism," February 6, 2014, http://www.youtube.com/watch?v=WCE2KQxCPGE.

33. Lawrence Pintak and Budi Setiyono, "The Mission of Indonesian Journalism: Balancing Democracy, Development, and Islamic Values," *International Journal of Press/Politics*, 16 (2010): 185–209.

34. Herbert J. Gans, *Deciding What's News: A Study of* CBS Evening News, NBC Nightly News, Newsweek, *and* Time (New York: Pantheon Books, 1979).

35. Edward Said, *Orientalism* (New York: Vintage, 1979); Edward Said, *Covering Islam* (London: Vintage, 1997).

36. Thomas Friedman, "Broadway and the Mosque," *New York Times*, August 3, 2010.

37. Mitchell Stephens, *A History of News* (New York: Viking, 1988).

38. Nick Davies, *Flat Earth News* (London: Vintage Book, 2009).

39. Shawn Powers, "Examining the Danish Cartoon Affair: Mediatized Cross-Cultural Tensions?" *Media, War & Conflict* 1 (2008): 339–359.

40. Owen Bennett Jones, "Terry Jones, Pastor," *The Interview*, BBC World Service, October 4, 2010. http://www.bbc.co.uk/programmes/p009zklg.

41. Steven Maras, *Objectivity in Journalism* (Cambridge: Polity, 2013).

42. Raphael Cohen-Almagor, "The Limits of Objective Reporting," *Journal of Language and Politics* 7 (2008): 138–157; Jay Rosen, *What Are Journalists For?* (New Haven, CT: Yale University Press, 1999); Gaye Tuchman, "Objectivity as Strategic Ritual: An Examination of Newsmen's Notions of Objectivity," *American Journal of Sociology* 77 (1972): 660–679.

43. Kelly McBride, "How to Report on Quran Burning and Other Hate Speech," Poynter.org: Everyday Ethics, September 9, 2010.

44. Frank La Rue, *Report of the Special Rapporteur on the Promotion and Protection of the Right to Freedom of Opinion and Expression*, United Nations General Assembly, September 7, 2012, A/67/357, 20.

45. Mark Potok, interview by author, February 20, 2015.

46. Yazuv Baydar, interview by author, March 1, 2013; Pinar Sevinclidir, "Hate Speech on the Rise in Turkish Media," *BBC Monitoring*, October 30, 2014.

47. "IFJ Declaration of Principles on the Conduct of Journalists," International Federation of Journalists, 1986, http://www.ifj.org/about-ifj/ifj-code-of-principles.

48. "SPJ Code of Ethics," Society of Professional Journalists, 2014. http://www.spj.org/ethicscode.asp.

49. "Principles of Journalism," Pew Research Journalism Project. Accessed September 1, 2014. http://www.journalism.org/resources/principles-of-journalism/. [Available at: http://journalistsresource.org/tip-sheets/foundations/principles-of-journalism.]

50. "Editorial Guidelines," BBC, 2011; Reuters, "Handbook of Journalism," Thomson Reuters.

51. Geoff Elliott, *Reporting Diversity: How Journalists Can Contribute to Community Cohesion* (Cambridge: Society of Editors, and London: Media Trust, 2005); Debra L.

Mason, ed. *Reporting on Religion: A Primer on Journalism's Best Beat* (Westerville, OH: Religion Newswriters Association, 2006); Verica Rupar, *Getting the Facts Right: Reporting Ethnicity & Religion* (Brussels: International Federation of Journalists, 2012).

52. Majid Tehranian, "Peace Journalism: Negotiating Global Media Ethics," *Harvard Journal of Press/Politics* 7 (2002): 58–83; Rukhsana Aslam, "Peace Journalism: A Paradigm Shift in Traditional Media Approach," *Pacific Journalism Review* 17 (2011): 119–139.

53. Gita Widya Laksmini Soejoatmodjo, "Peace Journalism in Indonesia," in *International Journalism and Democracy: Civic Engagement Models from around the World*, ed. Angela Romano (New York: Routledge, 2010), 180–194.

54. Liz Fawcett, "Why Peace Journalism Isn't News," *Journalism Studies* 3 (2002): 215.

55. Lee Seow Ting, "Peace Journalism: Principles and Structural Limitations in the News Coverage of Three Conflicts," *Mass Communication and Society* 13 (2010): 361–384.

56. Thomas Hanitzsch, "Deconstructing Journalism Culture: Toward a Universal Theory," *Communication Theory* 17 (2007): 367–385.

57. Mitch Stacy, "Minister: 'Burn a Quran Day' to Go as Planned on September 11," *Huffington Post*, September 7, 2010, http://www.huffingtonpost.com/2010/09/07/burn-a-quran-day-to-go-as_n_707823.html.

58. Thomas Kent, "Fighting Hate Speech: UN Can Treat the Press as a Partner," *Media Asia* 40 (2013): 308.

59. Ibid., 309.

60. Rupar, *Getting the Facts Right*, 58.

61. Garry Trudeau, "The Abuse of Satire," *Atlantic*, April 11, 2015; Steve Sack, Remarks at Opening Forum, 6th Pulitzer Prize Winners Workshop, Hong Kong Baptist University, October 28, 2015.

62. Dan Gillmor, *We the Media: Grassroots Journalism By the People, For the People* (Sebastopol, CA: O'Reilly Media, 2006).

63. Kimberly Meltzer, "Journalistic Concern about Uncivil Political Talk in Digital News Media Responsibility, Credibility, and Academic Influence," *International Journal of Press/Politics* 20 (2015): 85–107.

64. Jay Rosen, "The People Formerly Known as the Audience," *Press Think*, June 27, 2006.

65. Cherian George, "Public Accountability Brings Rewards and Risks: Interview with A. S. Panneerselvan," *Media Asia* 41 (2014): 13.

66. Ibid.

67. Elisabeth Noelle-Neumann, "The Spiral of Silence: A Theory of Public Opinion," *Journal of Communication* 24 (1974): 43–51.

68. Emma Goodman, *Online Comment Moderation: Emerging Best Practices* (Darmstadt, Germany: WAN-IFRA, 2013), 58.

69. "Manila Principles on Intermediary Liability," 2015. https://www.manilaprinciples.org/principles.

70. Rainer Forst, "Civil Society," in *A Companion to Contemporary Political Philosophy*, ed. Robert E. Goodin, Philip Pettit, and Thomas Pogge, 2nd ed. (Malden, MA: Blackwell, 2007), 452–462.

71. http://www.hatebase.org.

72. http://fightagainsthate.com.

73. http://www.nohatespeechmovement.org.

74. Iginio Gagliardone et al., *Countering Online Hate Speech* (Paris: United Nations Educational, Scientific, and Cultural Organization, 2015).

75. *Intellectual Freedom Manual*, 8th ed. (Chicago: American Library Association, 2010); "Interpretations of the Library Bill of Rights," American Library Association, n.d., http://www.ala.org/advocacy/intfreedom/librarybill/interpretations.

76. "Library Bill of Rights," American Library Association, http://www.ala.org/advocacy/intfreedom/librarybill.

77. American Library Association. "Support for Dealing with Challenges." *Banned & Challenged Books*, n.d., http://www.ala.org/bbooks/challengedmaterials/support.

78. Willem Velthoven, "*Fitna* the Movie. We're Tired of Waiting. So, Let's Do It Ourselves! Sorry!" *Mediamatic*, March 17, 2008, http://www.mediamatic.net/33851/en/fitna-the-movie.

79. "The Pink Chaddi Campaign," 2009, http://thepinkchaddicampaign.blogspot.de/.

80. Bill Chappell, "'Muslim Rage' Explodes on Twitter, but in a Funny Way (Yes, Really)," *NPR.org*, September 17, 2012. http://www.npr.org/sections/thetwo-way/2012/09/17/161315765/muslim-rage-explodes-on-twitter-but-in-a-funny-way-yes-really.

81. Mark Potok, interview by author, February 20, 2015.

82. Justin Huggler, "Lamps Go out All over Germany in Backlash against Anti-Immigrant Protests," *Telegraph*, January 5, 2015, http://www.telegraph.co.uk/news/

worldnews/europe/germany/11326516/Lamps-go-out-all-over-Germany-in-backlash
-against-anti-immigrant-protests.html.

83. Liesbet van Zoonen, Farida Vis, and Sabina Mihelj, "Performing Citizenship on
YouTube: Activism, Satire and Online Debate around the Anti-Islam Video *Fitna*,"
Critical Discourse Studies 7 (2010): 249–262.

84. Tara Morrow, interview by author, February 24, 2015.

85. "A New Conversation," New Evangelical Partnership, accessed November 1,
2015, http://www.newevangelicalpartnership.org/christianmuslimdialogue.

86. Kay Campbell, "Amendment One to Outlaw 'Foreign Law' in Alabama? Not
Such a Good Idea, Some Christians Say," *AL.com*, October 30, 2014, http://www
.al.com/news/huntsville/index.ssf/2014/10/how_will_you_vote_on_amendment
.html.

87. Randy Brinson, interview by author, February 20, 2015.

88. Robert P. George, "Defend Religious Liberty for Muslims," *Firstthings*, June 5,
2012.

89. Matthew Schmitz, "Fears of 'Creeping Sharia,'" *National Review*, June 13, 2012.

Chapter 8

1. Matthew Duss et al., *Fear, Inc. 2.0* (Washington, DC: Center for American Progress, 2015).

2. Larry Diamond and Leonardo Morlino, "The Quality of Democracy: An Overview," *Journal of Democracy* 15 (2004): 24.

3. Doug McAdam, Sidney Tarrow, and Charles Tilly, *Dynamics of Contention* (Cambridge: Cambridge University Press, 2001), 6.

4. Joseph R. Gusfield, *Symbolic Crusade: Status Politics and the American Temperance
Movement* (Urbana: University of Illinois Press, 1963); Louis A. Zurcher Jr. et al.,
"The Anti-Pornography Campaign: A Symbolic Crusade," *Social Problems* 19 (1971):
217–238.

5. William Mazzrella and Raminder Kaur, "Between Sedition and Seduction: Thinking Censorship in South Asia," in *Routledge Handbook of Media Law*, ed. Monroe E.
Price, Stefaan G. Verhulst and Libby Morgan (Abingdon, UK: Routledge, 2013),
308–309.

6. Tom Porter, "Germany: Radical Imam Abu Bilal Ismail Faces Charges after Calls
for Destruction of Zionist Jews," *International Business Times*, February 25, 2015,
http://www.ibtimes.co.uk/germany-radical-imam-abu-bilal-ismail-faces-charges
-after-calls-destruction-zionist-jews-1489440.

7. Jeremy Sharon, "Marton Gyongyosi of Jobbik Party Calls for List of Jews Who Are Threat to Country; Jewish Groups: Reminiscent of Nazi Policy," *Jerusalem Post*, November 27, 2012, http://www.jpost.com/International/Hungarian-rightist-List -Jews-who-pose-security-risk.

8. Jim Yardley, "Europe's Anti-Semitism Comes Out of the Shadows," *New York Times*, September 23, 2014, http://www.nytimes.com/2014/09/24/world/europe/ europes-anti-semitism-comes-out-of-shadows.html.

9. Anshel Pfeffer, "Hungarian Jews: Angry About the Holocaust but Unworried About Today's Anti-Semitism," *Haaretz*, February 24, 2015, http://www.haaretz .com/jewish-world/jewish-world-features/.premium-1.644077.

10. Farid Hafez, "Shifting Borders: Islamophobia as Common Ground for Building Pan-European Right-Wing Unity," *Patterns of Prejudice* 48 (2014): 479–499.

11. Mary E. McCoy, "Purifying Islam in Post-Authoritarian Indonesia: Corporatist Metaphors and the Rise of Religious Intolerance," *Rhetoric & Public Affairs* 16 (2013): 294.

12. Asifkhan Pathan, interview by author, July 1, 2015.

13. Haj Yazdiha, "Law as Movement Strategy: How the Islamophobia Movement Institutionalizes Fear Through Legislation," *Social Movement Studies* 13 (2014): 273.

14. Nathan Lean, interview by author, February 23, 2015.

15. Paul Duggan, "Metro Says No to Issue-Oriented Ads," *Washington Post*, May 28, 2015, https://www.washingtonpost.com/local/trafficandcommuting/metro-says-no -to-issue-oriented-ads/2015/05/28/ee182bec-0572-11e5-8bda-c7b4e9a8f7ac_story .html.

16. Rowan Williams, "A Common Word for the Common Good," Dr Rowan Wil- liams, 104th Archbishop of Canterbury, July 15, 2008, http://rowanwilliams .archbishopofcanterbury.org/articles.php/1107/a-common-word-for-the-common -good.

17. Miranda Blue, interview by author, February 23, 2015.

18. Charles Tilly, *Popular Contention in Great Britain, 1758–1834* (Cambridge, MA: Harvard University Press, 1995).

19. "True Tolerance," Focus on the Family, n.d., http://www.truetolerance.org/.

20. Sherry Machlin, "Banned Books Week: And Tango Makes Three," New York Public Library, September 23, 2013, http://www.nypl.org/blog/2013/09/23/banned -books-week-and-tango-makes-three.

21. Varghese K. George, interview by author, April 22, 2015.

22. Priscilla Marie Meddaugh and Jack Kay, "Hate Speech or 'Reasonable Racism?' The Other in Stormfront." *Journal of Mass Media Ethics* 24 (2009): 254.

23. Annelies Verdoolaege, *Reconciliation Discourse: The Case of the Truth and Reconciliation Commission* (Amsterdam: John Benjamins, 2008), 89.

24. Anand Dibyesh, "The Violence of Security: Hindu Nationalism and the Politics of Representing 'the Muslim' as a Danger," *The Round Table: The Commonwealth Journal of International Affairs* 94 (April 2005): 203–215.

25. "Digvijaya Hits out at Modi and Shah for Carrying out a 'Communal Campaign'," *IBN Live*, May 5, 2014, http://www.ibnlive.com/news/india/digvijaya-hits -out-at-modi-and-shah-for-carrying-out-a-communal-campaign-685704.html.

26. Jason Burke, "Narendra Modi: India's Saviour or Its Worst Nightmare?" *Guardian*, March 6, 2014, http://www.theguardian.com/world/2014/mar/06/ narendra-modi-india-bjp-leader-elections.

27. Dibyesh, "The Violence of Security."

28. "No Guilty Feeling about Gujarat Riots, Says Modi," *Hindu*, July 13, 2013, http:// www.thehindu.com/news/national/no-guilty-feeling-about-gujarat-riots-says-modi/ article4908704.ece.

29. Wajahit et al., *Fear, Inc.: The Roots of the Islamophobia Network in America* (Washington, DC: Center for American Progress, 2011).

30. Matthew Duss et al., *Fear, Inc. 2.0* (Washington, DC: Center for American Progress, 2015).

31. Ian Shapiro, *The State of Democratic Theory* (Princeton, NJ: Princeton University Press, 2003), 85.

32. United Nations Human Rights Committee, *General Comment no. 34, International Covenant on Civil and Political Rights—Article 19: Freedoms of Opinion and Expression*, September 12, 2011, CCPR/C/GC/34.

33. Nick Cohen, *You Can't Read This Book* (London: Fourth Estate, 2012).

34. Erasmus, "How to Combat Hate," *Economist*, June 5, 2015, http://www .economist.com/blogs/erasmus/2015/06/tony-blair-religion-and-free-speech.

35. "A European Model Law for the Promotion of Tolerance and the Suppression of Intolerance," The European Council on Tolerance and Reconciliation, 2015.

36. Michael Blake, "Tolerance and Theocracy: How Liberal States Should Think of Religious States," *Journal of International Affairs* 61 (2007): 1–17.

37. The words, "You can turn around and go home," are borrowed from Atticus Finch's face-off with a mob in Harper Lee's Alabama-based novel, *To Kill a Mockingbird* (1960).

38. "The Publicity Dilemma," The Church of Jesus Christ of Latter-Day Saints, March 9, 2009, http://www.mormonnewsroom.org/article/the-publicity-dilemma.

39. *"Book of Mormon* Musical: Church's Official Statement," The Church of Jesus Christ of Latter-Day Saints, February 7, 2011, http://www.mormonnewsroom.org/article/church-statement-regarding-the-book-of-mormon-broadway-musical.

40. Office of the High Commissioner for Human Rights, "Rabat Plan of Action on the Prohibition of Advocacy of National, Racial or Religious Hatred That Constitutes Incitement to Discrimination, Hostility or Violence" Conclusions and Recommendations Emanating from the Four Regional Expert Workshops organized by the OHCRR in 2011 and Adopted by Experts in Rabat, Morocco, October 5, 2012.

41. Robert Post, "Hate Speech," in *Extreme Speech and Democracy*, ed. Ivan Hare and James Weinstein (Oxford: Oxford University Press, 2009), 135.

42. John M. Cotter, "Sounds of Hate: White Power Rock and Roll and the Neo-Nazi Skinhead Subculture," *Terrorism and Political Violence* 11 (1999): 111–140.

43. The Editorial Board, "Free Speech vs. Hate Speech," *New York Times*, May 6, 2015, http://www.nytimes.com/2015/05/07/opinion/free-speech-vs-hate-speech.html.

44. "Rabat Plan of Action," 2.

45. Article 19, *The Camden Principles on Freedom of Expression and Equality* (London: Article 19, 2009), 3.

46. Mark Potok, interview by author, February 20, 2015.

47. Teesta Setalvad, interview by author, July 6, 2015.

48. Agnes Callamard, "Comments and Recommendations on ECRI General Policy Recommendation No. 15 on Combating Hate Speech," Global Freedom of Expression, Columbia University, May 20, 2015.

49. "S.A.S. v. France: The European Court's Decision in Light of Human Rights Doctrine on Restricting Religious Dress," *International Justice Resource Center*, July 11, 2014.

50. Adam Liptak, "Muslim Woman Denied Job Over Head Scarf Wins in Supreme Court," *New York Times*, June 1, 2015, http://www.nytimes.com/2015/06/02/us/supreme-court-rules-in-samantha-elauf-abercrombie-fitch-case.html.

51. Eric Michael Mazur, *The Americanization of Religious Minorities: Confronting the Constitutional Order* (Baltimore: Johns Hopkins University Press, 1999).

52. Ossama Bahloul, "The Gift of Difficulty," presented at TEDxNashville, Nashville, Tennessee, May 7, 2013, http://tedxtalks.ted.com/video/The-Gift-of-Difficulty-Ossama-B.

53. Corey Saylor, interview by author, February 23, 2015.

54. Samuel Issacharoff, *Fragile Democracies* (New York: Cambridge University Press, 2015), 21.

55. Shapiro, The State of Democratic Theory, 96–97.

56. Edward Aspinall, "How Indonesia Survived," in *Democracy and Islam in Indonesia*, ed. Mirjam Künkler and Alfred Stepan (New York: Columbia University Press, 2013), 126–146.

57. "Millions in Multiculturalism Funding Going Unspent," *CBC News*, June 30, 2013, http://www.cbc.ca/news/politics/millions-in-multiculturalism-funding-going-unspent-1.1311570.

58. Michael Dewing, "Canadian Multiculturalism." Background Paper, Ottawa, Canada: Library of Parliament, 2013, http://www.parl.gc.ca/content/lop/researchpublications/2009-20-e.pdf

59. Peter Molnar, "Interview with Robert Post," in *The Content and Context of Hate Speech*, ed. Michael Herz and Peter Molnar (New York: Cambridge University Press, 2012), 26.

60. Frank La Rue, *Report of the Special Rapporteur on the Promotion and Protection of the Right to Freedom of Opinion and Expression*, United Nations General Assembly, September 7, 2012, A/67/357.

61. Camilla Slok, "Here I Stand: Lutheran Stubbornness in the Danish Prime Minister's Office during the Cartoon Crisis," *European Journal of Social Theory* 12 (2009): 231–248.

62. Sidney Jones, interview by author, July 17, 2015.

63. Post, "Hate Speech," 133.

64. Lorenz Langer, Religious Offense and Human Rights: The Implications of Defamation of Religions (Cambridge: Cambridge University Press, 2014), 376.

65. Martha C. Nussbaum, *The New Religious Intolerance: Overcoming the Politics of Fear in an Anxious Age* (Cambridge, MA: Belknap Press, 2012).

66. Ibid.

67. Amartya Sen, *Identity and Violence: The Illusion of Destiny* (New York: W. W. Norton, 2006), xiv.

68. Ibid., 176.

69. Ibid., 175.

References

Abaza, Khairi. *Political Islam and Regime Survival in Egypt*. Policy Focus #51. Washington, DC: The Washington Institute for Near East Policy, January 2006. http://www.washingtoninstitute.org/html/pdf/PolicyFocus51.pdf.

ACT! for America. *Education or Indoctrination? The Treatment of Islam in 6th through 12th Grade Assessment Textbooks*. 2011. http://www.actforamerica.org/downloads/Full_Report_version_7.31.12.pdf.

Ali-Fauzi, Ihsan, and Ben Hillman. "Confronting Intolerance: New Hope for Indonesia's Religious Minorities." *East Asia Forum* 7, no. 1 (March 2015). http://www.paramadina-pusad.or.id/publikasi/kolom/confronting-intolerance-new-hope-for-indonesias-religious-minorities.html.

Ali-Fauzi, Ihsan, Samsu Rizal Panggabean, Nathanael Gratias Sumaktoyo, H. T. Anick, Husni Mubarak, Testriono, and Siti Nurhayati. *Disputed Churches in Jakarta*. Edited by Tim Lindsey and Melissa Crouch. Translated by Rebecca Lunnon. Reprint. Jakarta: Pusat Studi Agama dan Demokrasi, Paramadina Foundation, 2014.

Allen, Pam. "Challenging Diversity?: Indonesia's Anti-Pornography Bill." *Asian Studies Review* 31 (2007): 101–115.

Anti-Defamation League. *David Yerushalmi: A Driving Force Behind Anti-Sharia Efforts in the U.S.* Anti-Defamation League, 2013. http://www.adl.org/assets/pdf/civil-rights/david-yerushalmi-2012-1-11-v1.pdf.

Ahluwalia, Pal, and Toby Miller. "The Politics of Free Speech." *Social Identities: Journal for the Study of Race, Nation and Culture* 18 (2012): 627–628.

Anand Patwardhan v. Union of India and Ors on July 19, 1996 (AIR 1997 Bom 25).

American Bar Association. *Resolution 113A*, August 8–9, 2011. http://www.americanbar.org/content/dam/aba/directories/policy/2011_am_113a.authcheckdam.pdf.

American Library Association. *Intellectual Freedom Manual*, 8th ed. Chicago: American Library Association, 2010. http://www.ala.org/advocacy/intfreedom/iftoolkits/ifmanual/intellectual.

American Library Association. "Support for Dealing with Challenges." In *Banned & Challenged Books*, n.d. http://www.ala.org/bbooks/challengedmaterials/support.

American Library Association. *Library Bill of Rights*. 1939, amended 1980. http://www.ala.org/advocacy/intfreedom/librarybill.

Arifianto, Alexander R. "Unpacking the Results of the 2014 Indonesian Legislative Election." *ISEAS Perspective*, no. 24 (April 17, 2014). http://www.iseas.edu.sg/images/pdf/ISEAS_Perspective_2014_24.pdf.

Article 19. "Indonesia: Human Rights NGOs Argue 'Defamation of Religions' Law Contravenes Freedom of Expression, Freedom of Religion and Equality In Legal Brief to Constitutional Court." Press Release, March 23, 2010. https://www.article19.org/data/files/pdfs/press/indonesia-human-rights-ngos-argue-defamation-of-religions-law-contravenes-fr.pdf

Article 19. *The Camden Principles on Freedom of Expression and Equality*. London: Article 19, 2009. http://www.article19.org/data/files/pdfs/standards/the-camden-principles-on-freedom-of-expression-and-equality.pdf.

Article 19. *Broadcasting Genocide: Censorship, Propaganda and State-Sponsored Violence in Rwanda 1990–1994*. London: Article 19, 1996. http://www.article19.org/pdfs/publications/rwanda-broadcasting-genocide.pdf.

Article 19 and Aliansi Jurnalis Independen. *Freedom of Expression and the Media in Indonesia*. London and Jakarta, December 2005. http://www.article19.org/data/files/pdfs/publications/indonesia-baseline-study.pdf

As'ad, Muhammad. "Ahmadiyah and the Freedom of Religion in Indonesia." *Journal of Indonesian Islam* 3 (2009): 390–413. http://jiis.uinsby.ac.id/index.php/JIIs/article/view/56/56.

Aslam, Rukhsana. "Peace Journalism: A Paradigm Shift in Traditional Media Approach." *Pacific Journalism Review* 17 (2011): 119–139.

Aspinall, Edward. How Indonesia Survived. In *Democracy and Islam in Indonesia*, ed. Mirjam Künkler and Alfred Stepan. 126–146. New York: Columbia University Press, 2013.

Aspinall, Edward, Marcus Mietzner, and Dirk Tomsa. The Moderating President: Yudhoyono's Decade in Power. In *The Yudhoyono Presidency: Indonesia's Decade of Stability and Stagnation*, ed. Edward Aspinall, Marcus Mietzner and Dirk Tomsa. 1–21. Singapore: Institute of Southeast Asian Studies, 2015.

Atton, Chris. *Alternative Media*. London: Sage Publications, 2002.

Australian Broadcasting Corporation. *Editorial Policies: Principles and Standards*. 2011, updated 2015. http://about.abc.net.au/wp-content/uploads/2015/09/EdPols2015.pdf.

Baker, C. Edwin. *Media, Markets, and Democracy.* Cambridge: Cambridge University Press, 2002.

Bald, Margaret. *Banned Books: Literature Suppressed on Religious Grounds.* Rev. ed. New York: Facts On File, 2006.

Barlow, John P. "A Declaration of the Independence of Cyberspace." E-mail circular, February 8, 1996. http://w2.eff.org/Censorship/Internet_censorship_bills/barlow_0296.declaration.

Basu, Amrita. The Long March from Ayodhya: Democracy and Violence in India. In *Pluralism and Democracy in India: Debating the Hindu Right,* ed. Wendy Doniger and Martha C. Nussbaum. 153–173. New York: Oxford University Press, 2015.

Bayuni, Endy M. "Porn Bill Debate Exposes Culture War Fault Lines." *The Jakarta Post,* March 27, 2006. http://www.thejakartapost.com/news/2006/03/27/porn-bill-debate-exposes-culture-war-fault-lines.html.

BBC. "Editorial Guidelines." BBC, 2011. http://www.bbc.co.uk/guidelines/editorialguidelines/.

Benesch, Susan. "Words as Weapons." *World Policy Journal* 29 (2012): 7–12.

Benford, Robert D., and David A. Snow. "Framing Processes and Social Movements: An Overview and Assessment." *Annual Review of Sociology* 26 (2000): 611–639.

Bilal Ahmed Kaloo v. State Of Andhra Pradesh on August 6, 1997 (7 SCC 431).

Bilgrami, Akeel. "The Clash within Civilizations." *Daedalus* 132 (2003): 88–93.

Blake, Michael. "Tolerance and Theocracy: How Liberal States Should Think of Religious States." *Journal of International Affairs* 61 (2007): 1–17.

Blumberg, Phillip I. *Repressive Jurisprudence in the Early American Republic.* Cambridge: Cambridge University Press, 2010.

Bowen, John. Contours of Sharia in Indonesia. In *Democracy and Islam in Indonesia,* ed. Mirjam Künkler and Alfred Stepan. 149–167. New York: Columbia University Press, 2013.

Boyer, Paul S. 2002. *Purity in Print: Book Censorship in America from the Gilded Age to the Computer Age.* 2nd ed., 276–324. Madison: University of Wisconsin Press.

Boyle, Robert P. *Books Challenged or Banned 2013–2014.* Chicago: American Library Assocation, 2014. https://www.ila.org/content/documents/bbw_2014_short.pdf.

Brandenburg v. Ohio. 395 U.S. 444 (1969).

Brass, Paul R. *Theft of an Idol: Text and Context in the Representation of Collective Violence.* Princeton, NJ: Princeton University Press, 1997.

Brass, Paul R. *The Production of Hindu-Muslim Violence in Contemporary India*. Seattle: University of Washington Press, 2003.

Bukovska, Barbora, Agnes Callamard, and Sejal Parmar. "Towards an Interpretation of Article 20 of the ICCPR: Thresholds for the Prohibition of Incitement to Hatred." Article 19. A Study Prepared for the Regional Expert Meeting on Article 20, Organized by the Office of the High Commissioner for Human Rights, Vienna, February 8–9, 2010. http://www.ohchr.org/Documents/Issues/Expression/ICCPR/Vienna/CRP7Callamard.pdf.

Buchanan, Patrick J. "Address to the Republican National Convention." Republican National Convention, Houston, Texas, August 17, 1992. http://www.americanrhetoric.com/speeches/patrickbuchanan1992rnc.htm

Bump, Philip "How Sharia Law Became Embedded in Our Political Debate." *The Washington Post*, January 8, 2016. https://www.washingtonpost.com/news/the-fix/wp/2016/01/08/how-sharia-law-became-embedded-in-our-politics.

Bush, Robin. Religious Politics and Minority Rights during the Yudhoyono Presidency. In *The Yudhoyono Presidency: Indonesia's Decade of Stability and Stagnation*, ed. Edward Aspinall, Marcus Mietzner and Dirk Tomsa. 239–257. Singapore: Institute of Southeast Asian Studies, 2015.

Byman, Daniel L. "Terrorism in North Africa: Before and After Benghazi." *The Brookings Institution*, July 10, 2013. http://www.brookings.edu/research/testimony/2013/07/10-terrorism-north-africa-before-after-benghazi-byman.

CAIR. *Legislating Fear: Islamophobia and Its Impact on the United States*. Washington, DC: Council on American-Islamic Relations, 2013. http://www.cair.com/islamophobia/legislating-fear-2013-report.html.

CAIR. "CAIR Video Calls Out Fox News' Faux 'Condemn Islamic Extremism' Challenge to Muslim Leaders." Washington, DC: Council on American-Islamic Relations, 2014. http://www.cair.com/press-center/american-muslim-news/12734-cair-calls-out-fox-news-faux-condemn-islamic-extremism-challenge.html.

Callamard, Agnes. "Comments and Recommendations on ECRI General Policy Recommendation No. 15 on Combating Hate Speech." Global Freedom of Expression, Columbia University, May 20, 2015. https://globalfreedomofexpression.columbia.edu/publications/comments-and-recommendations-on-ecri-general-policy-recommendation-no-15-on-combating-hate-speech/.

Castells, Manuel. "A Network Theory of Power." *International Journal of Communication* 5 (2011): 773–787.

Center for Human Rights and Democracy. *Indonesia: Submission to the UN Universal Periodic Review. Thirteenth Session of the UPR Working Group of the Human Rights Council*. Faculty of Law, University of Brawijaya, Indonesia, May 2012. http://lib.ohchr

.org/HRBodies/UPR/Documents/session13/ID/CHRD_UPR_IDN_S13_2012_Center HumanRightsDemocracy_E.pdf.

Center for Security Policy. *Shariah: The Threat to America.* Washington, DC: Center for Security Policy, 2010. http://shariahthethreat.org/.

Chatterji, Angana, Lise McKean, and Abha Sur. *Genocide in Gujarat: The Sangh Parivar, Narendra Modi, and the Government of Gujarat.* Coalition Against Genocide, 2005. http://www.coalitionagainstgenocide.org/reports/2005/cag.02mar2005.modi.pdf.

Chenoy, Kamal Mitra, Vishnu Nagar, Prasenjit Bose, and Vijoo Krishnan. "Ethnic Cleansing in Ahmedabad: A preliminary report by the SAHMAT Fact Finding Team to Ahmedabad, 10-11 March 2002." *Outlook* (March) (2002): 22.

Chua, Amy. *World on Fire: How Exporting Free Market Democracy Breeds Ethnic Hatred and Global Instability.* New York: Doubleday, 2003.

Church of Jesus Christ of Latter-Day Saints. "The Publicity Dilemma." March 9, 2009. http://www.mormonnewsroom.org/article/the-publicity-dilemma.

CHRD. *Indonesia: Submission to the UN Universal Periodic Review.* Thirteenth Session of the UPR Working Group of the Human Rights Council. Center for Human Rights and Democracy, Faculty of Law, University of Brawijaya, Indonesia.

Cohen-Almagor, Raphael. "The Limits of Objective Reporting." *Journal of Language and Politics* 7 (2008): 138–157.

Cohen, Nick. *You Can't Read This Book.* London: Fourth Estate, 2012.

Concerned Citizens Tribunal—Gujarat. 2002. "Crime Against Humanity." Mumbai: Anil Dharkar for Citizens for Justice and Peace, 2002. http://www.sabrang.com/tribunal/tribunal1.pdf.

Cornell University Law School Legal Information Institute. "Obscenity." https://www.law.cornell.edu/wex/obscenity.

Cotter, John M. "Sounds of Hate: White Power Rock and Roll and the Neo-Nazi Skinhead Subculture." *Terrorism and Political Violence* 11 (1999): 111–140.

Crouch, Melissa. "Judicial Review and Religious Freedom: The Case of Indonesian Ahmadis." *Sydney Law Review* 34 (2012): 545–572.

Curran, James. Rethinking Media and Democracy. In *Mass Media and Society,* ed. J. Curran and M. Gurevitch. 120–154. London: Arnold, 2000.

Curran, James. What Democracy Requires of the Media. In *The Institutions of American Democracy: The Press,* ed. Geneva Overholser and Kathleen Hall Jamieson. 120–140. New York: Oxford University Press, 2005.

Dalmia, Archana. "Jekyll and Hyde Syndrome Spells Danger for Nation." *New Indian Express*, May 11, 2014. http://www.newindianexpress.com/columns/Jekyll -and-Hyde-Syndrome-Spells-Danger-for-Nation/2014/05/11/article2217530.ece.

Datta, Saurav. "Why It Is Open Season for Hate Speech in India's Elections." *Index on Censorship* 28 (April) (2014). http://www.indexoncensorship.org/2014/04/open -season-hate-speech-indias-elections/.

Davie, Grace. Resacralization. In *The New Blackwell Companion to the Sociology of Religion*, ed. Bryan S. Turner. 160–177. Chichester, UK: Blackwell, 2010.

Davis, Richard H. "Book Review: *Shivaji: Hindu King in Islamic India*, by James W. Laine." *Journal of the American Academy of Religion* 72 (2004): 1047.

Davies, Nick. *Flat Earth News*. London: Vintage Book, 2009.

Diamond, Larry. "Thinking About Hybrid Regimes." *Journal of Democracy* 13 (2002): 21–35.

Diamond, Larry, and Leonardo Morlino. "The Quality of Democracy: An Overview." *Journal of Democracy* 15 (2004): 20–31.

Dibyesh, Anand. "The Violence of Security: Hindu Nationalism and the Politics of Representing 'the Muslim' as a Danger." *Round Table: The Commonwealth Journal of International Affairs* 94 (April 2005): 203–215.

Doniger, Wendy. "India: Censorship by the Batra Brigade." *New York Review of Books* (May 8) (2014). http://www.nybooks.com/articles/2014/05/08/india-censorship -batra-brigade/.

Douglas, Mary. *Purity and Danger: An Analysis of Concepts of Pollution and Taboo*. London: Routledge & Kegan Paul, 1966.

Downing, John D. H. *Radical Media: Rebellious Communication and Social Movements*. Thousand Oaks, CA: Sage, 2001.

Ducol, Benjamin. A Radical Sociability. In *Defense of an Online/offline Multidimensional Approach to Radicalization." In Social Networks, Terrorism and Counter-Terrorism: Radical and Connected*, ed. Martin Bouchard. 82–104. Abingdon, Oxford: Routledge, 2015.

Duss, Matthew, Yasmine Taeb, Gude Ken, and Ken Sofer. *Fear, Inc. 2.0*. Washington, DC: Center for American Progress, 2015. https://cdn.americanprogress.org/wp -content/uploads/2015/02/FearInc-report2.11.pdf.

Dworkin, Ronald. Foreword. In *Extreme Speech and Democracy*, ed. Ivan Hare and James Weinstein. v–ix. Oxford: Oxford University Press, 2009.

Election Commission of India. "Handbook for Candidates." 1998, reprint 1999. http://eci.nic.in/archive/handbook/CandidateHB_EVM_.pdf.

Election Commission of India. "Model Code of Conduct for the Guidance of Political Parties and Candidates." 2014. http://eci.nic.in/eci_main/MCC-ENGLISH _28022014.pdf.

Elliott, Andrea. "The Man Behind the Anti-Shariah Movement." *New York Times*, July 30, 2011. http://www.nytimes.com/2011/07/31/us/31shariah.html.

Elliott, Geoff. *Reporting Diversity: How Journalists Can Contribute to Community Cohesion*. Cambridge: Society of Editors, and London: Media Trust, 2005). http://mediadiversity.org.

Elliott, Justin. "How the 'Ground Zero Mosque' Fear Mongering Began." *Salon*, August 16, 2010. http://www.salon.com/2010/08/16/ground_zero_mosque_origins/.

Equal Rights Trust. *Stakeholder Submission to the Universal Periodic Review of the Republic of Indonesia*. Submitted to the United Nations Human Rights Council, 2011. http://lib.ohchr.org/HRBodies/UPR/Documents/session13/ID/ERT_UPR_IDN_S13 _2012_EqualRightsTrust_E.pdf.

European Council on Tolerance and Reconciliation. *A European Model Law for the Promotion of Tolerance and the Suppression of Intolerance*. 2015. http://ectr.eu/en -projects-and-initiatives/national-statue-for-the-promotion-of-tolerance.

ERT. *Stakeholder Submission to the Universal Periodic Review of the Republic of Indonesia, 2011*. London: The Equal Rights Trust, 2011.

Fawcett, Liz. "Why Peace Journalism Isn't News." *Journalism Studies* 3 (2002): 213–223.

Forst, Rainer. Civil Society. In *A Companion to Contemporary Political Philosophy*. 2nd ed., ed. Robert E. Goodin, Philip Pettit and Thomas Pogge. 452–462. Malden, MA: Blackwell, 2007.

Fox, Jonathan. *Religion, Civilization, and Civil War: 1945 Through the New Millennium*. Lanham, MD: Lexington Books, 2005.

Fox, Jonathan. "World Separation of Religion and State Into the 21st Century." *Comparative Political Studies* 39 (5) (2006): 537–569.

Fox, Jonathan. Integrating Religion into IR Theory. In *Routledge Handbook of Religion and Politics*, ed. Jeffrey Haynes. 273–292. Abingdon, Oxford: Routledge, 2009.

Fox, Jonathan, and Deborah Flores. "Religions, Constitutions, and the State: A Cross-National Study." *Journal of Politics* 71 (2009): 1499–1513.

Fraser, Nancy. Rethinking the Public Sphere: A Contribution to the Critique of Actually Existing Democracy. In *Habermas and the Public Sphere*, ed. Craig Calhoun. 109–143. Boston: MIT Press, 1992.

Freedom House. "Resolutions on Defamation of Religions Do Not Belong at United Nations, Organizations Say." November 10, 2009. https://freedomhouse.org/article/resolutions-defamation-religions-do-not-belong-united-nations-organizations-say.

Freedom House. "Freedom in the World 2013." Washington, DC: Freedom House, 2013. https://freedomhouse.org/report/freedom-world/2013/india#.VRV83UayxA9.

Freedom House. "Freedom in the World 2015—Discarding Democracy: Return to the Iron Fist." Washington, DC: Freedom House, 2015. https://freedomhouse.org/report/freedom-world/freedom-world-2015.

Freedom House. "Freedom in the World 2015—Indonesia." Washington, DC: Freedom House, 2015. https://freedomhouse.org/report/freedom-world/2015/indonesia

Friedman, Thomas. "Broadway and the Mosque." *New York Times*, August 3, 2010. http://www.nytimes.com/2010/08/04/opinion/04friedman.html.

Frydman, Benoit, and Isabel Rorive. "Fighting Nazi and Anti-Semitic Material on the Internet: The Yahoo! Case and Its Global Implications." Paper presented at the "Hate and Terrorist Speech on the Internet: The Global Implications of the Yahoo! Ruling in France" conference, Cardozo Law School, New York, February 11, 2002.

Gagliardone, Iginio, Danit Gal, Theo Alves, and Gabriela Martinez. *Countering Online Hate Speech*. Paris: United Nations Educational, Scientific and Cultural Organization, 2015.

Gamson, William A. *The Strategy of Social Protests*. 2nd ed. Belmont, CA: Wadsworth, 1990.

Gamson, William A. Injustice Frames. In *The Wiley-Blackwell Encyclopedia of Social and Political Movements*, ed. David A. Snow, Donatella Della Porta, Bert Klandermans, and Doug McAdam. Oxford: Blackwell Publishing Ltd, 2013. http://doi.wiley.com/10.1002/9780470674871.wbespm110.

Ganguly, Sumit. "The Crisis of Indian Secularism." *Journal of Democracy* 14 (2003): 11–25. doi:10.1353/jod.2003.0076.

Gans, Herbert J. *Deciding What's News: A Study of CBS Evening News, NBC Nightly News, Newsweek, and Time*. New York: Pantheon Books, 1979.

George, Cherian. "Public Accountability Brings Rewards and Risks: Interview with A. S. Panneerselvan." *Media Asia* 41 (2014): 8–15.

George, Robert P. "Defend Religious Liberty for Muslims." *Firstthings,* June 5, 2012. http://www.firstthings.com/blogs/firstthoughts/2012/06/defend-religious-liberty-for-muslims/.

George, Varghese K. "India: A Hindutva Variant of Neo-Liberalism." *Hindu*, April 4, 2014. http://www.thehindu.com/opinion/lead/a-hindutva-variant-of-neoliberalism/article5868196.ece.

Gillmor, Dan. *We the Media: Grassroots Journalism by the People, for the People*. Sebastopol, CA: O'Reilly Media, 2006.

Goodman, Emma. *Online Comment Moderation: Emerging Best Practices*. Darmstadt, Germany: WAN-IFRA, 2013.

Gopal Vinayak Godse v. Union Of India and Ors on August 6, 1969 (AIR 1971 Bom 56).

Guha, Ramachandra. "A Play in Five Acts—Narendra Modi and the RSS." *Telegraph*, December 12, 2015. http://www.telegraphindia.com/1151212/jsp/opinion/story _57928.jsp#.VnlBqPGyxA8.

Guha, Ramachandra. *Patriots & Partisans*. London: Penguin Books, 2013.

Gusfield, Joseph R. *Symbolic Crusade: Status Politics and the American Temperance Movement*. Urbana: University of Illinois Press, 1963.

Handyside v. The United Kingdom, 5493/72, Council of Europe: European Court of Human Rights, November 4, 1976. http://www.refworld.org/docid/3ae6b6fb8.html.

Hafez, Farid. "Shifting Borders: Islamophobia as Common Ground for Building Pan-European Right-Wing Unity." *Patterns of Prejudice* 48 (2014): 479–499.

Hamelink, Cees J. *Media and Conflict: Escalating Evil*. Boulder, CO: Paradigm Publishers, 2011.

Hamayotsu, Kikue. "The Limits of Civil Society in Democratic Indonesia: Media Freedom and Religious Intolerance." *Journal of Contemporary Asia* 43 (2013): 658–677.

Hanitzsch, Thomas. "Deconstructing Journalism Culture: Toward a Universal Theory." *Communication Theory* 17 (2007): 367–385.

Hanitzsch, Thomas, Patrick Lee Plaisance, and Elizabeth A. Skewes. Universals and Differences in Global Journalism Ethics. In *Global Media Ethics: Problems and Perspectives*, ed. Stephen J. A. Ward. 30–49. Chichester, UK: Wiley-Blackwell, 2013.

Hanitzsch, Thomas. "Populist Disseminators, Detached Watchdogs, Critical Change Agents and Opportunist Facilitators: Professional Milieus, the Journalistic Field and Autonomy in 18 Countries." *International Communication Gazette* 73 (2011): 477–494.

Haraszti, Miklos. Foreword: Hate Speech and the Coming Death of the International Standard before It Was Born (Complaints of a Watchdog). In *The Content and Context of Hate Speech: Rethinking Regulation and Responses*, ed. Michael Herz and Peter Molnar. xiii–xviii. New York: Cambridge University Press, 2012.

Hare, Ivan. Extreme Speech Under International and Regional Human Rights Standards. In *Extreme Speech and Democracy*, ed. Ivan Hare and James Weinstein. 62–80. Oxford: Oxford University Press, 2009.

Hare, I., and J. Weinstein, eds. *Extreme Speech and Democracy*. New York: Oxford University Press, 2011.

Hardgrave, Robert L. "India: The Dilemmas of Diversity." *Journal of Democracy* 4 (1993): 54–68. doi:10.1353/jod.1993.0052.

Hart, William, Dolores Albarracín, Alice H. Eagly, Inge Brechan, Matthew J. Lindberg, and Lisa Merrill. "Feeling Validated versus Being Correct: A Meta-Analysis of Selective Exposure to Information." *Psychological Bulletin* 135 (2009): 555–588.

Hefner, Robert W. *Civil Islam: Muslims and Democratization in Indonesia*. Princeton, NJ: Princeton University Press, 2000.

Herz, M., and P. Molnar, eds. *The Content and Context of Hate Speech: Rethinking Regulation and Responses*. New York: Cambridge University Press, 2011.

Heyman, Steven J. Hate Speech, Public Discourse, and the First Amendment. In *Extreme Speech and Democracy*, ed. Ivan Hare and James Weinstein. 158–181. Oxford: Oxford University Press, 2009.

Hibbard, Scott W. *Religious Politics and Secular States: Egypt, India, and the United States*. Baltimore: Johns Hopkins University Press, 2010.

Hamayotsu, Kikue. "The Limits of Civil Society in Democratic Indonesia: Media Freedom and Religious Intolerance." *Journal of Contemporary Asia* 43 (2013): 658–677.

Hofstadter, Richard. *The Paranoid Style in American Politics, and Other Essays*. New York: Knopf, 1965.

Holcomb, Jesse, and Amy Mitchell. Cable: By the Numbers. In *State of the News Media 2013*. Washington, DC: Pew Research Center, 2013., http://www .stateofthemedia.org/2013/cable-a-growing-medium-reaching-its-ceiling/cable-by -the-numbers/.

Horwitz, Paul. "Amendment One Is Useless, Costly, and Wrong." *AL.com*, October 30, 2014. http://www.al.com/opinion/index.ssf/2014/10/amendment_one _is_useless_costl.html.

Horwitz, Robert B. *America's Right: Anti-Establishment Conservatism from Goldwater to the Tea Party*. Cambridge: Polity, 2010.

Human Rights Watch. *We Have No Orders to Save You: State Participation and Complicity in Communal Violence in Gujarat*. New York: Human Rights Watch, April 30, 2002. http://www.hrw.org/reports/2002/india/gujarat.pdf.

Human Rights Watch. "Indonesia: Religious Minorities Targets of Rising Violence." Human Rights Watch, February 28, 2013. https://www.hrw.org/news/2013/02/28/ indonesia-religious-minorities-targets-rising-violence.

Huntington, Samuel P. *The Clash of Civilizations and the Remaking of World Order.* New York: Simon & Schuster, 1996.

I.A. v. Turkey, 42571/98, Council of Europe: European Court of Human Rights, September 13, 2005. http://merlin.obs.coe.int/iris/2005/10/article3.en.html.

ImamsOnline.com. "British Imams Condemn ISIS." Video. July 11, 2014. https://www.youtube.com/watch?v=KKjAt6lIlgY

Inayatullah, Sohail. "Understanding the Postmodern World: Why Khomeini Wants Rushdie Dead." *Third Text* 4 (1990): 91–98.

International Crisis Group. "Indonesia: Implications of the Ahmadiyah Decree." Asia Briefing no. 78. Jakarta/Brussels: July 7, 2008. http://www.crisisgroup.org/~/media/Files/asia/south-east-asia/indonesia/b78_indonesia___implications_of_the_ahmadiyah_decree.pdf.

International Crisis Group. "Indonesia: 'Christianisation' and Intolerance." Policy Briefing No. 114, November 24, 2010. http://www.crisisgroup.org/~/media/Files/asia/south-east-asia/indonesia/B114%20Indonesia%20-%20Christianisation%20and%20Intolerance.pdf.

International Federation of Journalists. "IFJ Declaration of Principles on the Conduct of Journalists." 1986. http://www.ifj.org/about-ifj/ifj-code-of-principles/.

Issacharoff, Samuel. *Fragile Democracies.* New York: Cambridge University Press, 2015.

Jahangir, Asma, and Doudou Diène. *Report of the Special Rapporteur on Freedom of Religion or Belief, and the Special Rapporteur on Contemporary Forms of Racism, Racial Discrimination, Xenophobia and Related Intolerance, Further to Human Rights Council Decision 1/107 on Incitement to Racial and Religious Hatred and the Promotion of Tolerance.* United Nations Human Rights Council, A/HRC/2/3, September 20, 2006. http://www.choike.org/documentos/rapporteur_religion.pdf.

Jaitly, Rishi. "Intermediary Liability and the Future of the Internet in India." Google Public Policy Blog, October 14, 2007. http://googlepublicpolicy.blogspot.hk/2007/10/intermediary-liability-and-future-of.html.

Janmohamed, Zahir. "Gujarat: A Tale of Two Cities." *Hindu*, May 25, 2015. http://www.thehindu.com/todays-paper/tp-opinion/gujarat-a-tale-of-two-cities/article7242288.ece.

Jersild v. Denmark. 36/1993/431/510, Council of Europe: European Court of Human Rights, August 22, 1994. http://www.refworld.org/docid/3ae6b6fc0.html.

Jones, Sidney. Indonesian Government Approaches to Radical Islam Since 1998. In *Democracy and Islam in Indonesia*, ed. Mirjam Künkler and Alfred Stepan. 109–125. New York: Columbia University Press, 2013.

Jones, Sidney. "Briefing for the New President: The Terrorist Threat in Indonesia and Southeast Asia." International Crisis Group, June 25, 2008. http://www.crisisgroup .org/en/regions/asia/south-east-asia/op-eds/jones-briefing-for-the-new-president-the -terrorist-threat-in-indonesia-and-southeast-asia.aspx.

Jordan, Guy. "The Politics of (Mere) Presence: The Islamic Center of Murfreesboro, Tennessee." Conversations: An Online Journal of the Center for the Study of Material and Visual Cultures of Religion. 2014. http://mavcor.yale.edu/conversations/essays/ politics-mere-presence-islamic-center-murfreesboro-tennessee.

Journalism.org. "Principles of Journalism." Pew Research Journalism Project, n.d. Accessed September 1, 2014. http://www.journalism.org/resources/principles-of -journalism/.

Karataş v. Turkey. Application no. 23168/94, Council of Europe: European Court of Human Rights, July 8, 1999. https://www.article19.org/resources.php/resource/2561/ en/karatas-v.-turkey.

Kaye, David. "Expression, Opinion and Religious Freedoms." Keynote speech at the "Expression, Opinion and Religious Freedoms in Asia" Regional Consultation, Jakarta, Indonesia, June 3, 2015.

Kent, Thomas. "Fighting Hate Speech: UN Can Treat the Press as a Partner." Media Asia 40 (2013): 306–309.

Khan, Saeed A. "Sharia Law, Islamophobia and the U.S. Constitution: New Tectonic Plates of the Culture Wars." University of Maryland Law Journal of Race, Religion, Gender and Class 12 (2012): 123–139.

Kohl, Uta. "Google: The Rise and Rise of Online Intermediaries in the Governance of the Internet and beyond (Part 2)." International Journal of Law and Information Technology 21 (2013): 187–234.

Kohut, Andrew, Carroll Doherty, Michael Dimock, and Scott Keeter. "Continuing Divide in Views of Islam and Violence." Washington, DC: The Pew Research Center for The People & The Press, March 9, 2011. http://www.people-press.org/files/ 2011/03/714.pdf.

Kohut, Andrew, Scott Keeter, Carroll Doherty, Michael Dimock, Luis Lugo, Alan Cooperman, and Greg Smith. "NYC Mosque Opposed, Muslims' Right to Build Mosques Favored – Public Remains Conflicted Over Islam." Washington, DC: Pew Research Center, August 24, 2010. http://www.pewforum.org/files/2010/08/Islam -mosque-full-report.pdf.

Kovaleski, Sergei F., and Brooks Barnes. "From Man Who Insulted Muhammad, No Regret." New York Times, November 25, 2012. http://www.nytimes.com/2012/11/26/ us/from-the-man-who-insulted-islam-no-retreat.html.

Kumar, Aishwary. *Radical Equality: Ambedkar, Gandhi, and the Risk of Democracy.* Stanford, CA: Stanford University Press, 2015.

Künkler, Mirjam. How Pluralist Democracy Became the Consensual Discourse Among Secular and Nonsecular Muslims in Indonesia. In *Democracy and Islam in Indonesia*, ed. Mirjam Künkler and Alfred Stepan. 53–72. New York: Columbia University Press, 2013.

La Porta, Alphonse F. "Indonesia's Presidential Election: Will Democracy Survive?" *CSIS PacNet*, no. 55 (July 15, 2014). http://csis.org/publication/pacnet-55-indonesias-presidential-election-will-democracy-survive.

La Rue, Frank. *Report of the Special Rapporteur on the Promotion and Protection of the Right to Freedom of Opinion and Expression.* United Nations General Assembly, August 10, 2011, A/66/290. http://daccess-dds-ny.un.org/doc/UNDOC/GEN/N11/449/78/PDF/N1144978.pdf.

La Rue, Frank. *Report of the Special Rapporteur on the Promotion and Protection of the Right to Freedom of Opinion and Expression.* United Nations General Assembly, September 7, 2012, A/67/357. http://daccess-dds-ny.un.org/doc/UNDOC/GEN/N12/501/25/PDF/N1250125.pdf.

Lagouette, Stephanie. "The Cartoon Controversy in Context: Analyzing the Decisions Not to Prosecute under Danish Law." *Brooklyn Journal of International Law* 33 (2008): 379–404.

Lal, Ratan Mani. "Decoding Amit Shah's Campaign: How He Conquered Uttar Pradesh." *Firstpost*, May 23, 2014. http://www.firstpost.com/politics/decoding-amit-shahs-campaign-how-he-conquered-uttar-pradesh-1538759.html.

Laine, James W. *Shivaji: Hindu King in Islamic India.* Oxford: Oxford University Press, 2003.

Langer, Lorenz. *Religious Offence and Human Rights: The Implications of Defamation of Religions.* Cambridge: Cambridge University Press, 2014.

Larsen, Signe Engelbreth. "Towards the Blasphemous Self: Constructing Societal Identity in Danish Debates on the Blasphemy Provision in the Twentieth and Twenty-First Centuries." *Journal of Ethnic and Migration Studies* 40 (2014): 194–211.

Lean, Nathan. *The Islamophobia Industry: How the Right Manufactures Fear of Muslims.* Chicago: University of Chicago Press, 2012.

Lee, Seow Ting. "Peace Journalism: Principles and Structural Limitations in the News Coverage of Three Conflicts." *Mass Communication & Society* 13 (2010): 361–384.

Lemons, Katherine, and Joshua Takano Chambers-Letson. "Rule of Law: Sharia Panic and the US Constitution in the House of Representatives." *Cultural Studies* 28 (2014): 1048–1077.

Liang, Lawrence. "Legal Notice for Violation of Rights of Readers." February 14, 2014. https://www.documentcloud.org/documents/1018093-notice-to-penguin-by-alternative-law-forum.html.

Liddle, R. William, Saiful Mujani, Mirjam Kunkler, and Alfred Stepan. Indonesian Democracy. In *Democracy and Islam in Indonesia*, 24–50. New York: Columbia University Press, 2013.

Lilla, Mark. The Return of Political Theology. In *The Rule of Law and the Rule of God*, ed. Simeon O. Ilesanmi, Win-Chiat Lee and J. Wilson Parker. 15–29. New York: Palgrave Macmillan, 2014.

Lim, Merlyna. Islamic Radicalism and Anti-Americanism in Indonesia: The Role of the Internet. In *Policy Studies 18*. Washington, DC: East-West Center Washington, 2005. http://scholarspace.manoa.hawaii.edu/bitstream/handle/10125/3520/PS018.pdf?sequence=1.

Linz, Juan José, and Alfred Stepan. *Problems of Democratic Transition and Consolidation*. Baltimore: Johns Hopkins University Press, 1996.

MacKinnon, Rebecca, and Ethan Zuckerman. "Don't Feed the Trolls." *Index on Censorship* 41 (2012): 14–24. http://ioc.sagepub.com/content/41/4/14.

Magnis-Suseno, Franz. Christian and Muslim Minorities in Indonesia. In *Democracy and Islam in Indonesia*, ed. Mirjam Kunkler and Alfred Stepan. 73–85. New York: Columbia University Press, 2013.

Mahaprashasta, Ajoy Ashirwad. "The Riot Route." *Frontline*, October 4, 2013. http://www.frontline.in/the-nation/the-riot-route/article5134119.ece.

Mahaprashasta, Ajoy Ashirwad. "The Rule of Unreason." *Frontline* 28 (November 5–18, 2011), http://www.frontline.in/static/html/fl2823/stories/20111118282312500.htm

Manzar Sayeed Khan v. State of Maharashtra & Anr on April 5, 2007 (Appeal (crl.) 491 of 2007).

Maras, Steven. *Objectivity in Journalism*. Cambridge: Polity, 2013.

Marzouki, Nadia. "Moral Offense versus Religious Freedom." [English] *Revue Francaise de Science Politique* 61 (2011): 1–25.

Mason, D. L., ed. *Reporting on Religion: A Primer on Journalism's Best Beat*. Westerville, OH: Religion Newswriters Association, 2006. http://www.religionlink.com/pdf/primer2006.pdf.

Mazur, Eric Michael. *The Americanization of Religious Minorities: Confronting the Constitutional Order*. Baltimore: Johns Hopkins University Press, 1999.

Mazzrella, William, and Raminder Kaur. Between Sedition and Seduction: Thinking Censorship in South Asia. In *Routledge Handbook of Media Law*, ed. Monroe E. Price, Stefaan G. Verhulst and Libby Morgan. 303–323. Abingdon, Oxford: Routledge, 2013.

McAdam, Doug, Sidney Tarrow, and Charles Tilly. *Dynamics of Contention*. Cambridge: Cambridge University Press, 2001.

McBride, Kelly. "How to Report on Quran Burning and Other Hate Speech." Poynter.org: Everyday Ethics, September 9, 2010. http://www.poynter.org/latest-news/everyday-ethics/105487/how-to-report-on-quran-burning-and-other-hate-speech/.

McCombs, Maxwell, and Tamara Bell. The Agenda-Setting Role of Mass Communication. In *An Integrated Approach to Communication Theory and Research*, ed. Michael B. Salwen and Don W. Stacks. 93–110. Mahwah, NJ: Lawrence Erlbaum, 1996.

McCoy, Mary E. "Purifying Islam in Post-Authoritarian Indonesia: Corporatist Metaphors and the Rise of Religious Intolerance." *Rhetoric & Public Affairs* 16 (2013): 275–315.

McLaughlin, Nicole. "Spectrum of Defamation of Religion Laws and the Possibility of a Universal International Standard." *Loyola of Los Angeles International and Comparative Law Review* 32 (2010): 395–426.

McGonagle, Tarlach. A Survey and Critical Analysis of Council of Europe Strategies for Countering 'Hate Speech. In *The Content and Context of Hate Speech: Rethinking Regulation and Responses*, ed. Michael Herz and Peter Molnar. 456–498. Cambridge: Cambridge University Press, 2012.

Mohd. Haroon and Ors. v. Union of India on March 26, 2014 (5 SCC 252).

McLaughlin, Nicole. "Spectrum of Defamation of Religion Laws and the Possibility of a Universal International Standard." *Loyola of Los Angeles International and Comparative Law Review* 32 (2010): 395–426.

Meddaugh, Priscilla Marie, and Jack Kay. "Hate Speech or 'Reasonable Racism?' The Other in Stormfront." *Journal of Mass Media Ethics* 24 (2009): 251–268.

Mehta, Pratap Bhanu. Hinduism and Self-Rule. In *World Religions and Democracy*, ed. Larry Diamond, Marc F. Plattner and Philip J. Costopoulos. Baltimore: Johns Hopkins University Press and the National Endowment for Democracy, 2005.

Mekay, Emad. "The Muhammad Movie: Look Who Fanned the Flames." *Columbia Journalism Review* 7 (January) (2013). http://www.cjr.org/behind_the_news/egypt_and_the_muhammad_movie_l.php.

Meltzer, Kimberly. "Journalistic Concern about Uncivil Political Talk in Digital News Media Responsibility, Credibility, and Academic Influence." *International Journal of Press/Politics* 20 (2015): 85–107.

Mendel, Toby. Does International Law Provide for Consistent Rules on Hate Speech? In *The Content and Context of Hate Speech: Rethinking Regulation and Responses*, ed. Michael Herz and Péter Molnar. 417–429. New York: Cambridge University Press, 2012.

Millie, Julian. "One Year after the Cikeusik Tragedy." *Inside Indonesia*, no. 107 (January–March 2012). http://www.insideindonesia.org/one-year-after-the-cikeusik -tragedy.

Mishra, Pankaj. "Another Incarnation." *New York Times Book Review*, April 24, 2009. http://www.nytimes.com/2009/04/26/books/review/Mishra-t.html.

Molnar, Peter. Interview with Robert Post. In *The Content and Context of Hate Speech*, ed. Michael Herz and Peter Molnar. 11–36. New York: Cambridge University Press, 2012.

Monasebian, Simone. The Pre-Genocide Case against Radio-Television Libre Des Milles Collines. In *The Media and the Rwanda Genocide*, ed. Allan Thompson. 308–329. Pluto Press, 2007.

Mooney, Chris. *The Republican Brain: The Science of Why They Deny Science—and Reality*. Hoboken, NJ: John Wiley & Sons, 2012.

Moynihan, Michael. "The Repentant Radical." *Daily Beast*, September 17, 2013. http://www.thedailybeast.com/articles/2013/09/17/ahmed-akkari-repents-violent -opposition-to-danish-cartoons-lampooning-islam.html.

Mozzafari, Mehdi. "The Rushdie Affair: Blasphemy as a New Form of International Conflict and Crisis." *Terrorism and Political Violence* 2 (1990): 415–441.

Mullally, Claire. "Banned Books." First Amendment Center Website, September 13, 2002. http://www.firstamendmentcenter.org/banned-books.

Muzakki, Akh. "Contested Islam: Examining the Material Base of Islamic Discourse in New Order Indonesia." *Graduate Journal of Asia-Pacific Studies* 6 (2010): 71–88.

Nair, Neeti. "Beyond the 'Communal' 1920s: The Problem of Intention, Legislative Pragmatism, and the Making of Section 295A of the Indian Penal Code." *Indian Economic and Social History Review* 50 (2013): 317–340.

Narayanan, Dinesh. "RSS 3.0." *Caravan*, May 1, 2014. http://www.caravanmagazine .in/reportage/rss-30.

New York Times Co. v. Sullivan. 376 U.S. 254 (1964).

Nisbet, Erik, and Kelly Garrett. "Fox News Contributes to Spread of Rumors about Proposed NYC Mosque." Ohio State University, October 14, 2010. http://rkellygarrett .com/wp-content/uploads/2014/05/Nisbet-Garrett-Fox-News-contributes-to-spread -of-rumors.pdf.

Noelle-Neumann, Elisabeth. "The Spiral of Silence: A Theory of Public Opinion." *Journal of Communication* 24 (1974): 43–51.

Noman, Helmi. "In the Name of God: Faith-Based Internet Censorship in Majority Muslim Countries." *OpenNet Initiative*, August 1, 2011. http://opennet.net/sites/opennet.net/files/ONI_NameofGod_1_08_2011.pdf.

Noorani, A. G. "Penguin & the Parivar." *Frontline*, April 4, 2014. http://www.frontline.in/social-issues/penguin-the-parivar/article5787832.ece.

Norris, Pippa, and Ronald Inglehart. *Sacred and Secular: Religion and Politics Worldwide*. Cambridge: Cambridge University Press, 2004.

Norris, Pippa, and Sina Odugbemi. Evaluating Media Performance. In *Public Sentinel: News Media & Governance Reform*, ed. Pippa Norris, 3–30. Washington, DC: World Bank Publications, 2010.

Nurun, Nisa. "Constitutional Court Rejects Judicial Review of Religious Defamation Law." *Wahd Institute Monthly Report on Religious* 29 (April) (2010): 1–3.

Nussbaum, Martha C. *The New Religious Intolerance: Overcoming the Politics of Fear in an Anxious Age*. Cambridge, MA: Belknap Press, 2012.

O'Donnell, Guillermo, and Philippe C. Schmitter. *Transitions from Authoritarian Rule: Tentative Conclusions about Uncertain Democracies*. Baltimore: Johns Hopkins University Press, 2013.

Olesen, Thomas. *Global Injustice Symbols and Social Movements*. New York: Palgrave Macmillan, 2015.

Olesen, Thomas. From National Event to Transnational Injustice Symbol: The Three Phases of the Muhammad Cartoon Controversy. In *Dynamics of Political Violence: A Process-Oriented Perspective on Radicalization and the Escalation of Political Conflict*, ed. Lorenzo Bosi, Chares Demetriou and Stefan Malthaner. 217–236. Farnham, UK: Ashgate, 2014.

Olesen, Thomas. "Transnational Injustice Symbols and Communities: The Case of Al-Qaeda and the Guantanamo Bay Detention Camp." *Current Sociology* 59 (2011): 717–734.

Olesen, Thomas. "The Muhammad Cartoons Conflict and Transnational Activism." *Ethnicities* 9 (2009): 409–426.

Organization of American States. *American Convention on Human Rights*, November 22, 1969. http://www.oas.org/dil/treaties_B-32_American_Convention_on_Human_Rights.htm.

Organization of the Islamic Conference. *Cairo Declaration on Human Rights in Islam*, August 5, 1990. http://www.oic-oci.org/english/article/human.htm.

Organization of the Islamic Conference. "1st OIC Observatory Report on Islamophobia." Presented to the 35th Council of Foreign Ministers, Kampala, Uganda, June 18–20, 2008. http://www.oic-oci.org/uploads/file/Islamphobia/islamphobia_rep_may_07_08.pdf.

Panggabean, Rizal, and Ihsan Ali-Fauzi. *Policing Religious Conflicts in Indonesia*. Translated by Natalia Laskowska. Jakarta, Indonesia: Center for the Study of Religion and Democracy (PUSAD), Paramadina Foundation, 2015. http://www.paramadina-pusad.or.id/pustaka/policing-religious-conflicts-in-indonesia-2.

Panizza, Francisco. Introduction: Populism and the Mirror of Democracy. In *Populism and the Mirror of Democracy*, ed. Francisco Panizza. 1–31. London: Verso, 2005.

Patel, Faiza, Matthew Duss, and Amos Toh. *Foreign Law Bans: Legal Uncertainties and Practical Problems*. Washington, DC: Center for American Progress, 2013. http://www.brennancenter.org/sites/default/files/publications/ForeignLawBans.pdf.

Pedrioli, Carlo A. "Constructing the Other: U.S. Muslims, Anti-Sharia Law, and the Constitutional Consequences of Volatile Intercultural Rhetoric." *Southern California Interdisciplinary Law Journal* 22 (2012): 65–108.

People For the American Way. *Texas Textbooks: What Happened, What It Means, and What We Can Do About It*. Washington, DC: People For the American Way, 2010, http://www.pfaw.org/sites/default/files/rww-in-focus-textbooks.pdf.

People For the American Way. *Book Wars: The Right's Campaign to Censor Literature, History, and Science*. Washington, DC: People For the American Way, 2014. http://www.pfaw.org/rww-in-focus/book-wars-right-s-fight-redefine-america-0.

People's Alliance for Democracy and Secularism. "India: Statement on 2014 General Elections." May 24, 2014. http://sacw.net/article8763.html.

Pew Research Center. "Partisanship and Cable News Audiences." Pew Research Center, October 30, 2009. http://www.pewresearch.org/2009/10/30/partisanship-and-cable-news-audiences/.

Pew Research Center. "The Global Religious Landscape." Washington, DC: Pew Research Center's Forum on Religion & Public Life, December 2012. http://www.pewforum.org/2012/12/18/global-religious-landscape-exec/.

Pew Research Center. "Global Religious Diversity: Half of the Most Religiously Diverse Countries are in the Asia-Pacific Region." April 4, 2014, http://www.pewforum.org/files/2014/04/Religious-Diversity-full-report.pdf.

Pew Research Center. "Indians Reflect on Their Country & the World." March 31, 2014. http://www.pewglobal.org/2014/03/31/chapter-1-indians-in-a-sour-mood/.

Pew Research Center. "How Americans Feel About Religious Groups." July 16, 2014. http://www.pewforum.org/2014/07/16/how-americans-feel-about-religious-groups/.

Pintak, Lawrence, and Budi Setiyono. "The Mission of Indonesian Journalism: Balancing Democracy, Development, and Islamic Values." *International Journal of Press/ Politics* 16 (2010): 185–209.

Posner, Eric. "The World Doesn't Love the First Amendment." *Slate.com*, September 25, 2012. http://www.slate.com/articles/news_and_politics/jurisprudence/2012/09/the_vile_anti_muslim_video_and_the_first_amendment_does_the_u_s_overvalue_free_speech_.html

Posner, Eric. *The Twilight of Human Rights Law.* Oxford: Oxford University Press, 2014.

Post, Robert. Hate Speech. In *Extreme Speech and Democracy*, ed. Ivan Hare and James Weinstein. 123–138. Oxford: Oxford University Press, 2009.

Powers, Shawn. "Examining the Danish Cartoon Affair: Mediatized Cross-Cultural Tensions?" *Media, War & Conflict* 1 (2008): 339–359.

Prijosusilo, Bramantyo. "A Year after the Murders in Cikeusik, Why Is the Govt Going Soft on Hard-Liners?" *Jakarta Globe*, February 6, 2012. http://jakartaglobe.beritasatu.com/archive/a-year-after-the-murders-in-cikeusik-why-is-the-govt-going-soft-on-hard-liners/

R.A.V. vs City of St Paul. No. 90–7675, 505 US 377 (1992).

Ramsay, Gilbert, and Sarah Victoria Marsden. "Radical Distinctions: A Comparative Study of Two Jihadist Speeches." *Critical Studies on Terrorism* 6 (2013): 392–409.

Radsch, C. C., ed. *World Trends in Freedom of Expression and Media Development.* Paris: United Nations Educational, Scientific and Cultural Organization, 2014. http://unesdoc.unesco.org/images/0022/002270/227025e.pdf.

Rajan, Rajeswari Sunder, and Anuradha Dingwaney Needham. Introduction. In *The Crisis of Secularism in India*, ed. Rajeswari Sunder Rajan and Anuradha Dingwaney Needham. 1–44. Durham, NC: Duke University Press, 2007.

Ramesh s/o Chotalal Dalal v. Union of India and Ors on February 16, 1988 (1 SCC 668).

Rao, Mohan, Ish Mishra, Pragya Singh, and Vikas Bajpai. "Communalism and the Role of the State: An Investigation into the Communal Violence in Muzaff Arnagar and its Aftermath," *Economic & Political Weekly*, December 2013. https://blog-cafedissensus.files.wordpress.com/2014/01/independent-fact-finding-committee-report-on-muzaffarnagar-riots.pdf.

Raychaudhuri, Diptendra. "Elections 2014: RSS Swallows the Great Indian Media." *Mainstream Weekly* 52 (May 17, 2014). http://www.mainstreamweekly.net/article4925.html.

Reidenberg, Joel R. "Yahoo and Democracy on the Internet." *Jurimetrics* 42 (2002): 261–280.

Reimann, Mathias. "Introduction: The Yahoo! Case and Conflict of Laws in the Cyberage." *Michigan Journal of International Law* 24 (2003): 663–672.

Reuters. "Handbook of Journalism." Thomson Reuters, 2008. http://handbook .reuters.com/index.php/Main_Page.

Robert Faurisson v. France. Communication No. 550/1993, United Nations Human Rights Committee, U.N. Doc. CCPR/C/58/D/550/1993(1996). http://www1.umn .edu/humanrts/undocs/html/VWS55058.htm.

Robertson, Geoffrey. "Looking Back at Salman Rushdie's *The Satanic Verses.*" *Guardian*, September 14, 2012. http://www.theguardian.com/books/2012/sep/14/looking -at-salman-rushdies-satanic-verses.

Rosen, Jay. *What Are Journalists For?* New Haven, CT: Yale University Press, 1999.

Rosen, Jay. "The People Formerly Known as the Audience." *Press Think*, June 27, 2006. http://archive.pressthink.org/2006/06/27/ppl_frmr.html.

Rosen, Jeffrey. "Google's Gatekeepers." *New York Times Magazine*, November 28, 2008. http://www.nytimes.com/2008/11/30/magazine/30google-t.html.

Rosenfeld, Michel. Hate Speech in Constitutional Jurisprudence: A Comparative Analysis. In *The Content and Context of Hate Speech*, ed. Michael Herz and Peter Molnar. 242–289. New York: Cambridge University Press, 2012.

Rupar, Verica. *Getting the Facts Right: Reporting Ethnicity & Religion*. Brussels: International Federation of Journalists, 2012. http://ethicaljournalisminitiative.org/assets/ docs/107/024/7d0676b-793d318.pdf.

"*S.A.S. v. France*: The European Court's Decision in Light of Human Rights Doctrine on Restricting Religious Dress." International Justice Resource Center, July 11, 2014. http://www.ijrcenter.org/2014/07/11/s-a-s-v-france-the-european-courts-decision -in-light-of-human-rights-doctrine-on-restricting-religious-dress/.

Sachs, Jeffrey D. *Common Wealth: Economics for a Crowded Planet*. New York: Penguin Books, 2008.

Said, Edward. *Orientalism*. New York: Vintage, 1979.

Said, Edward. *Covering Islam*. London: Vintage, 1997.

Sakr, Naomi. "Enriching or Impoverishing Discourse on Rights? Talk about Freedom of Expression on Arab Television." *Middle East Journal of Culture & Communication* 3 (2010): 101–119.

Sampath, G. "Mandate 2014: Triumph of the Spin." *Mint*, May 20, 2014. http:// www.livemint.com/Opinion/hNdjVFTqfkl0nEd690YsDK/Mandate-2014-Triumph -of-the-spin.html.

Sandoval, Marisol, and Christian Fuchs. "Towards a Critical Theory of Alternative Media." *Telematics and Informatics* 27 (2010): 141–150.

Scammell, Margaret, and Holli A. Semetko. The Media and Democracy. In *The Media, Journalism and Democracy*, ed. Margaret Scammell and Holli A. Semetko. xi–xlix. Burlington, UK: Ashgate, 2000.

Schauer, Frederick. Uncoupling Free Speech. In *The Price We Pay: The Case against Racist Speech, Hate Propaganda, and Pornography*, ed. Laura Lederer and Richard Delgado. 259–265. New York: Farrar, Straus and Giroux, 1995.

Schedler, Andreas. "What Is Democratic Consolidation?" *Journal of Democracy* 9 (1998): 91–107.

Scher, Bill. "How Republicans Lost the Culture War." *Politico Magazine*, October 12, 2014. http://www.politico.com/magazine/story/2014/10/how-republicans-lost-the-culture-war-111822.html.

Schmitter, Philippe C., and Terry Lynn Karl. "What Democracy Is ... and Is Not." *Journal of Democracy* 2 (1991): 75–88.

Schmitz, Matthew. "Fears of 'Creeping Sharia.'" *National Review* 13 (June) (2012). http://www.nationalreview.com/article/302280/fears-creeping-sharia-matthew-schmitz.

Schweiker, William. Monotheistic Faith and the Cosmopolitan Conscience. In *The Rule of Law and the Rule of God*, ed. Simeon O. Ilesanmi, Win-Chiat Lee, and J. Wilson Parker. 31–49. New York: Palgrave Macmillan, 2014.

Sen, Amartya. *The Argumentative Indian: Writings on Indian History, Culture and Identity*. New York: Penguin, 2006.

Sen, Amartya. *Identity and Violence: The Illusion of Destiny*. New York: W. W. Norton, 2006.

Sen, Amartya. *The Idea of Justice*. London: Penguin Books, 2009.

Sen, Amartya. The Politics of History. In *Pluralism and Democracy in India: Debating the Hindu Right*, ed. Wendy Doniger and Martha C. Nussbaum. 21–34. New York: Oxford University Press, 2015.

Sevinclidir, Pinar. "Hate Speech on the Rise in Turkish Media." *BBC Monitoring*, October 30, 2014. http://www.bbc.co.uk/monitoring/hate-speech-on-the-rise-in-turkish-media.

Shapiro, Ian. *The State of Democratic Theory*. Princeton, NJ: Princeton University Press, 2003.

Shah, T. S., A. Stepan, and M. D. Toft, eds. *Rethinking Religion and World Affairs*. New York: Oxford University Press, 2012.

Silverstone, Roger. *Media and Morality: On the Rise of the Mediapolis.* Cambridge: Polity, 2007.

Slok, Camilla. "Here I Stand: Lutheran Stubbornness in the Danish Prime Minister's Office during the Cartoon Crisis." *European Journal of Social Theory* 12 (2009): 231–248.

Society of Professional Journalists. "SPJ Code of Ethics." 2014. http://www.spj.org/ethicscode.asp

Soejoatmodjo, Gita Widya Laksmini. Peace Journalism in Indonesia. In *International Journalism and Democracy: Civic Engagement Models from around the World,* ed. Angela Romano. 180–194. New York: Routledge, 2010.

Spaaij, Ramón, and Mark S. Hamm. "Key Issues and Research Agendas in Lone Wolf Terrorism." *Studies in Conflict and Terrorism* 38 (2015): 167–178.

Spellberg, Denise A. *Thomas Jefferson's Qur'an: Islam and the Founders.* New York: Alfred A. Knopf, 2013.

Spivak, Gayatri C. "Reading The Satanic Verses." *Third Text* 4 (1990): 41–60.

State Of Maharashtra and Ors. v Sangharaj Damodar Rupawate and Ors on July 9, 2010 (5 Bom CR646).

Stedman, Stephen John. "Spoiler Problems in Peace Processes." *International Security* 22 (1997): 5–53.

Stepan, Alfred. Religion, Democracy, and the 'Twin Tolerations. In *World Religions and Democracy,* ed. Larry Diamond, Mark F. Plattner and Philip J. Costopoulos. 3–23. Baltimore and London: Johns Hopkins University Press, 2005.

Stepan, Alfred, and Mirjam Künkler. "An Interview with Amien Rais." *Journal of International Affairs* 61 (2007): 205–216.

Stephens, Mitchell. *A History of News.* New York: Viking, 1988.

Stiglitz, Joseph. *Globalization and Its Discontents.* New York: Penguin, 2003.

Sujato Bhadra v. State of West Bengal on September 22, 2005 (3 CALLT 436 HC).

Surek v. Turkey. Application no. 26682/95, Council of Europe: European Court of Human Rights, July 8, 1999. https://www.article19.org/resources.php/resource/3102/en/echr:-surek-v.-turkey (no.-1).

Tarrow, Sidney. *Power in Movement: Social Movements and Contentious Politics.* 2nd ed. Cambridge: Cambridge University Press, 1998.

Tarrow, Sidney. "Transnational Politics: Contention and Institutions in International Politics." *Annual Review of Political Science* 4 (2001): 1–20.

Tehranian, Majid. "Peace Journalism: Negotiating Global Media Ethics." *Harvard Journal of Press/Politics* 7 (2002): 58–83.

Thapar, Romila. Secularism, History, and Contemporary Politics in India. In *The Crisis of Secularism in India*, ed. Anuradha Dingwaney Needham and Rajeswari Sunder Rajan. Durham, NC: Duke University Press, 2007.

Tilly, Charles. *Popular Contention in Great Britain, 1758–1834*. Cambridge, MA: Harvard University Press, 1995.

Tripathi, Salil. *Offence: The Hindu Case*. London: Seagull Books, 2009.

Trudeau, Garry. "The Abuse of Satire." *Atlantic*. April 11, 2015. http://www.theatlantic.com/international/archive/2015/04/the-abuse-of-satire/390312/.

Tsesis, Alexander. *Destructive Messages: How Hate Speech Paves the Way For Harmful Social Movements*. New York: New York University Press, 2002.

Tuchman, Gaye. "Objectivity as Strategic Ritual: An Examination of Newsmen's Notions of Objectivity." *American Journal of Sociology* 77 (1972): 660–679.

Turner, Bryan S. Religion in a Post-Secular Society. In *The New Blackwell Companion to the Sociology of Religion*, ed. Bryan S. Turner. 649–667. Chichester, UK: Blackwell, 2010.

US Department of State. *International Religious Freedom Report for 2013—Indonesia*. Washington, DC: US Department of State, Bureau of Democracy, Human Rights and Labor, 2014. http://www.state.gov/j/drl/rls/irf/religiousfreedom/index.htm?year=2013&dlid=222133.

United Nations. "Charter of the United Nations." October 24, 1945. http://www.un.org/en/charter-united-nations/index.html].

United Nations General Assembly. *Universal Declaration of Human Rights*, December 10, 1948, 217 A (III). http://www.un.org/en/documents/udhr/.

United Nations General Assembly. *International Covenant on Civil and Political Rights*. United Nations, Treaty Series, vol. 999, December 16, 1966. http://www.ohchr.org/en/professionalinterest/pages/ccpr.aspx.

United Nations General Assembly. *Declaration on the Elimination of All Forms of Intolerance and of Discrimination Based on Religion or Belief*. November 25, 1981, A/RES/36/55. http://www.un.org/documents/ga/res/36/a36r055.htm.

United Nations General Assembly. *Resolution 66/168: Elimination of All Forms of Intolerance and of Discrimination Based on Religion or Belief*. A/RES/66/168, December 19, 2011. http://www.un.org/en/ga/search/view_doc.asp?symbol=%20A/RES/66/168.

United Nations General Assembly. *Report of the Working Group on the Universal Periodic Review—Indonesia.* Human Rights Council, July 5, 2012, A/HRC/21/7. http://daccess-dds-ny.un.org/doc/UNDOC/GEN/G12/150/17/PDF/G1215017.pdf.

United Nations General Assembly. *Summary Prepared by the Office of the High Commissioner for Human Rights in Accordance with Paragraph 5 of the Annex to Human Rights Council Resolution 16/21—Indonesia.* March 9, 2012, A/HRC/WG.6/13/IDN/3. http://daccess-dds-ny.un.org/doc/UNDOC/GEN/G12/118/12/PDF/G1211812.pdf.

United Nations Human Rights Committee. *General Comment no. 34, International Covenant on Civil and Political Rights—Article 19: Freedoms of Opinion and Expression,* September 12, 2011, CCPR/C/GC/34. http://www2.ohchr.org/english/bodies/hrc/docs/gc34.pdf.

United Nations Human Rights Council. *Combating Defamation of Religions.* Resolution 7/19, March 27, 2008. http://ap.ohchr.org/documents/E/HRC/resolutions/A_HRC_RES_7_19.pdf.

United Nations Office of the High Commissioner for Human Rights. "Rabat Plan of Action on the Prohibition of Advocacy of National, Racial or Religious Hatred That Constitutes Incitement to Discrimination, Hostility or Violence." Conclusions and Recommendations Emanating from the Four Regional Expert Workshops organized by the OHCRR in 2011 and Adopted by Experts in Rabat, Morrocco, October 5, 2012. http://www.ohchr.org/Documents/Issues/Opinion/SeminarRabat/Rabat_draft_outcome.pdf.

United States Commission on International Religious Freedom. *USCIRF Annual Report 2015—Tier 2: Indonesia.* May 1, 2015. http://www.refworld.org/docid/554b355b11.html.

United States Senate. "Violent Islamist Extremism, the Internet, and the Homegrown Terrorist Threat." Majority and Minority Staff Report, United States Senate Committee on Homeland Security and Governmental Affairs, May 8, 2008. http://hsgac.senate.gov/public/_files/IslamistReport.pdf

Van Bruinessen, Martin. "What Happened to the Smiling Face of Indonesian Islam? Muslim Intellectualism and the Conservative Turn in Post-Suharto Indonesia." *RSIS Working Paper Series.* Singapore: S. Rajaratnam School of International Studies, January 6, 2011.

Van Susteren, Greta. "My Offer to Muslim Leaders—Come on 'On the Record' and Condemn Islamic Extremism." *On the Record with Greta Van Susteren,* October 6, 2014. http://www.foxnews.com/on-air/on-the-record/2014/10/07/greta-my-offer-muslim-leaders-come-record-and-condemn-islamic-extremism.

Van Zoonen, Liesbet, Farida Vis, and Sabina Mihelj. "Performing Citizenship on YouTube: Activism, Satire and Online Debate around the Anti-Islam Video Fitna." *Critical Discourse Studies* 7 (2010): 249–262.

Verdoolaege, Annelies. *Reconciliation Discourse: The Case of the Truth and Reconciliation Commission*. Amsterdam: John Benjamins, 2008.

Venu, M. K. "Modi and the Numbers Game." *Hindu*, June 12, 2013. http://www.thehindu.com/opinion/lead/modi-and-the-numbers-game/article4804449.ece

Wajahit, Ali, Eli Clifton, Matthew Duss, Lee Fang, Scott Keyes, and Faiz Shakir. *Fear, Inc.: The Roots of the Islamophobia Network in America*. Washington, DC: Center for American Progress, 2011, https://www.americanprogress.org/issues/religion/report/2011/08/26/10165/fear-inc/.

Waldron, Jeremy. Hate Speech and Political Legitimacy. In *The Content and Context of Hate Speech: Rethinking Regulation and Responses*, ed. Michael Herz and Peter Molnar. 329–340. New York: Cambridge University Press, 2012.

Waltman, Michael, and John Haas. *The Communication of Hate*. New York: Peter Lang, 2011.

Weber, Anne. *Manual on Hate Speech*. Strasbourg: Council of Europe Publishing, 2009. https://book.coe.int/eur/en/human-rights-and-democracy/4197-manual-on-hate-speech.html.

Weiss, Michael. "Guilt and the 'Innocence of Muslims.'" *World Affairs*, September 2012. Accessed 8 August 2015. http://www.worldaffairsjournal.org/article/guilt-and-innocence-muslims.

"What the BJP's Election Campaign CD 'Bharat Ki Pukar' Presents—Excerpts from the Transcript." *Hindu*, April 7, 2007. http://www.thehindu.com/todays-paper/tp-national/article1824857.ece.

Whillock, Rita Kirk. The Use of Hate as a Strategem for Achieving Social and Political Goals. In *Hate Speech*, ed. Rita Kirk Whillock and David Slayden. 28–54. Thousand Oaks, CA: Sage Publications, 1995.

Winseck, Dwayne R. Intermediary Responsibility. In *International Encyclopedia of Digital Communication and Society*, ed. Robin Mansell and Hwa Ang Peng. Oxford: Wiley-Blackwell, 2015., 10.1002/9781118767771.wbiedcs143.

Wise, Lindsay. "Amr Khaled vs Yusuf Al Qaradawi: The Danish Cartoon Controversy and the Clash of Two Islamic TV Titans," *Transnational Broadcasting Studies*, 16 (2006). http://stuff.jworld.ch/al-jazeera/19%20Vertiefungstext%2010.pdf.

Whetstone, Rachel. "Our Approach to Free Expression and Controversial Content." Google Official Blog, March 9, 2012. http://googleblog.blogspot.sg/2012/03/our-approach-to-free-expression-and.html.

Wilson, Ian. "Resisting Democracy: Front Pembela Islam and Indonesia's 2014 Elections." ISEAS Perspective, no. 10 (February 24, 2014). http://www.iseas.edu.sg/documents/publication/ISEAS_Perspective_2014_10-Resisting_Democracy.pdf.

Wong, Cynthia, and James X. Dempsey. *The Media and Liability for Content on the Inernet*. London: Open Society Foundations, 2011. http://www.opensocietyfoundations .org/sites/default/files/mapping-digital-media-liability-content-internet-20110926 .pdf.

Woischnik, Jan, and Philipp Muller. "Islamic Parties and Democracy in Indonesia." *Konrad Adenauer–Stiftung International Reports*, no. 10 (2013): 59–79.

Wood, Graeme. "What ISIS Really Wants." *The Atlantic*, March 2015. http://www .theatlantic.com/features/archive/2015/02/what-isis-really-wants/384980/.

Yates v. United States. 354 US 298 (1957).

Yazdiha, Haj. "Law as Movement Strategy: How the Islamophobia Movement Institutionalizes Fear Through Legislation." *Social Movement Studies* 13 (2014): 267–274.

Yerushalmi, David. *CLE Course on Draft Uniform Act: American Laws for American Courts*. Law Offices of David Yerushalmi, P.C., November 7, 2012, accessed July 23, 2015, http://www.davidyerushalmilaw.com/CLE-Course-on-Draft-Uniform-Act --American-Laws-for-American-Courts-b25-p0.html.

Yudhoyono, Susilo Bambang. "Keynote Speech by President of the Republic of Indonesia." Sixth Global Forum of the United Nations Alliance of Civilizations, Nusa Dua, Bali, Indonesia, August 29, 2014. http://www.setneg.go.id/index.php?option =com_content&task=view&id=8155.

Zubrzykci, Genevieve. Religion and Nationalism: A Critical Re-Examination. In *The New Blackwell Companion to the Sociology of Religion*, ed. Bryan S. Turner. 606–625. Chichester, UK: Blackwell, 2010.

Zurcher, Jr, and A. Louis. "R. George Kirkpatrick, Robert G. Cushing, and Charles K. Bowman. "The Anti-Pornography Campaign: A Symbolic Crusade." *Social Problems* 19 (1971): 217–238.

Index